D0425876

MOLDING
JAPANESE
MINDS

THE STATE IN EVERYDAY LIFE

Sheldon Garon

PRINCETON UNIVERSITY PRESS

PRINCETON, NEW JERSEY

Library of Congress Cataloging-in-Publication Data
Garon, Sheldon.
Molding Japanese minds : the state in everyday life / Sheldon Garon.
p.   cm.
Includes bibliographical references and index.
ISBN 0-691-04488-0 (alk. paper)
1. Japan—Social policy.   2. Japan—Social conditions—1868–   .
3. Social control—Japan—History.   I. Title.
HN723.G39   1997
306'.0952—DC20   96-33488

This book has been composed in Sabon and Charlemagne

The following articles have been reprinted in revised form with
permission from the *Journal of Japanese Studies*:
Sheldon Garon, "State and Religion in Imperial Japan, 1912–1945,"
Journal of Japanese Studies 12.2 (Summer 1986): 273–302.
Sheldon Garon, "Women's Groups and the Japanese State: Contending
Approaches to Political Integration, 1890–1945," *Journal of
Japanese Studies* 19.1 (Winter 1993): 5–41.

To Sherrill, Thea, and Claire

Contents

Illustrations

FIGURES

TABLES

Abbreviations

DNTGS	*Dai Nihon teikoku gikai shi*
NARA	National Archives and Records Administration
NFMSS	*Nihon fujin mondai shiryō shūsei*
NSHZS	*Nihon shakai hoshō zenshi shiryō* (Shakai hoshō kenkyūjo)
SCAP	Supreme Commander for the Allied Powers
SSUK	*Shin seikatsu undō kyōkai 25 nen no ayumi* (Shin seikatsu undō kyōkai)
WAAF, CI&E	Women's Affairs Activities File, Civil Information and Education Section (SCAP)
WCTU	Women's Christian Temperance Union
Zen chifuren	Zenkoku chiiki fujin dantai renraku kyōgikai

Preface

THE SPECTER of impending crisis is never far from the minds of those who govern Japan. In June 1990, American newspapers ran the story of a powerful finance minister, Hashimoto Ryutarō, who had become alarmed at the precipitous decline in Japan's birth rate. If such trends continued, he worried, Japan would soon face acute labor shortages and soaring welfare costs, as too few wage earners were forced to support too many elderly. European leaders had voiced similar concerns about birth rates in their own countries, but Hashimoto's proposed solution was to intervene in the lives of women in a manner that the Europeans would not have considered. Reasoning that increasing numbers of young women were deferring childbearing to attend colleges and universities, the finance minister urged the cabinet to reconsider the government's postwar policy of encouraging women to obtain a higher education. The cabinet did not act on Hashimoto's recommmendation to roll back the numbers of women in colleges and universities, although it immediately ordered the formation of a commission to recommend various means of persuading women to have more children. Hashimoto himself went on to become prime minister in 1996.

Just a short distance from the site of that cabinet meeting, elite bureaucrats in the Ministry of Health and Welfare were working to devise programs that would address Japan's "aging-society problem" without incurring the substantial expenditures of European welfare states. The ministry had already spent a decade dampening public expectations of a more generous welfare policy, deftly playing upon the widely held belief that Japan's vaunted three-generation families—particularly middle-aged wives—were the most appropriate caregivers. Meanwhile, on the other side of downtown Tokyo, in the neoclassical ediface that houses the Bank of Japan, the staff of the Central Council for Savings Information was supervising an ongoing savings campaign by coordinating women's organizations, local school systems, and community groups to persuade families to spend less and save more. The bureaucrats' work left them little time to ponder why the government was aggressively promoting household savings after it had ostensibly accepted the 1986 Maekawa

Report's recommendations to stimulate consumption on a massive scale. A group of young officials later confided to me that they could no longer harangue the people to "save, save, save" as in the days before 1945 or during the early postwar era; their current mission was to find less imperious ways of persuading the populace to save while instilling in the nation's children the values of hard work and frugality.

Although there have been recurring calls for greater moral leadership in our own country, few of the Americans who shape public opinion believe that government should or even could mold the values and habits of citizens. They respond to evidence to the contrary by either ignoring it or dismissing it. When the American press does report on the Japanese government's efforts at exhortation, these policies are invariably treated as the exotic relics of a dying style of rule that laughably flies in the face of a modern secular society. "Surprisingly quaint" and "turning back the clock" was how a *New York Times* editorial described Hashimoto's proposal to discourage women from pursuing a higher education.[1] Yet such episodes are hardly isolated incidents in the postwar history of Japan. Indeed, they are simply the most recent manifestations of a powerful pattern of governance in which the state has historically intervened to shape how ordinary Japanese thought and behaved—to an extent that would have been inconceivable in the United States and Britain, and would probably have strained the limits of statism in continental Europe. I term this phenomenon "social management," for the government devoted considerable resources to managing not only the economy but society itself. The authorities' chief managerial tool has been moral suasion, a method no doubt influenced by traditional forms of statecraft practiced before the establishment of the modern Japanese state in 1868. The refinement of techniques for managing society, however, dates most immediately to processes at work during the first half of the twentieth century.

To chronicle the development of social management in modern Japan, this book presents four case studies in the changing relationships between the state and society from the late nineteenth century to the present. The first four chapters deal with prewar Japan from 1868 to 1945. Chapter One examines the evolution of a "Japanese-style" welfare system whose architects self-consciously sought to avoid the perceived ills of European welfare states, while strengthening the traditional familial and communal bases of mutual assistance. Chapter Two deals with the formulation of a "religions policy," in which the regime gradually incorporated the more established religions into the state apparatus, while violently suppressing several charismatic "new religions" that challenged both official orthodoxy and the intelligentsia's ideas of modernity. The next two chapters explore seldom discussed issues of gender and sexuality to uncover more subtle intrusions into everyday life by the state and middle-class groups. Chapter Three reconstructs the highly charged debate between the opponents of Japan's extensive system of licensed prostitution and the system's defenders. To a degree that would astound Americans, most Japanese favorably regarded the officially regulated brothels; they viewed the licensed quarters as a legitimate part of the state's managerial project of preserving the Japanese "family system," promoting economic development, and augmenting national power. Chapter Four retells the story of Japan's nascent women's organizations. It argues that their growth between the two world wars reflected an interplay between the government's efforts to mobilize women on behalf of new programs of social management, on the one hand, and the inclination of most women's groups to cooperate with the bureaucracy in numerous campaigns to improve the lives of women and children, on the other. The final three chapters assess the changes and remarkable continuities in the patterns of social management from 1945 to this day.

The history of these various aspects of social management illuminates the mechanisms by which the Japanese state obtained not simply passive compliance from the people but the enthusiastic participation of many private groups in its ambitious programs to manage society. Social scientists, journalists, and policymakers have generated myriad accounts of the contemporary Japanese economy and industrial policy, but few have come to grips with the modern Japanese state's singular success in cultivating the social underpinnings of national economic advance. Government welfare expenditures in Japan are among the lowest in industrialized societies, as families continue to bear much of the burden of supporting the elderly; Japan's impressive levels of capital formation are unquestionably related to high rates of household savings, which have prevailed since the early 1930s; and large-scale women's organizations—which many Westerners assume would resist official initiatives—work closely with the state to socialize youth, control crime, promote savings, and protect Japanese producers. These distinctive features of contemporary Japan can best be understood in the context of developments that span the entire twentieth century.

It is my intention neither to criticize nor defend the cooperative arrangements that exist between the Japanese state and society. Rather I seek to instill a new appreciation of the complex interrelationships that contributed to the formation of Japan's political economy during the twentieth century. Only by doing so, I believe, will Americans be able to deal realistically with a nation that shows few signs of embracing norms and policies prevalent in the United States.

Given the diversity of the cases, I could not have proceeded without the cooperation of friends and colleagues in a number of fields. I benefited enormously from close readings of the manuscript by Chalmers Johnson, T. J. Pempel, and Daniel Rodgers. There is scarcely an area of this work

that has not been improved by years of intellectual exchange with Andrew Gordon. Bill Mihalopolous has been indefatigable in expanding my
theoretical horizons, particularly with respect to the literature on social
control. Andrew Fraser and my former students Harald Fuess and Jamie
Hood generously shared their research. Many others graciously critiqued
individual essays—including David Ambaras, James Bartholomew, Judith Babbitts, Peter Brown, Dipesh Chakrabarty, Samuel Coleman, Martin Collcutt, Desley Deacon, Natalie Davis, Laura Engelstein, Elizabeth
Frierson, Helen Hardacre, Sally Hastings, David Howell, Marius Jansen,
William Jordan, Gregory Pflugfelder, Mark Ramseyer, Richard Samuels,
Robert Smith, Lawrence Stone, James White, and David Williams.
Soowon Kim of Princeton's Gest Library was extraordinarily helpful in
securing Japanese materials. I cannot begin to thank my undergraduate
assistant Emily Lin for her long hours and overall thoughtfulness at several phases of the project. Brigitta van Rheinberg, Margaret Case, Lauren
Osborne, and others at Princeton University Press have been wonderful in
their support and excellent suggestions during the publication process.

I am equally grateful to those who assisted my research activities in
Japan over the past decade. They range from Gyōten Toyoo, former vice
minister of finance, to Nitta Kunio, chief priest of the sect Shintō
Shūseiha, and Miyazaki Reiko, a home economist who opened my eyes to
the persistence of "daily life improvement campaigns" in Japan today.
Katō Masayo, Katsube Mieko, and Yoshida Sumi similarly arranged interviews and introductions to several archives. Special thanks go to my
academic hosts: Nakamura Masanori (Hitotsubashi University), William
Steele (International Christian University), Miura Fumio (Japan College
of Social Work), and Igarashi Takeshi and Mitani Taichirō (both of the
University of Tokyo). Narita Ryūichi profoundly influenced my thinking
on the role of modernity in state-society relations. Also invaluable were
many conversations with my colleagues: Abe Tsunehisa, Akazawa Shirō,
Endō Kōichi, Gomi Yuriko, Ichibangase Yasuko, Ishida Takeshi, Itō
Takashi, Kano Masanao, Miki (Takizawa) Tamio, Nakajima Kuni, Nakajima Michio, Nishinarita Yutaka, Ōbinata Sumio, Suzuki Yūko,
Utsumi Takashi, Watanabe Osamu, Yasumaru Yoshio, and Yui Ma-
saomi. In addition, I wish to thank Oikawa Ryōko (Japan College of
Social Work), Yoshida Hiroshi (Central Council for Savings Information), Hamamura Takatō (Association to Build the Japan of Tomorrow),
and the staffs of the Women's Suffrage Hall and Ie no Hikari Kyōkai for
going beyond the call of duty in making their collections available.

Research and writing was made possible by grants from the Japan
Foundation, Social Science Research Council and American Council of
Learned Societies, National Endowment for the Humanities, Program in
Women's Studies (Princeton University), and Research School of Pacific

Studies (Australian National University). My visiting fellowship in Australia made me aware, as never before, of the fallacy of equating "the West" with the United States and of the pitfalls in assuming that the Japanese state is somehow unique in seeking to manage society. For this and other insights, I thank Dani Botsman, Peter Drysdale, Mark Elvin, C. Andrew Gerstle, Jill Matthews, Gavan McCormack, and Sandra Wilson.

Following East Asian practice, Japanese surnames precede given names, excepting those Japanese whose English-language works have been cited. Macrons in Japanese words have been omitted in well-known Japanese words (such as, Shintō) and the place names Tōkyō, Ōsaka, Kyōto, and Kōbe.

Finally, I wish to thank my family. My wife and fellow historian Sherrill Cohen has been a tremendous inspiration and an incisive critic. Her own work on gender and prostitution in Europe encouraged me to broaden my study of Japanese political history in directions I could scarcely have imagined fifteen years ago. Our twin daughters Claire and Thea have also inspired me with their energy and delightful zaniness. It is through my children, moreover, that I experienced firsthand the politics of everyday life. In suburban New Jersey, that means contentious annual referenda on local school budgets. As a leader of our town's pro-education group, I gained a new appreciation of the more ordinary aspects of state-society relations in Japan—not the least of which are the gendered differences in how women and men participate in public life. These insights have resulted in few school-election triumphs thus far, but I believe I have become a better historian.

MOLDING
JAPANESE
MINDS

Poster from the Moral Suasion Mobilization Campaign, 1929. Devils flee the revitalized Japan, symbolized by the rising sun. Calligraphy by the pioneer entrepreneur Shibusawa Eiichi reads: "When the people's spirit is roused, the national crisis will pass." Mombushō, *Kyōka dōin jisshi gaikyō*.

Social Management:
An Introduction

The purpose of policing is to ensure the good fortune
of the state through the wisdom of its regulations, and
to augment its forces and its powers to the limits of its
capability. The science of policing consists, therefore,
in regulating everything that relates to the present
condition of society, in strengthening and improving it,
in seeing that all things contribute to the welfare of the
members that compose it.

—JOHANN VON JUSTI, *Éléments généraux de police*
(1768)[1]

NATION states have intervened in
the everyday life of people to a greater degree and more effectively during
the twentieth century than at any other time in history. Many have celebrated these interventions, citing improvements in the health and welfare
of the general populace. Others—conservatives in the United States and
free-market "liberals" elsewhere—have vehemently condemned state regulation for distorting markets or usurping parental authority. The most
provocative reassessments of interventionism in recent years, however,
have come from critics on the Left. These observers seek to expose the
efforts of states and powerful groups to "discipline," "police," or "regulate" the rest of society. The last two decades have seen a flurry of books
and articles that invoke the concept of "social control," generally as a
pejorative.

What is meant by "social control" varies considerably. During the first
several decades of the twentieth century, the term carried positive, even
progressive connotations. American sociologists and social workers defined social control as the process by which society imposed restraints on

the "antisocial" behavior of individuals. It could refer to socializing children, teaching the poor to be productive members of society, or constraining the activities of greedy businessmen by means of labor legislation.[2] As disillusionment with welfare programs and state power set in during the late 1960s, however, progressive historians and social scientists in the United States and Britain increasingly portrayed social control as a set of mechanisms and policies by which the dominant classes advanced their interests by imposing their values and behavior on the lower classes and those whom they classified as deviant. Individual studies detected social control at work in a number of realms—education, social work, medicine, psychiatry, the juvenile court system, and the military. The new scholarship argued, for example, that public welfare programs did not primarily result from humanitarian impulses but from the elites' desires to regulate the poor so as to force the underclass into the low-wage labor market and prevent upsurges in violence.[3] "Social control" became a major explanation of why the bourgeois capitalist order had triumphed and maintained itself with a minimal use of force against the working class.

Michel Foucault and other French thinkers provided the study of social control with more elaborate theoretical underpinnings in the late 1970s and 1980s. Although he seldom used the words "social control," Foucault formulated a general theory of how modern societies came to discipline their members. He traced these processes back to the eighteenth century, when the belief spread that individuals could be trained in both mind and body to become better soldiers, workers, and subjects. From that period on, he contended, institutions such as the army, schools, factories, and hospitals strove to normalize thinking and behavior—that is, to discipline and correct "that which does not measure up to the rule." Foucault also suggested that the rise of middle-class professionals—educators, engineers, social reformers, doctors, and psychiatrists—served to extend disciplinary mechanisms throughout society.[4]

Theories of social control captured the attention of a great many historians in English-speaking countries, but its scholarly adherents soon faced a barrage of opposition. They have been criticized, first for exaggerating the unity of purpose on the part of the controllers, second for denying those who were controlled any autonomous role in resisting or initiating the processes of socialization, and third for equating the ambitious aims of the controllers with the often disappointing results.[5] Yet what most bothers historians who think about the rest of the world is that the debate is culturally bound.[6] Ironically, the main body of literature on social control applies to three of the most liberal democratic polities in the world—the United States, Britain, and France. How effective, how concerted could social control have been, asked the critics, in nations whose states were relatively weak and where many alternative institutions and value systems existed for those wishing to escape control? The point was not lost on Foucault and his followers. They have readily admitted that the French state did not necessarily coordinate and initiate the many disciplinary projects since the eighteenth century; rather the disciplinary mechanisms became dispersed throughout society. Precisely because liberal states do not openly engage in molding everyday behavior, most students of social control dedicate themselves to unmasking the subtle ways in which states and their allies in society intrude on the autonomy of individuals.[7]

In modern Japan, efforts to mobilize the populace were not so subtle. Accounts of social control in Japan necessarily highlight the direct role of the state. Long before theories of social control became popular in Anglo-American and French historiography, Japanese intellectuals were wrestling with the problem of why the Japanese people (and they themselves) had not resisted the growth of authoritarianism, repression, and militarism prior to Japan's devastating defeat in World War II. They concluded overwhelmingly that the prewar state successfully controlled the people by means of an elaborate "emperor system," which the regime strategically created following the Meiji Restoration of 1868. In structural terms, the "emperor-system state" was administered by a small corps of military officers, civilian bureaucrats, and police. Situating themselves *above* society, Japanese officials perceived themselves to be officials of the emperor rather than servants of the public. According to the dominant version of the emperor-system thesis, even landlords and bourgeois capitalists—whose interests the bureaucrats could not entirely ignore—constituted at best junior parties in the emperor-system coalition. Armed with enormous powers of repression, the police systematically suppressed Communists, anarchists, and others who offered genuine alternatives to the state's orthodoxy.[8]

Yet adherents of the emperor-system thesis also recognized that the imperial state did not rely on repression alone in its efforts to increase national power, promote economic development, and maintain social order. In more positive terms, the government energetically disseminated an "emperor-system ideology" to the public, inculcating patriotism, loyalty to the emperor, and the virtues of diligence and thrift. The state did so by utilizing a highly centralized set of institutions: the national school system, the military, a network of State Shinto shrines, and numerous hierarchically organized associations. If social control in the West implies society's regulation of its members or one group's domination over another *within* society, its Japanese analogue—the emperor system—refers to the unrelenting drive by a transcendent state to control society as a whole between 1868 and 1945.

This book tells the story of the extraordinary efforts to transform the Japanese people into active participants in the state's various projects. I have termed the process one of "social management" to distinguish it both from Western theories of social control and the prevailing Japanese paradigm of the emperor system. The prominent roles played by Japanese private groups in managing everyday life do bear some resemblance to the type of social control described by scholars of Western democracies. Nevertheless, the term "social control" assumes the presence of a relatively weak state. In many European nations during the eighteenth and nineteenth centuries, successive challenges by groups in civil society weakened the hold of early modern monarchical states, resulting in the transformation and diffusion of disciplinary mechanisms. In Japan, by contrast, following the overthrow of the Tokugawa shogunate in 1868, leaders of the new government constructed a *more* interventionist, centralized state to replace the shogunate and autonomous domains. In this context, the term "social control" can be misleading.

I have avoided utilizing the Japanese concept of emperor system, on the other hand, because its adherents generally portray the state bureaucracy as acting alone and from above in controlling society. As we shall see, Japanese officials and groups within society frequently interacted in formulating and implementing programs to manage society. Furthermore, the centrality of the emperor in the term "emperor-system ideology" obscures more than it illuminates. Reverence for the emperor and his state was only one aspect of the values and behavior that the government and its allies attempted to instill in the populace.[9] Official campaigns were just as likely to promote improvements in health and sanitation, better child-rearing techniques, and other reforms that the public associated with modernization.

Compared to either "social control" or "emperor system," the term "social management" best describes how Japanese bureaucrats and private groups themselves envisioned their task throughout the twentieth century. The term "control" implies a rigid style of governance, in which the controllers demand a particular type of behavior from the people and systematically punish deviations. Not until the crisis years of the 1930s did the Japanese government commonly invoke the word "control" (*tōsei*), and then primarily in the context of controlling the economy. Officials preferred to speak of "regulation" (*torishimari*), as in the "regulation of public morality" or the "regulation of the religions." "Regulation" connoted not so much the suppression of popular activity (although suppression occasionally occurred); rather, regulation meant that the authorities officially recognized certain activities and groups, while placing them within supervised frameworks or "zones." The regulations governing religious organizations was one such instance, and the system of officially supervised prostitution within licensed quarters was another. The state's approach in these cases was managerial in the sense that groups and individuals might function fairly autonomously within these zones—unless, of course, they attempted to scale the walls and operate beyond administrative supervision.

Officials before 1945 further described their programs in terms of an ongoing, managerial process of persuading or teaching the masses to internalize appropriate values. They explicitly spoke of "management" in two contexts. The first involved efforts, beginning in the mid-nineteenth century, to cultivate in peasants and the urban poor the spirit of "self-management" (*jiei*)—that is, a commitment to diligence, thrift, and other good habits so that individuals and families would avoid relying on public assistance. Second, the government sought to manage everyday life as a major part of programs to strengthen national power and the economy. The most obvious examples were the state's adoption of thoroughgoing "postwar management" (*sengo keiei*) following the Russo-Japanese War (1904–1905) and World War I.

The word that officials employed most frequently in their campaigns to influence and mobilize the people before 1945 was *kyōka*. Few Western scholars have appreciated the power of this term in prewar Japan, and *kyōka* lacks an accepted English translation.[10] The very difficulty of translation bespeaks the cultural divide between East Asian and Anglo-American societies in assessing the proper relationship between political authority and daily life. I have translated *kyōka* as "moral suasion," although "moral reform" or "moral education" would also be appropriate in certain contexts. *Kyōka* is a direct Japanese translation of an ancient Chinese word *jiaohua*, used by Buddhists and Confucianists alike. In Japan, China, and Korea, Buddhists defined *kyōka* (or *kyōke*) to mean instructing and guiding humankind to goodness through the teachings of Buddha. The more politicized ideology of Confucianism prescribed that the wise ruler instill proper behavior in his people so as to maintain order in human relationships and prosperity within the realm.[11] During Japan's Tokugawa or early modern era (1600–1868), authorities of the shogunate and various domains regularly exhorted peasants to work hard, pay their taxes, and avoid luxury. The leaders of the modern state inherited and systematized moral suasion on a nationwide scale. Elaborate bureaucracies sprang up, devoted to running moral suasion campaigns, coordinating local moral suasion groups, disseminating "social education," and effecting "spiritual mobilization."

A Nation at War in Peace

The past hundred years of governance in modern Japan constitute the century of the moral suasion campaign. These campaigns were central in the state's relationships with religious groups, women's organizations, social work leaders, and the poor. The drives were often traditional in rhetoric, but they employed new "technologies" in organizing society that first appeared at the beginning of the twentieth century.[12] Prior to 1900, the fledgling modern government lacked the unity of purpose and administrative apparatus necessary to mount nationwide moral suasion campaigns successfully. During the first half of the 1870s, for example, some leaders of the new regime launched an ill-fated drive to transform indigenous Shinto practices into a national religion. They concurrently sought to rally the people behind mass education, military conscription, the new postal savings system, and the state's other modernizing reforms. Reliance on Shinto and Buddhist priests to promote such Western innovations as postal savings accounts proved less than effective, however.[13] By the late 1880s, intellectuals, local elites, and officials broadly agreed on the need to foster "a sense of nation" in the masses if Japan were to modernize and compete with Western rivals. One result was the government's Imperial Rescript on Education of 1890, which called on subjects to practice filial piety, be loyal to the emperor, obey the laws, and "offer yourselves courageously to the State."[14] Although the imperial rescript was thereafter read daily to the nation's schoolchildren, the government established few other channels to convey its message to the rest of the country during the 1890s.

As the twentieth century dawned on Japan, a new generation of elite bureaucrats became convinced that the state would have to do more to mobilize and manage its human resources. They argued that Japan could not expect to compete with the much stronger and wealthier Western powers unless it generated a "unity of the people's spirit" on behalf of greater austerity in daily life.[15] In the wake of Japan's victory in the Russo-Japanese War, the government embarked upon a program of "postwar management." Eager to safeguard its geopolitical position in northeast Asia and the western Pacific, the leadership carried out a massive military buildup while committing substantial funds to administer Japan's newly acquired territories in Korea, southern Manchuria, and the southern half of Sakhalin. The cabinet simultaneously undertook to modernize the nation's industrial infrastructure—railroads, telephones, harbor and river works. The government immediately faced the problem of how to finance its ambitious policies. The Russo-Japanese War had been very costly. The Japanese had depended on large-scale loans from American and British financiers, and the government had further saddled its people with unprecedented tax increases. When Japan in 1905 failed to extract from the Russians an indemnity with which to compensate creditors and the people, thousands of Tokyo residents rioted over what they perceived as overly generous terms given to the defeated foe.[16]

The regime's postwar management quickly assumed the form of social management, as officials strove to persuade the public to bear the new burdens of the nation's great-power status. No sooner had the military campaign ended than the moral suasion campaign began. Seeking to bring the modern state into the lives of Japanese adults as never before, the powerful Home Ministry launched the Local Improvement Campaign (1906–1918). The bureaucracy concentrated on the villages and small towns, where most Japanese lived and where officials could rely on more stable local leadership than in the cities. The drive did not stop at exhorting peasants to pay taxes but also endeavored to create productive subjects who would constitute the basis of industrial competitiveness and national power. Inoue Tomoichi, an influential Home Ministry bureaucrat, openly worried that Japan was falling behind the other powers, as measured by several indices of national strength. Not only were the Japanese people working far fewer hours than Western counterparts, even their hens appeared to be less than diligent—laying a mere forty eggs per year, compared to seventy in Germany. The key to "managing a nation," concluded Inoue, was "making a people who work harder."[17] In 1908, this message was formalized in the Boshin Imperial Rescript. The emperor instructed his subjects to be "frugal in the management of their households . . . to abide by simplicity and avoid ostentation, and to inure themselves to arduous toil without yielding to any degree of indulgence."[18]

The Local Improvement Campaign mobilized the populace on several fronts. In the realm of administration, the Home Ministry sought to shore up local finances and eliminate replication by having village and town offices take over many of the responsibilities that previously had been handled by the traditional governing units, the hamlets. The most intrusive of these efforts involved the ministry's drive to dismantle the hamlets' Shinto shrines, where most Japanese had previously worshiped, and to replace them with one state-supported shrine per administrative village. The consolidation of local administration and shrines was designed to strengthen the villager's sense of identification with the central state and the emperor. Home Ministry bureaucrats also argued that the rationalization of local administrative and ritual life reduced the number of festivals, which they believed diverted villagers from working hard and paying their taxes.[19] Civil servants worked closely with "customs reform" groups to eliminate wasteful consumption in drinking, weddings, and funerals.

What particularly distinguished the Local Improvement Campaign from earlier campaigns was the creation of several intermediary mechanisms that enabled the state to convey its messages more effectively through local associations. Between 1900 and 1918, various ministries incorporated grass-roots groups into national hierarchical organizations: these included federations of agricultural cooperatives, the *hōtokusha* (village mutual assistance societies), young men's and young women's groups, and military reservists' associations.[20]

One might have expected the bureaucracy to lessen its reliance on moral suasion campaigns during the era of democratization and rapid urbanization following World War I. Yet rather than pull back, governments between the two world wars sponsored moral suasion drives in unprecedented numbers and variety. In 1919, once again under the banner of "postwar management," the Home Ministry launched the Campaign to Foster National Strength (Minryoku Kan'yō Undō). Local officials were instructed to encourage, even compel, the public to worship at State Shinto shrines and place Shinto altars in their homes so as to cultivate a "sound sense of the State." Combining economics and morality, the Campaign to Foster National Strength also aimed at eliminating the habits of "luxury and self-indulgence" that had developed as the result of Japan's rapid economic expansion during World War I. Officials blamed reckless consumption for the postwar inflation and rising foreign debt; these were important factors in Japan's declining power to compete in world markets in the 1920s. The solution, they believed, lay in gaining the "thorough understanding and cooperation of all the people" on behalf of "restraint in consumption."[21] The government's emphasis on savings promotion and austerity continued under the Campaign to Encourage Diligence and Thrift (Kinken Shōrei Undō, 1924–1926) and the Moral Suasion Mobilization Campaign (Kyōka Dōin Undō, 1929–1930).

Although the interwar campaigns flowed out of the earlier Local Improvement Campaign, there were significant changes, not the least of which was a new focus on the cities in addition to the countryside. The Local Improvement Campaign had paid relatively little attention to mobilizing urban residents before World War I because of difficulties in securing the cooperation of intermediary groups and community leaders. But by the early 1920s, a number of social problems had become associated with the cities. Hundreds of thousands of urban dwellers had rioted over the soaring price of rice in 1918, and surveys revealed distressing levels of destitution among the working poor. Growing numbers of workers took part in labor unions and strikes, and some of them embraced socialism, anarchism, and communism. Under the Campaign to Foster National Strength, officials and private groups responded by redoubling their efforts to organize urban life. They were further prodded to action by the anarchy and vigilantism that followed the Great Kantō Earthquake, which destroyed large parts of Tokyo and Yokohama in September 1923. One month later the government promulgated the "Imperial Rescript regarding the Promotion of National Spirit" (Kokumin Seishin Sakkō ni kansuru Shōsho), an exhortation to counteract dangerous tendencies in popular sentiments in the cities.

Officials thereupon encouraged the formation and coordination of "moral suasion groups" (kyōka dantai) that would "spiritually guide the people's sentiments and elevate and improve public morals."[22] These groups encompassed religious organizations, private charities and social services, temperance associations, and thousands of volunteers (hōmen iin) who visited the homes of the poor.[23] In 1924, the Home Ministry established a national Federation of Moral Suasion Groups (Kyōka Dantai Rengōkai). The Ministry of Education in 1925 counted seven or eight hundred moral suasion groups, estimating their membership in the tens of thousands. In the city of Osaka alone, some five thousand "moral suasion commissioners" (kyōka iin) served as liaisons among local moral suasion groups in 1926.

Whereas campaigns in the countryside generally relied on the local branches of state-sponsored associations, official drives in the cities tended to work through these more autonomous moral suasion groups. The active cooperation of the emerging urban middle classes was vital in this respect. To make their programs attractive to this stratum, the architects of the interwar campaigns were compelled to formulate more positive messages than the bleak imperatives of austerity and sacrifice. During the early 1920s, to be sure, the Campaign to Foster National Strength harangued urban consumers to return to the "beautiful customs of diligence and thrift." At nearly the same time, however, the Ministry of Education embarked upon the first of several "daily life improvement campaigns" (seikatsu kaizen undō), which proved more appealing to the middle classes. The improvement campaigns similarly urged the populace to be thrifty, yet they also introduced methods of bettering the quality of life by means of scientific budgeting, better nutrition and hygiene, and avoiding wasteful spending on festivals, alcohol, and tobacco.[24]

Initially aimed at the cities, the daily life improvement campaigns later, during the Depression years of the 1930s, focused on the "economic revitalization" of the villages. In a particularly vivid montage, the agricultural cooperative movement's popular magazine Ie no hikari (Light of the home) photographically profiled the various things villages were doing to improve work habits and reduce waste (see Figure 1).[25]

FIGURE 1. "The Latest in Daily Life Improvement," 1934. Upper row (left to right): An inexpensive cotton kimono for the bride; a communal clock that fosters "attention to, and respect for time"; one cooperative lends out funereal accoutrements to reduce the costs of ritual; and "civilians, too, are turning to communal cooking." Lower row: A stele proclaims: "This village gave up alcohol"; a model "improved kitchen"; and functional, "efficient" clothes for women who work at home and in the fields.

The interwar campaigns intervened in daily life to an extent that would not have been possible under the earlier Local Improvement Campaign. Central and local bureaucracies had grown, as had the numbers of co-operative volunteers.[26] At the height of the Campaign to Foster National Strength, the Home Ministry could send a directive inquiring about "programs to encourage frugality in consumption" and receive exhaustive reports from district chiefs, with detailed village-by-village information on the time spent on funerals and weddings and, in the case of weddings, the numbers attending, the type of cermemony, and what was served at the banquet.[27] The state's capacity to inundate the country with its messages reached awesome proportions by the time of the Moral Suasion Mobilization Campaign in 1929. The campaign's official history lists thousands of hortatory lectures given by officials and community leaders to women's associations, youth groups, religious organizations, and other civic groups. In the space of two months in rural Toyama prefecture, to take a random example, the campaign sponsored more than 300 public lectures and exhibitions and an additional 260 meetings of participating local groups and educators. The government's outreach was unquestionably aided by new technologies. The campaigns increasingly employed motion pictures; villages often distributed handbills to every household; and organizers blanketed public buildings with colorful posters conveying the nation's desperate need for savings and frugality (see Figure 2).[28]

The Japanese campaigns remind one of wartime drives launched by the Anglo-American powers to maintain popular morale and promote savings and austerity during the two world wars. Like their Japanese counterpart, governments in Britain and the United States attempted to use patriotism and non-market appeals to change everyday behavior.[29] But the differences may be more telling, for the modern Japanese state has managed its society in peacetime much as Western democracies have done only while at war. The blurring of wartime and peacetime mobilization can be explained in part by the fact that Japan was engaged in hostilities during nearly half of the years between 1894 and 1945: in the Sino-Japanese War (1894–1895), the Russo-Japanese War (1904–1905), World War I (1914–1918), and the "Fifteen Years War" (1931–1945). And when not at war, the government was often occupied with "postwar management" or preparations for the next war.

Nonetheless, even when the country was neither at war nor getting ready for one, Japan's social managers repeatedly invoked the image of war and the country's vulnerability. Following both the Russo-Japanese War and World War I, the public was warned again and again of Japan's "coming peacetime economic war" with the Western powers and the need to work hard, make sacrifices, and rally behind the state.[30] It is noteworthy that Hamaguchi Osachi's government was the first to adopt the military term "mobilization" in its Moral Suasion Mobilization Campaign in 1929, even though it was vigorously working to reduce Japan's military presence overseas at the time. Moreover, the wartime National Spiritual Mobilization Campaign (1937–1940) was not an unprecedented response to the needs of total war, but evolved from the peacetime moral suasion campaigns of the 1920s and early 1930s. Nor did the government abandon social management as a technique of economic

FIGURE 2. Poster from the Campaign to Encourage Diligence and Thrift, 1925. Caption reads: "Diligence and Thrift, the Seeds of Human Happiness." This idealized depiction of the gendered division of labor conveys the government's emerging message that motherhood and women's other domestic roles contribute to the national economy no less than males' productive labor.

development after World War II, despite the nearly universal consensus that Japan would never again be a military power. Nationalistic appeals continued to be used in numerous postwar campaigns to revive the nation's economy, increase savings, "rationalize" consumption, and encourage consumers to purchase Japanese products.

THE CASES

The moral suasion campaigns were an indispensable tool of social management in Japan, yet they were simply one aspect of the state's recurrent interventions into everyday life during the twentieth century. To capture the complexity of interrelationships between the state and society, the first four chapters of this book examine the evolution of welfare programs, policies toward religious organizations, the regulation of prostitution and illicit sexuality, and relationships between the state and emerging women's groups. I have chosen these cases in part because each represents a significant aspect of modern Japanese history that is little known to Western readers. The cases also exhibit several common features that deepen our understanding of the practice of social management.

As diverse as these issues may seem to Americans, in the years before 1945 the four programmatic areas came under the administrative jurisdiction of a cohesive set of elite bureaucrats located in the Home Ministry and, to a lesser extent, in the Ministry of Education. One result was that Japanese officials approached the issues as interrelated facets of larger social problems. By the early twentieth century, the Home Ministry functioned as a veritable general staff for domestic regulation. The ministry's higher civil servants were discouraged from specializing in any one policy area in the course of their careers. They typically rotated among the Home Ministry's many bureaus, which supervised the national police and handled matters relating to health and sanitation, licensed prostitution, social welfare, the State Shinto shrines, religious organizations (until 1913), labor policy (after 1922), and electoral reform (including the question of women's suffrage). The Home Ministry was also responsible for administering Japan's forty-seven prefectures, and most of its higher civil servants gained firsthand experience in integrating various programs of social management in their posts as district chiefs (*gunchō*), chiefs of the prefectural internal affairs and police affairs departments, and prefectural governors. The Ministry of Education initially played a smaller role in areas unrelated to the schools, but by the 1920s education officials were actively regulating religious organizations and disseminating "social education" and moral suasion among adults and youths who were no longer in school.[31] Few policy areas—or even the promotion of economic development—escaped the administrative purview of the two ministries. Whereas campaigns to augment national savings in Western nations were usually run by economic ministries, for example, the Home Ministry or Ministry of Education coordinated every savings drive until the wartime efforts of the late 1930s.

Regarding themselves as the enlightened "shepherds of the people" (*bokuminkan*), Home Ministry officials were supremely confident that there existed no problem that could not be solved by persuasion and the carefully supervised organization of intermediary groups.[32] Welfare policy thus became a matter of coordinating private relief efforts and reforming the habits of the poor so that public monies would not have to be spent on material assistance. The nation's religions figured prominently in programs of social management, both as subjects and objects. They offered the state a means of influencing great masses of people, though any religious organization potentially threatened the state and the rest of society by propagating heterodox beliefs and practices. Imperial Japan's extensive system of licensed prostitution existed not simply to prevent the spread of venereal diseases but to reinforce differences in sexual and gender roles that contributed to national efficiency, in the eyes of many Japanese. And the state's ongoing drives since the 1920s to integrate women into civic life stemmed from an interest in mobilizing women to manage other women and everyday life, as the local community became an extension of the domestic sphere.

All four areas reveal the substantial involvement of outside groups in helping to devise and implement the government's programs of social management. What appear to be instances of top-down control by the state turn out often to have resulted from demands by nongovernmental groups, which looked to the bureaucracy to advance their agenda. Established Buddhist and Christian denominations pressed officials to do something about their competitors, the "new religions"; community activists in the cities urged the government to formulate comprehensive programs for rehabilitating the poor; women's leaders contributed to the emerging consensus that the most appropriate public role for women was as agents of "daily life improvement"; and Protestants who wished to abolish licensed prostitution called upon the state to impose their own version of public morality. The activist groups in one story often appear in the other three, as well. Particularly prominent were Christian moral and social reform associations and the many local moral suasion groups, which took an interest in everything from socializing youth to organizing welfare and sanitation activities. These organizations were overwhelmingly middle-class in character. They were dominated by neither the great landlords nor big businessmen but rather by the old middle class of small farmers and petty entrepreneurs, and by the new middle class of educators, social workers, physicians, and the wives of salaried employees. Their middle-class nature rested, above all, on the common desire to improve the morality and behavior of the ordinary people below them.

Rethinking Japanese Political History

Most historical accounts of twentieth-century Japan posit a sharp divide between society and a powerful bureaucratic state. Sometimes the people appear to resist the regime; more often they acquiesce, but rarely are they depicted as cooperating actively with the state. This portrait of state-society relations has led historians on both sides of the Pacific to divide— not totally convincingly—the first half of the twentieth century into two distinct periods. The 1910s and 1920s are generally seen as a time of conflict between a conservative state and a progressive, urbanizing civil society that included labor unions, feminist organizations, liberal intellectuals, modernist writers, and Marxist social scientists.[33] The years between 1932 and 1945, by contrast, are described as a period when military and bureaucratic elites clamped down on this once-flourishing civil society and mobilized an obedient, passive population behind authoritarianism and war.[34]

Japan has enjoyed peace and unbroken parliamentary democracy since 1945, yet curiously the postwar era has been periodized much like the previous decades. Scholars write of the profound alienation of the urban populace from the ruling conservative politicians and bureaucrats between 1945 and 1960; thereafter, except for the brief citizens' movements, the middle and working classes resumed their passive support of the regime. Karel van Wolferen, who has offered the only serious analysis of present-day Japanese social management, put it bluntly: " 'civil society'—the part of the body politic outside the active Government and power system—is virtually unknown."[35]

Historians of Japan are just beginning to question these depictions of the people as simply the opponents or victims of the state. Carol Gluck pointedly challenges those Japanese scholars who contend that state officials single-handedly manufactured an oppressive "emperor-system ideology" between 1890 and 1915. She instead emphasizes the crucial role played by "popular" (*minkan*) ideologues—journalists, educators, and local notables—in creating a national orthodoxy.[36] Miles Fletcher does much the same for the 1930s, when many progressive intellectuals, enamored with European models of fascism and national socialism, took an active role in policymaking bodies and were responsible for introducing statist schemes that subordinated private interests.[37] A growing number of Japanese scholars similarly examine "grass-roots fascism," highlighting the often enthusiastic participation of ordinary people in the authoritarian mobilization drives of World War II.[38] Rich in potential, this new work nonetheless remains focused on two discrete eras, 1890–1915 and 1931–1945. What we need now are longer-term analyses of the processes by which groups within society, including progressive middle-class elements, joined government officials to manage the people throughout the twentieth century.

In examining the historical evidence, three themes will be important in reconceptualizing the relations between state and society: the role of the middle classes, the appeal of modernization, and the significance of gender in political history.

The Middle Classes and the State

Recent studies relate growing interventionism by Western states to the emergence of new middle classes. Many middle-class experts—social workers, educators, doctors, and psychiatrists—became civil servants, whereas others advised the authorities or administered social services with official support. The participation of these professionals encouraged states to undertake new forms of intervention, such as propagating better child-rearing techniques or investigating conditions of the poor.[39]

Few students of Japanese history, on the other hand, have explored the impact of the middle classes on the state. This may be because nearly all accounts depict the guardians of that state, the elite bureaucrats, as occupying a firmly autonomous space above the rest of society. Indeed, a strong case for bureaucratic transcendence may be made. Following the Meiji Restoration, the social gap between officials and most Japanese was enormous. The vast majority of the first generation of bureaucrats were former samurai, the warrior/administrative elite of the Tokugawa era.[40] Moreover, the modern bureaucracy was already in place by the early 1890s, before a sizable middle class appeared in the cities. A national parliament, the Imperial Diet, was not established until 1890, and loose collections of politicians—comprising landlords, businessmen, and some professionals—did not begin to form disciplined national parties until 1900. The two major political parties did become a significant part of the state from 1918 to 1932, when they organized a series of party-led cabinets.[41] But with the erosion of the parties' influence in cabinets during the crisis-filled years of the 1930s, career bureaucrats and military men once again made themselves synonymous with the "state" in the eyes of society.

By the 1920s, however, higher civil servants had much more in common with members of the new middle class than has been recognized. Both groups advanced primarily on the basis of mastering Western knowledge. In the late 1880s and 1890s new rules required most candidates to pass competitive examinations. With the establishment of Tokyo Imperial University in 1886 and thereafter other universities, higher education—not aristocratic pedigree—emerged as the acknowledged route to officialdom.[42] At the universities, which were concentrated in Tokyo and other big cities, would-be civil servants rubbed shoulders with those who would make up the new middle class of lawyers, journalists, educators, engineers, physicians, and salaried employees.[43] In cultural terms as well, during the early twentieth century, bureaucrats and their families adopted middle-class life styles that were associated with Westernization and urbanization.

Common backgrounds and experiences contributed to the growth of close relationships between influential officials and the middle-class activists who championed the modernization and Westernization of Japanese society. One of the earliest instances of such collaboration in policymaking occurred when higher civil servants and social policy scholars jointly surveyed labor conditions and formulated protective factory legislation at the turn of this century.[44] In the decades before World War II, the bureaucracy also relied extensively on the expertise of prominent Japanese Christian reformers, who served as conduits for information on the latest Western programs in the areas of social work, education, and moral uplift.

The boundaries between the higher civil servants and middle-class activists further blurred during the 1920s and 1930s.[45] To confront new social and economic problems, party cabinets and various ministries routinely convened authoritative study commissions, while private individuals and organizations established large numbers of policy-related discussion groups. Whether governmental or unofficial, these forums brought together bureaucrats, party politicians, journalists, academic experts, physicians, women's leaders, and other representatives of private associations.[46] The arenas of interaction expanded and became more formal during the latter half of the 1930s; officials and middle-class groups cooperated in supra-ministerial policy boards and on wartime councils that coordinated campaigns to mobilize the populace. Some historians judge that the state dominated this process of knowledge sharing.[47] Yet the frequent instances of collaboration often resulted, on the contrary, in high-ranking officials adopting middle-class commitments to the modernization of popular beliefs, daily habits, and gender relations.

Modernization and Social Management

This shared belief in modernization helps to explain the puzzling alliances between the state and progressive middle-class groups that are described in the chapters that follow. The imperial state before 1945 may strike contemporary Americans as unreservedly reactionary. It stamped out "new religions" as if they were premodern heresies, and it railed against the populace's embrace of "luxury and self-indulgence," just as the Tokugawa shogunate had harangued the peasants to be diligent and thrifty. To urban and Westernizing Japanese, however, the state was a more complicated entity. On one hand, the regime occasionally intruded on their freedom of expression and maintained the offensive institution of licensed prostitution. On the other hand, the middle classes in a late-developing nation like Japan generally regarded the state as a progressive agent in the transformation of daily life. Their mission and that of the government frequently became one: to eliminate the "evil customs of the past," in the words of the Charter Oath, which enunciated the principles of the Meiji regime in 1868.[48] So it was that the intellectuals could cheer on police who suppressed "superstitious" new religions; that middle-class women could cooperate with officials to introduce "scientific" methods of child rearing to rural and lower-class women; or that West-ern-educated Protestant social reformers could join with Confucian-minded bureaucrats to teach the poor the virtues of hard work, savings, and self-help.[49]

This book further argues that moral suasion campaigns became a fix-ture in Japanese governance during the twentieth century because, to a significant degree, they enjoyed broad support from the middle classes. This was particularly true in the case of the interwar campaigns to im-prove daily life. The government formally solicited the advice of women's leaders, educators, and other specialists. These middle-class experts, in turn, sought to use the authority of the state to improve the diet, hygiene, work habits, housing, consumption patterns, and ritual life of the Japa-nese people. It is not at all ironic that the democratizing decade of the 1920s would witness both the emergence of an urban middle-class culture and the growing use of moral suasion campaigns. In the postwar era, these "daily life improvement campaigns" continued to thrive under the name of "New Life campaigns." Their modernizing agenda united bu-reaucrats, conservative politicians, social democrats, and women's lead-ers, even during the latter half of the 1950s, when members of the Liberal Democratic and Socialist parties were literally slugging it out on the floor of the Diet over other issues. Clearly the government's success in managing Japanese society during this century rests in part on its ability to combine the mission to modernize and Westernize everyday life with the statist objectives of extracting savings, improving the quality of the work force, and maintaining social harmony.

Gender in the Study of Japanese Political History

In recent years one of the newest fields in history, the study of gender, has begun to influence one of the oldest, the study of politics and government. The analysis of gender, notes Joan Scott, developed in part as a reaction to another emerging subfield, women's history, which tended to examine women in isolation from males and the world of politics. The study of gender, on the other hand, permits historians to examine how societies constructed relations between the sexes and the roles of both women and men. Political historians are increasingly employing, in Scott's words, gender as "a useful category of historical analysis" to discuss such questions as regulated prostitution and state ideologies toward the family.[50] For example, Theda Skocpol and others explain cross-national variations in welfare policies in terms of prevailing conceptions of gender roles and the particular demands made by women's organizations in each country.[51]

To students of Japanese politics and political history, gender offers an especially useful category with which to provide fuller explanations and pose new questions. As I began this study of social management, it soon became obvious that one could not hope to comprehend relations between the Japanese state and society without examining the roles of women, sexuality, and other aspects of gender. The savage suppression of several new religions during the 1930s, for example, makes little sense unless we recognize that these sects attracted large numbers of married women and challenged widely held notions of public morality.

Looking at the interaction of state and society through the lens of gender also opens up whole new areas of inquiry. Policymakers and scholars have long debated the question of how the Japanese attained and maintained high rates of personal savings in the postwar era. Yet few economists and political scientists have seriously considered the century-long efforts of the government and private associations to mold a culture of savings and frugality by means of the moral suasion campaigns. One reason for the neglect, I suspect, is that the main actors in the campaigns are unknown to specialists on savings behavior. The savings drives developed in line with new perceptions of gender roles in society, as responsibility for household consumption became associated with wives, and women's groups emerged as key local agents in the campaigns. The category of gender, in short, is critical in understanding the pervasiveness of the modern Japanese state in daily life.

Finally, a book like this will be read by some as an exposé of the many Japanese who "collaborated" with the wartime regime between 1932 and 1945. That, however, is not my intention. I have deliberately adopted a century-long perspective because I seek to explain why officials and intermediary groups cooperated in programs of social management before, during, and after World War II. Rather than dwell on the transformation of leading progressives into statists, I am more interested in demonstrating how their participation in the formulation and administration of policy contributed to the relative success of Japanese social management.

Nor do I wish to deny the existence of conflict between various societal groups and the state in modern Japan. There were Communist party members, socialist feminists, and others who never accepted the "orthodoxy" put forward by the state and their allies. Even those organizations that welcomed some aspects of state intervention often criticized the government's other intrusions. Accordingly, this book explores the incidence of contention, as well as consensus. A work of this breadth and time span necessarily omits considerable detail and areas of analysis. These deficiencies, I can only hope, will inspire others to delve more deeply into the complex relationships between the Japanese state and everyday life.

PART ONE

*State and Society
before 1945*

The Evolution of
"Japanese-Style"
Welfare

THE MIDDLE of the twentieth century was a heady time for the proponents of state-sponsored welfare throughout the industrial world. By the 1960s the trend toward comprehensive, universal coverage appeared unmistakable. Reflecting the era in which they lived, historians scoured the past for the "origins of the welfare state" in various nations.[1] Although few non-Western states had developed welfare programs on the order of Western Europe and Australasia, scholars presumed that they would do so as their societies reached comparable levels of urbanization, industrialization, and national wealth. The history of welfare was thus bound up with the universal process of modernization, whose take-off points and end points seemed clear. Put simply, societies "progressed" in their responses to hardship and poverty in many aspects: from laissez-faire to state intervention; from viewing destitution as the result of individual failings to recognizing it as a "social problem"; from familial and communal support to public assistance; from fiscal conservatism to the guarantee to all of an established minimum standard of living; from charity to the citizen's entitlement or "right" to welfare benefits; from the social stigma of poor laws and poorhouses to unconditional, universal coverage by means of national health plans, old-age pensions, and various forms of social insurance; and from an emphasis on the moral reform of the poor to emphasis on the provision of material assistance.

This story of progress appealed to many Japanese during the 1960s and early 1970s. Optimists applauded Japan's achievements in "catching up" to the West, while more skeptical scholars pointed to aspects of modern welfare programs that the Japanese state and society had yet to accept fully. Yet both sides agreed that the European "welfare state" represented the standard against which Japan's welfare policies should be measured. When the Diet passed a slew of social legislation during the early 1970s, the media proclaimed 1973 "the first year of welfare." The process of convergence appeared to have entered the final stage.

The fragility of Western welfare states in the late twentieth century, however, forces us to rethink not only their future, but their past. It has become clear that welfare has not necessarily progressed, irreversibly, from premodern charity and relief to the modern welfare state; rather the various polarities presented above constitute arenas of ongoing contention, whose outcome is far from obvious. In the United States, politicians and the public have reacted angrily to "entitlements" and the alleged moral debilitation inherent in public assistance programs. Thatcherism in Britain revived the message of "self-help" as an antidote to dependence on state welfare. And many polities—notably France in 1995—struggled over how and whether to pay for increasingly expensive social programs. In Japan from the mid-1970s, the ruling Liberal Democratic party and the bureaucracy openly rejected the trajectory of European welfare states. They sought instead to build a "Japanese-style welfare society" (*Nihongata fukushi shakai*), in which families and communities provide the bulk of social welfare.

Contemporary Japan's ideological challenge to the "welfare state" suggests that a nation's shared values and history powerfully conditions how it defines "welfare" and formulates social policies. Indeed, during the first half of the twentieth century, government officials and many in the social work community strove to devise "Japanese-style" solutions to the growing problem of poverty. The authorities actively intervened to alleviate poverty, yet emphatically avoided major commitments to European-style public assistance and costly social programs. To those like the influential Home Ministry bureaucrat Inoue Tomoichi in 1912, "relief work" did not revolve around poor laws, but rather constituted "the most important task in managing a nation."[2] As he and others made clear, the successful management of relief lay in "improving the morals of the poor," organizing private social work, and preventing the growth of dependency on the state for assistance.[3] Between 1868 and 1945, the state and private groups combined efforts at managing society with various concrete programs to cope with destitution.

EARLY MODERN ANTECEDENTS

In a study of modern social politics in Britain and Sweden, Hugh Heclo observes that the twentieth-century social programs of the two welfare superstates did not arise in a vacuum. Both nations inherited attitudes and interventionist policies dating back to the establishment of extensive national poor-law systems in the late sixteenth century.[4] Much the same may be said for modern Japan, where welfare policies and moral suasion efforts were profoundly shaped by earlier ideas and the many programs that aimed at relieving destitution during the Tokugawa era (1600–1868).

The relief of poverty emerged as a central concern of the Tokugawa shogunate and individual domains. Just as municipalities and some national governments in early modern Europe assumed greater responsibility for poor relief in part to curb indiscriminate alms giving by the Catholic Church, Japanese rulers took over many of the welfare functions that had been performed in medieval times by Buddhist temples.[5] There were, however, critical differences between Japanese and European relief systems in terms of premises, scope, and operation. Writing in 1909, the Home Ministry official Inoue Tomoichi astutely observed that early modern relief programs in England and in German municipalities were characterized both by the existence of an "obligation" on the part of local governments to provide assistance, and by their "ongoing" nature such that public bodies aided indigents on a long-term basis.[6] Under England's Poor Law of 1601, the central government made parishes legally responsible for granting assistance to the poor—who might include male adults and their families in cases of unemployment and inadequate wages.[7]

In Japan, on the other hand, the concept of relief was embedded in a more personal, hierarchical relationship between the lord and his subjects. Chinese Confucianism sank its deepest roots during the Tokugawa period. This intensely political ideology extolled the virtues of the "kingly way" and "benevolent rule," by which the wise ruler ameliorated the misery of his people through timely doses of the "lord's relief" (osukui). In the words of Ikeda Mitsumasa, a daimyo (domainal lord) renowned for his philanthropy, "the lord [shogun] is entrusted by Heaven with the people of Japan." To demonstrate both his compassion and his moral authority the first shogun, Tokugawa Ieyasu, bequeathed to his son 30,000 pieces of gold and 13,000 kan of silver—the sum to be used solely for relief.[8] Japanese authorities considered natural disasters to be the principal source of destitution, and intervened to assist victims of crop failures, fires, typhoons, and floods.

The opportunity came often enough. Tokugawa society experienced at least three nationwide crop failures, in the 1730s, 1780s, and 1830s. Confronting a bad harvest in 1783, the domain of Shirakawa, for example, spent the enormous sum of 210,000 kan of silver to purchase rice, which it distributed to the families of retainers and peasants until the crisis passed. The daimyo Matsudaira Sadanobu, who later spearheaded the shogunate's Kansei reforms, may have financed the entire operation from his stepmother's personal wealth.[9] The provision of "lord's relief" became standard by the time of the devastating Tempō famine in the 1830s. Governments set up shelters, dispensed free rice, and employed artisans in relief construction projects.[10]

The primary objective of relief in the Tokugawa era was to maintain the millions of small-peasant households whose taxes were vital to the shogunate and domains. Nothing worried officials more than the specter of impoverished peasants abandoning their fields en masse. Although the lord self-consciously bestowed emergency assistance as an act of benevolence, villagers often came to expect disaster relief as an obligation of the ruler.[11] What Stephen Vlastos has called the "political economy of benevolence" reinforced Confucian ideology. Because of "fluctuations in yields and periodic crop failure," explains Vlastos, "peasants could not survive without judicious adjustments in fiscal policy, and benevolence appeared to protect the interests of both lord and peasant."[12]

As in most poor-relief systems, early modern Japanese officials attempted to set limits on seigneurial largess for moral and fiscal reasons. To this end, they designated the categories of those who merited assistance. The category of indigents requiring long-term, nondisaster relief was particularly circumscribed. Ogyū Sorai (1666–1728) and other Japanese Confucian scholars urged rulers to provide ongoing assistance only to those "who have no one to turn to" (mukoku no mono) or to "the helpless" (kanka kodoku—literally, "widows and orphans"). Few favored aid to the able-bodied and their families who might be temporarily down on their luck. Yamaga Sokō (1622–1685), an influential thinker on poor relief, defined the deserving poor as orphans, the severely ill or disabled, and those old people without offspring to take care of them.[13] Though he called on lords to relieve the "destitute" (kyūmin), Yamaga advised local functionaries to distinguish types of poverty, lest relief programs create more of "the indolent" (damin). If "idlers" (yūmin) were forced to reclaim new land, counseled Yamaga, the problem of poverty could be not merely relieved but prevented.[14] Officials most commonly responded to the able-bodied poor not with relief, but with "moral suasion" (kyōka)—exhorting the peasantry to practice the virtues of diligence and thrift. "Idlers" threatened a status-based order in which peasants, artisans, and merchants were expected to perform assigned productive roles.[15]

Although they upheld the lord's ultimate responsibility, the shogunate and domains further minimized their costs by delegating the primary tasks of relief to the family and community. In a formulation cited by generations of future Japanese leaders, Yamaga Sokō prescribed that, first and foremost, the poor should be helped by relatives; if one lacked relatives, the "village as a whole" bore the obligation to assist; but if the village itself were too impoverished to do so, a "magistrate should carefully investigate and, in the last resort, assistance should be granted from above."[16]

Studies confirm that early modern relief systems often operated much as Yamaga described them, with many villages vigorously assisting the destitute through various forms of mutual assistance. Because Tokugawa-era peasants paid taxes collectively as a village or a "five-family group," wealthier peasants commonly bore the burdens of less fortunate neighbors. Those with surplus land might also employ collateral relatives and other villagers. To forestall assuming an even greater portion of the communal tax burden, taxpaying peasants—like the domain itself—had a stake in maintaining the viability of weaker households. The system of collective responsibility similarly furnished a strong incentive for prosperous villagers to preach the virtues of diligence and thrift to less successful neighbors.[17]

Mutual assistance did not necessarily spring up spontaneously among the people. In many cases communal relief mechanisms were introduced and closely supervised by the authorities. Officials in the domain of Fukuoka, for example, were shocked by the weakness of local solidarity during the Kyōhō famine in the 1730s. In Shingū, one merchant hoarded his wealth while a third of the villagers died. By the mid-nineteenth century, donations by well-to-do villagers in Fukuoka had become commonplace, but only after the domain encouraged a sense of benevolence among them. Philanthropic commoners received official "letters of praise" and sometimes such samurai privileges as permission to wear a short sword or use a surname.[18] The elaborate system of village-level emergency granaries is another case in point. Rice was accumulated in good times for the purposes of feeding needy residents in times of crop failures and soaring prices. By the nineteenth century, many villages proudly maintained the granaries as communal institutions. Nonetheless, stern directives from the ruler were often initially required to persuade peasants to contribute a portion of their rice harvest to the granary.[19]

The authorities of early modern Japan in large part succeeded in containing the problem of poverty within villages by means of seigneurial "benevolence" and informal, albeit managed, mechanisms of mutual assistance. Shogunal and domain officials rarely dealt with the poor on an individual and ongoing basis, preferring to grant relief to entire villages in cases of disaster, or after rich peasants petitioned that they had exhausted their own resources in helping the poor.[20] In the big cities, however, administrators were forced to create more institutionalized programs of public assistance and indoor relief. Large numbers of peasants—many of them poor—migrated to the rapidly growing cities, particularly in the late seventeenth and early eighteenth centuries. Begging and vagrancy became major problems of public order.

Administered directly by the shogunate, the cities of Edo (present-day Tokyo) and Osaka initially responded to urban poverty in the mid-seventeenth century by establishing temporary relief shelters. Vagabonds were given food and immediately sent back to their homes in the countryside. Gradually the cities developed more permanent facilities, which Yoshida Kyūichi, the pioneer historian of Japanese social welfare, has compared to those run by European cities prior to England's Poor Law of 1601.[21] During the late seventeenth and early eighteenth centuries, Edo and Osaka constructed several poorhouses (*hiningoya*) in an effort to keep vagrants off the streets and house the sick and homeless.[22] Established in 1670, the *hiningoya* in the castle town of Kanazawa also doubled as workhouses and job-placement centers for the able-bodied.[23]

In Edo, the Temmei famine—coupled with massive rioting in 1787— sparked another round of institution building. The shogunate opened a new type of workhouse, the *ninsoku yoseba*, on the island of Ishikawa-jima in 1790. The facility aimed to remove the "non-criminal homeless" from Edo while teaching them work skills prior to resettlement elsewhere. Daniel Botsman has noted that new strains of neo-Confucianism and nativism (*kokugaku*) held out the possibility of morally reforming commoners, including vagrants. Shogunal officials took the task of rehabilitation so seriously that they appointed a leading scholar of "practical ethics" (Shingaku) to give three day-long lectures each month to inmates. From the start, coercion coexisted with moral suasion as means of instilling a work ethic. Authorities punished laziness and bad behavior by binding an inmate's hands, and those who attempted to escape were to be decapitated. After it began incarcerating convicted criminals in the 1820s, the *ninsoku yoseba* became less of a welfare institution for the homeless and more of a penal institution.[24]

Also in the early 1790s, the shogunal chief councilor Matsudaira Sadanobu introduced Tokugawa Japan's most extensive system of ongoing outdoor relief in Edo. City officials created an endowment that was financed by a shogunal donation and the substantially larger "seventy-percent reserve fund"—so called because it amounted to seventy percent of a special levy on the townspeople of Edo. A new town office, the *machi-kaisho*, was established to administer the fund along with three granaries to store relief rice. Assistance was divided into "temporary relief" for disaster victims and "ongoing relief" for those elderly, young children, and chronically ill who lacked relatives to support them. An estimated 1,826 people, or 4 of every 1,000 townspeople in Edo, received ongoing assistance in 1805, a fairly typical year without major disasters.

This ratio far exceeded the proportion aided by modern Japanese public assistance programs before the 1930s. In addition, twenty times between 1802 and 1868 the *machi-kaisho* provided temporary relief to more than 5,000 people a year. In several instances recipients numbered more than half of the non-samurai population of Edo. Though supervised by the shogunate, the *machi-kaisho* was managed by wealthy merchants and other townspeople. Edo's poor-relief apparatus thus constituted a more rationalized, public, and ongoing institution than either seigneurial benevolence or the ad hoc mutual assistance schemes found in the villages and other cities.[25]

One final ingredient in the early modern response to poverty was the emergence of a more optimistic philosophy of self-help among the peasantry itself. From the ranks of prosperous farmers arose several agricultural reformers, the best-known of whom was Ninomiya Sontoku (1787–1856). These reformers traveled the countryside promoting new methods for improving productivity and, together with itinerant religious figures, attempted to inculcate the Confucian virtues of filial piety and diligence.[26] Yet the reformers distinguished their teachings from the orthodox Confucian view of a static social order, in which peasants were not to accumulate surplus wealth. Even the poorest peasant could enrich himself by his own efforts, they insisted. One farming primer instructed: "Let two men be equally lucky, one will succeed and the other fail by reason of differences in skill."[27] Relying on the "lord's relief," warned the reformers, would only destroy the moral capacity of the poor to help themselves. In the 1830s, Ninomiya Sontoku sternly advised the daimyo of Odawara: "Grants in money, or release from taxes, will in no way help them in their distress. Indeed, one secret of their salvation lies in withdrawing all monetary help from them. Such help only induces avarice and indolence, and is a fruitful source of dissensions among the people."[28] To Ninomiya, whether one lived in wealth or poverty depended on the degree of one's own diligence (*kinrō*), thrift (*bundo*), and willingness to yield to others (*suijo*). To be diligent, one needed to practice "self-management" (*jiei*)— that is, to restrain one's innate "indolence and selfishness."[29]

These efforts to instill values of self-help profoundly influenced official and popular attitudes toward welfare in modern Japan. Robert Bellah has argued that such doctrines served as the equivalent of the Protestant ethic in fostering indigenous capitalism before the import of Western industrialization.[30] They also may have given rise to the "Protestant" notion that if an individual was not prosperous, he or she must be lazy and spendthrift. However, Ninomiya and other reformers by no means reduced the sources of poverty to individual failings, nor did they necessarily relegate the task of rescue to the individual and the family. On the contrary, Ninomiya strongly encouraged villagers to engage in mutual assistance and provide no-interest loans to the poor.[31] Although he advanced the message of economic recovery by "self-reliance" (*jiriki*), he defined "self" to mean the entire community, not the individual.[32] Other reformers similarly promoted indigenous welfare mechanisms within the villages.[33]

The movement toward self-help in the late Tokugawa era thus bequeathed a complex legacy to modern Japan. On one hand, a belief grew among local elites that official relief fostered indolence in individuals. On the other hand, many within and outside the government became convinced that poverty could be eliminated outright if the community and state worked together to reform the morals of the poor.

"Mutual Fellowship" and Malthus

The Tokugawa order came crashing down in 1868 when a number of powerful domains defeated shogunal forces and installed a government that ruled in the name of the emperor. The decade following the Meiji Restoration witnessed a flurry of changes that affected nearly every aspect of Japanese institutional and everyday life. Faced with foreign and domestic challenges, leaders of the new government transformed the existing patchwork of shogunal lands and some 250 autonomous domains into a centralized nation state. In 1871, the domains were abolished, replaced by French-style prefectures administered by centrally appointed governors. The process astounded the British minister to Japan, who observed that similar episodes of unification in Europe had required years of warfare.[34] Determined to create a modern nation on the order of its Western rivals, the regime thereupon introduced universal education, military conscription, and other radically new institutions.

What "modernization" and "Westernization" meant in the context of social welfare, however, is less obvious. Japan did not have anything approaching a comprehensive public assistance law until 1929. Some scholars detect a gradual modernization of policies toward the poor during the late nineteenth century, as many Japanese came to view destitution as the result of social and economic causes—not personal failings—and accordingly looked to state intervention to ameliorate poverty.[35] Others charge the Japanese government with having shirked the responsibilities of a modern state to assist the poor.[36] But in measuring late-nineteenth-century poor relief by the standards of the mid-twentieth-century welfare state, neither group of scholars examines the evolving welfare programs on their own terms. The chief areas of contention rarely revolved around whether the authorities should or should not be responsible for social welfare. As in the early modern era, most Japanese officials believed that the central state (as successor to the shogun and daimyo) bore responsibility for mobilizing the resources of the nation, at all levels, to assist the destitute. The questions that most divided officials and politicians before 1945, however, were to what extent the state should impose central control over the provision of relief, and how the financial burden would be allocated among the state, local governments, communities, and families.

The Tokugawa approach to the poor loomed large in the first years of the Meiji era (1868–1912). In its opening proclamation, the Restoration government sought to legitimize its rule in Confucian terms much the same as those used by the first Tokugawa shogun. The declaration extolled the virtues of the "lord's relief of the people," noting that "the king's treasure is his people."[37] The Meiji government also inherited the tendency to concentrate relief efforts on maintaining the agrarian population of taxpayers. Efforts to protect children remained a priority. Shogunal and domain officials had long endeavored to discourage peasants from the widespread practices of infanticide and abandonment. In 1871, the new regime similarly instructed local governors to provide 126 liters of rice annually for the upkeep of abandoned children until they reached fifteen years of age. Two years later the government began granting poor families cash payments of 5 yen upon the birth of their third child.[38]

Like their early modern predecessors, the Meiji leaders responded most generously to destitution brought on by natural calamities. They furnished assistance not only to prevent impoverished farmers from leaving the land but also to mollify the many discontented peasants who took part in organized protests (as they had in the late Tokugawa years). Within months of taking power in 1868, Restoration leaders ordered governors of the former shogunal lands to use local funds in aid of victims of floods and fires. Central officials drew heavily on Tokugawa precedents over the next decade, taking control of local emergency granaries and deferring land-tax payments when entire villages suffered bad harvests.[39]

In 1880, the government formulated the innovative Agricultural Distress Fund Law (Bikō Chochikuhō), which blended indigenous practices of emergency granaries with land-tax relief regulations found in Westphalia and the Rhenish provinces of Prussia. Drafted by a German employee, Paul Mayet, the measure instituted substantial central and prefectural reserve funds, which made grants or loans to victims of bad harvests or "undeserved misfortunes." Between January 1881 and March 1886, 3.8 million victims were granted money to sustain themselves, and 880,000 families received additional assistance in the form of grants or loans to rebuild houses, purchase farm implements and seeds, or pay land taxes. Several newspapers and journals in Germany, which had just pioneered social insurance for workers, praised Japan's system of agricultural insurance as a model worthy of consideration. To Mayet's dismay, the Agricultural Distress Fund system was drastically cut back in 1890, after the state ceased contributing an annual 1.2 million yen to the reserve funds.[40]

One of the most elaborate welfare programs of the early Meiji years was aimed not at the most destitute but at members of Japan's warrior elites, the samurai. A great many samurai had fallen into debt before the Meiji Restoration. They suffered further during the 1870s, as the reforming state abolished their feudal privileges and commuted their stipends into inconvertible bonds. Out of compassion—and no doubt fears of armed insurrection—the leadership offered a number of relief measures that included low-interest loans and the resettlement of former samurai on reclaimed lands.[41]

In contrast to samurai, disaster victims, and abandoned children, the chronically poor neither constituted an organized threat to the new state nor did their existence significantly weaken the agrarian tax base. From the start, the Meiji leadership distinguished those requiring long-term relief from other destitute subjects, and the former generally were provided with public assistance at lesser amounts and on a much smaller scale. In 1874, the regime promulgated the Relief Regulations (Jukkyū Kisoku). Because this rather modest piece of legislation persisted as Japan's only general poor law for the next fifty-five years, its underlying assumptions merit close attention.

The officials who drafted the Relief Regulations may have been aware of European poor laws, but the provisions and very language of the ordinance flowed entirely out of Tokugawa-era precedents. Indeed, the statute was more a restatement of early modern Japanese norms than a detailed poor law. The preamble declared that "relief of the poor and destitute should be based on mutual fellowship among the people" (*jimmin no jōgi*). The one group—and by implication, the only group—that required state assistance according to the provisions of the Relief Regulations were "the poor who have no one to turn to" (*mukoku no kyūmin*). In keeping with shogunal and domain policies that had excluded the able-bodied and their families, the ordinance limited relief to those who "were extremely poor and without family" in the following categories: the crippled; those aged seventy and older who suffered from "severe illnesses and decrepitude of old age"; the chronically ill; and children aged thirteen and younger. In each case except that of children, recipients had to be incapable of working. The regulations did, however, permit assistance to those indigents whose only living relatives were elderly or children.[42]

Even as the Relief Regulations invoked the categories and parlance of the past, in other important respects they marked a sharp break from the poor-relief programs of the Tokugawa era. The ordinance "modernized"

Japanese social welfare insofar as it centralized and standardized the myriad relief programs administered by the shogunate, domains, and big cities. In practice, the modernization of Japanese welfare often meant enormous reductions in local relief programs that had previously assisted whole families, the able-bodied, and other categories not covered by the Relief Regulations. The reasons were in large part fiscal. The new regime found itself in financial crisis, inheriting the debts and expenditures of the shogunate and domains while struggling to build Japan into a world power.[43]

In addition to fiscal motivations, Restoration leaders were determined to strengthen the hand of the central bureaucracy vis-à-vis local self-governing entities. While praising "mutual fellowship among the people"—that is, the ad hoc efforts of local people to help their destitute neighbors—the Meiji government took a dimmer view of civic institutions in the big cities that dispensed relief in the form of public assistance. The fate of the substantial "seventy-percent reserve fund" in Tokyo (formerly Edo) is a telling illustration. The ranks of the city's poor swelled amid the dislocations of the late Tokugawa era and early Meiji years. In 1868, the town office or *machi-kaisho* gave temporary assistance to a staggering 941,686 people (18.7 percent of the population), and granted ongoing assistance to 16,568 people (0.3 percent) the following year. Given the scale of this assistance program, prefectural authorities complained that they could not hope to compete for the "loyalty" of the people if the "wealthy merchants of the city" continued to oversee the provision of poor relief.[44] Alarmed by the huge expenditures and by the competiton for influence, the new Tokyo prefectural government abolished the *machi-kaisho* in 1872. Their action severely curtailed the provision of poor relief in Tokyo.

Under the watchful eyes of the newly created Home Ministry, the Relief Regulations became the linchpin in a dual policy aimed at centrally managing the provision of relief and minimizing its costs. In 1875, the Home Ministry directed prefectural officials to investigate all applicants for state relief. Applicants, the directive warned, might qualify "in name" because of age or disability, but "even those aged seventy and older and cripples" must prove their inability to work. The ministry also ordered the authorities to refuse relief to anyone who might be supported by family members or the community (although state funds could supplement communal assistance if it was deemed to be insufficient).[45] Local officials, in fact, devoted considerable efforts to locating relatives who could maintain the applicant and save the state some money. In several instances, officials compelled an elderly applicant to adopt an unrelated adult as a son, persuading the younger man to assume responsibility for supporting his new parent.[46]

Guided by such directives, the Japanese bureaucracy held the costs of state relief at remarkably low levels during the last three decades of the nineteenth century. The number of those receiving relief nationwide under the Relief Regulations ranged from 2,521 in 1876 to 18,545 in 1892. As measured against the entire population, recipients accounted for a mere .018 percent between 1876 and 1885, and .041 percent between 1886 and 1895. Moreover, the provision of relief bore little relation to the actual incidence of destitution. At a time of acute recession and large-scale migration to the cities, only 25 indigents were granted state relief in all of Tokyo prefecture in 1885. Regional disparities could be profound, particularly within Japan's poorest area, the northeast. Between 1885 and 1889, the annual number of recipients in Aomori prefecture rose as high as 1,740, while the numbers peaked at a mere 3 people in neighboring Iwate prefecture and 2 in nearby Miyagi prefecture.[47]

The Home Ministry stringently administered the Relief Regulations, not only to maintain the national treasury but also to prevent moral degeneration among the poor, including those not able to work. In a memorial to the Council of State in May 1875, the ministry warned that "if *the elderly, sick, poor and, decrepit* grow accustomed to relief, in the end, will not good people lapse into idleness and lose their sense of diligence?" Worst of all, recipients would "lose their spirit of independence and, in particular, become reliant on the government." The ill effects of "recklessly" providing relief were already apparent in Western nations, where poor laws were the subject of intense debate, observed ministry officials.[48]

If the Home Ministry's attitudes evoke the Malthusian critique of poor relief, this was not entirely coincidental. British theories of laissez-faire and individualism became influential in Japan during the 1870s, in part because they squared with indigenous beliefs that praised self-reliance and criticized official relief for fostering indolence. In his famous *Essay on Population* (1798), Thomas Robert Malthus had inveighed against the English poor laws, arguing that poor relief increased the number of paupers and lowered the wages of industrious laborers. Morally, relief subverted the peasantry's "spirit of independence," encouraged "carelessness and want of frugality," and weakened "sobriety and industry."[49]

From wealthy farmers to Tokyo journalists and officials, Japanese devoured translations of works by Malthus, John Stuart Mill, and Adam Smith. The *Essay on Population* appeared in translation in 1876, supplemented in 1887 by Henry Fawcett's invective against public relief, *Pauperism: Its Causes and Remedies.* Most widely read was Samuel Smiles' *Self-Help,* which preached the value of individual self-improvement as against charity and relief.[50] Several leaders of the Meiji government encountered popularizations of the Malthusian critique firsthand while on the Iwakura mission to Britain, the United States, and other Western nations in 1872–1873. Some went well beyond Tokugawa-era thinking—which had viewed official relief as encouraging indolence—to regard poverty itself as the product of individual failings. Upon returning to Japan, the mission's leader, Prince Iwakura Tomomi, offered this assessment in 1873: "Those whom we call 'the poor' are lazy and unwilling to work diligently. Clearly, they have brought their poverty upon themselves. Shizoku [samurai] are different. They have fallen into difficulties because of political changes. Lumping them together with 'the poor' knows no parallel."[51]

Official and popular attitudes toward poverty were also influenced by the growth of liberal thought within Japan itself. Back from his round-the-world tour, the publicist Fukuzawa Yukichi described the British poor-law debates as early as 1866 in his widely read *Seiyō jijō* (Conditions in the West). Fukuzawa denounced indiscriminate charity in virtually the same terms as those later employed in 1875 by the Home Ministry concerning the Relief Regulations. Such practices, he charged, "accustom the good people of the realm to the ways of idleness." He instead proposed the establishment of a national relief law, but only if, like England's New Poor Law of 1834, it aimed at driving the indigent off the dole by establishing workhouses whose conditions were worse than those of the lowest class of independent laborer.[52] Fukuchi Gen'ichirō, chief editor of the pro-government *Tōkyō nichinichi shimbun*, stated the case for laissez-faire succinctly in 1874: "It is evident that relief is not the business of government." And in a sign that the public did not necessarily equate the Meiji emperor with the new state during the 1870s, Fukuchi cavalierly dismissed the premodern Confucian tenet that "the emperor is father and mother to the people." Concluded the newspaperman with characteristic bluntness: "the government, it has become evident, is not father and mother to the people, and there is no reason why it should grant relief."[53]

Furthermore, as in Western nations, early democratization increased grass-roots pressures for lessening the costs of public relief.[54] No sooner had the government created prefectural assemblies in the late 1870s than local notables introduced several measures to abolish or curb the use of prefectural taxes for relief expenditures.[55] In 1881, the Tokyo prefectural assembly eliminated funds for free medical treatment and the Tokyo Poor House. One member, the liberal economist Taguchi Ukichi, repudiated the very principle of publicly funded assistance: "to save the poor, we are, in fact, levying local taxes on one set of poor to assist another. . . . If assemblymen with extra wealth take pity on the prefecture's poor, they should gladly give their own money."[56] When the popularly elected Lower House of the Imperial Diet first met in 1890, representatives vehemently attacked the government's poor relief bill (kyūmin kyūjo hōan), a modest attempt to expand the Relief Regulations. Asked one deputy, a student of English liberalism, "Are the poor made sick by society? Are they made idle by society? Are they made negligent by society?" No, he replied, and the state therefore had no obligation to assist them.[57]

Although the imported doctrine of laissez-faire reinforced the Meiji government's determination to avoid large expenditures on poor relief, Japanese officials categorically rejected the liberal principle that the state should play a minor role in managing the welfare of its people. Whereas liberal thinkers hoped that people would aid their unfortunate neighbors out of a sense of moral duty, the authorities did their utmost to manage the provision of relief at the local level so that "mutual fellowship among the people" would become reality. Viewing poor relief as an obligation of families and communities, they were also less concerned than British contemporaries in assessing whether one's poverty was the result of individual failings.[58] The Home Ministry enforced the Relief Regulations not simply to screen out applicants but in a more positive manner to arrange familial and communal support for the many poor who were ruled ineligible for state relief. Officials received explicit legal authority to make the family the basis of social welfare after the Civil Code of 1898 required family members and even distant relatives to support their poor.[59] "Laissez-faire" would have been the last word to describe the many instances in which the state intervened to force families and neighbors to aid the poor.

At the prefectural level, officials actively encouraged (and occasionally compelled) the local rich to bear the primary costs of relief during the 1880s and 1890s. The Meiji regime continued Tokugawa-era practices of commending subjects who aided the destitute.[60] To coordinate private and public relief work, governmental agencies also conducted detailed surveys that enumerated and classified the poor. In 1885, the Tokushima prefectural office counted 81,524 "poor people who faced starvation." Their plight was somewhat eased by donations from local "charitable worthies" (yūshisha), who furnished nearly half of the prefecture's disaster relief funds.[61] That same year in Saitama prefecture, the Satte district office reported that an extraordinary 30 percent of the district's inhabitants were receiving relief rice from the wealthy.[62]

The government reined in the costs of state, prefectural, and municipal relief by aggressively organizing private relief efforts while reserving public assistance as the last resort. This managed system of welfare unquestionably prevented widespread starvation and endemic social unrest. The system worked as well as it did, argues Ikeda Yoshimasa, because during the early Meiji period Japan was still an overwhelmingly agrarian society. In contrast to early modern England where the increasing concentration of landowning created large numbers of destitute wanderers and prompted the Elizabethan Poor Law, the number of farm households in Japan declined very slowly between the Meiji Restoration and the end of World War II. The chief sources of relief for most of Japan's poor remained families, stable villages, and mutual assistance networks.[63]

Nevertheless, by the 1890s intellectuals and bureaucrats were openly questioning whether the state's reliance on private relief activities could cope with new types of poverty arising from urbanization and industrialization. The recession of the mid-1880s may not have dispossessed Japanese peasants to the degree that England's enclosure movement did, but many indebted farmers did leave for the cities in search of work. In Tokyo and Osaka, highly visible slums sprang up as day laborers, rickshaw drivers, artisans, mechanics, and female textile operatives crowded into disease-infested neighborhoods. A survey by the Tokyo Metropolitan Police in 1890 classified 5,736 of the prefecture's population as "poor," including 291 individuals who were "on the verge on starvation."[64]

The specter of hungry masses rising up in social revolution prompted one group of scholars and bureaucrats to propose a comprehensive alternative to both the laissez-faire and state-managed/privately funded approaches to poverty. The movement's leading figures were Professor Kanai Noburu of Tokyo Imperial University and Gotō Shimpei, chief of the Home Ministry's Bureau of Hygiene during most of the 1890s. Both men had been inspired by their studies of "social policy" in Bismarck's Germany. Together with followers, they held that the state—in the interests of maintaining order and raising productivity—had an obligation to advance the well-being and health of its people by means of various social programs. The so-called social policy school proposed to shift the focus from the traditional relief of the elderly, sick, and crippled to improving the welfare of the more numerous working poor.[65] Gotō's innovative proposal for worker's sickness insurance was drafted in 1898 by his protégé in the Bureau of Hygiene, Kubota Shizutarō. Repudiating the "principle of pure charity" inherent in the Relief Regulations, Kubota called for an ambitious European-style program that combined nationally legislated public assistance for the poor with social insurance funded in part by workers' contributions.[66]

For all their intellectual vitality, the German-inspired champions of expanded public assistance proved no match for the combined forces of managed poor relief and liberal individualism in a series of parliamentary and bureaucratic skirmishes.[67] The first such episode occurred in 1890, when the government submitted the poor relief bill to the Diet. Drafted by the Home Ministry, the measure fell short of the extensive programs later proposed by Gotō Shimpei and his disciples, but it nonetheless departed significantly from the Relief Regulations of 1874. The Home Ministry's spokesman, Vice Minister Shirane Sen'ichi, pointedly condemned the government's previous reliance on private charity, communities and family: "You cannot relieve poverty in cases when there is neither mutual assistance among neighbors nor even a neighborhood. Nor relatives. Or when there are relatives, but they lack the resources to offer assistance."[68] To overcome the limits of the Relief Regulations, the poor relief bill emulated English and German poor laws in establishing a centrally supervised system that assigned municipalities the responsibility of assisting the poor out of public funds.[69]

Despite the legislation's modest scope, the Lower House overwhelmingly rejected the poor relief bill. In addition to citing the debilitating effects of relief on the poor, opponents predicted that local governments and taxpayers would bear the major share of the increased costs. Besides, some insisted, there were relatively few indigents in Japan, and they could be adequately aided by private philanthropy.[70] The government, which had done little to lobby for the poor relief bill, did not again sponsor a general poor relief measure until 1929. The grandiose programs formulated by Gotō Shimpei's Bureau of Hygiene failed to gain the endorsement of the Home Ministry, much less the cabinet. Gotō's proposed sickness insurance legislation remained a bureaucratic vision, and the Lower House in 1897 summarily pigeon-holed two public assistance bills that the Bureau of Hygiene had apparently drafted.[71] As the proponents of European public assistance faltered, others rushed in, determined to modernize Japan's indigenous welfare practices.

WELFARE AS MORAL REFORM

In 1902, three members of the Lower House introduced yet another poor relief bill. They found themselves face to face with a representative of the Home Ministry who was quite unlike the Bureau of Hygiene's proponents of German social policy. Inoue Tomoichi denounced the bill for resembling the public assistance laws of England and Germany. He warned that, if effected, the measure's "obligatory assistance would foster indolence, vastly increase the numbers of the poor, and siphon off national funds."[72] Inoue had returned one year earlier from a tour of the West, where he attended the International Social Work Conference in Paris and surveyed welfare programs in several advanced nations. He quickly emerged as the government's spokesman on poor relief, and in 1909 he published Kyūsai seido yōgi, a 550-page tome on Western and Japanese relief programs. As chief of the Prefectural Section (Bureau of Local Affairs) from 1897 to 1912 and governor of Tokyo prefecture from 1915 until his death in 1919, Inoue dominated thinking on welfare during the twentieth century's first two decades and beyond. He personified a new breed of bureaucratic experts and social work leaders. He was cosmopolitan and well acquainted with the latest trends in Western social policies. He was also intimately aware of the growing pessimism among Europeans concerning their own poor laws. Like others in the Home Ministry and social work community, Inoue fervently believed that Japanese solutions could forestall the explosion of poverty that had accompanied industrialization elsewhere.

Whereas Home Ministry officials had acknowledged the deficiencies of the Relief Regulations when they were considering European-inspired legislation during the 1890s, ministry leaders after 1900 presented the Relief Regulations as the ideal basis of Japan's distinctive and successful solution to poverty. Although the early Meiji government had couched its relief programs in traditional language, Inoue Tomoichi and his allies pointedly defined Japanese welfare policy in terms of how it differed from the poor laws of England, Germany, and other European nations:

> Our Relief Regulations system has never embraced the principle of obligating [the State or local governments] to grant assistance. Furthermore, . . . the healthy poor have been placed entirely outside the system. A fixed amount of assistance is provided as an act of mercy by the State (*kuni no onten*), but the right of the destitute to request assistance is not recognized. Also, the task of providing assistance is not left to the discretion of the local government; rather, the State administration possesses the sole authority to decide when assistance is permitted.[73]

The Japanese government, judged Inoue, had theretofore administered the Relief Regulations under the "principle of strictly limited assistance," and it remained wary of transforming Japan into a nation with a European-style "ongoing relief system" that aided the "healthy, able-bodied poor."[74]

Home Ministry spokesmen increasingly strove to persuade the public that the essential qualities of the Japanese made substantial public assistance unnecessary. Relief in Japan, according to Inoue, was based on the "ideals of pure philanthropy (*hakuaishugi*)"—that is, wealthy people's spirit of "charity and benevolent love" toward the poor of their communities.[75] Others like Tokonami Takejirō, chief of the Bureau of Local Affairs in 1910 and later an influential home minister, emphasized the role of the Japanese family. In Western countries, where "individualism" flourished, elaborate welfare programs treated members of families as individuals, but "in Japan, the family is the unit of society. A parent must raise a child, and a child must help his parent. Brothers must be kind to each other. . . . It is a family shame to send one of its own out to bother outsiders and to depend on others for assistance. This has been the social organization of our country since ancient times." The reliance on the family, asserted Tokonami, explained why there were so few poor in Japan, despite "extremely low expenditures" on charity and relief. In contrast, he noted, the weak family structure of Britain had forced that government in 1909 to commit the equivalent of 85 million yen for pensions covering all elderly.[76]

The more Japanese bureaucrats learned of expanding European welfare states the more obsessed they became with the need to prevent "the evils of excessive assistance (rankyū)" in their own country. They were haunted by the case of England, where costs and number of recipients had skyrocketed, notwithstanding efforts to limit the scope of the Poor Law in the reform of 1834.[77] The Home Ministry's determination to escape England's destiny produced tangible results. By 1908, Inoue Tomoichi could boast that administrators had succeeded in reducing the annual number of new recipients of aid under the Relief Regulations from 12 per 10,000 Japanese in 1892 to only 3 each in 1903, 1904, and 1905 (see Table 1 for total numbers of recipients). Even if one counted relief spending by prefectural and municipal governments, in addition to that by the state, he estimated that total annual expenditures rose very little between 1897 and 1906, from 319,000 yen to 400,000 yen. To Inoue, this was evidence of the central state's ability to control relief spending by local governments, as well. Convinced that tough-minded relief policies staved off fiscal and moral decline, Inoue boasted: "Comparing these [statistics in Japan] with those of Western countries, we see the differences between Heaven and Earth, and we must call this a great happiness without parallel in the world."[78]

Presumably Inoue became even happier after May 1908, when Tokonami Takejirō, chief of his Bureau of Local Affairs, directed prefectural governors "to correct excessive assistance in nationally funded assistance by encouraging cooperative assistance" at the local level. The new policy resulted in a sharp reduction of recipients of state relief from 13,106 in 1907 to fewer than 3,000 annually in 1910–1912—or from 0.28 recipients per 1,000 Japanese to only 0.05 recipients (see Table 1). Municipalities gradually assumed most of the burden of poor relief, but the cutbacks had a devastating impact on the cities in the short term. The Home Ministry slashed the city of Osaka's 1909 poor relief budget to one-fifth of the previous year's allocation, forcing the city temporarily to suspend all payments of state-funded relief. Remarkably enough, between 1907 and the end of 1917—a time of rapid urbanization, inflation, and a 14 percent rise in total population—the central government reduced its expenditures on poor relief from 216,907 yen to only 29,365 yen.[79]

As in the 1870s, the government's retrenchment in relief spending did not mean an end to official intervention in the realm of social welfare. On the contrary, the Home Ministry's directive of 1908 marked the begin-

TABLE 1
Public Assistance under Relief Regulations (1892–1931) and
Relief and Protection Law (1932–1944)

Year	Recipients of assistance	Recipients per thousand of total population	Expenditure on assistance (yen)
1892	18,545	0.46	127,504
1895	16,715	0.40	141,450
1900	15,211	0.35	183,006
1905	14,183	0.30	192,840
1907	13,106	0.28	216,907
1908	9,335	0.19	193,863
1909	3,753	0.08	62,979
1910	2,877	0.06	37,864
1912	2,402	0.05	49,565
1915	7,247	0.14	134,583
1917	7,355	0.14	163,520
1920	7,565	0.13	427,053
1925	8,577	0.14	401,045
1930	17,403	0.27	727,384
1931	18,118	0.28	624,228
1932	157,564	2.37	3,607,934
1933	213,462	3.17	5,176,214
1937	236,565	3.35	6,423,434
1940	182,696	2.54	—
1944	143,000	1.92	—

Source: Kōseishō, Kōseishō 50-nenshi, 2:815–16, 818–19.

ning of a new welfare policy that actively worked to prevent poverty by morally instructing the poor. In his case against European-style poor relief, Inoue Tomoichi insisted that "a system to prevent poverty is the root, whereas a system to relieve poverty is the branch." And the best way to prevent poverty, he concluded, was "to improve the general morals of the poor and develop their industry while establishing programs to encourage their diligence, thrift, and vigorous efforts."[80]

Although early modern Japanese thinkers had similarly recommended preventive works over relief, Home Ministry officials claimed to have been immediately inspired by Western trends toward using "moral suasion" as the key to preventing poverty.[81] Ironically, these bureaucrats, whose ministry was ruthlessly controlling socialism at the time, were strongly influenced by the theories of the British Fabian socialists, Sidney and Beatrice Webb. As a member of the Royal Commission on the Poor Law (1905–1909), Beatrice had written the well-known Minority Report, which advocated the breakup of the Poor Law, and the couple published *The Prevention of Destitution* in 1911 (translated into Japanese in 1914). Demanding an end to "relief by a money dole," the Webbs instead urged the adoption of preventive measures, such as compulsory labor exchanges, minimum wages, education, and medical services for the poor.[82] They also called for "more effort to 'reform' the habits and the conduct of the unemployed." Accordingly, the Webbs opposed the Liberal party government's proposed unemployment insurance legislation because it would assist all unemployed workers, including those who lost their jobs due to misconduct and idleness.[83] Home Ministry bureaucrats were therefore delighted when the Webbs visited Japan in 1911 and declared: "Japan has the great fortune not to have had a Poor Law." The British socialists further advised their hosts to emphasize prevention, so as to discourage the poor from developing the consciousness of a right to receive relief.[84]

The Japanese government did not introduce minimum wages and it established only a few labor exchanges before the 1920s. The state did, however, take several concrete steps to remedy what the Webbs called the "moral factor" in destitution. Even as they decimated the national budget for poor relief in 1908, senior Home Ministry bureaucrats shifted 22,000 yen of the resulting savings to a "fund to encourage relief work," primarily by private groups. Civil servants took pains to distinguish "relief work" or "reformatory and relief work" from the provision of poor relief. "Relief work" implied various social services to teach youth and the destitute how to avoid falling into poverty or how to escape from poverty. Reformatories for juvenile delinquents headed the agenda after 1908, when the revision of the Reformatory Law mandated the establishment of a reformatory in every prefecture.[85] By the end of 1910, the chief of the Bureau of Local Affairs could report rapid progress in reformatory and relief work, citing the total numbers of services in operation: 107 orphanages and other institutions that raised children, 86 clinics for the poor, 53 reformatories, 28 schools for the blind, deaf, and mute, 26 day care centers for the children of poor workers, 19 services to protect ex-convicts, 17 employment services, and 13 old-age homes.[86]

To a striking degree, officials formulated the new welfare policy within a broader set of programs designed to manage the lives not only of the very poor but of the general populace. When Inoue Tomoichi proclaimed in 1911 that relief work was "the most important task in managing a nation," he referred both to cultivating youth and "making a people who will work harder" in order to rise out of poverty. Managing society took on a new urgency for the state following the Russo-Japanese War (1904–

1905). Inoue was at the forefront of those Home Ministry officials who linked Japan's newly achieved great-power status to the creation of a self-reliant people who worked selflessly for national prosperity while making few demands on the state. As part of "postwar management," the government drastically cut the poor relief budget in 1908 to help pay for Japan's continued military buildup.[87] In 1908, Home Minister Hirata Tōsuke instructed relief workers: "Reformatory and relief work does not, in reality, stop at the objective of benevolently relieving the individual. We aim to teach and guide these people to be better, . . . and will devote our energies to making them good subjects of the State."[88]

Tokugawa-era authorities and the early Meiji state had generally delegated the tasks of moral suasion and mutual assistance to families and self-governing villages, towns, and neighborhoods. By the first decade of the twentieth century, however, even the defenders of the Relief Regulations acknowledged that communal bonds in the villages were weakening as urban culture intruded and many migrated to the cities. Within the cities, the growth of poor working-class families and slums particularly challenged the official policy of relying on communities and assisting only individuals without families. In 1911, the Bureau of Local Affairs recognized the extent of the problem when it applied Anglo-American methods to conduct the first of the Home Ministry's scientific surveys of poor households in the city of Tokyo.[89] During her visit that same year, Beatrice Webb judged the slums of Osaka to be "as bad as anything in London," observing widespread malnutrition, neglect of children, and inadequate ad hoc relief efforts (see Figure 3).[90] At the same time, the working poor emerged as a greater threat to the social order after the Russo-Japanese War. The first of several large-scale urban riots broke out in Tokyo's Hibiya Park in 1905, followed by a major miners' riot in 1907.[91]

The government's solution was to embark on a number of related campaigns to re-create the traditional community and in some cases to establish new intermediaries between the state and the people. In the Bureau of Local Affairs's 1908 directive to "correct excessive assistance," Tokonami Takejirō concurrently ordered prefectural officials to "work to make neighborly mutual assistance a reality." The new policy departed somewhat from the Relief Regulations. Local public bodies (municipalities), as well as private charities, became the prime agents in providing "neighborly mutual assistance."[92] Nonetheless, the government's welfare policies before the 1920s remained centered on the state's organization and management of private relief work.

In the countryside, these activities took the form of the Home Ministry's highly intrusive Local Improvement Campaign (1906–1918). As Kenneth Pyle has written, officials sought to organize community groups

FIGURE 3. A Tokyo slum, ca. 1927–1928.

into centrally supervised federations. Although the government's ultimate
goal was to mobilize the people in pursuit of national power, these organizations were also designed to improve popular welfare. The state-
regulated agricultural cooperatives (*sangyō kumiai*), for example, increasingly functioned as credit societies for villagers. The Bureau of Local
Affairs also institutionalized the teachings of the Tokugawa-era reformer
Ninomiya Sontoku on behalf of mutual assistance and "self-management." Led by Inoue Tomoichi, the Home Ministry joined forces with
Ninomiya's local followers, who had already established several local

hōtokusha ("repaying virtue societies"). In 1906, the ministry founded the Central Hōtokukai (Chūō Hōtokukai) to coordinate the creation of hōtokusha in villages throughout Japan.[93]

Organizing Japan's enormous cities and provincial centers was a more daunting task. The government chose instead to enlist the services of local notables and private charities. In 1908, the Home Ministry sponsored the first "Reformatory and Relief Works Seminar," a five-week course that encouraged local leaders to undertake social work in their own communities. Another twenty-eight seminars were held at the national and provincial levels over the next fifteen years. Participants included charity workers, local elites, civil servants, philanthropists, educators, and clerics. Although the study courses involved some training in techniques of social work, officials also instructed relief workers in methods of moral exhortation in order to prevent socialist thought, discourage dependency on material relief, and strengthen the family's obligation to support its own.[94] In addition, the Home Ministry began working closely with private charitable and relief organizations. Ministry officials, former bureaucrats, and prominent social work leaders in 1908 founded the Central Charity Association (Chūō Jizen Kyōkai) to research poverty problems and coordinate relief work. That same year the Home Ministry and imperial household instituted the practice of making donations to many charitable groups—including several Christian organizations. Government spokesmen freely admitted that the state sought to supervise private charity work and guide its development. Unlike Western nations, reasoned officials, Japan lacked a history of independent charity groups that could do the job themselves.[95]

One of the best-kept secrets in Japanese history is that middle-class Christians played a central role in formulating the government's programs of social management after 1900. At a time when many Japanese viewed Christians as disloyal foreign agents, Home Ministry bureaucrats depended on Christian social workers for their expertise and knowledge of welfare programs in the West. Christians had, for example, founded twelve of the nation's twenty-two new orphanages between 1878 and 1897. The Home Ministry's growing interest in moral reform and the prevention of poverty in fact owed much to intense lobbying by Christian pioneers in orphanage and reformatory work.

The most influential of these Christians was Tomeoka Kōsuke, a former Protestant prison chaplain who studied social work and prison reform in the United States and returned to found his own model reformatory.[96] The Bureau of Local Affairs employed Tomeoka as its authority on reformatories and social work from 1900 to 1914. The Home Ministry also hired as temporary "commissioned officers" (*shokutaku*) several other prominent Protestant social reformers, notably Namae Takayuki

and the Salvation Army's Yamamuro Gumpei.[97] Ironically the Home
Ministry official most responsible for introducing the indigenous self-help
teachings of Ninomiya Sontoku to the architects of the Local Improvement Campaign was not an ardent traditionalist, but Tomeoka, the cosmopolitan Christian. He and other Protestants lauded Ninomiya for pre-
scribing hard work and thrift as the means of preventing poverty.
Whereas Ninomiya and late nineteenth-century officials had emphasized
the community's obligation to relieve the poor, Tomeoka helped to persuade Home Ministry leaders of the importance of disseminating the
values of individual self-help and "self-management."[98] Tomeoka could
state—with no less conviction than Inoue Tomoichi—that Japan was
"fortunate to have escaped the evils of excessive assistance, nor have we
witnessed the ill effects of encouraging the indolent."[99]

No discussion of Japan's emerging welfare policy would be complete
without mention of philanthropy by the imperial household. Drawing on
early modern practices, the government commonly identified relief and
relief work with the emperor's benevolence. Although the emperor increasingly contributed to disaster relief and other charitable projects during the late nineteenth century, Home Ministry leaders institutionalized
and vastly expanded the practice of imperial donations following the
Russo-Japanese War. Proclaiming an act "unparalleled in Western countries," Home Minister Hirata Tōsuke announced in 1908 that the emperor would contribute to newly established "charity and relief funds" in
each prefecture.[100] These funds were generally used to subsidize private
charity and relief organizations, and they stimulated a major expansion
of social work projects at the municipal and prefectural levels during the
1910s. In 1911, the imperial household made its largest single gift in direct response to the execution of twelve anarchists who had been charged
with plotting to kill the emperor. Seeking to ameliorate the sources of
political radicalism, the emperor donated 1.5 million yen to create a program of free medical care for the poor. The donation was supplemented
by contributions from businesses, civil servants, and local notables, total-
ing 25.9 million yen. A nominally private foundation, the Saiseikai (Society to Assist Livelihood), was thereupon established to administer the
fund.

The Saiseikai summed up the government's overall approach to poverty between 1900 and 1918 in several respects. The state was moving to
address growing social problems, albeit not primarily by means of public
assistance. The Saiseikai's enormous endowment dwarfed the amounts
spent on poor relief under the Relief Regulations (only 135,000 yen in
1913, including central and local expenditures). Second, the state continued to rely on private funds even as it centralized the management of
"neighborly mutual assistance." Many donors to the Saiseikai com-

plained of being coerced by officials. Prefectural governors reportedly had been ordered to pressure the local rich into making contributions. As Beatrice and Sidney Webb described it at the time, this was nothing less than "extorted 'benevolence.'"[101]

Finally, the government emphasized imperial benevolence not only to foster popular loyalty to the state but also to discourage the Japanese people from developing a consciousness of the "right" to receive relief as in the more impersonal systems of public assistance in the West. Prefectural governments typically contributed more to the charity and relief funds than the emperor, yet, as in the case of the Saiseikai, officials portrayed the funds as examples of imperial largess, pure and simple.[102] When the price of rice soared in 1918, the government set up a national relief fund. Although the emperor's donation was relatively small, sacks of relief grain bore the label "Imperial Gift Rice." Authorities in Toyama prefecture directed officials and police to urge the poor to respond with gratitude, instructing that recipients be "kindly counseled and advised that [such imperial beneficence] would not become customary practice. The recipients should be directed to make greater efforts."[103] Japanese-style welfare was to be administratively simple, strongly didactic, relatively immune from taxpayers' opposition to public assistance, and embedded in the traditional relationship between the benevolent ruler and his subject.

MODERNIZING "NEIGHBORLY MUTUAL ASSISTANCE"

Inoue Tomoichi did not live to see the 1920s. That may have been just as well. The era between the two world wars witnessed a dramatic expansion in both governmental social programs and private social work. Whereas prefectural and municipal governments had spent approximately 1.4 million yen in 1917 on various social services including poor relief, the figure soared to 25 million in 1922.[104] The boom in Japanese manufacturing during World War I accelerated the onset of social problems associated with industrialization and urbanization. In 1918, an estimated one to two million people, mainly urban dwellers, took part in the Rice Riots to protest rising rice prices. The immediate postwar period was also a time of strike waves and the widespread formation of labor unions. Japan emerged as one of the victorious Big Five at Versailles in 1919, further convincing many Japanese that their nation must modernize and even democratize its institutions lest it lag behind the "civilized" powers. Defying Inoue's warnings, Home Ministry bureaucrats, middle-class reformers, and party politicians looked to the elaborate public welfare and labor programs of contemporary Britain and Weimar Germany as the basis of a new social policy. The American model of professional social work similarly gained influence.

The government responded to these changes by rapidly developing a social bureaucracy. Poor relief and social work had been merely one of several functions of the Home Ministry's Bureau of Local Affairs. Acknowledging the need for a more specialized agency, the Home Ministry created a small Relief Section within the bureau in February 1917. This was expanded in 1920 into a Bureau of Social Affairs, which dealt with poor relief, veterans' assistance, children's welfare, and unemployment. In 1922, the Home Ministry placed jurisdiction over labor and welfare matters in a newly established super-bureau (also named the Bureau of Social Affairs or Social Bureau). Tokyo, Osaka, and other big cities inaugurated their own social bureaus. As Sally Hastings has shown, the city of Tokyo's Bureau of Social Affairs actively sponsored labor exchanges, cheap lodging houses, public pawnshops, day nurseries, and settlement houses.[105]

I have elsewhere described the rising young officials who staffed these agencies as the "social bureaucrats."[106] They boldly challenged the precepts that had been put forward by Inoue Tomoichi, Tokonami Takejirō, and others. The social bureaucrats did not deem Japan fortunate to have been without a major public assistance law. Nor were they convinced that the problem of poverty could be successfully addressed by relying primarily on the nation's family system and closely knit neighborhoods. The Relief Regulations, in the words of the Social Bureau's Yamazaki Iwao, "do not correspond to the times."[107] Japan in the mid-1920s, reported Social Bureau officials, spent a mere 400 thousand yen annually on public assistance at all levels of government, while Britain spent the equivalent of 200 million yen. Rather than condemn the British for "excessive assistance," the bureaucrats concluded: "it is abundantly clear that not all of the poor [in Japan] are receiving sufficient relief."[108]

The Social Bureau's Ōno Rokuichirō, a proponent of British-style relief policies, castigated his own country's relief system as "nothing more than negativism, which leaves matters to nature." While surveying European social policies, Ōno visited Albert Mosse, the influential German scholar whom the Japanese government had employed to help formulate the Meiji Constitution and a modern system of municipal administration some four decades earlier. The venerable Mosse told the young Japanese bureaucrat that times had changed and Japan could no longer get by "while boasting of its unique family system." Ōno was equally unimpressed by his government's moralistic focus on "raising the self-respect" of the poor: "The problem that must be considered is what to do about these people who, through no fault of their own and no matter how hard they work, cannot survive."[109]

What further distinguished the new generation of civil servants was their emphasis on "society" as the unit for relieving poverty. In the years following World War I, the term "social work" replaced "relief work" and "charity work" in official and private circles alike. The change was more than cosmetic. Except for the small social policy school of the 1890s, previous Home Ministry officials had assigned the obligation to support the indigent to families, extralegal communal arrangements, and in the last resort to municipal governments. Led by the first chief of the Bureau of Social Affairs in 1920, Tago Ichimin, the new social bureaucrats instead embraced the contemporary French theory of "social solidarity" and comparable Western ideas. These theories held that society as a whole—and its representatives, the state and local governments—bore a public responsibility to care for the poor, who as members of society possessed the "right to survive."[110]

At the same time, most social bureaucrats remained wary of jettisoning Japan's putative differences in favor of fully emulating European welfare programs. Tago Ichimin himself maintained that social work must necessarily evolve differently in his country from the way it had in Western nations because Japan is "a nation with a family system."[111] Tomeoka Kōsuke, the influential Christian social work leader and former Home Ministry employee, criticized "social solidarity" thought for propounding the rights of the poor without teaching them duties and spiritual improvement.[112] In 1926, a special committee of the government's Investigative Commission on Social Work arrived at a seemingly contradictory consensus. On the one hand, the committee called for the adoption of "obligatory assistance by public bodies," judging that "the Japanese family system has gradually broken down" and "neighborly mutual assistance" was no longer effective. Members, nonetheless, recommended that a new poor law, if enacted, must not "destroy Japan's family system, lead to excessive assistance or unstoppable assistance, instill a spirit of dependency on others, or turn [recipients] into idlers."[113]

The bureaucracy's continued faith in a Japanese-style welfare system helps to explain why the government moved so slowly to revise the Relief Regulations during the 1920s. There were other reasons, as well. As one of the Social Bureau's strongest proponents of revision sadly noted in 1922, neither the general public nor scholars demanded the revision of the Relief Regulations, despite the widespread awareness of their inadequacy. In terms of priorities, the first wave of government-sponsored social legislation concentrated on improving the welfare of industrial workers in medium-sized and large enterprises. Workers were better organized, more crucial to the national economy, and potentially more threatening to the social order than the very poor. The Social Bureau successfully championed legislation instituting labor exchanges (1921),

workers' health insurance (1922), tougher restrictions on hours for working women and children (1923), mandatory retirement and severance pay
(1936), and seamen's insurance (1938).

Second, social bureaucrats and social work leaders had great difficulty
determining which European model to emulate. Some insisted on adopting a comprehensive public assistance law, while others, like Tago Ichimin, argued that the advanced nations had moved beyond poor laws to
separate laws assisting the elderly, the disabled, children, and mothers.[114]
Immobilized by division, neither of the government's two commissions
on relief and social work (convened in 1918 and 1921) recommended
revising the Relief Regulations. A third panel, the Investigative Commission on Social Work, did not propose an expanded public assistance law
until 1927.

While the Home Ministry pondered the question of new public assistance legislation, the most remarkable innovations occurred at the local
level with the development of the district commissioner (hōmen iin) system. In 1917, the governor of rural Okayama prefecture appointed a
number of distinguished subjects to serve as unsalaried "relief counsel-
ors," who visited and assisted the poor. The district commissioner system
itself originated in Osaka prefecture in October 1918 in the wake of the
Rice Riots. The system was the brainchild of Ogawa Shigejirō, a prominent scholar of social work and a former commissioned officer in the
Home Ministry. At the time he served as a special advisor to the governor
of Osaka. Ogawa divided Osaka prefecture by school district. In each
school district, authorities selected local "people of virtue" (tokushika) as
unpaid commissioners so that each was responsible for two hundred
households in his or her neighborhood. District commissioners in turn
elected a representative to an executive council, which deliberated on important cases once a month. Applying Western "social survey" techniques, Ogawa instructed the district commissioners to record detailed
information about poor households and their living conditions on index
cards. The commissioners functioned as intermediaries between the poor
and social services, public and private. The visitors might counsel families
in better hygiene or savings habits, or they might help the poor secure
employment, medical care, relief in money or goods, or funds that would
make it easier for the children to attend school.

Osaka's district commissioner system quickly became a model for municipalities and prefectures throughout Japan. In 1931, district commissioners were sponsored by 43 prefectures, 14 cities, 106 towns, and 3
private groups. The numbers of commissioners grew rapidly from 10,545
(1925), to 27,907 (1931), and finally to 74,560 (1942), including 4,537
women. Commissioners became a presence in the countryside during the

1930s. By 1942, the system had been adopted by 10,753 cities, towns, and villages (or 99 percent of all municipalities).[115]

Although the district commissioner system arose as a series of local experiments, the social bureaucrats soon endorsed it as "the key to solving social problems."[116] In 1928, the home minister declared the commissioners to be "the central institution of social work" in Japan.[117] The system's appeal to the Home Ministry is not difficult to understand. Social Bureau officials frequently remarked on the cost savings in deploying unpaid volunteers rather than professional social workers. In 1924, it cost a mere 30,000 yen to field 10,600 commissioners nationwide.[118] Moreover, Ogawa Shigejirō had designed the institution so that commissioners would discourage the poor from applying for public assistance, offering instead "spiritual relief," and steering the needy to social services. The bureaucrats also envisioned the district commissioners as the state's agents in monitoring the lives of the underclass; commissioners would help maintain public order, prevent unemployment, boost household savings, and thereby forestall the need for relief payments. One of the commissioners' central tasks, explained a Social Bureau official, was to "correct household registers," enabling the authorities to "track down relatives [who could furnish support], no matter how far away they live."[119]

Other civil servants noted that the district commissioner system permitted the government, for the first time, to help the working poor who were not totally destitute; the commissioners could provide timely advice or social services, such as medical care and job placement, before families fell apart.[120] The social bureaucrats further regarded district commissioners as a modern yet essentially Japanese solution. To Ozawa Hajime of the Social Bureau, the commissioners' mission was to "revive the neighborhood system" of premodern Japan and, in the words of Ninomiya Sontoku, to "teach the way to self-help and self-management."[121]

Official encouragement notwithstanding, the district commissioner system was more than an instrument of control imposed from above. In a path-breaking essay on the Osaka commissioners, Ōmori Makoto demonstrates that the rise of the district commissioners was closely related to the growing role of the old middle classes in urban neighborhoods after World War I. Whereas the Home Ministry had previously looked to the wealthy and the prominent as its local agents in managing the poor, Ogawa Shigejirō strove to deputize the "middle class" because its members had "much contact with the proletarian classes" on an everyday basis.[122] Indeed, most urban commissioners appear to have been the owners of small stores or workshops, with a smattering of doctors, teachers, priests, and professional social workers. These middle-class

かび上つた。

カード階級から浮

二組の家庭だけが

救助を辞退した

方面委員に ――

のうち、

七十組

FIGURE 4. Reforming the poor. The mass-circulation magazine *Ie no hikari* (1935) caricatures the urban poor as indolent and "spiritually bankrupt." Here, a Tokyo district commissioner gives stern advice to indigents. The caption quotes another commissioner: "Of my seventy cases, only two families managed to rise out of the card class [the most destitute]; they did so by refusing any material assistance offered by the district commissioner [succeeding by their own efforts]."

elements became further integrated into the state apparatus during the 1920s. Many district commissioners concurrently headed neighborhood sanitation associations and youth associations, served in ward assemblies, or functioned as "moral suasion commissioners" in the government's ongoing drives to encourage household savings, promote loyalty to the emperor, and cultivate good morals.[123]

The old middle classes, in turn, provided much of the dynamism in managing the poor. Many shopkeepers and small-scale manufacturers eagerly volunteered to be commissioners because they were genuinely concerned about the poverty and disorder around them and because this

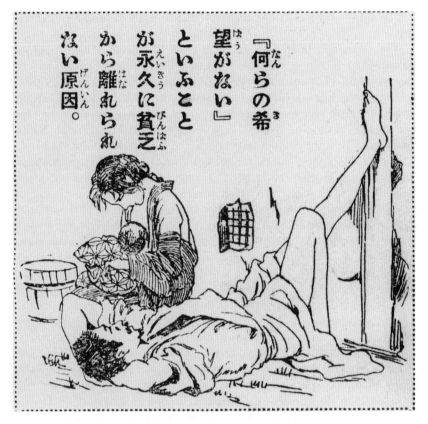

「何らの希望がない」といふことが永久に貧乏から離れられない原因。

FIGURE 5. A self-pitying couple languishes beneath the words: "The reason they'll never get out of poverty is all they do is utter 'woe is us.'"

public post elevated their status within the neighborhood. According to one Tokyo commissioner, commissioners sought, above all, "to prevent the worsening of thought" or political radicalization among their cases.[124] They often competed with the truly rich to be the guardians of the poor. In some instances commissioners refused charitable donations for their work from philanthropists out of the conviction that "donating money does no good" in terms of rescuing the destitute. Portraying themselves as self-made men, middle-class commissioners insisted that they were in a better position to teach struggling families the values of self-help and frugality (Figures 4 and 5).[125] When moral injunctions were insufficient, individual commissioners frequently gave hapless families money from their own pockets or helped organize charitable support groups of commissioners and other benefactors. With unconcealed delight, the Social Bureau in 1933 reported the existence of 683 support groups, which "in actuality bear a considerable part of the burden of funding relief and protection."[126]

The expansion of the district commissioner system played a pivotal role in the enactment and operation of the Relief and Protection Law (Kyūgohō) in 1929. Although the Social Bureau drafted the legislation in 1928, the cabinet of Tanaka Giichi evinced little enthusiasm. The bill would not have been introduced to the Diet, much less passed, were it not for pressure from Mutō Sanji, a socially minded businessman whose small party held the balance of power in the Lower House. In addition, a nationwide lobbying campaign by thousands of district commissioners and other social workers decisively strengthened the hand of the Social Bureau and impressed many Diet members. Ogawa Shigejirō had intended the district commissioners to be an alternative to public assistance, but the commissioners soon found that their most frequent activity was securing relief money and goods for impoverished families. Their awareness of the acute insufficiency of public assistance led to demands for a more expansive poor law in the late 1920s. The district commissioners mounted a second, larger campaign to effect the Relief and Protection Law after the Diet enacted the bill in 1929, but the succeeding cabinet attempted to delay funding the law for fiscal reasons. The commissioners eventually persuaded the government to implement the public assistance law on January 1, 1932, after directly appealing to the emperor himself.

Once effected, the Relief and Protection Law substantially enlarged the scope of public assistance. During its first year of operation in 1932, 157,564 individuals received assistance, as compared to only 18,111 the previous year under the old Relief Regulations (see Table 1). The Relief and Protection Law lowered the age of eligibility to sixty-five and liberalized the existing means test, which had required recipients to demonstrate the absence of other sources of support. The legislation added the benefits of medical care, childbirth expenses, occupational rehabilitation, and funeral expenses, although relief in money and goods still composed the bulk of annual expenditures. In a reversal of the post-1908 policy of placing the burden of public assistance overwhelmingly on local governments, the state also agreed to pay half of the cost of relief and protection, while prefectural and municipal governments split the remainder.

Nevertheless, the Relief and Protection Law did not represent a major departure from many of the assumptions underlying the Relief Regulations of 1874. The new statute, like its predecessor, excluded all employable persons, male and female. Social Bureau director Nagaoka Ryūichirō defended the measure in much the same terms as officials had used in the 1870s: "We have, for the most part, the beautiful customs of the family system and neighborly mutual assistance. This bill is intended to provide assistance only to those who cannot be assisted by either the family system or neighborly mutual assistance—that is, the disabled who lack a family or assistance from neighbors."[127] The Relief and Protection Law neither recognized the right to receive relief nor provided a means for failed applicants to bring suit to gain relief. The moral critique of poor relief remained, as well. As interpreted by the law's author, relief and protection would not be granted in "cases in which conduct is conspicuously bad or lazy . . . and in which granting relief and protection would conversely produce indolence."[128]

Despite warnings that the Relief and Protection Law would bleed the treasury and "give rise to entitlements," the Social Bureau's chief of the Protection Section, Mochinaga Yoshio, happily reported as of 1936 that "the dreaded evils of excessive assistance have yet to be seen." In 1935, he noted, the law assisted fewer than one-third of those who were technically eligible. Mochinaga credited the district commissioners with having restrained demands on the law by providing alternative relief and services to the poor. Others agreed, yet observed that government's tight-fisted policies left the district commissioners little choice but to arrange private relief. The fact of the matter was that between 1932 and 1935 the government reneged on its promise to pay 50 percent of relief costs, and fully 3,000 of the nation's 11,400 cities, towns, and villages were spending nothing on relief and protection.[129]

Moral and fiscal concerns likewise constrained the growth of the state's interwar unemployment policies. The government began employing the jobless in public works projects after the 1923 earthquake in Tokyo and Yokohama. These programs expanded during the Depression of the early 1930s. But here, too, one sees official fears of the debilitating effects of relief. Although the state never provided direct relief without demanding work before 1945, the Home Ministry openly worried in 1932 that the very term "unemployment relief services" would encourage an unwelcome "consciousness of rights" among the workers.[130] The authorities accordingly took pains to make the public works projects as temporary as possible.

The government's social welfare programs underwent a significant transformation during Japan's China and Pacific wars (1937–1945). The exigencies of total war rapidly advanced interwar trends toward the state control of social work. The Social Work Law of 1938 gave the government long-sought powers to supervise private social work. That same year the cabinet established a full-fledged Ministry of Health and Welfare at the initiative of the Army Ministry. Military authorities had vigorously lobbied for more comprehensive policies for the health and welfare of its recruits and the populace in general. While continuing to limit general public assistance, the government was unusually forthcoming in providing monetary assistance to wounded soldiers and the families of soldiers killed in action. Ironically, of all of imperial Japan's social legislation, the revised Military Assistance Law of 1937 most resembled contemporary European public assistance measures. Military assistance was funded entirely out of the national treasury; the application process was relatively easy; there was no need to demonstrate the lack of familial support; recipients did not lose their right to vote (unlike the recipients of ordinary public and private relief); and one received the assistance directly from the municipal office, rather than incurring the stigma of having to request aid through the district commissioners.[131] As the war intensified, the district commissioner system itself came increasingly under the direction of the state. Officials made sure that nearly every town and village employed district commissioners. At the same time, the commissioners' activities shifted from an emphasis on assisting the poor to advancing the wartime regime's programs of austerity and forced savings.[132]

Wartime welfare also involved a shift in focus from those unable to work to programs designed to "mobilize and enhance the human resources" of the nation. In the area of child welfare, new policies sought to maintain and improve the health and welfare of ordinary children, rather than simply impoverished and handicapped children. Day care facilities, which had been confined to poor children, spread to the general population and especially to the villages in an effort to employ women workers during an era of acute labor shortage. The Mother-Child Protection Law of 1937, supported by both women's groups and the government, offered allowances to fatherless families. The National Health Insurance Law of 1938 represented Japan's first major piece of social legislation that covered the populace as a whole. Its passage, too, can be traced to official concern for the health of the nation's soldiers and working people.

The new welfare policy, in a word, reversed the priorities of Japan's early modern and prewar relief programs, which had assisted only those who were incapable of working. Wartime welfare work grossly neglected the elderly, the disabled, and others who did not constitute valuable "human resources" in the military-industrial mobilization. The neglect of the mentally ill reached tragic dimensions. In the Matsuzawa Hospital the annual death rate for mentally ill patients soared to 31 and 41 percent, respectively, in 1944 and 1945 (compared to 1 percent in 1956).[133]

In the search for the origins of Japan's present-day welfare policies, some American social scientists begin their story in the early postwar era. Others note the prewar and wartime advances in national health insurance.[134] Few consider the impact of pre-1945 policies toward poverty, perhaps because those policies do not appear as familiar signposts on the road to the European-style welfare state. Japan emerged from World War II lacking provisions for old-age pensions, unemployment insurance, and a minimum wage. Its only major public assistance measure, the Relief and Protection Law, covered a small fraction of the nation's poor who were unable to work.

Rather than dwell upon Japan's failure to adopt European welfare measures, we have here traced the development of an active, self-consciously "Japanese" approach to the relief and prevention of poverty. Public assistance programs expanded before World War II, it is true, but the most significant changes involved the evolution of elaborate mechanisms to manage and reform the poor at little cost to the state. By the eve of the Pacific War, officials could rely on an army of district commissioners located in nearly every city, town, and village. The local volunteers arranged for relief of the worst cases of poverty while reinforcing the unchanging message that families and the community represented the first line of defense against destitution. During the first half of the twentieth century, the Japanese state and its local allies succeeded in re-creating and modernizing the intermediary communal institutions that had regulated and relieved the poor in the early modern era. The district commissioner system survived World War II intact, and the legacy of concerted efforts to manage the provision of welfare has had lasting effects on Japanese social programs to this day.

Defining
Orthodoxy and
Heterodoxy

THE INTERWAR bureaucracy eagerly enlisted the support of the middle classes, old and new, in its programs of social management. Officials were less willing or able, however, to incorporate the many groups that sprang up among the lower classes following World War I. Curiously little has been written about what was unquestionably the largest and fastest growing popular movement in interwar Japan: the so-called new religions. At their peak in 1935, adherents may have numbered in the several millions. Whereas urban intellectuals and skilled workers flocked to liberal and socialist movements, the popular sects largely appealed to small-scale farmers, peddlers, shopkeepers, day laborers, and working women. Unlike the many Buddhist-influenced new religions in the postwar era, most of the interwar new religions were Shintoist in orientation and resembled the charismatic mass sects of the mid-nineteenth century. Yet, by and large, those that arose after World War I were independent of the thirteen officially recognized Shinto sects. By the 1930s, journalists and theologians spoke of a veritable "religious revival" (shūkyō fukkō) sweeping Japan.

Although the new religions tended to be politically conservative, their dramatic rise greatly worried officials of the imperial state. To the authorities, these were at best "pseudo religions" (ruiji shūkyō), and at worst, "evil cults" (jakyō). The leaders of such groups might just as well have been Communists, so severe was the governmental repression directed against them. Indeed, prosecutors commonly applied their toughest anti-Communist ordinance, the Peace Preservation Law, against organizers and members of the new religions. During the 1920s, the government arrested leaders of two major heterodox sects, Ōmotokyō and Tenri Kenkyūkai.

But the worst was yet to come. In 1935, the police embarked on an official campaign to "eradicate the evil cults" (*jakyō semmetsu*). As a first step, officials dissolved the enormous Ōmotokyō sect. On December 8, 1935, hundreds of police descended on Ōmotokyō headquarters near Kyoto. They subsequently arrested nearly one thousand leaders and followers. The authorities also ordered wrecking crews to smash the sect's main shrine and other holy buildings into wooden pieces of less than one *shaku* (a Japanese foot), fearing that anything larger could be used to reconstruct the edifices of the sect. Like the anti-Buddhist iconoclasts of the 1860s and 1870s, police defaced and decapitated statues of Jizō and Kannon. They added the modern touch of dynamiting a sacred worship hall and other stone structures.[1] During the latter half of the 1930s, the government crushed several other new religions, including the even larger Hitonomichi Kyōdan.

Nor were the more established sects and denominations of Buddhism, Shinto, and Christianity immune from heavy-handed control by the state. Cabinets sponsored two unsuccessful bills to regulate religious bodies during the late 1920s. Ten years later, amidst war with China, the Diet enacted the Religious Organizations Law of 1939. Under the legislation, the state acquired powers to disband any religious organization whose teachings or actions were deemed incompatible with the "Imperial Way." In November 1940, the government established the Shrine Board (Jingiin), which formally elevated the authority of State Shinto over all other religions.

The state's actions suggest an obsession with heresy that one does not usually associate with industrializing societies in the twentieth century. How does one explain such savage suppression and interference? Furthermore, what does it tell us about the values of the Japanese state and society during the 1920s and 1930s? The explanations of most Japanese scholars draw on the concept of the "emperor system": put simply, Japanese leaders in the Meiji era created a new orthodoxy centered around a sacrosanct emperor, who was to be worshiped by all subjects at government-sponsored shrines in a system called State Shinto. Once established, according to this interpretation, the emperor-system state dealt harshly with the new mass religions that dared to worship different deities. Its guardians freely invoked the charge of lèse-majesté to stamp out groups considered heretical. Writing of the first arrests of Ōmotokyō leaders in 1921, one historian offered what has become a typical argument: "As is well known, all religions quest for the Absolute. Thus, in a nation like prewar Japan, *where the emperor system was the source of all values*, any true religion inevitably came in conflict with the emperor system."[2]

Given such assumptions, it is little wonder that few Japanese historians have examined the issue of state and religion for the period between

1900 and 1945. If the emperor-system state was truly the source of all values, the question of why the government smashed assertive new religions would not be particularly challenging or interesting. Accordingly, most Japanese-language research on the state and religion focuses on the last three decades of the nineteenth century, when government officials were just beginning to formulate and disseminate "emperor-system ideology."[3]

We must be wary, however, of invoking the emperor system as an all-encompassing explanation of modern Japanese history before 1945. Contemporary officials did not speak of the "emperor system" in their defense of the established order. The term itself was introduced by the Communist International in 1932, and only after World War II did Japanese intellectuals widely apply the construct in an effort to explain why the people had not resisted the tragic growth of authoritarianism and militarism. I by no means wish to deny the existence of an emperor system between the 1890s and 1945. Employed with precision, the term denotes the evolution of a series of structural impediments to political democratization and the freedom of expression. In a strictly legal sense, the Meiji Constitution of 1889 indeed placed sovereignty in the hands of a mythic imperial house, making it difficult and dangerous for future generations to advocate rule by the people and parliament. The emperor system also refers to the emergence of powerful, unaccountable elites in the military, bureaucracy, and national police.[4]

Nevertheless, emperor-system theory is not very useful when analyzing the dynamics of the relationship between the modern Japanese state and religions. First, the interpretation tends toward the ahistorical, for its adherents assume a direct link between the Meiji regime's attempt to establish an absolute national religion in the early 1870s and the wartime creation of the Shrine Board in 1940. Japanese scholarship provides few answers as to why the new religions were generally tolerated between the 1880s and 1935, or why the government's efforts to enact restrictive religious legislation failed miserably during the 1920s.

Second, if religions were suppressed for their "heterodoxy," what constituted "orthodoxy" in a society where State Shinto was not technically a religion, and where Buddhism, Christianity, and popular Shinto sects coexisted? To equate orthodoxy with emperor-system ideology is to beg an important question and to overlook changes in its definition over time. Orthodoxy meant more than respecting the majesty of the emperor. In Japan, as elsewhere, the prevailing orthodoxy was also bound up with more secular notions of social order, public morality, and even modernity. The only effective way of gauging the specific meanings of orthodoxy and heterodoxy is to examine how Japanese at the time defined the terms, and how they acted on those definitions.

Finally, the "emperor-system" approach invariably traces all suppression back to the pre-1945 Japanese state—a state that appears omnipotent and eager to define unilaterally what is orthodox. Yet as we have seen in the case of welfare programs, such theories of top-down control ignore the vital role of middle-class and other nongovernmental groups in managing the rest of society. The fact is that established religious organizations and progressive intellectuals were often as likely as bureaucrats to call for the strict regulation of newly arisen sects. We must therefore re-examine relations between the Japanese state and society in terms of a more interactive model. This relationship was not simply one of antagonism but typically involved efforts by the religious bodies themselves to use state power to their advantage.

STATE RELATIONS WITH THE
ESTABLISHED RELIGIONS

One key to understanding the government's policies toward the new religions lies in the growing ties between the state and the more established religions during the first four decades of the twentieth century. In general, officials did not seek direct control over spiritual affairs, nor did most denominations and sects insist on the absolute freedom of religion. Rather, both sides developed an interest in cooperating within the framework of the state.

Viewed from the perspective of the state, the regime's "religions policy" (*shūkyō seisaku*) evolved through three distinct stages between 1868 and the 1920s: the assertion of an exclusive national creed, followed by passive toleration of existing religions, and finally the incorporation of the established religions into the ruling structure. Those in charge of the modern state's religions policy in its first years were often devout Shinto priests or nativist scholars. In an effort to create an emperor-centered national religion based on Shinto, they confiscated lands of Buddhist temples and attempted to disestablish Buddhism itself during the first half of the 1870s.[5] Officials adopted an even harsher policy toward Christianity, discouraging its propagation outside of the treaty ports. However, the leaders of the Meiji government soon recognized the futility of trying to eradicate Buddhism, the faith of the vast majority of Japanese. The drive for doctrinal absolutism under a national religion alienated a great many subjects and paradoxically hindered the regime's overall quest for political consolidation.

As a result, the government gradually shifted to a policy of benign neglect toward the existing religions. In 1884, the Council of State issued an ordinance that placed Buddhism on an equal legal footing with the Shinto sects. The measure granted Buddhist and Shinto organizations a large degree of autonomy, delegating regulatory powers to the officially recognized head of each body. Responding to pressures from both the Western powers and some Buddhist leaders, the regime promulgated the freedom of religious belief. According to Article 28 of the Meiji Constitution of 1889, "Japanese subjects shall, within limits not prejudicial to peace and order, and not antagonistic to their duties as subjects, enjoy freedom of religious belief."

This was not exactly a ringing endorsement of the principle of religious freedom, and the highly conditional nature of Article 28 unquestionably limited the exercise of religious liberties before 1945. In one famous case in 1891, authorities at the government's First Higher School forced the resignation of Uchimura Kanzō, then a lecturer, after the well-known Christian theologian refused to bow at the reading of the Imperial Rescript on Education.[6] Officials and legal scholars subsequently debated whether the freedom of religion clause protected "religious activity" and "religious association," or simply inner "religious belief."[7] Its ambiguities notwithstanding, Article 28 did inhibit later governments from interfering in the affairs of established religions. The last stage in the new policy of toleration and official recognition came in 1899, when a Home Ministry ordinance legally recognized Christian denominations under a somewhat looser system of regulation than that imposed on Buddhist and Shinto sects.[8]

Although officials had come to tolerate the existence of religious bodies, they displayed little interest in mobilizing the religions in the service of the nation. The government's administration of religion had itself become a bureaucratic backwater, confined to the dusty work of processing the reports of the self-regulating religious bodies. Whereas the early Meiji-era regime had created a full-fledged Ministry of Rites and Education (Kyōbushō) to propagate a religiously based orthodoxy, the succeeding Bureau of Shrines and Temples (1877–1900) and Bureau of Religions (1900–1913) were simply low-ranking divisions within the Home Ministry.[9] Despite their normal penchant for empire building, leaders of the prestigious Home Ministry shed few tears when the cabinet transferred the Bureau of Religions to the relatively weak Ministry of Education in 1913.[10]

Rather than harnessing the spiritual influence of the religions, the authorities at the turn of the century preferred to socialize the people directly through agencies of the secular state. In 1899, for example, the Ministry of Education attempted to cleanse the entire educational system of religious influence—Buddhist as well as Christian. The ministry's controversial Directive 12 prohibited all religious instruction and ceremonies in the public schools and in any private school that wished to retain for its pupils the privileges granted public school students (such as draft deferments and the qualifications to enter public higher schools).[11]

In no area did the government demonstrate its indifference toward existing religions more than in the emerging institution of State Shinto. Although the regime had failed to establish an exclusive national religion in the 1870s, officials gradually transformed local folk Shinto shrines into political instruments for inculcating emperor-centered patriotism and values of social harmony. Government spokesmen insisted that the state-sponsored shrines did not constitute a religion but rather were secular forums for honoring the emperor and nation. To affirm the separation between shrines and religion, the authorities after 1900 barred the independent Shinto sects, which *were* regarded as religions, from leading public worship at the shrines. Hence, the shrines, they concluded, in no way competed with Christianity and Buddhism nor interfered with the freedom of religious practice. There were, however, ample grounds for skepticism. Government-paid shrine priests in fact conducted many ceremonies that could be considered religious—from weddings and funerals to offerings to ancestors. In 1908, the state accelerated efforts to mobilize the populace by its own quasi-religious means. Citing the "centrality of the shrines" in local governance, the Shrines Bureau of the Home Ministry mounted a campaign to encourage, if not compel, pilgrimages and shrine worship by schoolchildren and youth organizations.[12]

To most Japanese historians, the expansion of State Shinto in the early twentieth century marked the triumph of the emperor-system state over popular religions and other alternative value structures. Yet one must not exaggerate the omnipotence of emperor-system ideology and organization. By 1912, influential bureaucrats were openly promoting a more positive religions policy, whereby the state sought the cooperation and incorporation of the "Three Religions": sect Shinto, Buddhism, and Christianity. Contrary to the views presented by emperor-system theorists, these civil servants recognized the limitations of relying solely on the shrines to guide popular thought. Indeed, the post-1906 drive to extend State Shinto aroused tremendous opposition from not only the Christians but also many Buddhist orders, particularly those associated with the largest denomination, Shinshū. Between 1913 and 1916, a number of local councils and an occasional prefectural governor attempted to compel shrine worship and the placement of Shinto altars (*kamidana*) in every home. Buddhists vehemently protested these actions, mobilizing sympathetic politicians to censure the government on the Diet floor. Christians and Buddhists also banded together to demand the elimination of all religious elements from the shrines.[13] So effective was the protest that the Home Ministry's Bureau of Shrines quickly retreated in 1916 and announced a new policy: everyone would be free to hold his or her own view of the shrines; although the authorities hoped the people would eventually accept the shrines, no one would be compelled to do so.[14] The Home Ministry maintained this essentially passive approach to State Shinto during the 1920s under increased pressure from Christian and Buddhist groups.[15]

Abandoning the drive for the "centrality of the shrines" almost as soon as it had begun, Home Ministry officials increasingly looked upon the established religions as natural allies in their managerial campaigns to improve social welfare, modernize daily habits, and ward off radical thought. The many Christian orphanages and reformatories had become crucial to the government's relief policies by the early twentieth century, and the Home Ministry employed some of the best-known Protestant social work leaders as commissioned officers. As part of the Local Improvement Campaign, the ministry also deputized the Protestant minister Kanamori Michitomo, who crisscrossed the country preaching the virtues of diligence and thrift.[16] Nor could the authorities afford to ignore the growing role of Buddhists in social work and moral reform. In an effort to recover their following and compete with the Christians, Buddhist denominations founded a spate of protective institutions for orphans and released offenders during the 1890s and 1900s.[17]

Chief architect of the rapprochement with the religions was Tokonami Takejirō, vice minister of home affairs and former chief of the Home Ministry's Bureau of Local Affairs. Tokonami personified a new breed of bureaucrats who sought to broaden the social bases of the state. The Home Ministry provided an excellent vehicle for their efforts, since the agency supervised local government, the police, and social work—as well as the administration of shrines and religions. Dedicated to integrating the populace into the nation state, these well-trained professionals differed from the exclusionist Shinto priest-officials of the early Meiji-era government. They also distanced themselves from contemporaries in the army and other ministries who espoused the "mistaken belief that Christianity advocates socialism," according to Home Minister Hara Takashi (Kei) in 1911.[18] The aims of the Home Ministry were decidedly "corporatist" in the sense that the agency systematically patronized a range of private, hierarchical organizations—from religious bodies to agricultural cooperatives—in order to supplement administrative efforts at the local level.[19]

Beginning in 1908, the authorities actively enlisted the support of Buddhist and Christian clergy in the Home Ministry's campaigns to encourage charitable activities, poor relief work, and the reform of wayward youths.[20] In 1912, Vice Minister Tokonami sponsored the first Assembly of the Three Religions (Sankyō Kaidō). Representatives of Buddhism,

Shinto, and Christianity pledged to "raise the morality of the people and improve social mores," while the government promised to "respect the fundamental authority of religion."[21] Confronted by rising labor and socialist movements after World War I, officials routinely called on the three religions to aid the government in propagating "moral suasion" to their adherents and the general populace.[22] In 1919, Tokonami, by then the home minister, periodically consulted Buddhist clerics on how best to ameliorate tensions between labor and capital.[23] The extremely conservative cabinet of Tanaka Giichi similarly appealed to the Congress of Japanese Religions in its crusade against communism in 1928.[24] Preferring to employ moral uplift in the service of a deflationary economic policy, the relatively liberal government of Hamaguchi Osachi rallied the major religious groups, as never before, in the Moral Suasion Mobilization Campaign of 1929. Religious organizations took up the charge with gusto, lecturing the public on the need to eschew luxuries and restrain overall consumption.[25]

Recognizing the growing value of the religions as allies, interwar officials moved to reduce the sources of tension between religions and the state. Most important to Christians and Buddhists, the Ministry of Education relaxed the Meiji-era ban on religious education in public and equivalent private schools in 1924. According to the chief of the Bureau of Religions, Directive 12 would thenceforth prohibit only the propagation of "teachings and beliefs that call for a single privileged religion or sect." In a major departure, the ministry actually encouraged the spread of religious instruction in a concerted drive to roll back radical thought.[26]

Religious groups occasionally complained about being "used" by a manipulative state.[27] But for the most part, the religions were delighted with their incorporation into the Japanese establishment. Tenrikyō, the rapidly growing sect that initially remained outside the official campaign to propagate national Shinto, had since 1887 energetically sought recognition. The sect enthusiastically supported the regime during the Sino-Japanese and Russo-Japanese wars, finally winning governmental recognition in 1908. In response to the anti-Buddhist policies of the 1870s, most Buddhist denominations had likewise thrown themselves into collaborating with the state. By so doing, they hoped to regain the privileged position enjoyed during the Tokugawa era.[28] Although some Christian leaders criticized any official interference in religious affairs, an impressive majority praised Tokonami Takejirō's Assembly of the Three Religions for placing their faith on an equal level with Buddhism and Shinto.[29]

The established religions and the government, moreover, shared a commitment to defending the capitalist order from the perceived Marxist threat. A few months after the Tanaka government arrested hundreds of suspected Communists on March 15, 1928, the Congress of Japanese Religions convened a special "committee on thought," chaired by the cosmopolitan scholar of religion, Professor Anesaki Masaharu. Consisting of Christian, Buddhist, and Shinto representatives, the congress unanimously approved the committee's resolution, which read:

> This Congress favors the eradication (*zetsumetsu*) of Communist associations and the Communist movement, which are utterly opposed to our national polity. . . .[30]
>
> The three most deplorable things in society today are the evil trend of thought, restless living and political corruption. In order to enlighten the people, solve present-day problems, and save society from these evil conditions, society must be reformed and a new culture created. We believe that this can not be brought about by morbid materialism and that religious faith in the highest and deepest sense of the term can alone accomplish this task. We religionists must try by self-examination, self-awakening, and hearty cooperation and mutual effort to help this holy era of Showa (Radiant Peace) to realize the true significance of the "Light from the East."[31]

This is not to say that the emperor-system state boldly led, while the established religions meekly followed during the 1920s. On the contrary, religious bodies behaved much like other effective interest groups. Religious leaders welcomed state intervention when it advanced the interests of their own organizations, but single-mindedly resisted intrusions that did not.

The government's religions bill (shūkyō hōan) of 1927 was notable in its intrusiveness. The proposed legislation granted tax-exempt status and various protections to legally recognized religious bodies, in exchange for a strong dose of state interference. Most remarkable, the bill empowered the authorities to restrict or prohibit the propagation of any teachings or the conduct of any ceremony that they "feared might be prejudicial to peace and order, corrupt morals, or be antagonistic to one's duties as a subject." Anyone found guilty of using "deceptive or fraudulent" means to propagate religious teachings or conduct ceremonies faced imprisonment of up to six months or a fine of 300 yen. The appointment of the head and the manager of each organization required the approval of the minister of education. The minister could also take "necessary steps to maintain its rules and order" in cases of internal disputes. The religions bill further barred anyone from preaching who had not graduated from middle school or its equivalent. The legislation was particularly hard on newly founded Shinto and Buddhist sects. They were denied the privileges of the officially recognized "religious bodies" (shūkyō dantai) and were instead subject to severe regulation as mere "religious associations" (*shūkyō kessha*).[32] Government spokesmen made it clear that this provision was designed "to prevent the ills of the evil cults."[33]

Despite its repressive thrust, the religions bill encountered few protests from the established religions on the grounds of the freedom of religion. Except for several Christian spokesmen and a small group of liberal Buddhists, the nation's religious organizations generally supported the legislation. And why not? The Buddhist orders had been demanding just such a law since the late 1890s as a means of regaining ownership of some of the temple grounds confiscated by the early Meiji regime. By authorizing the sale of these lands to the temples at nominal prices, the religions bill in effect bought the silence of the Buddhist leadership on other controversial issues.[34] Furthermore, what we might view as state interference was regarded by the Buddhist and Shinto establishments as friendly reinforcement of their hierarchies against internal fragmentation and competition from other religions. The legislation granted an order's chief abbot and main temple considerable legal powers over affiliated priests and branch temples. The fear of fragmentation was greatest among the thirteen recognized Shinto sects. Tenrikyō, once a vigorous critic of official intervention, now called on the government to strengthen the bill's projected controls over the qualifications for clerics and the formation of new religions. By no coincidence, Tenrikyō leaders were at the time locked in battle with a growing breakaway faction, the Tenri Kenkyūkai.[35]

The established religions most sympathized with the provisions of the religions bill that would regulate and marginalize the new religions. Having developed a full range of institutions to train their own clerics, the Buddhist orders and Shinto sects like Tenrikyō and Konkōkyō favored the legislation of tough educational qualifications for clerics—first and foremost, to eliminate competition from the often barely literate preachers of the new religions.[36] Even the Christian opponents of the bill commonly endorsed the regulation of certain sects, as one explained: "in the endeavor to discourage the ignorant religious 'quack,' who battens on human superstition, the Bill required certain standard education on the part of all religious teachers, an excellent idea so far as some 'religions' are concerned, but rather hard on the humble 'lay preacher' or Salvation Army worker!"[37]

Buddhist and Shinto support notwithstanding, the religions bill died in a committee of the House of Peers before it could reach the popularly elected Lower House. The government's somewhat more liberal religious organizations bill suffered the same fate in 1929. The failure of religions legislation in part reflects the greater acceptance of pluralism during the 1920s than at any other time in Japan before World War II. The religious organizations may have advanced narrow self-interests in the course of the debates, but influential members of the House of Peers committees took Article 28 of the Meiji Constitution seriously enough to quash the religions bills in the name of the freedom of religious belief.[38]

Second, the government was not at all united behind the attempt to establish an elaborate new system for regulating the religions. The initiative for the legislation had come from the Ministry of Education's low-ranking Bureau of Religions, whose frustrated officials sought a more substantial role. Representatives of the powerful Home Ministry, on the other hand, displayed little enthusiasm at the prospect of enforcing what many believed to be an unnecessary law.[39] They certainly perceived a threat to "orthodoxy" and the social order, but it came from the Communist party, not poorly educated preachers.[40]

Finally, when Ministry of Education officials attempted to impose administrative uniformity on three quite different religions, they inevitably displeased significant elements in all three. Buddhist priests who were not affiliated with the established Buddhist orders loudly protested the very inclusion of Christian denominations in the bills, not to mention the special privileges granted Christians to form independent churches. Many Christians, for their part, resented the state's proposed imposition of a Buddhist-type ecclesiastical absolutism on their denominations. They also feared the use of Japanese educational standards to disqualify foreign clerics.[41] In the end, legislation on religions failed in the 1920s because the definition of orthodoxy remained broad enough to include all three religions, plus the institution of State Shinto.

Orthodoxy versus the New Religions

Orthodoxy is best defined by what it chooses to exclude. Communism represented the unquestioned pariah in Japanese society throughout the interwar years. Yet to most leaders of the state and established religions, the "newly arisen religions" ranked a not-too-distant second. The phenomenon of new religions was in fact not so new. The majority of the thirteen officially recognized Shinto sects had themselves begun as charismatic, often persecuted religions during the late Tokugawa and early Meiji periods. The second wave of new religions occurred after World War I, cresting during the early 1930s against the backdrop of the Great Depression and Japan's increasing military involvement on the Asian continent. In 1924, the Ministry of Education classified 98 groups as new religions, of which two-thirds were Shintoist and the rest largely Buddhist. The number of groups increased dramatically to 414 in 1930 and finally to 1,029 in 1935.[42] Their followers may have numbered in the several millions. Ōmotokyō alone claimed one to three million adherents, although official estimates in the mid-1930s placed the figure closer to 400,000. The authorities considered Hitonomichi Kyōdan the boom religion of the 1930s. It grew from 100,000 (8 branches) in 1928 to at least 500,000 (98 branches) in 1936. Though not technically a "new religion" because it enjoyed governmental recognition, the fiercely evangelical Tenrikyō sect officially reported a membership of 4,256,000 in 1938.[43]

In his path-breaking study of local political culture, Kano Masanao portrays the new religions as the forgotten other side of the mass awakening following World War I.[44] The interwar new religions drew their greatest support from the cities and those rural areas most affected by industrialization and urbanization. The best-known sects got their start in the Kansai region encompassing Osaka, Kyoto, and Kobe. Ōmotokyō, the oldest of these new religions, emerged during the 1890s in a rural area of Kyoto prefecture, where the rapid influx of silk mills and railroads was already eroding traditional social relations and religious influences. The anomie of the metropolis was also a factor, for a great many urban converts had recently arrived from the villages, yearning for a new sense of community and spirituality to replace the organized Buddhism left behind.[45]

As in the case of their postwar counterparts, the success of the interwar new religions lay specifically in their ability to meet the worldly needs of such people.[46] Various forms of healing attracted the most followers, according to official surveys of arrested leaders and members.[47] The sects also offered spiritual guidance in dealing with marital problems, economic hardships, and existential crises. The highly practical Hitonomichi Kyōdan, for example, combined all of these elements. Originally centered on the merchant class of Osaka, Hitonomichi passionately preached the virtues of individual success. Its forerunner, Tokumitsukyō, had built up a following among petty speculators and gamblers, who were particularly enamoured of the sect's powers to divine the near future. Hitonomichi's founder, Miki Tokuharu, further inherited Tokumitsukyō's methods of healing. In one ritual called *ofurikae*, Tokuharu temporarily transferred the sickness or misfortunes of others to himself so that he might vicariously endure their sufferings. He and his clerics likewise interpreted divine oracles (*mioshie*) to help believers overcome everyday problems. The phenomenal growth of Hitonomichi spoke for the appeal of these practices. One leader remembered joining up after Tokuharu consulted the oracles to clarify the sources of the man's marital discord. Another entered the sect because the founder had cured his eldest son of bedwetting.[48]

The new religions owed much of their appeal to the charisma of founders or organizers, who were often promoted as living gods. The colorful Deguchi Ōnisaburō of Ōmotokyō was undoubtedly the best

FIGURE 6. Ōnisaburō reviews two of Ōmotokyō's paramilitary organizations in the 1930s. Astride his white horse, the patriarch not only mimics the emperor, but also incorporates the modern techniques of mass mobilization prevalent among fascist and other authoritarian movements in contemporary Europe.

known. Ōmotokyō grew out of the trances experienced in 1892 by Deguchi Nao, an elderly peasant woman with no formal education. A student of the Shinto tradition, the much younger Ōnisaburō married Nao's daughter and quickly emerged as the real organizer of Ōmotokyō. Just as Miki Tokuharu commanded the devotion of followers by virtue of his unique powers to heal, Ōnisaburō constructed his own cult of personality. He perfected the ritual of inducing a trance called *chinkon kishin* (pacifying the soul and returning to divinity), which united the believer with the spiritual world. Drawing on the traditional charisma of the female shaman, he wore brightly colored kimonos and occasionally dressed as a goddess. Ōnisaburō would enrage the public yet awe supporters by reviewing the sect's paramilitary organizations from atop a white horse— an act conventionally reserved to the emperor himself (Figure 6). Ōnisaburō's innate recklessness nearly cost him his life in 1924, when he led a ragtag army of five hundred on a futile quest to convert the Mongolians.[49]

The organizational skills of a Deguchi Ōnisaburō or Miki Tokuharu constituted the final ingredient in the spectacular rise of the interwar sects. For all the journalistic attacks on their antimodern doctrines, the new religions adopted some very modern techniques to mobilize far greater numbers of Japanese than labor or tenant-farmer unions between the two world wars. Hitonomichi Kyōdan's attractiveness, as Yamano Haruo and Narita Ryūichi observe, was based in part on its incorporation of several aspects of urban modernity. Reflecting the gradual shift from three-generation households to nuclear families in the cities, the sect encouraged husbands and wives to spend more time together. And like the more comfortable housewives of the new middle class, Hitonomichi women eagerly attended lectures that introduced new methods of washing clothes and keeping homes free of mosquitoes and flies.[50] Furthermore, to maintain control over the expanding Hitonomichi Kyōdan, Tokuharu rationally demarcated the administrative and ritual powers of his clergy according to a system of fifteen to eighteen rankings.[51] Ōmotokyō organized men, women, and youth into auxiliary organizations, frequently staging impressive parades of their uniformed members.

The big sects also proved adept at raising funds from believers. Nor were they shy about displaying their wealth in the form of lavish buildings, such as those at Hitonomichi's headquarters outside Osaka or Ōmotokyō's vast pilgrimage center at Ayabe. Finally, leaders skillfully relied on advertising and sect-owned newspapers to spread the word.[52] Their nineteenth-century predecessors had counted disciples in the tens of thousands; they, on the other hand, reached hundreds of thousands throughout the nation and Japan's overseas empire.

Although government officials had viewed the new religions with suspicion since the Meiji Restoration, they only gradually adopted a policy of outright suppression during the interwar decades. Under the 1884 system of indirect supervision of Shinto and Buddhist orders, the authorities tolerated religions like Ōmotokyō as long as those bodies were affiliated with one of the officially recognized sects or denominations.[53] Faced with a rising number of unaffiliated sects during World War I, the Bureau of Religions (Ministry of Education) directed prefectural authorities to strengthen surveillance over all unrecognized religious groups in March 1919. Bureau officials coined the contemptuous term "pseudo religions" to describe such organizations, for they "engage in activities resembling those of religions, yet do not belong to the denominations and sects of Shinto, Buddhism, and Christianity."[54] In essence, the state would determine what constituted a genuine religion.

In 1921, the government mobilized more than two hundred policemen to arrest three leaders of the rapidly growing Ōmotokyō. They were charged with committing lèse-majesté and violating the Newspaper Law's prohibition against printing materials disrespectful of the emperor and the imperial house. The sect had been preaching of an impending apocalyptic war with the United States, after which the emperor would reunite a defeated Japan from Ōmotokyō's sacred shrine at Ayabe outside Kyoto. Deguchi Ōnisaburō, the patriarch, was subsequently sentenced to five years at hard labor; the two other defendants received lesser sentences (see Figure 7).

On March 4, 1928, just a week and a half before massive raids against suspected Communists, the government moved against another Shintoist group, Tenri Kenkyūkai. The founder, Ōnishi Aijirō, had led his flock out of the officially recognized Tenrikyō in 1925, after criticizing the parent organization for having departed from its original teachings (which had not fully accepted the divinity of the emperor). The authorities became alarmed in 1927 when Ōnishi dispatched followers throughout the nation to circulate pamphlets warning of an imminent world war and the annihilation of Japan unless the Japanese accepted his own interpretation of the Tenrikyō creed. In contrast to the limited prosecutions of Ōmotokyō, judicial officials ordered the arrests of 467 leaders as well as followers of Tenri Kenkyūkai, indicting 180 on the charge of lèse-majesté.

However, the bureaucracy lacked both the unity and legal apparatus necessary to dissolve the leading "pseudo religions" during the 1920s. Ōnisaburō served only four months of his sentence before being released on parole. He was fully pardoned in 1927 as part of a general amnesty following the death of the Taishō emperor. The courts similarly suspended the sentences of every Tenri Kenkyūkai defendant but Ōnishi (and the Supreme Court acquitted him in 1930 on grounds of diminished mental capacity). Both sects soon regained their impressive momentum.[55]

As harsh as the government's actions of the 1920s might appear, they paled by comparison with those taken after 1935. When the chief of the Home Ministry's Police Bureau announced the campaign to "eradicate the evil cults" in 1936, he challenged the fundamental right to exist of several popular religions.[56] The problem of distinguishing the "evil cults" from other new religions did not seem to bother the bureaucrats—at least, not the resident expert on religions, Nagano Wakamatsu of the Special Higher Police. In an article addressed to ordinary policemen, Nagano cautioned against equating all "pseudo religions" with "heretical cults" (inshi jakyō). Nevertheless, he concluded, "a majority of the pseudo religions are in fact hotbeds of such religious crimes as lèse-majesté, fraud, obstructing medical treatment, and corrupting good morals."[57]

FIGURE 7. Dismantling one "evil cult." Police pose triumphantly before Ōmotokyō's holiest shrines, which they have finished gutting in the first raid on the sect
in 1921.

The government's sensational actions against Ōmotokyō on December 8, 1935, launched the new campaign. Some 550 police cordoned off
Ōmotokyō's sacred grounds in Ayabe and Kameoka, and soon afterward
there were raids on branches throughout Japan, its colonies, and occupied territories. A total of 987 adherents were arrested. Unlike the first
Ōmotokyō incident of 1921, this time the police came with orders to
destroy the religion itself. The extraordinary level of physical destruction
has already been described (see Figure 8). The zealous authorities subsequently auctioned off the sect's lands for one-hundredth of their real
value. Adding insult to injury, officials forced Ōmotokyō to bear the total
costs of its own destruction.[58] To insure the conviction of as many Ōmotokyō leaders as possible, prosecutors established the legal precedent of
dismembering religious organizations by means of the Peace Preservation
Law of 1925—the measure had theretofore been applied only against
left-wing elements. Under the law, some fifty-one leaders of Ōmotokyō
received stiff sentences for allegedly organizing an association with the

FIGURE 8. The remains of Ōmotokyō await the bonfire outside the Ayabe police station, following the second and final set of raids in 1935.

aim of "overthrowing the national polity"—that is, seeking to overturn rule by the emperor. As patriarch, Ōnisaburō was sentenced to life imprisonment with hard labor.[59]

The eradication of other new religions soon followed. In April 1937, the government dissolved the fastest growing new religion of the 1930s, Hitonomichi Kyōdan, and, as usual, prosecuted several elders for lèse-majesté. The case put the more respectable new religions on notice, for Hitonomichi Kyōdan, unlike Ōmotokyō, was still affiliated with one of the thirteen officially recognized Shinto sects. Henceforth, any charismatic sect—not only the unrecognized "pseudo-religions"—could be crushed as an "evil cult." Tenri Hommichi (formerly Tenri Kenkyūkai) and the evangelical Christian denomination, Jehovah's Witnesses, met similar ends in 1938 and 1940, respectively. In the case of Tenri Hommichi, officials employed some of the extralegal tactics learned in the suppression of Ōmotokyō. Without bothering to await the outcome of judicial proceedings, police drove the founder's family from its Osaka home and seized the sect's assets, of which two-thirds were appropriated for Japan's war effort. These three religious organizations were simply the largest or best known victims in the escalating campaign of religious persecution.[60]

It is difficult to fathom what it was about these hapless new religions that so threatened the state. Existing explanations tend to generalize on the basis of the rather exceptional case of Ōmotokyō. Several Japanese scholars portray Ōmotokyō as a "radical" or "revolutionary" lower-class movement that truly challenged the emperor-system state with a millenarian vision of remaking the world.[61] Ōmotokyō, it is true, possessed an elaborate eschatology, which prophesied the destruction of all evil and the "restoration and renovation of the world" (*tatekae tatenaoshi*). In addition, Ōnisaburō and his disciples freely condemned the privileged position of capitalists and landlords. A key feature of their utopia would have been the redistribution of all property by the Japanese emperor to the peoples of the world.

Whether Ōmotokyō's doctrines gave rise to radical behavior, however, is more questionable. When historians of Europe discuss millenarianism, they usually refer to movements among the "rootless poor," whose millenarianism was "violent, anarchic, at times truly revolutionary."[62] For all his talk of the rift between rich and poor, Ōnisaburō preached that relief lay in the spiritual world, not proletarian revolution. Ōmotokyō in fact vehemently rejected democratic movements led by organized labor and the urban intelligentsia.[63] Furthermore, the arrests of 1921 dampened whatever remained of the sect's visions of an imminent millennium. By the time of its obliteration in 1935, Ōmotokyō had ironically become one of the staunchest supporters of the emperor and the Japanese military.

One finds even less evidence of a class-based or millenarian threat to state and society from the other persecuted religions. It is noteworthy that police reports rarely ascribed millenarian traits to the "pseudo religions" during the 1930s. Rather, they acknowledged the sects' focus on the "simple, common interests of this world."[64] When officials arrested 467 leaders and followers of the putatively millenarian Tenri Kenkyūkai in 1928, they discovered that most were middle-aged or elderly farmers, shopkeepers, and artisans (nearly one-third were aged 51 to 79). Fewer than 10 percent had gone beyond higher elementary school, and almost one-fifth of those arrested were women, whose average age was 46.[65] In no way did these humble folk resemble the young intellectuals and class-conscious workers who formed secret Communist cells during the same period. Moreover, most of the new religions enthusiastically supported the government's expansionist policies on the Asian mainland after 1931. The ill-fated Hitonomichi Kyōdan, in particular, not only preached familialism and selflessness in work, but also drew thousands to daily morning worship services for the emperor and nation during the 1930s.[66] In their relation to the capitalist order, most of these sects resembled a postwar religion examined by Winston Davis, who noted: "Far from contradicting the practical achievement-orientation of industrial Japan, the practices of Mahikari seem to increase the capacity of its lower-class members for responsibility, self-denial, and toil."[67]

Historians have offered only one other explanation that might have justified the extreme actions of the state. According to this theory, the government suppressed Ōmotokyō in December 1935, hoping to avert a coup d'état by right-wing military officers. The officers allegedly received funds from Ōnisaburō's ultranationalist auxiliary associations.[68] Indeed, a group of Army officers did attempt to overthrow the cabinet on February 26, 1936. It is also true that Ōnisaburō had recently organized a new paramilitary organization, the Shōwa Shinseikai (Shōwa Sacred Association), which cooperated with other ultranationalist groups.

However, as Watanabe Osamu has persuasively shown, the civil authorities crushed Ōmotokyō as part of the campaign to "eradicate the evil cults"—not for its right-wing politics. Although after World War II some police officials justified their actions by pointing to Ōmotokyō's ultranationalism, the police at the time made no mention of the sect's political activities in their string of charges. The legal instruments used—lèse-majesté and the Peace Preservation Law—were ones enforced against religious organizations and leftists, rarely if ever against the Right. There were many nationalistic associations in Japan during the mid-1930s, yet only Ōmotokyō was so savagely suppressed. Most important, the Special Higher Police agents who masterminded the raids against Ōmotokyō worked in the religions subsection, rather than in the office responsible for monitoring nationalistic movements. They or their immediate successors went on to dismantle Hitonomichi Kyōdan, Tenri Hommichi, and the Jehovah's Witnesses. None of these religions, it should be noted, had anything to do with the radical Right. Their common denominator was heterodox religious activity, not dangerous politics.[69]

If the new religions did not pose a political threat to the state, what could possibly account for the increasingly ruthless campaign against them after 1935? Bureaucratic sectionalism was clearly one major factor. In yet another illustration of the "banality of evil," a repressive organ of state had run out of movements to repress. The Home Ministry had established a nationwide network of Special Higher Police units during the 1920s with the primary objective of destroying the underground Communist party and related groups. Success had its costs, however. Officials of the Special Higher Police had so thoroughly annihilated the Communist movement by 1933 that they faced the prospect of drastic retrenchment. *Their* salvation lay in convincing the government and the public of the need for a specialized "religions police" to control that other social movement—the new religions. The lobbying paid off in June 1935, when the cabinet centralized jurisdiction over controlling religions within the Police Bureau's Public Security Section and its Special Higher Police units in each prefecture. The scale of the newly formed "religions police" (shūkyō keisatsu) was simply extraordinary. Within the Tokyo Metropolitan Police, for example, the Special Higher Police Department in 1936 added a separate religions office, staffed by no fewer than twenty-one agents. Suddenly, previously harmless sects became "evil cults," which could only be controlled by His Majesty's Religions Police.

Lest the crackdown on new religions appear to be evidence of statism pure and simple, let us also consider the broad societal support for the drive to eradicate the cults. It would be comforting to see the repressive emperor-system state on one side and its victims—liberals, socialists, and religions—on the other. Yet this was hardly the case. As we have seen, most leaders of the three established religions favored, and even campaigned for, governmental control of the new religions. The leadership of Hitonomichi Kyōdan believed, with some justification, that the established religions had urged officials to arrest the sect's founder in 1936. The Buddhist order, Higashi Honganji, regarded Hitonomichi with particular enmity, having lost large numbers of adherents and some priests to the upstart religion. Higashi Honganji's chief abbot may have turned damning evidence over to the authorities, according to statements by Hitonomichi leaders.[70] The popular press, including some of the most liberal dailies, also legitimized the suppressions with lurid stories of orgies, mass hypnotic trances, and underground torture chambers.[71]

Prominent scholars, writers, and physicians played no less active roles in criticizing the new religions. The leading socialist thinkers Ōyama Ikuo and Kawakami Hajime openly worried about the "superstitious" tendencies of the expanding cults, perhaps because they, too, were fighting a losing battle against the popular sects for the hearts and minds of poor farmers and laborers.[72] As devout modernists, progressive intellectuals were further swayed by the emerging social science of abnormal psychology. In 1920, a psychologist named Nakamura Kokyō published a widely read study of Ōmotokyō leaders and followers. His book featured sympathetic introductions written by a number of well-known liberals, socialists, and academic specialists. Nakamura adduced Ōmotokyō to be "a band of paranoiacs (embracing the excessive bibliomania of the religiously deluded), the delusionally demented, superstitious individuals, and swindlers." As an instructor at the Tokyo Police Academy, Nakamura personally encouraged the somewhat reluctant home minister to take action against Ōmotokyō before the first arrests in 1921.[73] The crusading psychologist was still at it in 1937, when he urged the police to demolish the rest of the "false religions," beginning with the officially recognized Tenrikyō.[74]

Equally striking was the fanaticism of the "New Buddhists" (Shin Bukkyōtō), a group of liberal laymen that had generally opposed governmental interference in religious affairs since 1899. Led by Professor Takashima Beihō and other scholars from Waseda University, the New Buddhists sponsored a major rally in 1920 to convince the public and government of the dangers of Ōmotokyō and other "superstitious" religions. Takashima's good friend, the aforementioned psychologist Nakamura Kokyō, also addressed the meeting. In contrast to some in his movement, Takashima claimed to oppose outright suppression; he preferred merely to expose the "superstitious, heretical beliefs" of Ōmotokyō.[75] But directly following the second raids on Ōmotokyō in 1935, Professor Takashima heartily endorsed the emerging policy of sheer eradication: "I fervently hope that the Home Ministry will not stop at arrests of Ōmotokyō alone, but will stage one massive roundup, concentrating its fire on those groups possessed of quackery (inchikisei), whether they be established religious bodies or the newly arisen pseudo religions."[76] In a bizarre twist, the progressive Buddhist urged the authorities to invoke the Meiji Constitution's Article 28 for the express purpose of denying the freedom of religion to any cult they deemed "prejudicial to peace and order."[77]

Given the widespread societal sentiment against the new religions, it is clear that state officials were not acting totally autonomously. Nor did they simply manipulate public opinion to their advantage, as some have argued.[78] Rather, in many instances, the bureaucrats responded to the outside clamor for tough controls or, at the very least, based their policies on definitions of heterodoxy shared by intellectuals, psychologists, and established religious leaders.

Two questions naturally arise. In what specific areas did the new religions offend the general orthodoxy? And why did the state and society grudgingly tolerate the existence of popular sects in 1920s, yet demand their eradication during the latter half of the 1930s? Nagano Wakamatsu, architect of the "religions police," provided unusually frank answers to these questions in 1936. The "quack religions" (inchiki shūkyō), he explained, threatened the social order on several counts. They propagate lèse-majesté, he said; "bewilder the people" with superstition and sorcery; "obstruct medical treatment"; "fleece the wealth" of followers; and "corrupt public morals."[79] With a slight reorganization of Nagano's charges, one may summarize the government's essentially secular definition of heterodoxy as follows:

Lèse-majesté. To proponents of the emperor-system thesis, the state suppressed the new religions primarily because of perceived doctrinal challenges to the supremacy of the emperor. Yet lèse-majesté was simply one of several reasons for dismembering suspect religions, according to accounts by Nagano and other police officials. To be sure, prosecutors in 1921 and 1936 went to great lengths to prove that the teachings of Ōmotokyō denied the rule of the Japanese emperor; the sect allegedly revered the ancient gods, Susa-no-o and Kuni-toko-tachi—rather than the Sun Goddess, progenitor of Japan's imperial line. The government likewise charged Hitonomichi Kyōdan with lèse-majesté for worshiping the sun, which its doctrine innocently equated with the sacred Sun Goddess. Nevertheless, these charges appear little more than legal pretexts, deployed after the fact to cripple religions that had committed other offenses in the eyes of the authorities and society. Officials resolved to destroy Ōmotokyō in 1935, years after Ōnisaburō had squared his teachings with the imperial myth.[80]

The case of Hitonomichi Kyōdan is revealing. Convinced that the order was an "evil cult," the authorities had sought an excuse to immobilize the flourishing sect since 1931. The problem was that Hitonomichi's creed dutifully quoted the 1890 Imperial Rescript on Education, which called on Japanese subjects to be loyal to the emperor and filial in social relationships. The Special Higher Police redoubled their efforts during the autumn of 1936. In searches of the religion's branches throughout the nation, agents questioned more than two thousand people and sifted through numerous publications and documents. But by year's end, prosecutors were forced to admit that they still lacked hard evidence of lèse-majesté.[81] They eventually resigned themselves to demonstrating Hitonomichi's confusion of the sun and the Sun Goddess, although this doctrinal deviation had never bothered officials before. If the state had truly intended to eradicate any religion that questioned the absolute authority of the emperor, it would have started with the Christian denominations, not the new Shintoist orders.

Irrationality, Superstition, and Healing. Like many progressive intellectuals, Home Ministry officials despised the new religions for "denying the rationality of modern science" and "worshiping superstition and absolute nonsense."[82] The critique of superstition was not new. Domain governments in the Tokugawa era frequently attempted to eliminate such folk rituals as incantations and divination. In 1873, the Meiji regime similarly promulgated the first of several ordinances against those who impeded medical treatment by spells and charms.[83] The authorities nonetheless remained relatively tolerant of the popular sects throughout the nineteenth century, in part because officially sanctioned medical practices were not much more effective than spiritual healing.

Modernization ironically laid the groundwork for a much stronger assault on heterodox religions during the interwar era. The spread of

Western education, modern medicine, and social welfare bred a new determination in the "enlightened" state. The higher civil servants who directed the Special Higher Police were no ordinary policemen. Most had graduated from Tokyo Imperial University's prestigious Faculty of Law. Several then studied administrative policies in Europe and the United States. They regarded themselves as progressive bureaucrats responsible for preventing social unrest by repression, if necessary, but also by positive social policies. Some had previously served in the Home Ministry's reformist Social Bureau, while others, like Nagano Wakamatsu, went on to oversee labor and welfare administration within the Ministry of Health and Welfare.[84]

What made public health and welfare a particularly urgent issue during the 1930s was Japan's expansion into Manchuria and China. Military-industrial mobilization demanded healthy recruits and workers. Between 1936 and 1938, Home Ministry officials championed a whole new set of health and protective labor measures. Intent on improving the "health of the nation," the Special Higher Police vowed to "hammer" those "evil cults" that practiced healing to the exclusion of modern medicine. Officials were also livid about what Nagano termed the "religion biz" (shūkyō eigyō). The new religions allegedly amassed huge fortunes by extracting contributions and by selling pamphlets and amulets at unreasonable prices. Citing the government's stated commitment in 1936 to "stabilize the people's livelihood," Nagano pledged to arrest the many cult leaders who "robbed the general masses of their meager funds."[85]

Corruption of Public Morals. Although "corrupting public morals" (fūzoku kairan) may appear a mere pretext for suppressing religions, the charge had real meaning for most Japanese. Prewar Japanese orthodoxy extolled patriarchal authority, in law and often in practice. Yet the new religions attracted huge numbers of women, partly because women were associated with traditional shamanistic practices and partly because the sects emphasized the themes of family and marriage. Many women became preachers themselves, especially in those religions which drew little distinction between cleric and follower.[86] As in medieval and early modern Europe, the emergence of female proselytizers openly challenged the orthodox gender ideology of Japan. Women outside the home were considered sexually volatile.[87] Most of the new religions in fact, promoted familial values, but the general public stood ready to believe the wildest stories of countless perversions. Brimming with moral outrage, officials charged that many charismatic cult leaders seduced female followers, having taken advantage of their victims' "crazed faith and blind devotion." These "pseudo religions," the complaints continued, propagated sheer hedonism: "The results are well known. They stimulate the lust of their ignorant mass following. By evoking total looseness in matters of carnal love, they unabashedly propagate a gospel of extreme lewdness concerning sexual pleasure."[88]

Suspicion of sexual excesses could by itself justify suppression. One of Hitonomichi Kyōdan's gravest offenses, it seems, was to encourage mutual friendship, rather than hierarchical relations, between husband and wife. The order would sponsor "couples' discussion groups" and foot races between couples. Clerics also stressed the importance of sexual love as the key to a happy marriage.[89]

That was apparently the kiss of death, at least in the eyes of the earnest Special Higher Police agent responsible for religions in Osaka prefecture. Hitonomichi, he charged, imposed a "strict regimen of nightly sexual intimacy" on its followers. His horror stories reveal more about the mentality of the authorities than they do about Hitonomichi. In one, a woman developed a high fever after being instructed to sleep with her husband the night following childbirth. In another, a seventy-year-old woman obeyed an oracular commandment to engage in "yin and yang" every night. She ended up bedridden, the agent noted. Indeed, the Special Higher Police first moved against Hitonomichi on the suspicion of a sexual crime. Officials arrested Miki Tokuharu in September 1936, after a disgruntled branch head accused the founder of raping his fifteen-year-old daughter. Police subsequently claimed that Tokuharu had raped some ten other female assistants, aged thirteen to fifteen. The veracity of the charges is open to question, considering their sensationalism and timing. True or false, the original accusation of rape furnished the Special Higher Police with a pretext to search Hitonomichi branches throughout the nation for evidence of "the erotic corruption of public morals, the fleecing of wealth, and the obstruction of medical treatment."[90]

Organizational Autonomy. What ultimately sealed the fate of the new religions was not their teachings or rituals, but their rapid development outside the state-approved hierarchy of the established religions. Nagano Wakamatsu admitted as much in 1936. Although earlier "pseudo religions" had engaged in superstitious practices and healing, the police did not regard them as a serious challenge, precisely because they were generally folk religions with small local bases. The new religions, argued Nagano, became a "social evil" only after they attained nationwide organization and influence over hundreds of thousands amidst the "religious revival" of the early 1930s.[91] Their dramatic rise further clashed with the state's authoritarian drive to mobilize the nation's organizations behind the war effort during the latter half of the 1930s. Whereas wartime officials incorporated independent associations of workers, women, and others into state-supervised hierarchies, they dismissed the new religions as inherently uncontrollable "assemblages of the permanently traumatized and the mentally disabled."[92] Nothing alarmed the fastidious civil servants of imperial Japan more than an organization whose membership could not be accurately counted.

Finally, police and judicial officials increasingly portrayed the new religions as a dangerous threat to the economic and social order. Never mind the fact that the popular sects strenuously opposed Communism and labor unions. To the bureaucrats, Communism and the "evil cults" bore certain resemblances in organizational terms. Both appealed to the masses in a time of "social dislocation brought on by changes in the capitalist structure." Both contributed to the "unprecedented chaos" of the time.[93] And both, it would seem, had to be eradicated to preserve that amorphous, but very real, concept of orthodoxy and the social order.

THE TRIUMPH OF RELIGIOUS STATISM IN
WARTIME JAPAN

In 1937, Japan embarked on an all-out war against China. The conflict ushered in the final phase in the evolving religions policies of imperial Japan. The ruthless campaign against popular Shintoist religions continued unabated, while relations between the state and the established religions experienced significant changes. Prodded by the military, the authorities widened their dragnet to smash several Christian groups, notably the Jehovah's Witnesses and the Holiness Church. Christian and Buddhist bodies had largely escaped persecution before 1937, since officials judged their doctrines to be free of the "lèse-majesté and lawlessness" issuing from the Shintoist "evil cults." However, as one Ministry of Justice bureaucrat observed in 1939, what was harmless in peace could be considered an expression of "antiwar and antimilitary" sentiment in wartime.[94]

Second, the regime employed an increasingly statist form of incorporation to mobilize the support of religious bodies.[95] Whereas the religions had previously worked with the state on a voluntary and coequal basis, the wartime authorities virtually conscripted religious bodies into the service of the nation. The government's new policy toward religions enlisted the country's clerics to collect donations for the war, console families of the dead, and proselytize on the continent in the name of Japanism. In 1939, the Diet enacted the long-stymied Religious Organizations Law (Shūkyō Dantaihō), giving the state unprecedented powers to regulate religious bodies and associations. The following year, religious organizations fell victim to the authoritarian drive to rationalize and absorb labor unions, political parties, and most other autonomous associations into the Imperial Rule Assistance Association. Drawing on their new powers to license all religious groups, Ministry of Education officials compelled the twenty Christian denominations to merge into a mere two organizations. Even the Buddhists were forced to halve the number of their orders from fifty-six to twenty-eight.

Finally, the wartime state asserted a monopoly over the definitions of orthodoxy and social order. Previous governments, it will be recalled, had refrained from insisting on the supremacy of State Shinto over other religions. After 1937, bureaucrats also abandoned another historical understanding with the established religions—namely, that the charges of obstructing the "peace and order" and one's "duties as a subject" (as stipulated by the constitution's Article 28) would be applied, in most cases, only against the new religions. Led by the military, the state increasingly equated orthodoxy and "peace and order" with a rigid interpretation of Japan's "national polity" (*kokutai*). At the same time, government agencies pressured the established religions into eliminating alleged discrepancies between their teachings and the imperial myth.[96]

The subordination of all religions to the cult of the emperor became abundantly clear during the debates over the proposed Religious Organizations Law in 1939. Speaking before a Diet committee, Prime Minister Hiranuma Kiichirō codified the new definition of orthodoxy: "Let me emphasize that all religions must be one with the ideal of our national polity; they cannot be at odds with the spirit of our Imperial Way."[97] In 1940, the government created the independent Shrine Board on the model of the early Meiji era's Office of Shinto Rites (Jingikan).

After decades of denying that State Shinto was a religion, the statist Konoe Cabinet declared that it was the only religion. The Home Ministry revised the Peace Preservation Law in 1941 with the specific purpose of rooting out those religions, mainly Shintoist, which previously could not be successfully prosecuted on the charge of aiming to "overthrow the national polity." Under the revised law, officials could and did destroy such groups for propagating beliefs that simply "denied" (that is, varied from) the national polity or that "blasphemed the dignity of the Grand Shrine of Ise or the Imperial House."[98] In actuality, the overwhelming majority of religious bodies, including Christian denominations, adjusted to the new doctrinal absolutism and thus escaped direct persecution. Nevertheless, their acquiescence marked a sharp break with the once formidable power of the established religions to protect their institutional and doctrinal autonomy.

As tragic as the wartime suppression of Japanese religions was, we would do well to place the issue within the broader context of state-society relations and social management in the decades before 1945. The construct of the emperor-system state, I have argued, is of little utility in historical inquiry, for it exaggerates the unity, strength, and rigidity of the Japanese state from 1890 to the nation's defeat. Since all societies possess some notion of orthodoxy and the social order, it makes more sense to examine comparatively how the Japanese state and society defined the two terms over several decades. Modernization and Westernization reshaped, rather than eliminated, orthodox norms in Japan following the Meiji Restoration. A growing faith in scientific progress combined with traditional values of public morality and reverence for one's ruler. Elite bureaucrats, established religious leaders, and intellectuals had more in common than is usually recognized. The parameters of orthodoxy could accordingly be broad at times. During the 1920s, state and society tolerated the existence of most organizations as long as they did not advocate the overthrow of private property and the political system, which included the emperor. The social order proved capable of accommodating Christians, liberal intellectuals, trade unionists, and even local folk religions with deviant readings of the imperial myth.

On the other hand, one should hardly be surprised at the blatant suppression of new religions from 1935 or the severe regulation of all religions during the war. The emperor-system thesis is at its strongest when describing the repressive potential of the emerging bureaucratic structure after 1900. In its preoccupation with controlling "dangerous thought," the government created a sizable Special Higher Police force and corresponding "thought procurate" by 1930. Granted substantial discretionary powers in their campaign against Communists and anarchists, the political police proceeded to include the "pseudo religions" within their dragnet. When all is said and done, it was these bureaucratic specialists who ultimately translated public criticism of the new religions into systematic repression.

Nonetheless, forces within society played an important, if disturbing, role in shaping the state's evolving religions policy. By actively participating in moral suasion campaigns after 1900, they also enabled the bureaucracy to manage everyday life more effectively than before. Even at its broadest, the interwar Japanese definition of orthodoxy remained fundamentally hostile to the true freedom of religious belief and practice. Few within the established religions or intelligentsia were willing to apply the constitutional protections of Article 28 to the so-called pseudo religions or evil cults. Most religious orders insisted not so much on freedom from the state as inclusion within the national orthodoxy. Toward that end, religious leaders repeatedly turned to the state, expecting it to manage both their rivals and the general populace. Buddhists strove to use official recognition to strengthen themselves and weaken the Christians; Shinto leaders sought to apply legal sanctions against break-away factions. And almost all established religions called upon the state to defend their common visions of social order and public morality from the Communists, on one hand, and the new religions, on the other. Preferring orthodoxy to the toleration of divergent creeds, the established religions helped paved the way for the wartime assertion of a rigid state dogma—and inevitably for the regime's oppressive management of their own activities.

The World's Oldest Debate?
Regulating Prostitution and
Illicit Sexuality

O N SEPTEMBER 3, 1900, the offices of the *Niroku shimbun,* a Tokyo daily, received a desperate letter from a twenty-one-year-old prostitute named Nakamura Yae. A resident of the famed licensed quarters of Yoshiwara, Nakamura beseeched the socially progressive newspaper to assist her in leaving her occupation. Because vigilant keepers and police regulations made it difficult, even dangerous, for licensed prostitutes to venture outside the confines of the brothel quarters, the daily dispatched a lawyer to ascertain the woman's intentions. Two days later, the newspaper's president, the lawyer, and several staff members proceeded to the Asakusa police station to file Nakamura's report that she had ceased her trade and wished to have her name removed from the list of registered prostitutes. The station chief refused to accept the report on the grounds that the ordinances of the Tokyo Metropolitan Police required the brothel owner to countersign a prostitute's request for cessation of trade. When representatives of the newspaper returned to the brothel to urge the owner to sign, they confronted several angry toughs in the employ of the brothel keepers. Bolstered by reinforcements, the newspapermen fought back, sustaining several injuries. Just one day earlier, in another one of Tokyo's five licensed quarters, ruffians had severely beat Ensign Yamamuro Gumpei and a British major from the Japanese headquarters of the Salvation Army while the pair was on a similar rescue mission.

The incidents of 1900 brought home to Japanese officials that the regulation of prostitution could no longer be considered simply an administrative matter. The state's policies toward prostitutes threatened to embarrass the government domestically and internationally. The top brass of the Tokyo Metropolitan Police reacted swiftly to the melee in Yoshiwara. Protected by a contingent of sixty policemen, Nakamura Yae was permitted to leave the quarters so that she could personally file the report of cessation. Over the vehement protests of brothel owners, the commissioner of the Metropolitan Police also revised the police ordinances. Henceforth a prostitute could legally cease her trade even if the proprietor did not countersign the application.[1]

In retrospect, the battle over "free cessation" (jiyū haigyō) was but an opening skirmish in a protracted struggle over the fate of the system of licensed prostitution itself—a struggle that continued until the abolition of licensed prostitution in 1946 and the enactment of the Antiprostitution Law in 1956. Violent incidents in the brothel quarters did not cease. Yet the conflict moved increasingly into parliamentary chambers, prefectural assemblies, and bureaucratic offices, as well-organized groups of abolitionists on one side and brothel keepers on the other pressed their claims.

The discourse over the proper relationship between prostitution and the state may well be one of the world's oldest debates, dividing thinkers in ancient Greece and Rome as well as China and India.[2] As one classic study put it, prostitution has been such a universal phenomenon that in the range of official responses over time and across geographical boundaries, "the old adage holds—'There is nothing new under the sun.'" Authorities in a variety of polities have typically moved to and fro among policies of repression, laissez-faire, and regulation.[3]

In Japan, the protagonists frequently stated their case in terms heard elsewhere, although the defenders of licensed prostitution, in particular, made many assumptions about sexuality and gender roles for young women, wives, and male customers that were muted or absent in European society. The history of licensed prostitution in imperial Japan, moreover, bespeaks the state's fervent commitment to social management. Prior to 1946, elite bureaucrats sought to regulate people's sexuality in the service of a broader national agenda—much as they managed welfare and religious organizations. It was more than a matter of providing a hygenic, supervised outlet for male sexuality. Officials regarded licensed prostitution as an integral part of programs aimed at "regulating public morality," furthering economic development, and advancing national power.

Again we discover that the state did not act alone in defining public morality and managing society. Few abolitionists sought to remove the government from the realm of regulating extramarital sexuality, just as few in the established religions wished to strip the state of its considerable powers to supervise religions organizations. Rather, these middle-class reformers—no less than their opponents in the brothel trade—frequently looked to the state to propagate their own particular conceptions of public morality. Because some of the abolitionists were persecuted for their beliefs during the dark days of World War II, historians have understandably been reluctant to examine patterns of interaction between the imperial state and the moral reformers.

It has been especially difficult to discuss the abolitionists' participation in the official regulation of morality during the 1930s and early 1940s, for the abolitionist movement was led by several of Japan's most famous progressive politicians, educators, and social reformers, most of them Christian. Indeed, at the end of World War II, United States officials commonly represented these Christian leaders as American-style liberals whose influence had "been rigidly suppressed and silenced since 1931."[4] The label of "liberal," however, does little to advance our understanding of the Japanese abolitionists. By examining the areas of both contention and consensus among the moral reformers, the brothel owners, and the state, we achieve a more complete portrait of social management.

THE EVOLUTION OF LICENSED PROSTITUTION

British and American observers often condemned the licensed quarters as a relic of traditional Japan, but other Westerners recognized familiar features from their own societies. The modern system of regulated prostitution, like the Japanese state's other programs of social management, grafted European models onto indigenous practices that had developed in the centuries prior to the Meiji Restoration of 1868. Officially supervised prostitution dated at least as far back as the Kamakura period (1185–1333), when the shogunate created the office of "steward of prostitutes" (*yūkun betto*). The Ashikaga shogunate (1338–1573) formally recognized prostitution as a trade, and its Harlots Bureau (*Keiseikyoku*) began taxing the profession.

But the immediate roots of the modern system are to be found in the policies of the Tokugawa shogunate and domain governments. All five of modern Tokyo's licensed quarters were originally established by the shogunate in what was then called Edo. In 1618, the authorities set up the Yoshiwara quarters in an effort to concentrate scattered gangs of prostitutes. When a fire destroyed the district in 1657, the quarters were moved to the eastern outskirts and renamed New Yoshiwara, the site of the modern quarters. By the end of the seventeenth century, there were thirty-five licensed quarters throughout Japan. Yoshiwara and the Shimabara quarters (Kyoto) by themselves accounted for some two thousand and eight hundred prostitutes, respectively.[5]

Although Christian societies in the West generally viewed prostitution as an evil, albeit a necessary one, officials in early modern Japan expressed few moral reservations about the trade. The legal system appeared to encourage selling daughters into prostitution as a legitimate response to poverty. In 1733, one shogunal code addressed the common occurrence in which an impoverished "low-status" family offered a daughter to another household for adoption. Even if the foster family had the girl engage in prostitution, stipulated the code, "her true family may not lodge a complaint, regardless of their grievances."[6] Prostitution became morally objectionable only when the providers came from families of samurai status (this restriction did not apply to customers, of course). As late as 1876, the new central government, in defiance of its declared commitment to legal equality, instructed prefectural authorities that former samurai and their women must not be granted licenses to engage in the "shameful occupation" of running brothels or working as prostitutes or geisha, "no matter what their circumstances."[7]

Official attitudes were nonetheless shaken by the influx of Western ideas in the wake of Meiji Restoration. Leading figures in the new regime and intelligentsia began to criticize the human costs of the early modern system of regulation. In 1872, as would often be the case over the next several decades, an international incident precipitated a major change in policy. The Maria Luz, a Peruvian ship loaded with 230 Chinese indentured laborers, put into port at Yokohama. One of the Chinese swam to a nearby British warship, seeking to escape. Eager to demonstrate Japan's "civilized" status to the Western powers, the government detained the ship and ordered that the hapless passengers be returned to China. Peru's savvy minister to Japan protested. Because Japanese law permitted the sale of women and children into prostitution, he observed, traffic in human beings was perfectly legal. The Japanese court dismissed his claim, but the embarrassing nature of the incident persuaded an influential group of self-described "enlightened" bureaucrats that the entire system of regulated prostitution should be eliminated.[8]

In a remarkable reversal of inherited policies, the newly established Council of State issued the Ordinance Liberating Prostitutes in 1872. In addition to prohibiting the buying and selling of people, in general, the ordinance decreed that prostitutes, geisha, and "other indentured servants" be freed, with no recourse available to their masters. At the same time, the Justice Ministry, a bastion of the "enlightenment" clique, ruled that prostitutes and geisha would not have to repay monetary advances of their keepers, for "prostitutes and geisha are those who have lost rights over their bodies and thus are no different from cows and horses. It would not be reasonable to demand the return of goods from a cow or horse."[9]

Not only did the government's decrees do little to elevate the status of prostitutes as human beings, the Ordinance Liberating Prostitutes failed to have much impact on actual administration. The edict dictated a laissez-faire approach, tacitly permitting acts of prostitution themselves. Yet officials of the newly created prefectures were no more willing than the old shogunate to let matters take their course. Within days of the ordinance's promulgation in October 1872, authorities in Tokyo prefecture drafted rules that would strictly regulate prostitutes, geisha, and brothels.[10]

Aside from the Justice Ministry, the central government itself seemed more concerned with Japan's international reputation than with undertaking real reform. In 1873, the Board of the Left advised the government to "effect behind-the-scenes regulatory schemes . . . , and in so doing, we should, practically speaking, be able to maintain both the objects of the new Ordinance [Liberating Prostitutes] and [Japan's] good name in the eyes of other countries."[11] The central state formally delegated responsibility for regulating prostitution to the prefectures in 1876. The liberation ordinance had, for all practical purposes, been repudiated in favor of "behind-the-scenes" management from Tokyo.

During the next twenty-five years, the Home Ministry and prefectures worked together to expand and modernize the system of licensed prostitution. At the initiative of the Tokyo Metropolitan Police, the authorities emulated many of the regulatory practices of the Paris police.[12] To strengthen surveillance and check the spread of venereal diseases, Japanese prefectures similarly required registered prostitutes to submit to periodic medical inspections, and they restricted the brothel trade to designated areas. Regulation of the prostitutes themselves came under the central government in 1900, when the Home Ministry issued the Rules Regulating Licensed Prostitutes. That same year, the Administrative Enforcement Law (Gyōsei Shikkōhō) gave police extensive powers to arrest unlicensed prostitutes and order them to undergo medical examinations.[13] In addition, the authorities regulated the geisha and the barmaids-cum-prostitutes known as *shakufu*. As trained entertainers, geisha were prohibited from engaging in acts of prostitution, but one knowledgeable official estimated that three-fourths of all geisha in 1929 did so in fact.[14]

For all its similarities to the "French system," the Japanese system of licensed prostitution went much further in restricting the liberties of the prostitute in the interests of effective regulation. Although the authorities in nineteenth-century France and Italy would have preferred to concentrate all prostitutes in the licensed houses, they resigned themselves to allowing registered independent prostitutes to work outside the brothels. During the last decades of the century, the numbers of the independent *filles en carte* rapidly outstripped those of the brothel prostitutes in France. The sharp decline in the brothels reflected, according to Alain Corbin, a "European and even a worldwide phenomenon."[15]

Brothel prostitution may have been declining throughout Europe, but not so in Japan prior to the 1920s. The number of registered prostitutes in brothels increased by nearly 100 percent, from 28,432 in 1884 to 54,049 in 1916, although the population increased by less than 50 percent.[16] Moreover, in contrast to Western European regulations, the Rules Regulating Licensed Prostitutes effectively bound the women to the licensed houses and their keepers. Licensed prostitutes could neither work nor live outside the brothels. In addition, Article 7 barred them from venturing outside the licensed quarters at any time without permission of the police, unless prefectural rules specified otherwise.[17] Commenting on similar prefectural rules that immediately preceded the Home Ministry's Rules, the Nagoya District Court in 1900 found that "even at the death of parents it is with difficulty that [prostitutes] can get away," concluding that "there is scarcely no [sic] difference between their treatment and that accorded to convicts."[18] The press more commonly likened licensed prostitutes to "birds in a cage."

The autonomy of prostitutes was further constrained by their indentured relationships to the brothel owners. In a marked contrast to recruitment practices in Western European brothels, Japanese licensed houses by 1900 were offering sizable monetary advances to the young women or, in most cases, to their parents.[19] There is some debate as to whether proprietors primarily intended the advances as a bond to prevent prostitutes from running away in the middle of the contractual term.[20] Whatever the intention, if a prostitute quit without the keeper's permission before repaying the advance, her parents or guarantor was contractually liable for the debt. Recruiting agents typically signed contracts only with families or guarantors who had some visible property, such as furniture, which could be seized in the event the daughter decided to cease her trade. Families could lose "nearly everything, even to the straw mats on the floors, and the doors of the house."[21]

In 1899, a legally minded missionary named Ulysses Grant Murphy, together with a few Japanese pastors, set about to challenge the rules and practices that bound the prostitute. In a series of American-style "test cases," Murphy obtained court rulings the following year that declared contracts of prostitution to be null and void in accordance with the newly issued Civil Code of 1898, which invalidated contracts based on "immoral" intentions. These rulings—combined with subsequent agitation by the Salvation Army and progressive newspapers—persuaded Home Ministry officials to recognize the right of free cessation when they issued the Rules Regulating Licensed Prostitutes in October 1900.[22]

In practice, it remained difficult for prostitutes to leave the trade at will. The Supreme Court (Daishin'in), it is true, invalidated the provisions of contracts that specifically bound prostitutes to continue their trade in 1900. Yet the court upheld the obligation of the prostitute, family, or guarantor to repay the advance money and other debts that had accumulated during the term of service. Incredibly enough, the Supreme Court's decision stood until 1955.[23] Because many prostitutes who opted out of prostitution could not earn enough in other jobs to pay off their debts, policemen often discouraged acts of free cessation after 1900. According to Yamamuro Gumpei, the leading figure in the Japanese Salvation Army before World War II, when a young woman sought to quit, the police commonly called in the brothel keeper and her anxious parents. The officer might intimidate her into an out-of-court settlement, or he applied "a little persuasion" to cause her to change her mind about leaving.[24]

THE WORLD OF THE LICENSED PROSTITUTE

The system established in 1900 affected thousands of young women. The number of licensed prostitutes peaked in 1916 at 54,049, and remained at around 50,000 during the 1920s and early 1930s.[25] If we include the 79,348 geisha and 48,291 registered barmaids, one of every thirty-one young women—women between the ages of eighteen and twenty-nine—was working as a prostitute in 1925.[26] The licensed prostitutes worked in brothels in 550 licensed areas, which were located throughout the nation. The greatest concentrations of prostitutes were to be found in the big cities, port towns, and near military bases.[27]

Unquestionably, the prostitutes came from the poorest strata of society. Although 98 percent of school-age girls in Japan were attending school by 1913, 13 percent of the registered prostitutes in 1924 had never attended school, and only 28 percent had completed six years of compulsory elementary education.[28] Most were the daughters of farmers and laborers.[29] Surveys of Tokyo prostitutes, licensed and unlicensed alike, commonly reported disproportionately large numbers of women who had been recruited from the rural northeast, Japan's poorest region.[30] In a telling comment on the impact of class on options for young women, one missionary observed that more females worked as licensed prostitutes, geisha, and barmaids in 1925 (180,174) than attended the secondary-level higher girls' schools (176,808).[31]

Licensed prostitutes entered the brothels for a variety of reasons. But to a striking degree they echoed both the authorities and abolitionists in asserting that they had "sold themselves" to assist their impoverished families. In one typical survey of 809 licensed prostitutes by an Osaka prefectural official in 1918, 665 (82 percent) replied that they took up their trade to rescue their families from poverty, bail out failed family ventures, care for parents or siblings, or because of death or illness in the family. Another 130 (16 percent) singled out their own economic circumstances, mentioning indebtedness and child-related costs. A mere 4 (0.5 percent) asserted that they had "personally wanted" to be prostitutes.[32] The police, for their part, reinforced the message of filial obligation at the time of registration. As a matter of policy, the Home Ministry did not permit applicants to become licensed prostitutes unless they listed poverty as the reason.

There are, however, grounds to question the representation of the licensed prostitute as necessarily the passive victim of family poverty. In surveys of other categories of prostitutes in Tokyo in 1926 and 1927, 18 percent of the women asserted that they had personally wished to become geisha, and 19 percent had personally wished to be unlicensed prostitutes. Licensed prostitutes might have given similar replies had the regulations permitted them to list reasons other than poverty on the registration form.[33] Other surveys revealed that relatively few of the newly registered prostitutes in Tokyo during the mid-1920s were novices, freshly separated from their families. Most had worked previously as barmaids, geisha, or licensed prostitutes in other brothels. More than half of those surveyed in the Sūsaki quarter stated that they became licensed prostitutes to repay their own debts or improve their own circumstances.[34]

Abolitionists commonly portrayed Japanese prostitutes as sinking deeper and deeper into a morass of debt and moral degradation. Yet the reality came closer to the situation that the social investigator Parent-Duchâtelet found in Paris: "for the majority of public women prostitution is a transitory estate; . . . very few indeed remain until death."[35] Most Japanese licensed prostitutes left the trade before the expiration of their contractual terms, which was usually six years. According to one Home Ministry survey, 67 percent of Japan's licensed prostitutes in 1921–1923 had been working fewer than three years, and another 26 percent between three and six years. The average prostitute was in her early twenties, whereas those aged thirty or older constituted a mere 5 percent of all licensed prostitutes.[36]

Many a successful prostitute repaid the advance money and quit before the term's end, and contracts in Tokyo by the 1920s typically released the remaining women upon completing their terms, even if they had not fully repaid the advance money. In a survey of 685 prostitutes who removed their names from the police register in the Sūsaki quarter between 1925 and 1927, 27 percent had completed their terms with some debts outstanding; 20 percent had earlier repaid their advance money; 15 percent were redeemed by customers or in some cases by parents; and 14 percent simply quit without the consent of their keepers.[37] In some cases, however, prostitutes who became sick or could not otherwise attract many customers worked beyond six years in an effort to repay the advance money, as well as the brothel's monthly charges for food, clothing, room rental, and other items. Of those who removed their names from the register in the above survey, 24 percent in fact transferred to another brothel or quarter and then reregistered with the police. Some transferred by choice, but officials believed that many were unprofitable prostitutes, whose contracts and debts had been sold to other houses.[38]

What happened to the women who ceased their trade is not clear, but evidence suggests that most left lives of full-time prostitution to blend into the working classes. A governmental investigation of 1,563 former licensed prostitutes in 1931–1932 discovered that fewer than 19 percent returned to prostitution in any form, while another 7 percent became employees in brothels.[39] The Salvation Army, surveying the whereabouts of 304 licensed prostitutes rescued between 1931 and 1933 (a more skewed sample, to be sure), found that only 3 of the women reverted to prostitution, whereas 51 had secured factory jobs or other employment. Prostitution, of course, incurred some social stigma, although half (150) of the women in this sample went on to marry into or above their class. Their husbands were typically workers and petty merchants, but they also included several white-collar employees, a reporter, and a policeman.[40] American ethnographers working in the village of Suye Mura in 1935 similarly reported that women who left the village to become prostitutes could return home if they wished.[41]

It is likewise difficult to generalize about the quality of life within the brothels. Because the police required all customers to register at the brothels, we know that the sexual work load of a Japanese licensed prostitute was relatively light. In France, surveys in the 1890s estimated the average work load in the licensed houses to range between 4 and 8 customers per day, whereas licensed prostitutes in Tokyo averaged only 2.5 customers per day in 1924.[42] Nationwide, Japanese prostitutes on average took in only 1.2 customers per day in 1929, 1.6 in 1935, and approximately 1.9 in 1937.[43] Compared to ordinary prostitutes in many other societies, licensed prostitutes in Japan apparently spent more time eating, drinking, and flirting with clients.

Nonetheless, the fact remains that the prostitute's life was dangerously insecure. Venereal diseases and subsequent hospitalization were an ever-present threat, endangering health and hindering the ability to repay debts. If one averages the number of deaths over three years between 1921 and 1923, 649 prostitutes died annually—or 13 per 1,000 licensed prostitutes. An array of illnesses accounted for 496 of these deaths annually, although prostitutes succumbed to violence at far greater rates than the general population. Of the total of 649 fatalities, 93 women

FIGURE 9. Harimise. Displaying brothel prostitutes behind the grating in a licensed quarter, ca. 1915.

committed "double suicides" with lovers, and 60 fell victim to "unnatural deaths"—including individual suicides and murders by customers and others.[44]

Symbolic of the system's general dehumanization of the women was the practice of *harimise*, or displaying prostitutes behind gratings in rooms fronting upon the thoroughfares of Yoshiwara and other big-city quarters. The keepers used these "cages" to entice customers, who would then make their selections (Figure 9). The displays also attracted gawkers and the general public. Regulationists in nineteenth-century Europe generally strove to make "vice invisible." Italian laws prohibited brothel prostitutes from standing in windows or doors, and the windows of brothels had to be covered with smoked glass.[45] Yet in Yoshiwara, as one Western lawyer observed at the turn of the century, "To Europeans and Americans it is a strange sight to see family parties, including modest young girls, wending their way through the crowded streets on the night of the *Tori-no-machi* [festival], buying various knick-knacks and gazing at the painted beauties in their gorgeous dresses of glossy brocade and glittering gold."[46] Many former prostitutes recalled feeling like animals in a zoo. Writing in a noted women's journal, one summed up her five years of sitting inside the grating as "the greatest humiliation a woman can suffer."[47] Bowing in large part to foreign criticism, the authorities in Tokyo, Osaka, and other cities banned the *harimise* in 1916.[48]

Licensed Prostitution as Social Management

The authorities in early modern Japan had regulated prostitution for various reasons, but it was the emergence of a potent abolitionist movement in the late nineteenth century that called forth the modern state's comprehensive defense of licensed prostitution as a vital element in its policies to manage the economy, sexuality, and gender roles. From the start, Japanese Christians formed the core of the abolitionist forces. Protestants led the crusade, while Japanese Catholics generally accepted the need for regulated prostitution, as did most people in the Catholic nations of Europe. Although Japanese Protestants generally cooperated with the state in other areas of social management, the issue of licensed prostitution constituted an ever-present tension in this relationship. Composing less than one half of one percent of the population, Protestants nonetheless enjoyed considerable influence. They were well organized, active in social reform, and possessed international ties through missionaries from the United States and Great Britain. Indeed, Japanese moral reformers were directly inspired by the international abolitionist and social purity movements that emerged during the last three decades of the nineteenth century. Like abolitionists in France and the United States, they took their cues from Josephine Butler's successful campaign against regulation, which had culminated in the repeal of Britain's Contagious Diseases Acts in 1886.[49]

The first Japanese organization to oppose licensed prostitution consisted solely of women. In 1886, middle-class Japanese women established the Tokyo branch of the Women's Christian Temperance Union, the American organization that was at the time fighting attempts to regulate prostitution in several cities in the United States. The Tokyo branch was expanded in 1893 into the Japanese WCTU (Nihon Kirisutokyō Fujin Kyōfūkai), with branches throughout the country. The WCTU was joined in 1895 by the newly founded Japanese headquarters of the Salvation Army. By 1900, both groups had set up homes to rescue and reform prostitutes.[50] And in the protest to stop the rebuilding of the Yoshiwara quarters after a devastating fire in 1911, a group of predominantly male abolitionists formed the Purity Society (Kakuseikai) as a brother organization to the WCTU.

The abolitionists attacked licensed prostitution from a number of perspectives. The liberal or humanitarian critique attracted the broadest following among progressive politicians and thinkers, Christian and non-Christian alike. Abolitionists branded licensed prostitution a "system of slavery" in its fundamental "violation of human rights." The system, they charged, denied prostitutes the civil liberties guaranteed to Japanese subjects, particularly the freedoms to cease trade, choose one's customers, move about at will, and communicate unhindered with the outside world. What most offended the abolitionists was that the state lent its police powers to brothel keepers to suppress these liberties.[51] As in mid-Victorian Britain, many Japanese abolitionists concurrently championed a variety of other liberal causes, including universal suffrage and the freedom to organize labor unions.[52] The Japanese WCTU had, moreover, been agitating for the right of women to participate in political activities since 1890.[53] The Purity Society's leadership included several of Japan's most prominent progressive politicians, notably the Social Democratic party leader Abe Isoo (the society's second president), Katayama Tetsu (who became Japan's first socialist prime minister in 1947), and the liberal mavericks Shimada Saburō (the society's first president), Nagai Ryūtarō, and Ozaki Yukio.

Nonetheless, the abolitionist campaign should not be reduced to a purely liberal struggle, for the movement was not content merely to reform the license system so as to guarantee the liberties of prostitutes. The crusade against the "Social Evil" must also be seen as part of a conscious drive by Japanese Protestants to modernize the sexual mores of the populace along the lines of contemporary British and American societies. Prostitution challenged their religious beliefs that sexual relations should be confined to the institution of marriage.[54]

Japanese abolitionists struggled not simply to make society conform to its declared norms, as in Western nations, but to change the norms and laws of a non-Christian society that regarded marriage and the respective obligations of husband and wife in a different light. From its formation in 1886 until World War II, the leaders of the WCTU tirelessly petitioned the government to legislate and propagate the principle of strict monogamy. The problem, from their perspective, was that early modern Japanese customs and the government's new legal code in 1870 granted a concubine the same status as the wife. The Civil Code of 1898 eliminated the concubine's legal status and barred the children of concubines from inheriting the family name and property ahead of legitimate children. However, the code fell short of strictly protecting a wife's marital position. A husband could sue for divorce if his wife committed adultery, whereas adulterous actions by the husband did not constitute grounds for divorce.[55] The criminal codes similarly stipulated prison terms for wives who committed adultery, while permitting a husband's infidelities, unless his lover were a married woman.[56] The women of the WCTU demanded that the criminal and civil codes punish both husbands and wives for adultery, further insisting that the husband's liaisons with prostitutes, geisha, and concubines be considered adultery.[57]

Prostitution and concubinage further clashed with the fervent desire of Japanese Protestants to establish equality in gender relations. Few Protes-

tants endorsed full political equality and women's suffrage before the
1920s, but in its opening statement of principles in 1887 the Tokyo
WCTU vowed to eliminate the "evil customs" by which "men are respected and women despised." By becoming "playthings of men," prostitutes and concubines unwittingly contributed to the overall "denigration
of women."[58] Condemning the subordination of the wife in the early
modern Japanese family, Protestant abolitionists portrayed the modern
marriage as "a freely concluded union between those equal in human
character."[59] In their first petition to institute monogamy in 1889, WCTU
members argued that the "essence of marriage is love between a man and
woman." When a husband followed his "carnal desires" and shared his
love with other women, he destroyed the conjugal relationship and the
peace and prosperity of the family itself. Asserting that the indigenous
beliefs of Confucianism and Buddhism blessed the keeping of concubines
and the denigration of women, the Protestant women proclaimed that
Christianity alone could "save [Japan] from the evils of polygamy."[60]

Their opponents responded to the abolitionist challenge with an
equally confident defense of licensed prostitution based on reasons of
public policy, as well as markedly different assumptions about sexuality and gender roles. In addition to police and public-health officials in
the Home Ministry and local governments, the proponents of regulation
included many medical experts, politicians, publicists, and scholars.
They consistently cited two reasons for maintaining the system of licensed prostitution—the regulation of public morals and public hygiene.
These justifications had a long history in European societies, as well. To
Japanese officials, tightly regulated and segregated vice districts served as
a "breakwater" or "public latrine," protecting society and the "daughters of good families" from foulness. Just as St. Augustine in the fourth
century proclaimed, "suppress prostitution, and capricious lusts will
overthrow society," Japanese proponents warned that repressing the sexual desires of men would only lead to increased rape and other sex
crimes.[61]

Although Tokugawa-era officials had seldom utilized regulation to
prevent the spread of venereal diseases, by the 1890s public-health bureaucrats of the modern state became convinced of the effectiveness of
medical inspections.[62] Surveys by the Home Ministry's Bureau of Hygiene subsequently demonstrated that licensed prostitutes posed a significantly lower risk of contagion to customers than their unregistered rivals.
Physicians carried out nearly 3 million weekly examinations of licensed
prostitutes in 1927 and found venereal disease in only 2 percent of the
cases—compared to the rate of 32 percent for unlicensed prostitutes who
were arrested and examined that year.[63] Abolitionists countered that the
license system itself was ultimately responsible for Japan's relatively high

rates of venereal disease in the early twentieth century: its licit, deceptively safe nature vastly expanded the number of carriers by attracting otherwise risk-averse customers, and the licensed quarters encouraged the growth in adjacent areas of cheaper, clandestine prostitution with its attendant health hazards.[64] Bureau of Hygiene officials remained confident, however, that licensed prostitution formed the best defense against the specter of hundreds of thousands of unregulated prostitutes transmitting diseases throughout society.[65]

The government also valued the license system for other reasons, which appear more specific to Japanese society and derived from the government's managerial impulses. In many respects, both the abolitionists and regulationists were engaged in reformulating constructions of sexuality and gender in the context of Japan's modernization and Westernization after 1868. To the regulationists, rapid military-industrial modernization called for new types of men. Several remarked that conscription, expanded higher education, and the migration to the cities of large numbers of male workers—together with the low-wage nature of Japan's economic development—forced young men to postpone marriage or not to marry at all. The average age of marriage for men rose from 27.59 in 1899 to 28.68 in 1910, and it continued to rise during the 1920s.[66] Leading officials regarded the ready availability of "professional prostitutes" for these men as vital to maintaining the socioeconomic order.[67] Even the cosmopolitan thinker Fukuzawa Yukichi, who introduced Western concepts of monogamy and the equality of the sexes, asserted in 1885 that prostitution was "the only way to preserve social peace," considering the expected rise in the number of single men who lacked the wealth to marry.[68]

Other proponents spoke of the license system's contribution to Japan's rise as a major power. Referring to the naval race with the United States in 1935, one member of parliament boasted that the ample supply of prostitutes made it possible for Japanese officers to be away from home on naval maneuvers for extended periods. In the American navy, he noted scornfully, officers refused to be at sea longer than three months, complaining: "I miss my wife; I miss my children."[69]

As numerous regulationists explained, licensed prostitution maintained the Japanese "family system" and the unambiguous gender roles that permitted the nation to function efficiently. Hasegawa Yasushi, chief of the Bureau of Hygiene in 1900, considered prostitution to be necessary but hardly an evil, for the male body needed to satisfy sexual lust to maintain itself, just as a train would come to a halt if it did not burn coal. Distinguishing sexuality from marriage, he insisted that consorting with prostitutes was no more immoral than sex in marriage; the only differences related to time and place and whether a child was produced.[70]

The regulationists did not necessarily deny the innate sexuality of the wife, but they held that her physical desires needed to be restrained in the interests of the family. This imperative was based not simply on traditional Japanese values but also reflected a significant reformulation of gender ideology that occurred during the 1890s. Inspired by the pronatalist programs and theories of domestic science of their Western rivals, Japanese officials increasingly rejected the early modern subordination of the wife to the household head, her in-laws, and concubines. The government instead encouraged wives to become primarily responsible for managing the household and rearing children. The emergence of these new "duties" to the household and nation made it all the more important to prevent married women from taking on potentially subversive sexual roles. Such thinking explains why the Criminal Code of 1908 punished wives for committing adultery in all cases, but only penalized a husband when his partner was someone else's wife. Whereas Protestant abolitionists blamed philandering husbands for family disharmony, the responsibility for the stability of the modern Japanese family, by law and by convention, rested solely with the wife and mother.

Officials likewise sought to manage the sexuality of young women while reinforcing familial control. In the eyes of nineteenth-century European regulationists, women became prostitutes because of "libidinous" temperaments, criminal tendencies, laziness, or because they had fallen outside familial authority as they migrated to the cities.[71] Japanese authorities similarly feared the emergence of a huge class of hedonistic women, as daughters left home to become factory workers or housemaids. Yet in the Japanese case, such fears prompted the state to construct the category of the licensed prostitute, the paradoxically asexual daughter who honored the country's traditions of filial piety. As Prime Minister Itō Hirobumi explained to an English reporter in 1896, the woman who worked in the licensed brothel "does so often from a lofty desire to help her poor parents or relations; and, when she forsakes the life, by good conduct she is readmitted to society."[72] Furthermore, the practice of bonding the licensed prostitute through advance money, which was paid to parents or relatives, necessitated the recruitment of daughters directly from relatively stable families. The great strength of the license system was that the Home Ministry's standardized registration procedures effectively screened out any women who *personally desired to be a prostitute*, judged Kusama Yasoo, a noted reformist official in Tokyo's Bureau of Social Affairs.[73] The looser regulations governing geisha and barmaids failed to do so, alleged Kusama, resulting in significant numbers of "fallen women—lascivious, lazy, and frivolous—who embark on the road of prostitution not to help their poor parents or siblings; they immerse themselves in the mire because they personally want to."[74]

Responding to the abolitionists' liberal critique, regulationists were equally forthright about revealing the statist assumptions that underlay the license system. In the words of Ujihara Sukezō, the Home Ministry's leading spokesman on prostitution during the 1920s: because abolitionists in Western societies

> put the freedom of the individual first and regard the maintenance of public morals as of secondary importance, they judge those nations that have retained licensed prostitution and have placed the maintenance of public morals ahead of the freedom of the individual . . . to be backward. It is not easy for the Western savants of individualism to comprehend our distinctive system, which, even as it retains the license system, strictly regulates unlicensed prostitution and succeeds in preserving public morals.[75]

Another group of defenders similarly dismissed the abolitionists' charge that licensed prostitution demeaned women: "The State's objectives are to maintain order and improve the welfare of the greatest number, and if the interests of a few [women] must be sacrificed, this is truly inevitable in terms of the existence of the State."[76]

With respect to other areas of social management, the pleasure quarters also became central to the government's policies of crime control. The brothels attracted criminals, many of whom freely spent the proceeds of their misdeeds. Patrolmen and detectives relied on the keepers as informants. The authorities further required the brothels to register all customers for reasons of public security and monitoring of taxable profits, and those who gave false names were subject to harsh penalties. Close relationships developed between the police and the managers of the houses. Policemen would regularly eat and drink, free of charge, at the quarters' restaurants and bars. In exchange, the ordinary policeman returned runaway prostitutes, and he was loathe to enforce reformist changes in an institution that made his life easier.[77]

Finally, officials conceived of their managed system as the state's bulwark against the evils of clandestine prostitution. Confronted by rising numbers of unlicensed prostitutes, the Tokyo Metropolitan Police in 1916 attempted to eradicate illicit prostitution, while expanding the license system to woo customers back. Tokyo authorities even proposed lowering the minimum age for licensed women from eighteen to fifteen to divert the supply of adolescent girls from clandestine vice to the public sector. The minimum age was never lowered, but the police did simplify the building codes to encourage entrepreneurs to establish new brothels. In addition, emergency exits of Yoshiwara were opened to "make it easier for customers to come and go."[78]

Although a prime rationale for the licensed quarters was to sequester vice and protect the "daughters of good families," the logic of the system made regulated prostitution central to Japanese urban life. The annual number of visits by customers to the licensed houses rose from 22,360,000 in 1929 to approximately 30 million in 1937, considerably more than the 21 million Japanese males aged sixteen years or older in 1935.

REFORM VERSUS ABOLITION

Between 1909 and 1923, the abolitionist associations mounted several well-organized but generally unsuccessful campaigns to stop the rebuilding or relocation of Yoshiwara and other quarters. In 1926, however, the chief of the Police Bureau, Matsumura Giichi, instructed the annual conference of prefectural police chiefs to consider the question of reforming or abolishing the license system. This unexpected development was related to the rise of a socially reformist clique of higher civil servants within the Home Ministry, several of whom had already championed labor reform.[79] The bureaucracy was also responding to international abolitionist pressures emanating from the newly formed League of Nations. In 1925, Japan ratified the League's 1921 Convention for the Suppression of the Traffic in Women and Children. Few of the assembled police chiefs in 1926 favored abolition, but they did resolve to implement several reforms that centered on "respecting the liberties of prostitutes." For the first time, elite bureaucrats focused on the treatment of the women themselves from the standpoint of social policy. Matsumura directed prefectural authorities to enforce strictly the protections granted by the Rules Regulating Licensed Prostitutes of 1900 and to remove local restrictions on the freedom of movement. He also ordered that police no longer obstruct the prostitute's freedom to cease her trade.[80]

The Home Ministry's reforms, moreover, reflected long-term changes in Japanese society. The 1920s witnessed a dramatic rise in the public's concern for the "Woman Question." Young women were becoming better educated, and many, in their capacities as journalists, educators, nurses, and doctors, called for improving the status of women. Also, working-class women found new opportunities in manufacturing, services, and clerical work, which appeared preferable to a career in the brothels. Like many other women's groups, the Japanese WCTU began to focus its energies on gaining the vote for women as a means to abolition.[81]

Furthermore, many Japanese were beginning to question traditional conceptions of sexuality by which women were exploited for the pleasure of males. In the early 1920s, the literary feminist Hiratsuka Raichō and her proto-suffragist organization, the New Woman's Association (Shin Fujin Kyōkai), vigorously lobbied the Diet for a bill that would protect wives from venereal diseases picked up by their philandering husbands. In addition, conservative and semiofficial women's organizations placed new emphasis on safeguarding the chastity of young unmarried women. The Patriotic Women's Association (Aikoku Fujinkai), which was affiliated with the Home Ministry, engaged in major relief and rescue efforts in northeastern Japan, where devastating crop failures in 1934 compelled many farmers to sell their daughters into prostitution.[82]

Momentum for abolition grew rapidly during the late 1920s and early 1930s. Abolitionists organized several petition campaigns at the prefectural level. And for the first time, they successfully rallied major non-Christian organizations composed of Buddhists and social workers—as well as "moral suasion groups" and semiofficial associations for young men, young women, and adult women.[83] By 1934, half of Japan's forty-seven prefectural assemblies had either voted to abolish licensed prostitution in their locales or passed resolutions urging the centrally appointed governors to do so. After a report by the League of Nations' commission on traffic in women and children condemned Japan's system of licensed houses in 1932, the ever-sensitive Japanese government replied that abolition was under review. In May 1934, the Home Ministry announced that it would abolish licensed prostitution in the near future.[84]

It soon became clear, however, that the Home Ministry could not or would not draw up a viable plan to eliminate the licensed quarters. The abolitionists had done an impressive job of gaining influence among elite bureaucrats, but they proved no match for the well-organized political lobby mounted by the brothel trade. As one abolitionist bitterly observed, those who profited from the labor of prostitutes could be flogged in England, whereas in Japan brothel owners were considered "fine businessmen" and upstanding taxpayers who "may be municipal assemblymen, prefectural assemblymen, or members of parliament."[85] In 1924 the state-licensed trade associations of keepers united to form the National Federation of the Brothel Trade.[86] Brothel owners made large contributions to the political parties, and they were not shy about offering free favors to the many politicians who frequented the quarters.[87]

Nor were the friends of the brothels within the Diet shy about defending one of Japan's "beautiful customs." Their unabashed support of the license system sharply contrasts with the reluctance of late nineteenth-century French parliamentarians to discuss the question of prostitution openly.[88] When Purity Society members in 1931 introduced a bill in the Lower House that would abolish licensed prostitution, Yamazaki Dennosuke responded with a speech laced with obscenities and graphic language. Since lust was absolute, he argued, to try to repress it would only bring on masturbation, the chief cause of respiratory problems. Besides, he continued, was it not true that some of the "gentlemen" in the Lower

House kept concubines? Would this practice, too, be abolished? he asked mockingly.[89]

Provoked by the Home Ministry's declared intention of abolition, the brothel industry and their supporters in the Diet struck back. In March 1935, 270 members, or a majority of the Lower House, cosponsored a bill that would have strengthened the Home Ministry's Rules Regulating Licensed Prostitutes of 1900 by making them a statute. Supporters let the bill die in committee, content to make the point: "with a Lower House majority of 270 names, *our* position is public opinion."[90] Confronted by political pressures, Home Ministry bureaucrats quickly stepped back from considering the abolition of licensed prostitution. Abolition would not resurface as a serious political issue until after World War II.

A New Consensus: The Evils of Western-Style Sex

Most Japanese scholars who have chronicled this story dwell on the rise and fall of a liberal-minded popular movement that nearly persuaded the government to quit the business of managing prostitution. That depiction, I believe, ignores the complexities of the abolitionists' relationship with the imperial state. It also fails to recognize that licensed prostitution was simply one of several forms of extramarital sexuality of concern to officials and moral reformers alike. During the 1930s, leading abolitionists joined with unlikely allies, the licensed brothel owners, to pressure the government into suppressing dance halls, cafés, and clandestine prostitution. Although they attacked the license system for suppressing human freedom, the abolitionists frequently looked to the state to rectify immoral behavior.

During the 1910s and 1920s, abolitionists such as the WCTU's Kubushiro Ochimi insisted that they did not seek to eradicate clandestine prostitution.[91] The real problem, they maintained, was the pervasive system of licensed prostitution, by which the state sanctioned immorality and the exploitation of young women. Yet by the early 1930s, the abolitionists' attitudes toward both the state and the regulation of unlicensed prostitution had begun to change.

The precipitant was the emergence of café culture. While the number of licensed prostitutes remained around 50,000, the police counted 51,559 café waitresses in 1929, the number soaring to 111,700 in 1936.[92] The center of the new culture was the Ginza area of Tokyo, where a number of large neon-lit cafés, some employing tens of waitresses, mushroomed during 1930.[93] Higher civil servants and educators had earlier expressed

concerns about the many students who consorted with unregistered prostitutes in the Tamanoi and Kameido areas of Tokyo during the 1910s and
early 1920s. Nevertheless, the rise of cafés and dance halls challenged the
Japanese state and society to a much greater degree.

Japanese generally considered sexuality in the licensed quarters—
symbolized by the Tokugawa-era district of Yoshiwara—to be tradition-
ally Japanese, aesthetic, and for the sole pleasure of males. Cafés and
dance halls, on the other hand, were associated with modernism, individualism, and Western-style romantic relations between the sexes. The sexuality of waitresses could not easily be managed. The Tokyo official
Kusama Yasoo distinguished the waitresses from the filial daughters who
reputedly became licensed prostitutes for reasons of poverty. Waitresses,
lamented Kusama, chose their own jobs, concluded contracts directly
with employers, and "abandoned themselves" to "the pursuit of pleasure."[94] Contemporary literature and the press popularized café culture
with the phrases ero-guro-nansensu (eroticism, foolishness, and nonsense), moga (modern girls), and mobo (modern boys).[95] Waitresses and
dancers were not necessarily prostitutes, but their casual mingling with
"modern boys" of roughly the same age seemingly offended a society that
believed in arranged marriages and patriarchal authority. Many of the
Ginza-type cafés in fact promoted an atmosphere of eroticism. To attract
customers, waitresses were encouraged to entice male passers-by, sell
kisses, and sleep with the clientele after hours. Their employers' practice
of compelling the women to live on tips in lieu of wages was an added
inducement to cater to the whims of customers.[96]

The police and Home Ministry conducted the first campaign against
the cafés and dance halls between 1928 and 1930. The commissioner of
the Tokyo Metropolitan Police, Maruyama Tsurukichi, in July 1929
pledged to "deal a devastating blow" to "the red lights and jazz world
that pervade the capital." The Tokyo morals police, which had already
arrested more than three hundred waitresses and dancers in the first
months of 1929, also began rounding up forty to fifty "delinquent modern boys and girls" a night in a series of raids in August.[97] In 1934, the
Home Ministry's Police Bureau and the Metropolitan Police mounted
a second morals campaign, which continued unabated through World
War II.[98] Behind the crackdown lay a profound concern with the spread
of urban decadence and unregulated relations between young men and
women. Tokyo's metropolitan government prohibited students from
entering any café, bar, coffee or tea house that so much as employed
waitresses.[99] Police in rural Iwate prefecture began "expelling" cafés
from the villages with an eye toward uplifting the morals of youth.[100]

Middle-class Japanese Protestants had long propagated the "modern"
mores and gender ideals of nineteenth-century Western societies. Yet they

fully shared the authorities' anxieties about the *new modernity* of café culture. Abolitionists not only applauded the anti-café crusade of the mid-1930s, they demanded more state suppression. Kagawa Toyohiko in 1936 expressed alarm at the number of youth flocking to cafés and bars. "Frightening" was how the famous Christian social reformer described the evils of cafés, for they represented the influx of "French-style things" not found in Protestant countries. As for the causes of the rising sexual "looseness" of the Japanese people, Kagawa singled out "literature, which has grown erotic, and the authorities who simply wink at erotica."[101] Ieda Sakichi bemoaned the import of "Western lewd thought," which included notions of companionate marriages and trial marriages.[102] And the noted progressive Buddhist Takashima Beihō blamed the alleged widespread demands of women for "sexual liberation" on "queer foreign thought."[103]

Many an abolitionist greeted the outbreak of war against the Western powers in 1941 as a "fine opportunity" for a "great sweep-up" of immorality, in the words of Abe Isoo, the Purity Society's president and leader of the country's social democratic party.[104] Despite their denominational affiliations with North Americans and the British, some leaders of the Purity Society had likewise welcomed the conclusion of the Anti-Comintern Pact with Nazi Germany and Fascist Italy in 1937. The two authoritarian states were hailed as models for having taken "extremely strict positions toward the morals problem." The crisis brought on by the war in China that same year offered the long-awaited chance for the state to "wield a sharp knife at the morals problem," remarked spokesmen for the Purity Society.[105]

Abolitionists openly exploited the wartime atmosphere to agitate for restricting the operations of cafés and bars, all the time criticizing the supposed laxness of the Metropolitan Police.[106] Takashima Beihō, who was concurrently pressing the Home Ministry to stamp out all "quack" religions, praised the police for embarking on a campaign for the "eradication of the dance halls" in early 1938. Nonetheless, Takashima judged the crackdown to have come "rather late."[107] Prewar Japan's best-known liberal politician, Ozaki Yukio, urged the state to place "national morality" under "unified regulation." Commenting on the mass roundups of students in cafés and mah-jongg parlors in 1938, Ozaki demanded that the police also arrest their fathers, who frequented hostess bars (see Figure 10).[108]

In short, a new consensus had emerged by the mid-1930s between the bureaucrats and the "moral suasion" groups, including the abolitionists. The abolitionists privately recognized that, although licensed prostitution would continue, they would realize several of their objectives if they

FIGURE 10. Servants of the emperor, slaves to their desires? While police commissioners—pressed by moral reform groups—clamped down on café culture, other Home Ministry officials eagerly sampled the delights of Western-style sex. In 1931, the ministry's in-house journal *Chihō gyōsei* (Local administration) unabashedly carried this lurid book advertisement for *Tōkyō ero on pareedo* (Tokyo eros on parade). Sandwiched between notices of a new legal dictionary and a report on Japanese immigrants in South America, the blurb promises that this will be the "erotic book of erotic books"—the definitive guide to sex establishments in Tokyo. Higher civil servants presumably learned a great deal from the book, including where to find kisses for sale, the casino where "one gets a good peek at armpit hair," and even the "girl who swallows college mortarboards."

cooperated with the state in campaigns to stamp out cafés and educate youth in the virtues of chastity. The officials, for their part, would not have rushed into the morals crusade had they not discerned sizable support and even pressure emanating from community, education, and religious leaders. Completing the list of strange bedfellows were the licensed brothel keepers themselves. In 1933, Purity Society leaders and representatives of the brothel industry negotiated a settlement, though never implemented, whereby the houses would lose their licensed status but would retain de facto official recognition. The two sides also agreed to urge the Home Ministry to crush unlicensed prostitution.[109]

To mark the shift away from the focus on licensed prostitution, the League to Abolish Licensed Prostitution changed its name to the National Purification Federation (Kokumin Junketsu Dōmei) in 1935. Its nationalistic, eugenic emphasis on "purification of blood" (junketsu) complemented the state's needs for healthy recruits and mothers who were untouched by venereal diseases. Abandoning her laissez-faire position toward unlicensed prostitution, Kubushiro Ochimi, president of the Japanese WCTU, called on the state to eradicate all forms of prostitution. She had been inspired by her study of the United States government's crusade against prostitution in World War I.[110] In 1938, Kubushiro began coordinating discussions among educators, politicians, and Education Ministry and Metropolitan Police officials concerning the problem of students and the cafés.[111] As Japan's war with China and then the Western powers intensified, the abolitionists preached sexual continence and temperance to young men and women with the full support of the government.[112]

To read the abolitionist journals at the height of the Pacific War, one would think that the battle against prostitution had been won. Indeed, the Home Ministry severely clamped down on the nation's cafés and geisha houses and took steps to limit the numbers of new licensed prostitutes.[113] In reality, licensed prostitution had been shipped offshore and expanded tremendously. As recent exposés of the armed forces' use of "comfort women" have revealed, thousands of Japanese prostitutes were sent to service the needs of the empire's fighting men from 1937 to 1945. Tens of thousands more—primarily Korean girls, but also Taiwanese, Chinese, Southeast Asians and some Caucasians—were recruited, and, in most cases, forced or duped into becoming comfort women. George Hicks soberly estimates the total number of military prostitutes at 139,000, although others place the number much higher.

As in Japan, military authorities instituted the often meticulously regulated brothels primarily to reduce the incidence of venereal disease and satiate servicemen who would otherwise rape local women and girls. The plight of comfort women was incomparably worse, however, than that of Japanese licensed prostitutes back home. Comfort women could be forced into taking as many as thirty men in one day, with little recourse to legal and administrative protections. Many died from malnutrition, disease, and abuse—particularly in the desperate days at the end of the war. Thousands of others carried the psychological and physical scars of the experience for the rest of their lives. As the magnitude of this horror unfolds, we would do well to regard the wartime mobilization of comfort women as the tragic extension of Japan's system of licensed prostitution.[114]

MORAL REFORM AND STATISM

The history of licensed prostitution, although marginalized in most accounts of imperial Japan, reveals a great deal about relations between the state and society. The regulation of prostitution represented more than a vexing problem for urban police departments. It formed part of the national government's well-conceived program of managing society so that men would postpone the decision to marry, young women would employ their sexuality in a socially efficient and orderly manner, and wives would endure their husbands' infidelities in the interests of family stability. Although officials proved willing to reform the system of licensed prostitution at its edges, they continued to regard the regulation of prostitution as an instrument of state policy.

Alongside the wartime episode of the military comfort women, the most telling case of the continuities in official thinking occurred at the end of World War II. On August 18, 1945, just three days after the Japanese government announced its decision to surrender, the chief of the Police Bureau sent an urgent directive to prefectural governors. He instructed them to recruit geisha, licensed and unlicensed prostitutes, waitresses, barmaids, and "those who have committed the crime of habitual prostitution." In keeping with historical tendencies to marginalize the prostitute, the chief explained that these women would serve to "protect the Japanese people" against the foreign occupying forces. The directive did not conceal the fear of racial contamination, warning governors to prevent "Japanese" from consorting with these prostitutes, who would serve as a hygienic buffer. Eight days later, tens of thousands of women were organized into the Recreation and Amusement Association (RAA).[115] As one bureaucrat later recalled, Japanese officials reasoned that because the victorious Allied forces did not travel with their own comfort women, the soldiers would engage in widespread rape and create unimaginable disorder, if not properly supplied with prostitutes.[116]

It is also clear that the Japanese state did not formulate the social management of prostitution and sexuality in isolation. The prewar Japanese state was more than a small body of autonomous elite bureaucrats. The government's partners in regulating prostitution, the brothel keepers, not only assisted officials in articulating a defense of the system but also demonstrated their power to block the reformist efforts of higher civil servants. On the other side, abolitionist groups enjoyed close relationships with high-ranking bureaucrats. In the realm of social and educational policy, there existed seldom-discussed networks of discussion groups and other organizations which brought together higher civil servants, outside experts, and leaders of private associations.

As we have seen in previous chapters, Christians and other moral reformers played particularly prominent roles in this policymaking community. Committed to a small, inexpensive bureaucracy, the interwar Japanese government actively supported and sometimes subsidized the efforts of Christian social work organizations, notably the Salvation Army and the Women's Christian Temperance Union. These organizations in turn served the government, operating shelters for the poor and rescue missions for ex-prostitutes. Because of their knowledge of the West, Christians were also frequently consulted about social and educational policy innovations abroad. Even as he agitated for an end to the licensed quarters, the Salvation Army's Yamamuro Gumpei was employed by the Home Ministry in 1917 to survey poverty programs in the West.[117] As a result, many progressive Japanese, including social democrats, helped formulate the state's definitions of orthodoxy and public morality. Indeed, Home Ministry bureaucrats would probably never have contemplated the abolition of licensed prostitution had they not been associated with Christian social reformers. Similarly, the crusade against cafés and dance halls resulted from cooperation between the moral reformers and the state.

The close association between the moral reformers and the state is not surprising. Abolitionists and the bureaucrats of the Home and Education ministries shared a strong commitment to social management, and both groups worried about threats to social cohesion and moral standards. Many have viewed the abolitionists as philosophical liberals because they decried the restrictions placed on prostitutes. Yet their ultimate goal was neither a more humane license system nor the liberation of women from sexual double standards but rather the "rectification of morals" (kyōfū). For "moral rectification work" to succeed, observed several abolitionists long before the 1930s, the movement needed to cooperate with sympathetic officials so that licensed prostitution would be replaced by laws and programs designed to enforce the new moral standards.[118] Toward that end, the WCTU, like other Christian groups, earnestly participated in the government's periodic moral suasion campaigns, especially those aimed at cultivating the spirit of thrift, discouraging the purchase of imported luxuries, and eliminating the bad habits of smoking and drinking.[119]

Japanese moral reformers were hardly unique in embracing state intervention, but in few Western nations did antiprostitution movements press for the official repression of illicit sexuality with as little internal dissent or with as profound consequences for state-society relations as in Japan during the 1930s and early 1940s. In France, although evangelical morality societies agitated for the prohibition of extramarital relations in the late nineteenth century, the abolitionist movement remained under the domination of radicals and socialists, who recognized the right of prostitutes to practice their trade, if they did so discretely. What liberal French abolitionists most detested were the arbitrary actions of the police and medical establishments in regulating prostitution.[120] In pre-Fascist Italy, another strong bureaucratic state, the abolitionist movement similarly insisted on eliminating governmental intervention in the areas of prostitution and extramarital sexuality.[121] Following the repeal of regulated prostitution in Britain in the 1880s, many rank-and-file members of the Ladies' National Association joined vigilance societies and social purity alliances in pressuring the police to crack down on brothel keepers and prostitutes alike. But Josephine Butler and several other repeal leaders soon attacked the social purity movement for abusing the civil liberties of prostitutes.[122]

The experience of purity reformers in the United States most closely resembles that of the Japanese abolitionist movement. Compared to English and French abolitionists, American reformers from the 1880s more readily lobbied governments at various levels to carry out censorship and "the purification of society itself."[123] During the first two decades of the twentieth century, reformers successfully influenced municipal governments to suppress red-light districts in several big cities. At the height of World War I, many female leaders of Progressive movements actively participated in the federal government's repressive campaign to protect soldiers from venereal diseases. Thousands of women found near training camps were detained as suspected prostitutes.[124]

Nonetheless, the statism of the Japanese moral reformers stands out, even when compared with the American case. In the United States, the popular hysteria over venereal disease and allegedly promiscuous women was largely confined to the two years of American involvement in World War I. It did not recur during World War II. Moreover, both before and after World War I, prominent American feminists and liberals criticized the war on vice for targeting the prostitute, not her customers or pimp. Above all, the full consequences of the moral reformers' intolerance in the United States and Britain were tempered by their reliance on relatively weak states, which lacked central control over education and the police.

In Japan, on the other hand, moral educators frequently turned to a state that had the capacity to inculcate values and suppress deviance on a nationwide basis. For Japanese reformers, there was a much hazier line between moral suasion and suppression. The abolitionists hoped to teach youth the virtues of chastity and temperance, but in the meantime café waitresses and customers would be arrested and the dance halls shut down. If those Protestant activists who are widely held to have represented the flower of Japanese liberalism before World War II so strongly endorsed the techniques of social management, we must seriously reconsider the distinctions conventionally drawn between the oppressive imperial state, on one hand, and the liberal "civil society," on the other. The politics of regulating prostitution and illicit sexuality thus offers additional insights into understanding how many progressive middle-class groups helped shape the state's intervention into the lives of ordinary Japanese before 1945. And it may provide new ways of conceptualizing relationships between moral reformers and the state in other societies, as well.

Integrating Women into
Public Life: Women's Groups
and the State

THE STATE'S management of gen-
der relations did not stop at the regulation of prostitution and other
forms of extramarital sexuality. Indeed, it would be difficult to discuss the
history of Japanese women between 1890 and 1945 without reference to
the state. The legal system not only restricted the rights of licensed prostitutes and promoted a sexual double standard; the Civil Code of 1898 also
vested extensive powers in the head of the household, usually a male, and
it reduced women, upon marriage, to legal incompetents. Politically,
women were prohibited from sponsoring or attending political meetings
until 1922, nor were they able to join political parties before the end of
World War II. In social terms, as well, the government mobilized its centralized educational system to prepare girls to become the "good wives
and wise mothers" so essential to the nation's strength, prosperity, and
moral well-being.

Understandably, the Japanese state's heavy-handed intervention into
gender relations looms large in scholarship on Japanese women. Japanese
women's history has emerged in the past two decades as a dynamic field
dealing with a wide array of topics, from changing representations of
gender to the history of daily life.[1] Nonetheless, when it comes to scholarship on women's movements and women in politics, the history of Japanese women has, for the most part, been written in terms of resistance to
state power and ideology. Historians have generally focused on the careers of politically progressive women and literary feminists. Few Japanese scholars have gone beyond the concerns of Japanese women's history in the 1970s, when, observes Kano Masanao, the central question
was how women had liberated themselves or how they had been op-
pressed while trying to do so.[2] In English, Sharon Sievers' pioneering

work similarly traces "the development of feminist consciousness in the Meiji period," choosing to tell "the stories of the many women who refused to be victimized by that oppression [by the state], and who struggled against it."[3]

To many historians of the 1920s and early 1930s, the "women's movement" is nearly synonymous with the struggle to attain suffrage. The high point of this movement came in 1930 and 1931, when the Lower House of the Imperial Diet twice passed bills that would have granted to women "civic rights" (to vote and hold office) at the local level. Indeed, the story of the women's movement between the two world wars has become fused with the career of Ichikawa Fusae, who led the well-known suffragist organization, the League for Women's Suffrage (Fusen Kakutoku Dōmei). Following World War II, Ichikawa and her followers profoundly influenced the young field of women's history with numerous accounts of the suffrage movement.[4] American scholars, for their part, have been attracted to Ichikawa's insistence on gender equality and her repeated criticism of the state's efforts to co-opt the women's movement.[5]

Yet even as historians highlight the resistance of the women's movement to the prewar state, they have had to grapple with the fact that most women's leaders collaborated with the authoritarian regime during Japan's wars with China and the Western powers (1937–1945). No development seems to have divided these historians more than the Allied Occupation's purge of Ichikawa Fusae in 1947. The purge temporarily removed Japan's most famous suffragist from public life on the grounds that she had served as a director of the wartime Patriotic Press Association. Her defenders insist that Ichikawa and other women collaborated only to advance the interests of women amidst material deprivation and authoritarian rule.[6] In recent years, however, a younger generation of Japanese feminists has taken leaders of the prewar women's movement to task for their often enthusiastic participation in wartime mobilization.[7]

I have no quarrel with the quest of postwar Japanese feminists to discover an oppositional past, nor with the ongoing debate over wartime collaboration. But both approaches tend to isolate Japanese women's history from a broader set of questions concerning relations between the state and society. For one thing, most accounts describe the imperial state's actions as if they remained constant, although official policy in fact changed considerably between 1890 and 1941 in its attempts to define gender roles. Second, in their teleological search for the roots of "feminist consciousness," historians of Japan devote little attention to the vast majority of prewar women's groups, whose relations to the state were often ambiguous. The struggle for suffrage was only one of several issues raised by the disparate organizations that made up the "women's movement" during the 1920s and 1930s. These groups were just as likely to press for the abolition of licensed prostitution, lower prices for consumers, protection of mothers and children, modernization of Japanese mores, or promotion of household savings.

For all of the scholarly interest in it, Ichikawa Fusae's League for Women's Suffrage had enrolled a mere 1,511 members, clustered in the Tokyo area, at the height of the campaign for a local suffrage bill in 1930.[8] In contrast, the antiprostitution group, the Japanese Women's Christian Temperance Union (WCTU), reported 8,086 members in 155 chapters throughout Japan and its dominions in 1926.[9] Curiously, little has been written about the largest women's organization of the 1920s, the Federation of Women's Associations of Western Japan (Zen Kansai Fujin Rengōkai). Active in a wide array of social projects in addition to the suffrage drive, the federation claimed some 3 million members in 1927. The federation was composed in large part of local "women's associations" (fujinkai), many of which got their start with official patronage. Nevertheless, as recent scholarship has demonstrated, activist women often moved freely between these "officially created" associations, which worked closely with the state, and the "autonomous" women's movement.[10]

Such evidence suggests that the controversy over wartime collaboration is miscast, since both sides assume that cooperation between the regime and women's leaders was an aberration of the late 1930s and early 1940s. In actuality, these relationships first appeared in the 1920s, developing out of an interplay between the government's new efforts to mobilize women for peacetime goals and the desire of most autonomous women's groups to become integrated into the political system and the state. By 1930, officials, party politicians, and organized women agreed that women should play important roles in public or "civic" life. Just what form this integration would take was, of course, an ongoing source of contention. Ichikawa's suffragist wing campaigned for women's equal access to the parliamentary process by demanding the rights to elect representatives and join political parties. Elite bureaucrats, on the other hand, sought to mobilize women's groups on behalf of their own agenda of social work, savings promotion, moral reform, and eventually wartime mobilization.

Between these two camps lay most women's organizations, which not only looked to government intervention to improve the position of women but also concluded that organized women could better influence policymaking by allying with the bureaucracy, in preference to the parliamentary parties. As Paula Baker has written about American women before 1920, "In order to bring together the histories of women and of politics, we need a more inclusive definition of politics than is usually offered. 'Politics' is used here in a relatively broad sense to include any action, formal or informal, taken to affect the course or behavior of government or the community."[11] In Japan, wartime collaboration by women similarly signified not so much the end of the struggle for suffrage as a new phase in the long-term quest of women's organizations to gain power within the state-dominated political order.

THE POLITICAL EXCLUSION OF WOMEN
BEFORE 1919

The evolving relationships between women's groups and the state must be placed within the context of changes occurring in gender ideology since the late nineteenth century. Following the Meiji Restoration of 1868, the new government initially devoted little attention to the involvement of women in public life. In the late 1870s and 1880s, oligarchic leaders worried most about the challenge posed by the nascent political parties associated with the Popular Rights movement. When the regime responded to this movement with the restrictive Assembly Ordinance (Shūkai Jōrei) in 1880, women were neither singled out as a category nor prevented from attending political meetings or joining political associations. Influenced by Western liberal thought, several outspoken women in the Popular Rights movement joined their male comrades during the 1880s in calling for the establishment of a national assembly and for equal rights for women.[12] Some towns and villages even permitted women to vote for local assembly members and hold elected office if they met the same taxpaying requirements as males.

The initial absence of gender-related restrictions on women did not, however, imply a conscious recognition of women's rights. As the young regime centralized its rule, officials gradually eliminated the legal loopholes that had allowed women to engage in political activity. In 1884, the government foreclosed the possibility of local women's suffrage. In ward, town, and village assembly elections, both the franchise and office holding were thenceforth limited to males. In 1888, two basic laws regarding municipal government established that only an adult male could qualify as a "citizen" (kōmin)—literally, a "public person." That is, only males might exercise the "civic rights" to vote and serve in assemblies in villages, towns, and cities.[13]

To weaken the opposition parties, the government issued a new Law on Assembly and Political Association (Shūkai oyobi Seishahō) shortly before the first session of the Imperial Diet in 1890. For the first time, a law specifically prohibited women from joining political associations and from sponsoring or even attending meetings at which political discussion occurred. These provisions were carried over in the Police Law (Chian Keisatsuhō) of 1900. Article 5 of the Police Law barred women from joining political associations—along with soldiers, sailors, police officers, priests, teachers and pupils, minors, and those who had been divested of their civil rights. The second clause of Article 5 revealed much more about the government's views of gender. "Women and minors" were grouped together as the only Japanese who were permitted neither to sponsor nor attend political discussion meetings. Ex-convicts fared somewhat better. They, at least, could attend, though not sponsor, political meetings.[14]

Officials justified the political exclusion of women in terms of Japan's traditional gender distinctions. According to one treatise for police in 1920, the restrictions on women were based on the age-old Japanese ideal of the "good wife and wise mother." If they joined political associations, "not only would women be unable to fulfill their natural responsibilities, but this would destroy our country's time-honored beautiful customs that follow from the husband commanding and the wife obeying (*fushō fuwa*)."[15] Kiyoura Keigo, chief of the Home Ministry's Police Bureau and later a prime minister, similarly defended the Law on Assembly and Political Association before the Lower House in 1890:

> Women [in Japan] have always ruled inside the home. They are the ones who must attend to family education and other matters. What would happen if women joined political associations or engaged in political discussions? Family education would be hindered terribly. . . . If they are allowed to join political associations, they will neglect their duties as women (*joshi no hombun*). Such a situation would greatly disturb household management, as well as harm family education. . . . such a provision would produce grievous results for the future of the State.[16]

Despite repeated references to Japan's past, the government's rationale for politically excluding women rested on a significant reformulation of gender ideology that occurred against the backdrop of Japan's rapid modernization and Westernization. The ideal of the "good wife and wise mother" represented a new construction of the 1890s, substantially different from the image of the model samurai wife prevailing during the Tokugawa era. Early modern moral tracts had portrayed what Japanese would now call "the wife" as simply "the woman" (*onna*)—a rather lowly member of the three-generation household, who was admonished to obey her husband and parents-in-law. She lived as "a stranger in her husband's home," according to the widely circulated *Onna daigaku* (Greater learning for women) of the mid-Tokugawa period. In a world of in-laws, servants, and concubines even the primary responsibility for raising children did not necessarily reside with the wife. Describing women as dull-witted and temperamental, the author of *Onna daigaku* judged that "the woman" tended to spoil her child and hinder its development.[17] Among poorer families during the following Meiji era (1868–1912), young girls or *komori* were commonly hired to care for children, while mothers engaged in productive labor.[18] Not until the late nineteenth century did the authorities and middle-class Japanese exhort mothers to play the central role in child rearing, stimulated by the "social hygiene" drives and pronatalism of the nation's Western rivals.[19]

In proclaiming in 1890 that women's primary "duties" were household management and family education, the Home Ministry's Kiyoura in fact shared ground with several "enlightenment" publicists who sought to elevate the status of wives along the lines of contemporary Britain and the United States. Fukuzawa Yukichi condemned the servile position accorded women in *Onna daigaku*, arguing that wives working within the home should possess a status equal to their husbands.[20] The progressive journalist Tokutomi Sohō had in 1887 likewise urged Japanese society to recognize the modern woman's "mission" as "manager of the household."[21] Unlike the "enlightenment" thinkers, however, few officials before the 1920s respected women as the equals of men, even within their separate sphere.[22] Government spokesmen commonly denigrated the educational level of Japanese women, and they occasionally claimed that women were "excessively nervous" and would be harmed simply by hearing political speeches.[23]

The government's efforts to isolate women from politics did not go uncontested. In the first Diet in 1890, Ueki Emori, one of the era's outspoken liberals, argued passionately for the removal of the prohibition of women from attending political discussion meetings, sponsoring such meetings, and joining political associations. Dominated by the antigovernment "popular parties" during the early 1890s, the Lower House on three occasions passed amendments to the Law on Assembly and Political Association that would have eliminated all three prohibitions on women—only to be stymied each time by the conservative House of Peers. Other champions of women's rights pursued more limited goals, concentrating on securing the right merely to listen to "political discussion."[24] Joined by the major newspapers, the Japanese Women's Christian Temperance Union vigorously protested the government's decision in 1890 to bar women from sitting in the galleries of the Diet. Later that year the Lower House and the House of Peers voted to allow women to observe their proceedings. It was a small victory for women, but it led many members of parliament to question why the government continued to bar women from hearing political discussion while permitting them to witness partisan wrangling in the Diet.[25]

Although the regime could not totally prevent women from participating in political activities, it narrowed the range of acceptable public roles.

In the process, the state reshaped the strategies and composition of the nascent women's movement to a significant degree. Because officials equated "politics" with political parties and radical ideologies, their policies served to elevate the status of ostensibly nonpolitical moral reform drives among middle-class women. The chief beneficiary was the Japanese Women's Christian Temperance Union. The Christian organization escaped official persecution and quickly grew into one of the leading women's groups before the 1920s, despite its relentless crusade against licensed prostitution.[26] The government tolerated the WCTU's obviously "political" activities not only out of fears of offending the Americans and British but also because the WCTU worked closely with officials in other areas. The Christian women, for example, actively assisted the authorities on the home front at the time of the first Sino-Japanese War and Russo-Japanese War.[27]

In many other instances, however, the government invoked the Law on Assembly and Political Association and the succeeding Police Law to block the development of a politicized women's movement. What was "political" was, of course, determined by the authorities. In March 1920, the chairman of the Purity Society, which aimed at abolishing licensed prostitution, briefly mentioned the hotly debated question of universal manhood suffrage at a public meeting. The police promptly forced all two hundred women in attendance to leave the hall. In another case that same month, two prominent feminists, Hiratsuka Raichō and Ichikawa Fusae, were similarly expelled from a lecture entitled "How Intellectuals View the Present." Although the session began as a lecture meeting, officials later explained, it became a "political meeting" when the speeches touched upon the topics of the times.[28]

Aside from moral reform, the other major public role available to women was serving in associations that existed in large part to further the state's objectives. Yet officials did not appear eager to involve women in their otherwise determined efforts to create and mobilize local organizations before World War I. The government and prominent educators became caught in a paradox of their own making. They wanted women to serve the rapidly modernizing state at the local level, but they feared the consequences of encouraging new activities for women that went beyond the domestic roles of wives and mothers. During the mid-1890s, a few educators urged schools to cultivate a sense of "public-spiritedness" in girls. Most, however, agreed with Shimoda Utako, an influential woman teacher, who wrote in 1893 that the "prosperity and strength of the State" depended on women mastering "home economics" within the domestic sphere.[29]

The one major exception to the state's reluctance to involve women in public life occurred within the context of wartime mobilization. In 1901,

Okumura Ioko, the well-born daughter of the chief priest of a large Buddhist temple, founded the Patriotic Women's Association with the assistance of the Home Ministry and Army Ministry. Although the association's primary objective was to comfort wounded soldiers and the families of those who fell in battle, its founders also sought to "educate Japanese women about society" and to perform "charity works for the State" (*kokkateki jizen jigyō*).[30] Membership in the national organization rose to 464,000 at the height of the Russo-Japanese War in 1905, and nearly doubled to 807,000 in 1911. During its early years, the Patriotic Women's Association was more than a cozy alliance between the state and upper-class women. Among the original sponsors were several middle-class women educators, who pressed for integrating women into public life. Local branches included many schoolteachers, charity workers, farm wives, and even textile-mill workers. With the end of the war in 1905, the Patriotic Women's Association lost its earlier dynamism, becoming a moribund federation of wives of aristocrats, officials, and local elites.[31]

Following the Russo-Japanese War, local leaders and central bureaucrats gradually acknowledged the need for associations that incorporated women at the local level. As administrators of the pervasive Local Improvement Campaign, Home Ministry officials made some effort to mobilize women in drives for savings and frugality, improved public hygiene, charity work, and general "moral suasion."[32] Adult women, however, remained relatively unaffected by the new interventions. The state instead concentrated on establishing hierarchical federations covering farmers, veterans, young men, and young women.

Toward Political Integration

The decade and a half following the end of World War I witnessed an outpouring of public discussion of appropriate roles for women in society and politics. The debate reflected the rise of new categories of women whose lives and sometimes words challenged notions of the "good wife and wise mother." At the heart of these changes was the rapid spread of education for girls and young women. Between 1895 and 1920, the proportion of school-age girls attending elementary school doubled from 44 to 99 percent. The number of students in higher girls' schools (secondary-level institutions) nearly tripled to 151,288 between 1910 and 1920 alone. The expansion of female education resulted in the emergence of the professional women who led the interwar women's movement. Elementary-school teaching and nursing were two obvious areas of growth, but women also advanced as physicians in greater numbers in Japan than in contemporary America. Other women, like Ichikawa Fusae, became journalists as major dailies added women's columns, and the new industry of mass-circulation magazines for housewives and working women arose. Still others began to fill the clerical positions that proliferated with the rise of large stores and modern business offices in the big cities.[33]

These developments formed the basis for new women's organizations that demanded gender equality and political rights. Some activists had previously been associated with Hiratsuka Raichō's feminist journal *Seitō* (Bluestocking, 1911–1916). In December 1919, Hiratsuka joined with Ichikawa Fusae and Oku Mumeo to organize the New Woman's Association. The founders aimed at nothing less than the total liberation of women and women's suffrage.[34] As a first step, the New Woman's Association vigorously petitioned the Diet for the revision of Article 5 of the Police Law of 1900, so that women could fully participate in political activities.

In 1921, the Lower House passed an amendment to Article 5 that would have permitted women to attend and sponsor political discussion meetings. As had happened several times in the 1890s and 1900s, the measure subsequently failed in the House of Peers. Leading the attack, Baron Fujimura Yoshirō summed up the government's gender ideology since 1890:

> it is not a very good thing for [women] to engage in political movements on their own. First, speaking both physiologically and psychologically, this violates the laws of nature. Second, if we speak also of women's duties and mission (*hombun shimei*), it is not proper for women to take an active part along with men in political movements, in particular. Women's duties are in the home and in education and social work. Furthermore, when women do step out into society and engage in political movements, the results have been terrible. Look at Taira no Masako [1156–1225] and Sokuten Bukō [623–705], or, in another country, Queen Elizabeth. In each case, their involvement in politics had bad results. [Allowing women in politics] is contrary to our country's distinctive traditions, customs, and history. Finally, permitting women in these political movements would run counter to the family system, the basis of social organization in our country.[35]

The House of Peers, however, reversed itself the following year, approving the revision of Article 5 of the Police Law with little opposition. Having gained the right to attend and sponsor political discussion meetings, many women's groups turned their attention to the quest for suffrage.

Why did the Diet vote to expand women's rights in 1922 after more than thirty years of political exclusion? Most histories of Japanese women point to the activism of the New Woman's Association.[36] To be sure, the association deserves credit for raising the issue, rallying liberal politicians in all parties, and lobbying obstinate peers and party leaders. Nonetheless, few politicians appear to have been swayed by the organizational strength of women. The two major parties, the Seiyūkai and Kenseikai, expressed little interest in organizing women. Indeed, the ruling Seiyūkai adamantly opposed revising Article 5 so as to permit women to join political parties. The New Woman's Association in 1921 listed only 412 members, half of whom lived in the Tokyo area.[37] Moreover, the association was in disarray when the Diet voted to revise Article 5 in early 1922. Ichikawa had resigned, in large part over personality differences with Hiratsuka, and she was in the United States for a two-and-a-half-year stay. Hiratsuka was ill at home, and, overruling other leaders, she dissolved the New Woman's Association outright at the end of 1922.[38]

Viewed from a different perspective, the revision of Article 5 not only marked a breakthrough for organized women but also reflected major changes in how male elites perceived gender roles in public life. In the Lower House debates on Article 5 in 1920–1922, speaker after speaker noted that the world had changed since the passage of the Police Law in 1900. Few Western nations any longer barred women from taking part in political activities. On the contrary, observed several members, the expansion of women's political rights figured prominently in the new "trends of the world" following World War I. Britain and the United States had recently enacted national-level women's suffrage in 1918 and 1920, respectively, and a host of other countries—including Australia, Canada, the Philippines, Sweden, the Netherlands, and Germany—had extended the franchise to women in one form or another, they noted. Castigating Japan as a "police state," Tabuchi Toyokichi insisted that if Japan wished to be considered one of the "Big Five" in the postwar world, it must remove all obstacles to the freedom of expression—beginning with Article 5's restrictions on women.[39]

Although a few other Diet members joined Tabuchi in invoking women's rights, what united the nation's political elites—liberal and conservative—behind the revision of Article 5 was the growing belief that the political inclusion of women, in some form, would strengthen the Japanese state and society.[40] Diet speakers referred repeatedly to the active role played by women in supporting the war effort of Western nations during World War I. Even the outspoken liberal, Tabuchi Toyokichi, spoke of the British government's reliance on the "power of women" to sell war bonds, distribute food, and manufacture munitions. Turning to postwar Japan, Tabuchi pinpointed the state's problems in trying to harness the energies of apolitical women:

> [As prices of rice and other commodities soar], we are told to eat rice boiled in barley to foster national strength. But in the final analysis, it is women

who are being told this. Gentlemen, we talk of "the State, the State," but it is women who bear the consequences [of its policies]. And yet women are allowed to hear nothing about politics, nor can they attend political speeches or cast votes.

Women must be taught to be "members of the State," Tabuchi insisted, so that they could instill in their children the unselfish "sense to work for the State."[41]

Ichinomiya Fusajirō, the sponsor of the Seiyūkai's revision bill in 1921, similarly linked the politicization of women to service to society and the state. After describing the contributions made by Western women to their nations in World War I, Ichinomiya declared: "It is truly a demand of the times that women be encouraged to acquire political understanding to help out in tasks for the State and in social work." He did not repudiate the official ideal of "good wife and wise mother," but he forcefully asserted that "in a constitutional country, a woman cannot be a good wife and wise mother without a knowledge of politics." Drawing frequent applause from his fellow members in the Lower House, Ichinomiya concluded: "In short, today's woman must be liberated from her submissive position within the household and be encouraged to contribute socially, politically, and to the State."[42]

The political parties' efforts to amend the Police Law notwithstanding, the House of Peers would probably have continued to block any changes had the Home Ministry not dropped its long-standing opposition to the revision of Article 5. In 1920, Kawamura Takeji, chief of the ministry's Police Bureau, informed a Lower House committee that the government favored the immediate removal of the ban on women attending and sponsoring political meetings.[43] The following year Kawamura explained that the proposed revision of Article 5 was "in accord with the times." He did so in terms remarkably similar to those voiced by its liberal sponsors in the Diet. In the twenty years since the enactment of the Police Law, observed Kawamura, "we have witnessed a tremendous development in [women's] political knowledge" as education spread, women's groups sprang up, and articles about politics proliferated in newspapers and magazines read by women. The police chief also acknowledged that the Home Ministry was no longer rigorously enforcing Article 5, eschewing punishment in favor of occasional warnings to women's groups that engaged in "political" activities.[44]

At the same time, Home Ministry spokesmen made it clear that the government supported the revision of Article 5 primarily to encourage women "to acquire political knowledge," not to advance their political rights. Officials remained opposed to women joining political parties (or associations) because "enduring and ongoing" political participation diverted women from their principal responsibilities in the home. Nevertheless, Home Ministry officials no longer based their opposition on immutable gender differences, but simply stated that it was still "too early" for women to affiliate with parties.[45]

Like many of the Diet members who favored revising Article 5, Home Ministry officials promoted new public roles for women as Japanese interest in mobilizing women grew in the aftermath of World War I. Several agencies of the Japanese government had surveyed the home-front activities of European and North American belligerents during the war, and their reports highlighted the indispensable assistance of women's groups. In 1917, the Provisional Military Investigative Commission published the influential report, "The European War and Women in the Belligerent Nations." Declaring that "warfare in this day and age truly demands the total energies of the nation," the report observed that women's wartime activities necessarily transcended the confines of the "good wife and wise mother." Its authors further suggested that Japanese women must undertake such public activities in the next war.[46] In August 1918, the Home Ministry completed its own 242-page report on Western women and World War I. Surveying the wartime assistance of women in each country, ministry officials lauded their work in manufacturing, nursing, comforting the wounded and bereaved families, and other philanthropic activities. The Home Ministry also praised the patriotic activities of suffragist groups, especially in Britain. Japanese bureaucrats were beginning to recognize the advantages of mobilizing even the autonomous, politicized organizations.[47]

Indigenous developments combined with the perceived lessons of World War I to alter bureaucratic thinking on the relationship between women and the state. One could not speak of the rise of a coherent "women's policy" within the government, for the administrative responsibilities for women's matters remained scattered among the Home Ministry (welfare, law enforcement, suffrage), the ministries of Education (social education), Agriculture and Commerce (rural improvement), Finance (savings promotion), and other agencies. Nonetheless, the ministries shared an interest in involving women in the state's expanding programs of social management. To a degree unrivaled in earlier decades, interwar Japanese governments mounted a series of nationwide "moral suasion" campaigns. As the first step in the state's program of "postwar management" in 1919, the Home Ministry embarked on the far-reaching Campaign to Foster National Strength. This drive aimed, among other things, at boosting household savings rates, warding off socialist and democratic thought, and encouraging "public-spiritedness" and "the spirit of sacrifice."[48]

The campaigns of the 1920s and 1930s rested on a major reconceptualization of gender roles that was associated with the construction of the "housewife." Previous savings and frugality drives had rarely singled out adult women as a category to be mobilized. In 1900, few wives would have been considered the principal savers and consumers within the household, particularly among the urban working poor, shopkeepers, and farm families—who together comprised the vast majority of Japanese. Married women spent much of their time in productive work in or near the home, and the responsibility for managing the household often resided with parents-in-law or husbands.[49] As late as the 1930s in the remote village of Suye Mura, American ethnographers noted that the head of the household, in most cases a male, retained firm control over family finances.[50] When the Campaign to Foster National Strength sought to increase savings and dampen consumption in 1919–1920, officials did not initially mobilize adult women's groups, but rather worked through household heads' associations and young men's associations.[51]

By 1930, a savings campaign that did not draw upon the energies of women would have been unthinkable. Rapid urbanization and economic change during the first two decades of the twentieth century gave rise to a new middle class of salaried employees, professionals, and civil servants.[52] These men lived in smaller, often nuclear families and commanded incomes that made the productive labor of their wives less essential. As husbands removed themselves from the home, wives assumed control over household management and finances. The term "housewife" (*shufu*) became common in the 1910s and 1920s, and the magazine *Shufu no tomo* (The housewife's friend) found a sizable audience from the time of its appearance in 1917.[53] The phenomenon of the full-time housewife remained confined to the urban middle classes and provincial elites before World War II, but by the mid-1930s, hundreds of thousands of rural women, too, were reading magazines that provided advice on keeping household accounts, raising children, and other aspects of homemaking. Most influential was *Ie no hikari*, the attractively illustrated monthly that reached one million farm households by 1935 (Figure 11).[54]

Reflecting the changing gender ideology of middle-class society, various ministries began mobilizing women in their newly ascribed capacities as savers and consumers, as well as in their already recognized role as guardians of public morality. The early 1920s marked a turning point in state policy. Confronted by the postwar recession and persistently high prices, concerned officials tackled the problem of improving living standards, in addition to encouraging savings and frugality.

As one solution, the government increasingly created roles for women within the state apparatus. In October 1920, as part of its Campaign to Foster National Strength, the Home Ministry announced plans to promote the formation of local women's associations (*fujinkai*) throughout Japan. According to Soeda Keiichirō, the chief of the Bureau of Local

FIGURE 11. Cover of *Ie no hikari*, June 1934 (original in color). While the magazine encouraged rural women to become rational homemakers, motherhood and other domestic roles necessarily coexisted with farm work.

Affairs, existing organizations incorporated young men, young women, and household heads, but the time had come to encourage separate associations for adult women. Citing the improvements in the status of Western women as a result of World War I, Soeda spoke competitively of the need to cultivate in Japanese women an "awareness that does not lag behind the trends of the world." The women's associations were intended to "promote awareness and activity among women for the family, of course, but also for the State and society."[55] While praising the recent "spontaneous activity of women themselves" in the associations, the Home Ministry looked to local officials and other male elites to organize and guide women's associations.[56]

In tandem with the Home Ministry, Ministry of Education officials adopted new programs that made women the state's prime agents in improving "daily life." The initiative came from a rising group of bureaucrats who were charged with expanding "social education." The term referred to efforts to socialize the populace into loyal, yet modern, subjects. In 1920, the Ministry of Education launched the Daily Life Improvement Campaign (Seikatsu Kaizen Undō). A League for Daily Life Improvement (Seikatsu Kaizen Dōmeikai) was established as the campaign's coordinating and investigative organ. League members included several prominent women educators: Dr. Yoshioka Yayoi, Inoue Hideko, Hatoyama Haruko, Shimoda Utako, Yamawaki Fusako, Tsukamoto Hamako, and Ōe Sumi. Together, officials and educators aimed at improving the people's diet, hygiene, work habits, housing, consumption patterns, and ritual life. The government sponsored several short study courses, which enrolled women teachers from the higher girls' schools. In addition, between 1920 and 1926 the campaign appealed to housewives in the big cities and provincial centers with numerous public lectures and exhibitions.[57]

The Daily Life Improvement Campaign's hortatory rhetoric against wasting family resources on weddings and funerals recalled shogunal injunctions of the Tokugawa era. Yet by and large the drive's leaders employed the language of modernization. The Ministry of Education called on women to "sweep away the evil customs" of the past, and the league's specialists urged the universal adoption of Western clothing as being more economical and hygienic. Bureaucrats and educators lectured housewives on the need to practice "scientific diligence and thrift," "rational consumption" of inexpensive and healthy foods, and "rational, budgeted living and savings." Visitors to the traveling Reconstruction of Daily Life Exhibition in 1920 were greeted by a towering clock and the words: "Time is money."[58]

The bureaucrats further sought to integrate women into public life for the purpose of ameliorating the growing social problems of the interwar era. Within the Home Ministry, officials of the newly created Bureau of Social Affairs (and its successor, the Social Bureau) acted forcefully in this regard. In a book entitled *Shinjidai no fujin* (Women in the New Era), Tago Ichimin, an official and later chief of the Bureau of Social Affairs, wrote: "The patriots of the political [Meiji] restoration were men, but the patriots in the restoration of livelihood must be women."[59] Supported by the Bureau of Social Affairs, the Japan Women's College created a department of social work in 1921, and several of its graduates went to work for social affairs bureaus in prefectural, metropolitan, and central governments.[60]

The authorities also relied on women's organizations to carry out social work activities, particularly after the Great Kantō Earthquake of 1923. Forty-three women's groups, ranging from professional and religious associations to suffragist and socialist organizations, formed the Tokyo Federation of Women's Associations (Tōkyō Rengō Fujinkai). The federation worked closely with grateful city officials to aid the victims of the earthquake.[61] During the late 1920s and early 1930s, the Home Ministry encouraged district commissioners, the local volunteers who assisted the poor, to add more women to their ranks. Investing the female sex with the maternal traits of nurturing and compassion, the authorities maintained that women were well suited to the work since so much of a commissioner's job entailed caring for the sick.[62]

EXTENDING THE DOMESTIC SPHERE: THE ROLE OF ORGANIZED WOMEN

The bureaucrats of the Home Ministry and Ministry of Education preferred to integrate women into state structures without recognizing their autonomous demands for enfranchisement and other political rights. For their part, women's organizations, from socialist groups to many provincial women's associations, frequently criticized the government for opposing women's suffrage during the 1920s. Nonetheless, concerning most other issues, middle-class women's organizations not only cooperated with the state in its programs of social management but often helped shape the official discourse on gender.

Bureaucrats and politicians were not alone in advocating new public roles for women based on their assessment of the lessons of World War I. Women activists and male sympathizers similarly proclaimed the value of women to bolstering national power. According to Fukushima Shirō, male editor of the widely read women's newspaper *Fujo shimbun*, the war in Europe disproved that women were inferior, physically or mentally. Having filled men's jobs, "European women today [1917] fight the enemy indirectly as noncombatants." Anticipating Japan's post-war commercial and military competition with the Western powers, he concluded that Japanese women deserved equality for the sake of "national self-preservation." Their advance would "double our national strength."[63]

When Tago Ichimin and other officials in the Bureau of Social Affairs assigned women the separate sphere of reforming daily life, they drew upon arguments that were being advanced by women writers themselves in the media. Hiratsuka Raichō, the flamboyant leader of the New Woman's Association, had been particularly influential since 1916 in identifying women with motherhood. She increasingly wrote of the importance of women as mothers to society and the state.[64] Whereas Ichikawa Fusae, cofounder of the association, attempted to steer the New Woman's Association toward gender equality and suffrage, Hiratsuka strove to distinguish her group from Western women's movements. She characterized the latter as having "ignored or slighted the differences between men and women," demanding women's rights based on "individualism." The New Woman's Association, Hiratsuka asserted, did not call for suffrage primarily to discuss "as citizens, so-called political problems with men who are today called politicians." Rather, in the postwar world, "the time has come today for women to demonstrate fully their *special* qualities as women in social reconstruction," for "just as a family requires the power of women—especially a mother's love—society, too, needs the essential elements of women, which are different from those of men, for healthy cultural development."[65]

Whereas liberal feminists like Ichikawa distrusted a government that limited the liberties of women, Hiratsuka and many other women's leaders eagerly turned to the state bureaucracy to protect mothers and wives. Although the New Woman's Association is best remembered for the campaign to revise Article 5 of the Police Law between 1920 and 1922, the group may have devoted more energy to petitioning the Diet for a law to prohibit men with venereal diseases from marrying. More women signed these restrictive petitions than either of the association's two petitions on behalf of political rights, and they received strong support from the morally reformist Women's Christian Temperance Union.[66] The brainchild of Hiratsuka, the proposed law would have given a wife the right to obtain a divorce if her husband contracted venereal disease.

But Hiratsuka's draft proposal also reveals the statist proclivities of a significant wing of the interwar Japanese women's movement. The feminist leader explicitly granted the government extensive powers to restrict the liberties of men *and* women in order to protect wives and unborn children "from the standpoint of racial hygiene." Regardless of the bride's wishes, local mayors would be required to deny a marriage permit to any man who failed to obtain a medical certificate stating that he was free from venereal disease. Women would not be tested because, according to the Hiratsuka, most carriers were men. The draft legislation would have forbidden women from marrying or living in a de facto conjugal relationship with a man who had not obtained a marriage permit, and it stipulated a hefty fine (up to 300 yen) for male and female violators alike. The measure further required any man and woman who lived together to produce a marriage permit, if demanded by the authorities.[67] The Diet did not take up the marriage-prohibition petitions as legislation during the early 1920s. However, Hiratsuka remained keenly interested in eugenic policies. Together with other women's leaders, she later supported the enactment of the wartime government's National Eugenics Law (1940), which similarly aimed to prevent "those of inferior constitution carrying hereditary diseases" from reproducing.[68]

The government's enlistment of women's groups in social work and various campaigns was not simply a matter of co-optation. Before and, in many cases, after they embraced the cause of suffrage, most middle-class women's organizations concentrated on expanding the sphere of women into public areas concerned with improving the lot of women and children. Their members resembled the numerous American and British "social feminists," who placed moral reform, educational work, philanthropy, and the dissemination of child-rearing techniques ahead of the quest for equal rights during the nineteenth and early twentieth centuries.[69] Rather than resist state intervention, these Japanese groups more often urged the government to play an active role in the "social education" of women and girls. Women leaders and educators also shared with the bureaucrats a commitment to modernizing the mores and habits of ordinary women. The Daily Life Improvement Campaign proved particularly appealing to urban women. They attended the government's exhibitions in great numbers—drawn by discounted merchandise, economizing tips, and new labor-saving devices such as American washing machines.[70]

Indeed, middle-class women initiated the drive for improvements in daily life several years before the official campaigns of the 1920s. Hani Motoko, a well-known Christian educator, had been preaching the value of "rationalizing" daily life to urban women since 1908 in her magazine *Fujin no tomo* (The woman's friend). Her readers helped to spread the message through the organization of local *tomonokai* (friendship societies). In the early 1910s, the magazine mounted the first of several campaigns to encourage women to keep household account books, inspiring the government's later drives. Associated with several Christian socialists and liberals, Hani popularized the virtues of the Western-style "housewife," who was portrayed as the equal of her husband because she managed the domestic sphere.[71] Like several other prominent women educators, she frequently cooperated with the bureaucrats in sponsoring daily life improvement exhibitions and giving lectures.[72]

Influenced by Hani and others, organizations of middle-class women dedicated themselves to the mission of improving daily life even before the Ministry of Education and Home Ministry began mobilizing women's groups in 1920. In their founding statement of principles in November 1919, organizers of the Federation of Women's Associations of Western Japan pledged to "devote our energies to eliminating evil customs that are not in accord with the times and to reconstruct daily life."[73] At the federation's convention in October 1920, delegates from the Okayama prefectural chapter urged the organization to improve daily life by mounting moral reform campaigns that would "purify" the sexual mores of males and females, "spread the word about the dangers of alcohol poisoning," and "improve [Westernize] clothing from the perspectives of hygiene and good manners." In particular, they promised, "we will work for improvements in underwear," referring to the current campaigns to persuade Japanese women to replace their cumbersome traditional undergarments with Western underpants.[74] These champions of "daily life improvement" did not oppose the prevailing gender construction of the "good wife and wise mother," but they emphatically rejected the subordination of wives to their husbands. Rather, middle-class women's groups called on women to draw on their domestic talents as teachers and rational homemakers and take the lead in transforming society.

The case of the three-million-member Federation of Women's Associations of Western Japan also illustrates the difficulties in distinguishing the "officially created" women's organizations from the "autonomous" women's movement. On one hand, the federation was headed by liberal women activists based in Osaka. The Ōsaka asahi shimbun, a daily known for its support of social reform and universal suffrage, sponsored the founding of the federation in 1919, and the newspaper's branch offices assisted in the creation and maintenance of the affiliated prefectural confederations throughout western Japan. Committing themselves to women's suffrage in 1925, federation leaders mobilized their affiliates as no other Japanese women's organization could. They presented the Diet with 20,000 signatures in support of suffrage in 1927, 80,000 in 1929, and a staggering 100,000 each in 1930 and 1931.[75]

At the same time, the Federation of Women's Associations of Western Japan worked closely with state officials and local authorities. Nearly half of the federation's constituent groups were local women's associations, many of which were headed by mayors and male elementary school principals. During the 1920s and early 1930s, prefectural officials cooperated with local women and federation leaders to knit the local associations into prefectural confederations of women's associations. In the process, officials strengthened the federation's mass base and tacitly recognized the legitimacy of the suffrage movement. In exchange, activist women routinely lent their organizational support to the state's campaigns for daily life improvement, moral education, and "diligence and thrift."[76] To many women's leaders, the road to power and influence lay in assuming public roles, often in alliance with the state. By 1929, they viewed suffrage as an important means to achieving this goal, but it was not the only one.

THE QUESTION OF WOMEN'S SUFFRAGE

The converging efforts of women's groups, the parties, and bureaucracy to integrate women politically entered a new phase at the end of the 1920s. In 1929, a majority in the Lower House initially endorsed legislation that would grant to adult women the "civic rights" to vote and hold office at the prefectural and municipal levels. However, the Seiyūkai cabinet of Tanaka Giichi soon forced its party members to withdraw their support. In May 1930, members of both the ruling Minseitō and the opposition Seiyūkai parties supported a similar women's civic rights bill. The Lower House passed that measure, only to see it shelved by the House of Peers. Shortly thereafter, the Minseitō cabinet of Hamaguchi Osachi pledged to introduce its own women's civic rights bill to the next Diet, which would meet in early 1931. The government's bill would permit women to serve as mayors and other appointed officials, as well as to be elected to local assemblies. Unlike the Lower House members' bills in 1929 and 1930, the government's measure offered voting and office-holding rights to women only at the level of cities, towns, and villages— not at the prefectural level. Nonetheless, for the first time, a Japanese government had put forward a women's suffrage bill.

The civic rights legislation arose in part as a response to the growth of politicized women's organizations. Energized by the prospect of universal manhood suffrage (enacted in 1925), some middle-class women formed associations that demanded suffrage as their principal goal. The most prominent of these was the League for Women's Suffrage, established in December 1924 and soon dominated by Ichikawa Fusae. From its inception until 1929, the League concentrated on lobbying Diet members.[77] Socialist women's organizations, which were formed as auxiliaries to the new "proletarian parties" in 1927, also drew public attention to suffrage.[78]

As in the revision of the Police Law's Article 5 in 1922, however, agitation by suffragist organizations does not by itself explain the emergence of women's civic rights as a political question. Seiyūkai leaders resolved to introduce a women's civic rights bill in 1928 at a time of acute division and weakness among women's groups. Although a majority in the Lower House had signed on to civic rights bills for women by early 1929, the liberal *Tōkyō asahi shimbun* conceded that the "feeble women's movement" had done little to bring this about.[79] The reputed vanguard of the suffrage movement, the League for Women's Suffrage, had formed only two small branches outside of Tokyo before the Lower House passed a civic rights bill in May 1930.[80] Leaders of the larger, better organized Federation of Women's Associations of Western Japan frequently criticized Ichikawa's league as a few Tokyo-based "intellectuals" who were "content just to put up golden signs" and visit Diet members.[81] As one women's leader from Osaka remarked in April 1930, there were many men in the Diet who boldly advocated suffrage for women, but "what about women?"[82]

Rather than focus solely on the demands of women, we would do better to examine the areas of both contention and agreement in the arguments put forward by the political parties, bureaucrats, women's groups, and those conservatives who absolutely opposed civic rights legislation.

The Parties. It was the two major parties that put women's civic rights legislation on the political agenda, and they appeared to have done so primarily for partisan advantage. In June 1928, younger members of the Seiyūkai pressed party leaders to take up women's suffrage in an effort to restore the Seiyūkai's popularity among progressive voters.[83] Liberal backbenchers in the rival Minseitō responded by introducing their own civic rights bill to the Diet in January 1929, as the two parties scampered to appeal to the expected electorate of women. Sympathetic politicians sometimes lauded the efforts of the League for Women's Suffrage, but they seemed more interested in mobilizing the several million women who belonged to local women's associations. They were particularly impressed by the organizational potential offered by the Federation of Women's Associations of Western Japan, which hierarchically incorporated the local women's associations and their prefectural confederations in more than twenty prefectures.[84] At the national level, leading women educators formed the Women's Alliance (Fujin Dōshikai) in May 1930 as a thinly veiled support group for the Minseitō cabinet's civic rights bill and economic policies.[85]

In addition, several proponents of the civic rights bills appear to have been influenced by liberal thought and Western precedents. Suematsu Kaiichirō, chief sponsor of the Minseitō's civic rights bill in 1930, forcefully refuted theories of innate female inferiority and fixed gender roles. The rigid demarcation of women's duties had already broken down in

Western societies, he observed, and as Japanese women entered the workforce in greater numbers, they, too, required voting rights to advance their interests and reverse endemic discrimination.[86] Although neither the Minseitō nor Seiyūkai called for the immediate enfranchisement of women at the national level, spokesmen agreed that Japan should follow the path taken by most Western nations in gradually extending suffrage from the local to the national level.[87]

In terms of governance, the Minseitō's Hamaguchi cabinet sponsored its own civic rights bill in large part to secure the support of women's groups for its economic program. Upon forming in July 1929, the cabinet announced that Japan would soon return to the gold standard. In order to peg the yen at its prewar value, the government embarked on a deflationary campaign of "restraint in consumption" and retrenchment in public spending. Seeking to bring about "thrift in the kitchen of every home," cabinet ministers not only appealed to semiofficial women's groups and women educators as in the past, but also actively sought the assistance of the leading autonomous organizations, including the League for Women's Suffrage.[88] Except for the small socialist organizations, women's groups of all types enthusiastically responded by participating in the government's savings and frugality drive.[89] While urging Hamaguchi to give women the vote, Ichikawa Fusae declared that "never before has a government or cabinet so clearly appealed to women or attempted to borrow their power."[90] Another leader of the League for Women's Suffrage volunteered the services of the league and other women's groups in the "great task of propagating" the government's austerity message.[91]

Most women's organizations supported Hamaguchi's economic campaign not so much to obtain suffrage in exchange, but because they shared a commitment to lowering consumer and public-utility prices.[92] On August 15, 1929, the Federation of Women's Associations of Western Japan hosted a day of "Consumer Economy Lectures." Finance Minister Inoue Junnosuke himself was invited to speak to some three hundred representatives from the federation's affiliates. Onda Kazuko, the federation's president, promoted a more public role for Japanese women in their capacity as housewives who had a "mission and responsibility" at a time of "national economic crisis."[93] Proclaiming that economic recovery could only occur "with the cooperation of women, who hold the key to the consumer economy," the federation also sponsored the first annual All-Japan Women's Economic Conference later that autumn.[94]

The Bureaucrats. In contrast to the parties and women's organizations, the elite bureaucrats of the Home Ministry regarded the growing momentum for a women's civic rights law with apprehension. Over the past decade they had aggressively involved women in public life by means of local women's associations and nationwide campaigns. Yet ministry officials in the late 1920s remained opposed to granting civic rights to women at even the municipal level. Such legislation was "premature," considering "the conditions of our nation's family life and the degree of education of most women," judged the leading bureaucratic specialist on the subject.[95] The Lower House's support of civic rights legislation in 1929 and 1930, however, compelled the Home Ministry to formulate a new approach to "local self-government"—one that included civic rights for women. Charged with drafting the Hamaguchi cabinet's civic rights bill during summer 1930, Home Ministry officials approached the political integration of women with an eye toward stabilizing local society.

It soon became obvious that the ruling Minseitō and the bureaucrats disagreed over the meaning of the restriction of civic rights to cities, towns, and villages in the government's bill. Home Minister Adachi Kenzō, a veteran Minseitō politician, embraced the principle of "gradualism," declaring municipal-level civic rights to be simply the first step toward women's suffrage at the prefectural and national levels. In contrast, Home Ministry spokesmen insisted that women were innately qualified to participate in local government, whereas they had relatively weak connections to prefectural and national politics.[96] As voters and elected officials, women were expected to oversee aspects of local administration most related to family life—such as public utilities, sanitation, poor relief, construction of elementary schools and hospitals, and especially the protection of children.[97]

The bureaucrats also envisioned that middle- and upper-class women would help check the rise of radical male candidates from the ranks of workers and tenant farmers. In the words of one former Home Ministry official, the appearance of women in local governments would "impede the penetration of the partisan struggle to self-governing [local] bodies, alleviate discord between hamlet and hamlet, and, to a certain extent, serve as a palliative to strife between the classes."[98] In a pointed rejection of gender equality, the Home Ministry added a provision to the government's civic rights bill that required a successful woman candidate to obtain her husband's consent before taking office.

Although progressive politicians from both major parties criticized the illiberal features of the government's 1931 bill, they contended with the bureaucrats within the discourse on gender roles that had evolved since 1920. Nearly every speaker in the Lower House debate highlighted the special qualities that women would bring to local politics. Tago Ichimin (Seiyūkai), the former chief of Home Ministry's Bureau of Social Affairs, agreed with his old colleagues that "cities, towns, and villages are to a certain degree extensions of the household when it comes to, say, schools, sewers, or public toilets."[99] Based on their surveys of Western nations, the parties' advocates similarly asserted that women voters tended to be "conservative" and hostile to radical parties.[100] Home Minister Adachi was emphatic on this point: "women think conservatively. . . . Thus it will be enormously beneficial for women to take part in local government to maintain the order of State and Society (*kokka shakai*) by blocking radical change." France, he noted wryly, was one of the few Western countries that denied women the right to vote, and "it is, after all, a revolutionary nation." Terming women "pure in thought," Adachi further predicted that enfranchised women would "remedy the rottenness and corruption of today's local electoral politics."[101]

Women's Groups. Most middle-class women's organizations voiced grave disappointment with the government's civic rights bill in 1931 for its underlying notions of inequality. Few organizations demanded immediate national suffrage, but many leaders disputed the Home Ministry's claim that women lacked strong connections to prefectural politics. The Women's Christian Temperance Union was, after all, lobbying prefectural assemblies to abolish licensed prostitution and geisha houses at the time.[102] Led by the League for Women's Suffrage, thirteen women's organizations expressed "absolute opposition" to the government's "limited women's civic rights bill" at the second All-Japan Women's Suffrage Convention in February 1931.[103]

In actuality, these organizations were neither united nor absolute in their opposition. In the end, only one group—the rather small Women's Suffrage League (Fujin Sansei Dōmei)—joined the League for Women's Suffrage in pressing the cabinet for a "complete" civic rights bill. The pro-Minseitō Women's Alliance worked for the passage of the government's restrictive bill behind the scenes, and the mighty Federation of Women's Associations of Western Japan generally sat on the sidelines.[104] Many provincial women's groups, lamented Ichikawa Fusae, favored only local civic rights, believing women to have little role in national politics.[105]

The absence of effective opposition to the government's bill stemmed from more than the weakness of the women's movement. By 1930, bureaucrats, politicians, and middle-class women's organizations essentially agreed that women possessed special attributes that would substantially improve political life. The logic of the argument prompted most women's leaders to spotlight local government as the natural place for women. Even if women failed to obtain civic rights, remarked Onda Kazuko of the Federation of Women's Associations of Western Japan, they could do considerable work through local organizations "from the perspective of the housewife and mother" in the areas of post-earthquake reconstruction, parks, sewers, education, social work, and tax reform.[106] To broaden her group's appeal to ordinary women, Ichikawa Fusae— herself an outspoken advocate of gender equality—similarly argued that political participation by women would "purify today's rottenness to a large extent." Openly accepting the proposition of her conservative foes that men and women performed different "functions" (*shokunō*), she declared that political participation would enable women to "fulfill their work as women."[107] During the early 1930s, Ichikawa turned her attention to community organizing, explaining that "municipal government can be considered an extension of the household."[108]

Conservative Opponents. The strongest opposition to the government's civic rights bill of 1931 came not from progressive politicians and women's groups but from conservatives who had rejected the efforts of both the government and organized women since 1920 to integrate women into public life. In November 1930, the National Association of Mayors of Towns and Villages stated its opposition to granting civic rights to women in any form. Whereas the proponents of the civic rights bills, including Home Ministry officials, maintained that women would improve local government, the mayors thought otherwise. Women in local politics, warned the mayors' association, would bring about "complications in administration and confusion to the electoral world"; their involvement would, above all, "undermine the family system, the basis of our national polity (*kokutai*)."[109]

After the Lower House passed the government's civic rights bill in March 1931, the measure faced its ultimate test in the House of Peers. Composed primarily of titled nobles and distinguished retired bureaucrats and military men, the House of Peers represented an earlier generation of Japanese elites. Several members challenged the middle-class vision of the housewife in the nation's service, which had become dominant among women's leaders, politicians, and younger bureaucrats alike. As one liberal politician in the Lower House observed, "the families of the nobles in the House of Peers and *our* families are different." Concerning matters of schooling or sewers,

> the nobles of the House of Peers have numerous secretaries, clerks, butlers, and stewards, and they usually rely on these people to negotiate with schools about their children's education. However, in *our* families, the housewife herself goes to the school, and the housewife herself goes to the city or village hall to discuss matters. From the perspective of the families of the nobles in the House of Peers, [civic rights for women] may be unnecessary. But to *our* families, . . . if [women] do not have the vote and cannot be elected to local government, they cannot truly supervise [these matters].[110]

The parties and the government generally portrayed women as sober and "conservative," but several peers maintained that women were emotional and, in groups, they often engaged in "radical and odd behavior."[111] Baron Ida Iwakusu envisioned a particularly slippery slope:

> The day we grant women the right to vote, they will take their first steps away from the family system and out of the house. Women will set out on a straight course without restraint, insisting on right after right. Women will take on the same jobs as men. To put it bluntly, they will become masculinized, forgetting their womanhood. They will turn into women machines. Women will go beyond birth control and refuse to bear children at all. . . . The era of making humans in test tubes is at hand.[112]

These statements suggest that the main battle lines in interwar debate over women's suffrage lay not between women's groups and a monolithic state, but between opposing gendered representations of women, the family, and public life. On one side stood conservatives like Baron Ida, to whom the woman existed only as a subordinate element in the family system. Ranged along the other were organized women, politicians, and bureaucrats. This latter grouping had come to identify "family" with wives and mothers, and they envisioned civic life to be an extension of the family. As progressive observers were to discover, the older, conservative gender ideology proved remarkably resilient. On March 24, 1931, the House of Peers defeated a slightly modified version of government's civic rights bill by the decisive vote of 184 to 62.

WARTIME COOPERATION

The crushing defeat of the women's civic rights bill in 1931 marked the end of suffrage as a possible form of political integration in prewar Japan. Subsequent efforts to enfranchise women faced not only the formidable opposition of the House of Peers, but an increasingly illiberal political climate in the wake of Japan's occupation of Manchuria in 1931–1932. The parties lost the power to organize cabinets in 1932, and the cause of women's suffrage lost its most committed political allies. When suffragists met with government officials and demoralized party men during summer 1932, they heard a new refrain: universal *manhood* suffrage had been a "failure" or at least precipitous; women's suffrage would only compound the present political difficulties.[113]

The demise of women's civic rights legislation did not, however, bring an end to efforts within both the state and society to integrate women into public life. Various ministries continued the drive to expand bureaucratically supervised federations of local women's associations. In 1931, the

Ministry of Education established its own Greater Japan Federated Women's Association (Dai Nihon Rengō Fujinkai), and the Home Ministry took steps to revitalize the Patriotic Women's Association one year later. Also in 1932, the Army Ministry took control of the recently established Greater Japan National Defense Women's Association (Dai Nihon Kokubō Fujinkai). The association mobilized women to send off soldiers, comfort the wounded and bereaved, and perform social work. Some 10 million members strong at its peak, the National Defense Women's Association succeeded as no other women's federation—bureaucratic or autonomous—in reaching down to the village level and the lower classes. Its appeal was unquestionably related to the growing aspirations of ordinary women to undertake public roles as the nation's mothers and housewives.[114]

At the same time, the bureaucracy remained eager to secure the cooperation of autonomous women's organizations. To be sure, the Federation of Women's Associations of Western Japan and other women's groups openly resented the officially sponsored women's federations for drawing away large numbers of their own members.[115] Nonetheless, nearly all leading women's groups rallied behind the army's occupation of Manchuria in 1931–1932, except for the socialist Proletarian Women's League and Ichikawa's League for Women's Suffrage.[116] And most middle-class women's organizations maintained their enthusiasm about participating in the state's campaigns, not only out of patriotism but also to exercise influence in the public sphere.

Much attention has focused on the growing ties between Ichikawa Fusae's League for Women's Suffrage and the state during the 1930s.[117] In many respects, Ichikawa was not so much blazing a new trail as following the many other middle-class women leaders who had concluded during the 1920s that the most promising road to power and influence lay in cooperating with the bureaucratic state. As Ichikawa lost faith in the political parties' ability to improve the position of women, she and her followers made tactical alliances with civil servants at both the national and local levels. League leaders consciously sought to revitalize their organization by engaging in the activities that more closely conformed to the emerging gender representation of the civic-minded housewife and mother. In 1933, the League for Women's Suffrage worked with Tokyo city authorities to coordinate the cleanup of garbage in the hope of demonstrating the ability of women to exercise civic rights responsibly.[118] Ichikawa, whose league had committed itself in 1930 to the nonpartisan cleansing of electoral corruption "from the woman's perspective," eagerly accepted the Home Ministry's invitation to participate in the essentially anti-party "election purification" campaign of 1935–1936.[119] Noting that many women had been appointed to the Election Purification

Central League and local election purification councils, Ichikawa optimistically proclaimed the "acquisition of suffrage in actual fact."[120]

During the mid-1930s, the League for Women's Suffrage set aside the quest for suffrage in preference for welfare measures to protect mothers and children. Allying with other women's groups and the Home Ministry's welfare officials, the league successfully lobbied the Diet to enact the Mother-Child Protection Law in 1937. The statute provided assistance to impoverished mothers and their children who lived in fatherless families.[121] The passage of the Mother-Child Protection Law represented one more step in the emergence of a direct relationship between women and the state. As men left home for factories and the war during the 1930s, notes the historian Yoshiko Miyake, both women's groups and the government assigned mothers the central role in preserving the family system.[122] On tactical grounds, as well, women leaders discovered that they most effectively influenced policymaking when they furthered causes that appeared to lie within the special domain of women—particularly when their demands meshed with wartime eugenic campaigns to improve the health of mothers and children.

The evolving pattern of cooperation between autonomous women's groups and the state culminated in the formal integration of activist women into the government's mobilization structures at the time of the China and Pacific wars (1937–1945). In June 1938, the government appointed eleven women leaders—including Ichikawa Fusae, Dr. Yoshioka Yayoi, and Yamada Waka—to the Emergency Council to Improve the Nation's Ways of Living. Yoshioka became a director of the Central League of the National Spiritual Mobilization Campaign the following year, and Ichikawa and Takeuchi Shigeyo sat on the campaign's council. In addition, many women worked for the various ministries as commissioned officers or council members, dealing with wartime problems concerning factory women, families of deceased servicemen, price stabilization, and the conservation of scarce materials. In 1939, the Ministry of Finance dispatched Ichikawa, Hani Motoko, and twenty-nine other women leaders to exhort women's groups throughout the nation to increase household savings. The regime also enlisted the services of countless local women in its campaigns to curb luxuries and recycle materials.[123]

Like many activists, Ichikawa greeted the war with China in 1937 as an opportunity to elevate the position of Japanese women within the state, recalling the advance of women's power in Britain and the United States during World War I.[124] She had come to regard state mobilization itself as an agent in freeing women from the fetters of a household structure that dominated wives. On a visit to her home village in Aichi prefecture that August, Ichikawa chanced upon the inaugural meeting of the village's National Defense Women's Association branch. She listened po-

FIGURE 12. Women managing women during the China War, 1938. Doing its part to propagate austerity, the Tokyo branch of the upper- and middle-class Women's Patriotic Association holds a training course for leaders on how to make and wear *mompe*—the drab, coarsely made pantaloons which became the home-front uniform by the time of the Pacific War.

litely as the assembled women, some seven or eight hundred in all, were addressed by the regional regimental commander and local functionaries. Far from condemning the bureaucratically managed proceedings, Japan's most famous suffragist was euphoric: "for farm women who have had no time for themselves, to be liberated from the household for a half day to hear speeches is indeed women's liberation." Noting that the National Defense Women's Association was spreading from "village to village like wildfire," Ichikawa pronounced herself to be "quite pleased."[125]

In 1942, Ichikawa and many other well-known women leaders assumed prominent positions in the Greater Japan Women's Association, which had absorbed the National Defense Women's Association and all other women's organizations, autonomous and official. Followers of Hani Motoko, led by her daughter Setsuko, also actively assisted the wartime government in urging women to economize and "rationalize" their daily lives. These middle-class women had earlier advocated thrift in the name of "improving" and Westernizing daily life. Now, to aid the war effort, they called on women to eschew imported "luxuries," collect discarded goods, and generally get by on less (see Figure 12).[126]

The regime's deepening concern with social mores further empowered women in their maternal role as guardians of public morality. The Women's Christian Temperance Union earnestly took part in official campaigns aimed at stamping out smoking, drinking, and the frequenting of dance halls and cafés by potential recruits and future mothers. And many a white-aproned matron in the National Defense Women's Association stood on the street corner, haranguing women to "get rid of those permanents" and "gaudy clothes."[127] One may debate the extent to which the leaders of the prewar women's groups affected the basic policies of the wartime regime. Within the realm of everyday life, however, thousands of women—serving as deputies of the state—gained unprecedented influence over the lives of other women, children, and the elderly men who remained at home.

Relations between the imperial Japanese state and the women's organizations were dynamic and interactive, but they hardly constituted a partnership between equals. The government used its extensive powers to shape the contours and strategies of the women's movement from the 1880s through World War II. The police persecuted socialist women; Article 5 of the Police Law of 1900 prevented women from joining political parties until 1945; and the powerful bureaucracy did little to promote, and much to inhibit, the possibility of suffrage. The Home Ministry and Ministry of Education encouraged women to take on public or civic roles, yet they consistently endeavored to shield women from "politics."

Women's groups thus maneuvered within a heavily determined political order. Few women campaigned for political rights on the basis of strict equality between the sexes, and those who did, like Ichikawa Fusae, encountered formidable resistance from the government as well as from other women. Women proved more successful in influencing the official agenda when they embraced the modern state's ideology of separate spheres for men and women (the "good wife and wise mother"). In so doing, women's groups fashioned more authoritative roles within the family for housewives and mothers and, by extension, new public roles for women within the state—promoting economic development, social stability, and wartime mobilization. By highlighting their special abilities to manage daily life, the vast majority of organized women perceived like-minded bureaucrats to be their natural allies before 1945.

Just as the state occupied a growing place in the aspirations and actions of women's groups, changes in gender relations and gender ideology significantly affected the state's relations with society as a whole. Officials increasingly recognized the value of women as the nation's mothers, housewives, and community activists. The emergence of women as intermediaries in the project of social management, I would argue, permitted the bureaucracy between 1920 and 1945 to intervene in everyday life to a degree that had not been possible when male household heads served as the government's principal agents at the local level. The public involvement of women greatly aided official efforts to extract household savings and improve hygiene. And one has difficulty imagining how the regime could have imposed tremendous sacrifices on its people during World War II had it not been for the massive participation of ordinary women in managing local life. Following Japan's defeat in 1945, many observers expected women's groups to become fiercely independent of the bureaucracy. Yet the close relationships between organized women and the state persisted, enabling postwar governments to continue and, in some cases, extend their ambitious programs of social management.

PART TWO

Social Management in
Postwar Japan

Re-creating the Channels
of Moral Suasion

O N AUGUST 15, 1945, radios throughout Japan carried the unfamiliar voice of Hirohito announcing his empire's decision to surrender to the Allied powers. Recalling that "we declared war on America and Britain out of our sincere desire to ensure Japan's self-preservation and the stabilization of East Asia," the emperor followed with one of history's most famous understatements: "the war situation has developed not necessarily to Japan's advantage." He thereupon called on his war-weary subjects to "pave the way for a grand peace for all the generations to come by enduring the unendurable and suffering what is unsufferable."[1] The Japanese people, for their part, were left to ponder the nation's past and its future.

The war that had been waged in faraway places to ensure Japan's "self-preservation" ended in death and destruction throughout the Japanese archipelago. American bombers devastated more than 40 percent of the total urban area of the six most important industrial cities between early March and early June 1945. Similar fates befell large numbers of provincial cities and manufacturing centers.[2] In addition to Japan's 1.74 million military deaths in the China and Pacific wars, some 393,000 civilians died in the atomic bombings of Hiroshima and Nagasaki and the conventional bombings of sixty-four other cities, by the government's conservative estimate.[3] Those figures do not begin to include the millions made homeless, the maimed, nor the children malnourished as food became scarce in the course of the Pacific War. The fourteen-year "quest for autonomy" from the Western powers ironically cost Japan its very independence.[4] From 1945 to 1952, the Allied powers occupied their defeated foe, departing only after they had imposed a series of sweeping reforms.

The physical costs of World War II prompted some Japanese to reflect upon the close relationships between state and society that had undergirded social management in imperial Japan. The pervasive patterns of

popular cooperation with the regime, which had seemed so natural before and during the war, were sharply criticized after August 15, 1945,
for having permitted the government to lead an unquestioning populace
down the disastrous path of authoritarianism and militarism. Leaders of
the formerly illegal Communist party, one of the few organizations that
had not cooperated with the regime, insisted that purges and war crimes
trials target not only military and bureaucratic officials, but also the nongovernmental elites who had collaborated with them.[5] The liberal *Asahi
shimbun* warned against the continued influence of wartime women's
leaders "who were possessed by the power of the militarists and the spirit
of the times." Behaving like "private detectives," these self-appointed
guardians "took to the streets, instead of tending to their families, and
thrust leaflets into their sisters' hands, cajoling the passersby not to wear
kimonos embroidered with gold or silver threads" or sport permanent
waves.[6] To foster democratization from below, progressive intellectuals
appealed to the people to become the active subjects (*shutai*) of political
action, rather than remaining the objects of official campaigns.[7]

As the leading force in the Allied Occupation, American authorities
strongly encouraged these efforts to build a democratic "New Japan."
The Americans envisioned this society as one in which individuals and
nongovernmental associations undertook initiatives outside the control
of the state. Japanese officials thus confronted a group of foreigners who,
even within the Western world, were distinctive in their aversion to the
state's coordinated management of society. Other democratic states, such
as France or Britain, possessed centralized, interventionist police forces
or routinely deputized religious and other private organizations to administer schools and public services. The United States' plans to reform
Japan, on the other hand, reflected the long-standing American faith in
"the principles of decentralization and local self-government." American
reformers, moreover, came from a society that historically strove to separate religion and state. More recent New Deal thinking made them
equally determined to sever what they perceived as undemocratic connections between the Japanese state and putatively private organizations
(even if, in practice, governments in their own country frequently blurred
the distinction between public and private spheres—for example, subsidizing religious and charitable organizations to provide welfare services).
Particularly offensive to Americans were the thousands of intermediary
organizations, notably the neighborhood associations, which in wartime
and the early postwar months kept order, distributed food rations, and
performed other public functions. Regarding the neighborhood associations as the preserve of local bosses, the Americans aimed at creating a
more direct relationship between the state and individual. In 1947, mu-

nicipal and ward offices were ordered to assume all administrative functions previously undertaken by neighborhood associations.[8]

With a thoroughness and fervor that might shock a less confident America today, Occupation authorities—or SCAP (Supreme Commander for the Allied Powers)—set about dismantling the mechanisms of Japanese social management. SCAP began by directing the dissolution of the enormous wartime "patriotic" associations of workers, farmers, youth, women, and others. Second, the Japanese government was ordered to cease all support and supervision of Shinto shrines, effectively ending the system of State Shinto. Third, to prevent the state from mobilizing private groups to carry out governmental functions, Occupation officials inserted in the postwar constitution of 1946 the following:

> ARTICLE 89. No public money or other property shall be expended or appropriated for the use, benefit or maintenance of any religious institution or association, or for any charitable, educational or benevolent enterprises not under the control of public authority.

The coup de grâce came in 1947, when the Home Ministry itself was disbanded. In one stroke, the Japanese state lost much of its previous capacity to coordinate policies relating to the police, local government, welfare, new religions, Shinto shrines, prostitution, women's political activities, savings promotion, and other moral suasion campaigns.

Occupation reforms further encouraged the expansion of groups that were less likely than their prewar predecessors to look to the state bureaucracy to fulfill their objectives. The many repressive measures that had curtailed the freedoms of religion, expression, assembly, and association were abrogated. Politicized women's organizations quickly reemerged after defeat, bolstered by the newly granted right to join political parties and by the introduction of universal women's suffrage in 1946. Occupation-era guarantees of civil liberties and the right to organize labor unions similarly permitted forces on the Left to gain a degree of political influence that was unimaginable before 1945. The Japan Socialist party (JSP) grew to become the single largest party in 1947, and its president, Katayama Tetsu, briefly headed a coalition cabinet from 1947 to 1948. The Communist party failed to become a major party in the Diet, but it steadfastly opposed the conservative governments' attempts to revive the moral suasion policies of the prewar era.

The Occupation also played a crucial role in altering the ways in which Japanese envisioned their national mission and their very identity. With the armed forces disbanded and the postwar constitution renouncing war "as the sovereign right of the nation," the great majority of Japanese no longer expected their country to become a "first-rate" military power.

SCAP further shattered the presurrender equation of the state with the emperor, having instituted popular sovereignty in the new constitution. The Japanese government itself embraced the task of building a "democratic" nation. The official postwar mission became to construct a "peaceful nation," a "moral nation," and a "cultural nation."[9]

The Americans, nonetheless, failed to eradicate other powerful vestiges of imperial Japan. As the Occupation neared its end in 1952, civilian leaders of the old order staged a dramatic comeback. In 1951, SCAP "depurged" most of the former bureaucrats, politicians, and others who had been earlier purged from public life for their wartime activities. In the general election of October 1952, 139 of these depurged figures won seats in the Lower House—including more than 30 veterans of the former Home Ministry.[10]

By nearly all accounts, the conservative resurgence made the 1950s a decade of acute polarization between Left and Right. In the oft-quoted words of Yoshida Shigeru, the conservative prime minister who dominated the early postwar era, Japan—unlike Korea—had been spared outright partition during the Occupation, yet a "thirty-eighth parallel" divided the populace itself.[11] As historians commonly tell the story, on one side stood the "conservatives," who struggled to restore the bedrock of the prewar order—moral education, moral suasion campaigns, traditional gender roles, and a centralized police force and educational system. On the other side, scholars maintain, were the "progressives," who steadfastly resisted conservative governments' "feudalistic" efforts to tighten controls over the people. By the late 1950s, the Diet itself had become the scene of physical confrontations between members of the Left and the ruling Liberal Democratic party (established in 1955).[12] Although tensions subsided after 1960, observers generally agree that the existence of a sizable opposition bloc within the Diet—plus the postwar constitution and rapid urbanization—acted as powerful checks on the postwar state's capacity to manage society.[13] All in all, the conventional portrait of early postwar Japan is of a sharply divided polity.

If one looks beyond a few controversial issues, however, such as the role of the emperor or the status of the postwar military, we discover many areas of consensus between the progressive and conservative camps. It is the nature of this common ground that makes postwar Japan a very different society from the more liberal, individualistic United States. Like their conservative counterparts, self-styled progressive forces—activist women, socialists, and others—have frequently supported the use of state power to regulate public mores, socialize the populace, and modernize daily life. Relations between the state and society in postwar Japan underwent significant changes, to be sure, but hardly a revolution in the sense of a complete rupture with the past. Social management not only retained a central place in postwar governance, but actually gained strength in some spheres. Democratization and changes in gender roles generated new intermediaries who eagerly assisted the state in its interventions in daily life. Progressive and conservative campaigns to manage society did not always coincide, but the story of how many times they did surely deepens our understanding of postwar Japan.

One of the defining features of postwar social management in Japan has been the continued reliance on moral suasion campaigns. Drives to manage everyday life had united the bureaucratic state and middle-class groups in the cities and countryside since the 1920s. These forces remained convinced that Japan, a country poor in natural resources and racially isolated within a Western-dominated world order, had no alternative but to marshal its human resources to reenter the international economy in a competitive position. Indeed, in the wake of defeat, many progressive groups supported the state's moral suasion campaigns at the very moment that SCAP was encouraging democracy based on individualism and autonomous organization outside the government.

The postwar campaigns were a good deal more subtle than their prewar and wartime counterparts. To many urban Japanese today, they have become all but invisible. But if three strands in the state's ongoing programs of social management—savings drives, social education, and "new life" campaigns—are closely examined, the phenomenon becomes more visible and coherent. In the absence of a central command structure under the old Home Ministry, various agencies of the state necessarily directed the government's campaigns in these areas with somewhat different objectives. Yet the postwar programs of social management soon became intertwined.

ENCOURAGING SAVINGS: FROM STATE-LED
MOBILIZATION TO "DEMOCRATIC" CAMPAIGNS

In the months following the war's end, Japanese of various ideological stripes—from economic bureaucrats to Socialist party leaders—pressed for a revival of campaigns to persuade the populace to save more and consume less. Long a feature of prewar economic policy, savings promotion campaigns had become during the Pacific War "a major instrument of inflation control in Japan and have been so highly organized as to appear virtually compulsory," according to U.S. authorities.[14] Sponsored by the government, some 65,500 "national savings associations" were in operation in 1944, comprising 59 million members. The wartime savings associations were generally the responsibility of the state-supervised neighborhood associations, women's associations, youth associations, and other local organizations. Compelling the national savings associations to "digest" ever-increasing amounts of government bonds, the regime had by 1944 boosted the rate of household savings (as a percentage of disposable income) to an extraordinary 44 percent.[15]

The Japanese people emerged from World War II financially bled, but their plight did little to dampen the enthusiasm of the state and middle-class groups for savings promotion campaigns. If anything, immediate postwar conditions gave rise to a heightened sense of urgency. Acute scarcities in food and other commodities led to hyperinflation and sharp depreciations in the value of the yen. To bring inflation under control in autumn 1946, the Socialist party joined the major non-Left parties in the Lower House to establish the Currency Stabilization Committee (Tsūka Antei Taisaku Hombu). Diet members on the committee worked together with Bank of Japan officials to coordinate nationwide savings drives.[16]

In November 1946, the Bank of Japan, Ministry of Finance, and Currency Stabilization Committee kicked off the first of nine "National Salvation Savings Campaigns," which ran successively until the end of 1949. The campaigns were promoted by conservative and Socialist-led cabinets alike. As they would in other postwar applications of moral suasion, officials took pains to distance the National Salvation campaign from the top-down mobilization efforts mounted by the wartime state. In the words of Bank of Japan governor Ichimada Hisato, the campaign was to "develop democratically and autonomously and by the good sense and efforts of the people themselves."

In actuality, as one official history acknowledged, there was little to distinguish the early postwar campaigns from their predecessors. The goal of "national salvation" was telling. Saving for the good of the individual was clearly secondary to "maintaining the currency, augmenting savings, and furnishing the capital for industrial recovery." Postwar officials continued to envision "autonomous" participation much as prewar Home Ministry bureaucrats once worked to internalize state-centered values in the people so as to make coerced mobilization unnecessary. With no sense of the apparent contradiction, Governor Ichimada himself declared: "I desire the spontaneous cooperation of each and every person in this nation."[17]

The only force that might have derailed the state's penchant for savings campaigns came not from within, but from the United States government. In September 1949, an American mission headed by Carl Shoup pressed the Japanese government to check inflation primarily by means of increased tax collection, rather than by campaigns to promote household savings. Japanese officials sought to satisfy American demands by dissolving the Currency Stabilization Committee and terminating the National Salvation campaigns in December. Savings drives in fact continued at the local level under the direction of prefectural savings promotion committees with guidance from central authorities.[18]

Economic bureaucrats breathed a collective sigh of relief when the Occupation ended in April 1952. In its 1952 budget the government earmarked the rather hefty sum of 100 million yen—twenty times the previous year's allocation—to savings promotion programs. On April 15, officials unveiled the Central Council for Savings Promotion, a nominally "nongovernmental" organization whose secretariat would nonetheless be staffed by higher civil servants in the Bank of Japan's Savings Promotion Department.[19] In 1987, the organization changed its name to the Central Council for Savings Information, although its functions remained much the same. Together with the Bank of Japan, Ministry of Finance, and other national agencies, the Central Council constructed an elaborate hierarchy dedicated to encouraging household savings. It has mobilized not only the schools, prefectural governments, and municipal offices, but also the semiofficial prefectural savings promotion committees and myriad grass-roots groups.[20]

Although the Central Council supported the adoption of many material incentives such as preferential tax treatment for savings accounts, a major portion of its activities employed moral suasion, pure and simple. In its opening Commemoration of Independence Savings Campaign (1952–1953), the agency aimed "to revive the beautiful customs of diligence, thrift, and savings" and "to enlighten [the public] that popular savings forms the basis of our country's economic revival." Appealing to economic nationalism, the drives of the 1950s enjoined the people to advance national prosperity by means of individual austerity.

It may have been difficult for Japanese at the time to appreciate that the war had ended. To correct developing "excesses in consumption," the Promotion of Independence Savings Campaign (1953–1955) instructed the public to "make thoroughgoing cutbacks in expenditures" and, borrowing a wartime phrase, to promote "tendencies toward renovation in national life (kokumin seikatsu sasshin)." The language of sacrifice for the good of the nation pervaded the campaign's slogans: "Let's Save 10 Percent of Our Earnings"; "Let's Be Earnest about Conserving Money and Goods"; and "Let's All Change the Way We Live."[21] From 1957 to 1965, savings promotion officials further exhorted consumers to save money in order to "Promote Exports and Conserve Foreign Exchange." Rising personal spending contributed only to ominous increases in imported goods, Japanese were admonished; conversely, household savings would be productively invested in Japan's export industries.[22]

The Japanese people experienced rapid growth in their incomes and levels of consumption during the 1960s, and officials recognized grudgingly that "we will not make much of an impression if we thoughtlessly preach the virtues of economizing on consumption and of saving" for the sake of the nation or industry. Yet rather than abandon the use of suasion, the state maintained the drumbeat of savings promotion—albeit with greater emphasis on convincing the people of the immediate benefits of thrift. As Central Council's white paper explained in 1963,

> at a time when the message that "consumption is a virtue" has grabbed the attention of the masses and the leisure boom is surging, the best way to promote savings campaigns is . . . to encourage sound consumption and *act so that savings occur naturally*. It is vital to making consumption sound that one plans one's life, reduces waste, and works rationally for daily life improvement. The essence of savings campaigns involves a number of straightforward measures: getting people to keep household accounts and lead budgeted lives, guiding daily life so as to examine how families manage their finances, and investigating ways of simplifying ceremonial occasions, such as *chūgen* [when gifts are exchanged on the last day of the Bon Lantern Festival].[23]

To "guide" the people so that savings occurred "naturally," officials stitched together a vast network of public entities and private groups. Many of these cooperative relationships had first appeared in prewar and wartime savings drives. The government eliminated the legal compulsion to join savings associations in 1947, but the authorities continued to rely on the newly "autonomous" associations to encourage and accumulate the savings of millions of members at the grass roots. The money would then be deposited in postal savings and other financial institutions. By the early postwar era, savings associations had become so identified with local women's associations that they were dubbed "mothers' banks" (*hahaoya ginkō*). Leaders of savings associations assisted neighbors in the proper keeping of household accounts. Forming the front line in official campaigns, they regularly distributed government-issued household account books, which were designed to structure the ways in which people saved.[24]

In 1958, postwar bureaucrats systematized another wartime innovation, the model savings district. Local savings promotion committees designated groups or neighborhoods nationwide as model "districts" for three-year terms. There were 526 such districts in 1992. Group members distributed account books and other materials published by the Central Council for Savings Promotion, and they hosted lectures and study sessions to convince housewives and youth of the necessity of thrift. Composed overwhelmingly of local women's groups of various types, the model savings groups worked closely with neighborhood associations, "daily life improvement" groups, and youth associations. For their work on the government's behalf, model savings groups received small subsidies.[25]

Central authorities sought to inculcate the "spirit of thrift" in future generations, as well, through the institution of "children's banks," which first appeared in 1948. Established within elementary and junior high schools, children's banks were intended to teach pupils "how to spend money economically through fostering savings habits."[26] School officials encouraged children to make deposits, which were then placed in local financial institutions. At their peak in 1956, children's banks counted some 8,826,000 depositors in programs run by 29,105 schools. The high level of central coordination was unmistakable. In 1950, the Ministry of Finance—aided by the Ministry of Education and Bank of Japan—began hosting national and regional conferences of teachers in charge of children's banks.[27]

Finally, the postwar savings campaigns reveal the uses of new technologies of social management that did not exist or were less available before World War II. To disseminate its messages during the 1950s, the Central Council for Savings Promotion turned increasingly to radio and then television—in addition to posters, motion pictures, and magazines. Savings promotion was a regular feature of such popular programs for housewives as "The Woman's Hour," "The Housewife's Day," and "Make Our Neighborhoods Bright and Clean."[28] In recent years, the government has provided free computer consultation services "to assist the public in drafting individual life plans or to judge how appropriate a plan is."[29]

SOCIAL EDUCATION AS SOCIAL MANAGEMENT

Unlike the prewar Home Ministry, neither the Bank of Japan nor the Ministry of Finance possessed the administrative capacity to supervise local society. With the dissolution of the mighty Home Ministry in 1947, postwar savings campaigns and other programs of social management necessarily relied on the Ministry of Education to influence the citizenry. The Ministry of Education not only determined what Japanese schoolchildren would be taught but also supervised a national system of "social education" for adults and youth who had left or graduated from school.

Social education has attracted scant attention from students of Japanese politics. This is perhaps because "social education" in postwar Japan encompasses a broad array of activities, most of which strike observers as apolitical or the product of popular initiative. The Ministry of Education's Bureau of Social Education, for example, administers libraries, museums, art exhibitions, and other programs for the enlightenment of the general public. In most Japanese municipalities since the

Occupation era, the principal site of social education has been the citizens' public hall (*kōminkan*). These centers offer a variety of nonvocational classes, including instruction in the tea ceremony, literature, and homemaking. The citizens' public halls also provide meeting places for community groups.[30]

Moreover, postwar social education has by no means been the exclusive preserve of conservative governments. Occupation officials encouraged the growth of a decentralized system of adult education that would be operated by local citizens and respond to local needs. Advising SCAP to promote adult education in March 1947, the Allies' Far Eastern Commission broadly defined education as a "preparation for life in a democratic nation, and as a training for the social and political responsibilities which freedom entails. Emphasis should be placed on the dignity and worth of the individual, on independent thought and initiative, and on developing a spirit of inquiry."[31] At the time, progressive social educators in Japan similarly envisioned the citizens' public halls as places for open political discussion, including criticism of those in power.[32] During the 1950s and 1960s, citizens' public halls occasionally became the bases of citizens' movements that protested pollution, rearmament, and nuclear weapons.[33]

One runs the risk, however, of exaggerating the autonomous nature of postwar social education. Many Japanese—whether officials, educators, or social reformers—were less than enthralled by the Americans' emphasis on individual self-fulfillment and decentralization. It is worth noting that the Japanese retained the interwar term "*social* education," rather than adopting the Anglo-American concept of "adult education."

As they had since the inception of the Ministry of Education's social education and daily life improvement programs in the early 1920s, bureaucrats and middle-class reformers regarded social education as part of the state's obligation to educate its people for the purpose of producing a better society and a stronger nation. Prewar instruction had prominently promoted improvements in daily hygiene, "scientific" child rearing, household economizing, and methods of curbing juvenile delinquency and adolescent sexuality. Social education lost its independent identity at the height of the Pacific War, when the Bureau of Social Education was merged with agencies conducting propaganda and supervising religious organizations.[34]

Ministry of Education officials emerged from World War II eager to resurrect social education in its less militaristic prewar form. The Bureau of Social Education was reestablished in October 1945, charged with handling "matters concerning the promotion of national morality and the cultivation and enlightenment of the people." Highlighting the interwar partnership between social education officials and middle-class progressives, the minister appointed Sekiguchi Yasushi as the bureau's first chief. A liberal commentator at the *Tōkyō asahi shimbun* before the war, Sekiguchi had championed universal suffrage and the cultivation of a knowledgeable electorate through "civic education."[35] In a directive to prefectural governors, the new chief declared that the object of social education was the development of "personality and service to the state and society." Governors were instructed to heighten the "moral sense of the people" and "to cultivate religious sentiment, make efforts to improve physique, and encourage bright and magnanimous disposition among the people."[36]

To realize these objectives, Ministry of Education officials mobilized local youth and women's associations, much as they had before 1945. Japanese authorities complied with SCAP's requests to disband the bureaucratically supervised organizations, though hardly in a manner anticipated by the Americans. On September 25, 1945, the vice minister ordered prefectural governors to eliminate "the heretofore so-called government-manufactured or militaristic colors" among existing youth and children's associations. They were expressly told not to create a "nation-wide uniform organization." Nevertheless, the directive also instructed governors to establish youth and children's associations throughout each prefecture, lest young people "be left unorganized in their social life." These associations would "be managed under the guidance of the town- or village-chief, teachers, religious people and other people of knowledge, as purely non-official organizations." The associations were to be encouraged to develop "true to the purport of the Emperor's rescript announcing the end of the war"—that is, by "enduring the unendurable and suffering what is unsufferable." With no less sense of irony, the ministry directed governors on November 28 to encourage the establishment of a women's association in every elementary-school district, to be "carried on by the spontaneous activities and mutual help of the women themselves." The aims of the women's associations should be "to cultivate religious sentiment and respect for good manners and courtesy, and to promote home education, and the improvement of the next generation."[37]

To counteract the government's efforts to reassert control over private organizations engaged in social education activities, SCAP did its best to decentralize the administration of social education. And for a time, it appeared that the Americans had succeeded. Article 89 of the postwar constitution, which went into effect in 1947, explicitly barred governments at all levels from financially assisting "charitable, educational or benevolent enterprises not under the control of public authority." The Board of Education Law (1948) not only introduced popularly elected prefectural and municipal boards of education but also shifted responsibility for local social education from the Ministry of Education to social education sections attached to the new boards.[38] The Social Education Law of 1949 further promised to weaken the Ministry of Education's hold over women's associations, youth groups, and other organizations that assisted in social education work. The law prohibited the state and local governments from taking a "controlling leadership" over, or interfering with organizations related to social education. It also emphatically proscribed governments from giving subsidies to such organizations.[39]

Legislation was one thing. Persuading the Japanese state and outside organizations to abandon long-standing patterns of cooperation was quite another. The Ministry of Education was by no means keen on enforcing the new constitutional ban on public subsidies for private social education activities.[40] In many a locale, the cozy relationships of the past persisted. To the consternation of American authorities, Hyōgo prefecture was still distributing significant funds to ostensibly private groups in early 1948. A Military Government Team was particularly skeptical of the autonomy of Hyōgo's local women's associations and youth associations after discovering that the offices of their respective prefectural federations were located in, and maintained by, the prefectural government's social education section.[41]

Nor did the passage of the Social Education Law in 1949 put an end to official interference. Throughout the 1950s, governments found ways of subsidizing "organizations related to social education," frequently in ways that inhibited the development of truly autonomous associations. According to the Japan Housewives Association (Shufuren), local youth groups and women's associations desperately needed funds and welcomed public subsidies. The authorities often subsidized these organizations in fact, by cosponsoring events, paying for lecturers, or directly funding the social education activities delegated to the groups. In exchange for providing financial support, local social education officials routinely vetoed associations' selections of politically objectionable lecturers or imposed their own speakers and agenda on cosponsored meetings.[42]

Some of the best-publicized incidents of bureaucratic interference resulted from the Ministry of Education's policy in 1958 to rein in youth associations that engaged in activities judged undesirable by officials. In Kōchi prefecture, the board of education attempted to stop organizers of the annual prefectural youth congress from inviting seventeen of twenty-five requested speakers, most of whom were progressive professors or student leaders. The authorities further insisted that the congress not pass a final resolution, which customarily summed up the sense of a meeting. The youth organizations thwarted the intervention only by spurning the board's cosponsorship—no doubt at a major expense to themselves.[43]

The authorities had to engage in considerable artifice when circumventing the Social Education Law's ban on official subsidization and interference. Yet other provisions of the law openly permitted the central government to conduct social education as an instrument of state policy. One article required local boards of education to sponsor and encourage "meetings concerning scientific rationalization of daily living." Under this rubric, central authorities promoted household savings, "scientific" child rearing, and other inheritances of the prewar daily life improvement campaigns. In addition, heads of municipalities as well as "other government agencies" were empowered to use local social education facilities to propagate "necessary information." In practice, police stations and the Tax Administration Agency regularly enlisted the services of the citizens' public halls in nationwide campaigns aimed at traffic safety, crime prevention, and persuading citizens to pay their taxes.[44]

In a series of revisions to the original Social Education Law, beginning in 1951, the Ministry of Education and successive conservative governments further whittled away at the Occupation's safeguards against the central management of social education. Amendments placed prefectural and municipal social education in the hands of social education directors. These directors were trained in state-certified courses or by the government itself, and they increasingly functioned as an arm of the national bureaucracy.[45] In 1959, the intensely conservative cabinet of Kishi Nobusuke pushed through a major revision of the Social Education Law. The most controversial provision eliminated the previously unconditional prohibition of official subsidies. Public subsidies could thenceforth be given to nongovernmental groups engaged in social education, subject to approval by either the national-level Social Education Advisory Council or local social education committees. The fact was that Social Education Advisory Council members were appointed by the minister of education, and most social education committees were conservative politically and allied with the ruling Liberal Democratic party. The amended law, in effect, gave national and local governments free rein in subsidizing private associations that assisted the authorities.[46]

The contest over revising the Social Education Law in 1959 has gone down in history as one of the era's pitched battles between a backward-looking conservative cabinet and the forces of progress. Indeed, women's groups and prominent social educators attacked the government's bill on the grounds that subsidizing women's and youth associations would again, as before 1945, culminate in the official supervision of Japanese associational life. Within the Lower House, Socialist party members vehemently opposed the revision of Article 13. The governing Liberal Democratic party passed the amended Social Education Law only after the Socialists walked out of the chambers in protest.[47]

Progressive opposition to the revision of the Social Education Law should not, however, blind us to the widespread acceptance of close working relationships between the state and social education groups throughout the postwar era. The Socialist party had, after all, supported the passage of the original Social Education Law in 1949, despite several provisions that granted the state potent means of influencing the populace. Communist party members were virtually alone in opposing the measure.[48] Nor were the Socialists united in their opposition to Prime Minister Kishi's statist revision in 1959. Shortly before Socialists attempted to block the legislation in the Lower House, fellow party members in the House of Councilors had unanimously voted in favor of permitting public subsidies—in exchange for a rather minimal concession from the the LDP.[49] Socialist leaders might well have supported revisions to the Social Education Law in 1959 had they not been incensed by Kishi's confrontational tactics against their party over other issues— notably the revision of the Police Duties Law and the imposition of the teachers' rating system during the previous year.

For every national organization that unambiguously opposed the provision of subsidies, there were many others that looked forward to governmental support. Prior to the enactment of the Social Education Law of 1949, many youth and women's organizations joined prefectural social education associations to demand that subsidies be preserved.[50] When the Kishi Cabinet proposed to legalize social education subsidies in the late 1950s, the initiative was firmly backed by the National Coordinating Council of Citizens' Public Halls, the Boy Scouts of Japan, and several other youth and women's organizations. The enormous Japan National Council of Youth Associations did not endorse every provision of the 1959 revision, but the organization refrained from directly opposing the government's bill because it would permit the granting of badly needed support to the council's affiliates.[51]

Even critics of the revision bill, like the Housewives Association, often cosponsored events with the government at the time and since. After the passions unleashed in the Right-Left confrontations of the late 1950s cooled, the state's practice of mobilizing and subsidizing private associations—not to mention the overall project of social education—became unproblematic to most Japanese.[52]

A "NEW LIFE" FOR THE NEW JAPAN

Why progressives would support state-sponsored social education can be only partially explained by the chronically underfinanced state of private organizations in Japan. A fuller explanation rests on a basic, yet seldom acknowledged, fact of political life in postwar Japan. Progressives and conservatives generally agreed on the content of social education, which in one form or another aimed at the "improvement of daily life."

Officials, village leaders, and urban middle-class activists had allied in numerous campaigns to modernize and rationalize daily life since the early 1920s. After Japan embarked on a full-scale war with China in 1937, the government jettisoned the goal of "improving" living standards in favor of the "renovation of daily life" (*seikatsu sasshin*). Although the new thrust invariably resulted in heavy-handed campaigns to effect wartime austerity, many middle-class women and men who had been active in the interwar daily life improvement campaigns plunged into wartime drives with equal fervor, in part because the regime's interventions also included efforts to improve nutrition and establish day nurseries for the children of farmers during the busy summer months. So powerful was the Japanese belief in modernization, progress, and science that neither the contradictions of the wartime campaigns nor the nation's disastrous defeat in 1945 rent the alliance for daily life improvement in the postwar era. The most obvious change was cosmetic. Daily life improvement campaigns became more commonly known as "New Life campaigns" (*shin seikatsu undō*).[53]

Indeed, progressive forces played a central role in reviving the state's improvement campaigns after World War II. On June 20, 1947, the coalition cabinet led by Socialist prime minister Katayama Tetsu announced plans to launch the People's Campaign to Build a New Japan (Shin Nihon Kensetsu Kokumin Undō). The left-center government was keen to reconstruct Japan as a "democratic, peaceful, and cultural nation." The chief means to do so, proclaimed the Katayama cabinet, lay in the rapid development of a "New Life campaign." Prominent among the campaign's central objectives was the "establishment of rational and democratic habits in daily life."[54]

The inculcation of "democratic" habits had not been a part of prewar improvement drives, but in many other respects Prime Minister Katayama revitalized the state-directed project of daily life improvement, with all of its previous contradictions. On one hand, as in the interwar era, the cabinet sounded a strong note of modernization and betterment. The campaign was designed to persuade the people to "consider things rationally on an everyday basis and conduct themselves efficiently. Feudal customs will be cleared away, and enlightened, pleasurable, and democratic habits in daily life established. In so doing, we will promote inventions and improvements in the people's lives in all aspects of clothing, food, and shelter."[55] Even the symbols of rationality and efficiency remained much as they had since the early 1920s. In November 1947, the minister of education announced awards for those citizens' public halls that had done the most to advance culture within their communities. The prizes were none other than large communal clocks, which prewar proponents of daily life improvement had long argued were essential to fostering a respect for time among local residents.[56]

At the same time, the Katayama government left no doubt that the immediate objective in the rationalization of daily life was to strengthen the nation state and the national economy, rather than improve living conditions. As its prospectus made clear, Katayama's New Life campaign aimed, above all, at enlisting the cooperation of the people in confronting the hyperinflation, industrial stagnation, shortage of capital, and flagrant black-market activity that plagued the Japanese economy in the early postwar years. "Rationalization" promised more "pleasurable" living conditions at some later date, yet in the short run it was defined in negative terms reminiscent of wartime austerity drives. The cabinet called on the public, first and foremost, to "eliminate wastefulness in daily life and cut back on expenditures on luxuries."[57] In an "Appeal to the Nation" in August 1947, Katayama acknowledged that life was not improving, but he counseled that "the people of Japan must bear the pain of the great surgical operation of eliminating all economic ills." Because the nation's imports were far in excess of exports, he continued, "we are required to work harder by bearing all present hardships with the idea of sacrificing the present for a better future."[58] For the time being, the New Life looked pretty much like the old.

The most remarkable aspect of Katayama's New Life campaign was that a Socialist-led cabinet relied on the presurrender regime's techniques of moral suasion and social education in its efforts to solve the nation's economic problems. To induce citizens to save more, work harder, and avoid the black market, Katayama sought nothing less than the moral regeneration of the Japanese people. Echoing prewar and wartime bureaucratic pronouncements to an uncanny degree, the Socialist-led coalition noted with alarm that "morality is degenerating and thinking is in ferment. The result is that the social order is in chaos and the very basis of the national community (kokumin kyōdōtai) is becoming horribly fractured. . . . To ride out this crisis, we must awaken in all the people a powerful new spirit overflowing with the desire and passion to rebuild our homeland."[59] As in the prewar "diligence and thrift" campaigns, awakening this new spirit involved "elevating the will to work" among the people. And in an effort to further social welfare at minimal cost to the government, the New Life campaign similarly pledged to foster both the "sense of responsibility for one's own welfare and the spirit of comradeship through mutual assistance."

While insisting that this be a "people's campaign" based on the "initiative of each sector of society," the Katayama cabinet did not hesitate to rely on the state's hierarchically organized social education network to launch the New Life campaign. Following the precedents set by the Ministry of Education's social education officials, the cabinet proposed to "rouse to action" the schools, school-related groups, youth associations, women's associations, religious organizations, and other groups. It would also "work to establish the New Life . . . by making the most of citizens' public halls." In a concrete plan to effect the People's Campaign to Build a New Japan in 1948, the government further committed itself to establishing coordinating councils in each prefecture while sponsoring "people's forums" in each locale, workplace, and school.[60]

The Socialist party's endorsement of such a statist and moralistic campaign may appear puzzling. To some extent, the Katayama cabinet's promotion of "New Life" reflected the thinking of higher civil servants and the Socialists' more conservative coalition partners in the Democratic and People's Cooperative parties. The Katayama cabinet was not the first postwar government to encourage New Life explicitly. A cabinet formed by the Progressive party (predecessor to the Democratic party) had earlier unveiled a Campaign to Promote Economic Morality and New Life in February 1946.[61]

Nevertheless, the Socialists' support of official campaigns to promote New Life was motivated by more than a temporary alliance with conservatives. Leading socialists had since the 1920s believed that the state and intermediary groups should join together to extirpate "feudal customs" while bringing science and rationality to the people. A social democratic vision of the New Life appeared prominently in the Katayama cabinet's prospectus for the People's Campaign to Build a New Japan. The New Life did not necessarily mean increased levels of personal consumption, but it was predicated on "social justice" in that "public burdens would be shared fairly" and the value of work in rebuilding Japan would be respected, whether it be "brawn work or brain work." The New Life campaign also sought to foster "a sense of social solidarity," which would enable the people to "contribute to the welfare of society as a whole by means of mutual comradeship and cooperation."[62] Socialists and conservatives spoke of the New Life in somewhat different terms, but they agreed on the essentials. New Life campaigns would center on mobilizing groups to organize their communities in ways that generally furthered the state's agenda and rarely opposed it.

In addition to social democratic beliefs, Christianity played a major role in the postwar Socialists' interest in reforming popular habits. Socialist ministers in the Katayama cabinet overwhelmingly came from the party's right wing, which was dominated by a non-Marxist group of Protestant socialists and labor leaders. At least six members of the Katayama cabinet—five of them Socialists—were either practicing Christians or had been influenced by Christian teachings.[63]

Many of the Christian socialists, men and women, had been active in prewar and wartime savings drives, daily life improvement campaigns, and particularly the movement to abolish licensed prostitution. The prewar Purity Society had, after all, been headed by Abe Isoo, the veteran Christian socialist who concurrently served as chairman of the Social Masses' party during the 1930s. Some of the postwar Christian socialists had been influenced by such early twentieth-century Protestant social work specialists as Tomeoka Kōsuke, who emphasized the efficacy of inculcating sound morality and habits of thrift in the poor. Others were inspired by the Christian educator Nitobe Inazō and the social reformer Kagawa Toyohiko, both of whom took part in the semiofficial agricultural cooperative movement in order to improve the material and spiritual lives of the rural populace during the prewar era.[64]

Katayama Tetsu himself was a man with a mission. Japan's first Christian prime minister was less than meek when he declared that Japan's government, like his party, would be "guided by a Christian spirit of morality."[65] To Katayama, the nation's weakness resulted to a significant degree from the previous governments' failures to convey this morality to citizens, whether in the realm of sexual mores or everyday habits. Here was a man who, amid rampant unemployment and malnutrition, could advise his people against depending on official assistance with the platitude, "God helps those who help themselves."[66] As a leader of the prewar Social Masses' party, Katayama may have also been one of the first Japanese in the late 1930s to use the term "New Life campaigns," which he equated with the ongoing daily life improvement drives.[67] He apparently borrowed the phrase from China's New Life movement launched in 1934 by Chiang Kai-shek, head of the Nationalist government and a fellow Christian.[68]

The Katayama cabinet's propagation of the New Life was more memorable for the progressive camp's enthusiasm for official campaigns than for tangible results. The People's Campaign to Build a New Japan was just beginning to materialize when Katayama's government fell in March 1948. Succeeding cabinets did not undertake comparable drives during the late 1940s, some suggest, because no government could hope to persuade the public of the prospect of a "New Life" amid dire economic circumstances.[69]

The Japanese economy staged a dramatic recovery during the early 1950s, however, thanks to the Korean War, and official and grass-roots interest in New Life movements surged accordingly. In 1951, the Yomiuri

Shimbunsha, which published one of the nation's leading dailies, began awarding "Commendations for New Life Model Groups and Districts." The newspaper company further stimulated participation in local movements by publishing *Shin seikatsu* (New life), a daily newspaper sold primarily by women's groups to neighborhood women. National women's organizations also frequently sponsored New Life exhibitions and campaigns. To take one of many examples, at the local level Ibaragi prefecture witnessed the rapid expansion of a Daily Life Science movement in 1951. Mirroring the efforts of savings promotion and social education officials, governors in Hokkaido and several other prefectures established New Life councils within prefectural and municipal offices.

The government's renewed commitment to New Life campaigns flowed from a number of sectional interests. The Ministry of Education's social education bureaucrats remained the leading force, as they had in the interwar daily life improvement campaigns. The passage of the Social Education Law of 1949, along with the spread of citizens' public halls, gave the Ministry of Education unprecedented channels of influence over women and adolescents. From the start, the New Life campaigns relied on the activism of local women's associations and youth groups—that is, the organizations that were already routinely operating with the encouragement and financial assistance of social education officials. In addition, the Ministry of Agriculture and Forestry had been running its own New Life campaigns in the countryside through a nationwide network of "daily life extension officers." An Occupation-era innovation modeled after the U.S. Department of Agriculture's extension service, the extension officers promoted the formation of rural "daily life improvement groups" and 4–H clubs. Ministry of Health and Welfare bureaucrats, for their part, assisted in the New Life drives primarily to improve public hygiene. Their top priority was to secure the cooperation of local residents' organizations in a national movement to wipe out mosquitoes and flies.[70]

Official and nongovernmental movements for New Life coalesced in 1954. In December, the minister of education instructed the Social Education Advisory Council to formulate a plan for advancing New Life campaigns "from the perspective of social education." In its report of February 1955 the council expressed deep concern about the diffuse and temporary nature of the many existing New Life movements. The panel therefore proposed the immediate formation of a national organization that would coordinate the campaigns, all the time insisting that individual movements remain "spontaneous and autonomous."[71]

Acting upon the advisory council's recommendation, the newly formed government of Hatoyama Ichirō sponsored the creation of the New Life Campaign Association (Shin Seikatsu Undō Kyōkai) in September 1955.

The prime minister assured the public that the New Life campaign would not be one in which the government exhorted the people to "do this, do that."[72] The official financing of the campaign, nonetheless, limited the potential for autonomous grass-roots activism. The association's first annual budget of 50 million yen, a rather sizable sum, was funded entirely out of the Ministry of Education's special assistance monies for social education. The coordinating organization received the bulk of its funds from the central government until 1979.[73]

The establishment of the New Life Campaign Association demonstrated, as nothing else, the continued appeal of daily life improvement to postwar conservatives, liberals, and the moderate Left alike. Prime Minister Hatoyama, the campaign's enthusiastic sponsor, had been a jingoist prewar politician whom the Occupation had purged for his pro-fascist behavior. The former wartime Home Ministry bureaucrats Gotō Fumio and Yasui Seiichirō, who had similarly been purged and then depurged for ultranationalist activities, sat on the association's board of directors during the latter half of the 1950s. At the same time, the directors included the Christian pacificist Yanaihara Tadao and some of Japan's most famous socialists—Katayama Tetsu, Kagawa Toyohiko, and the official representative from the Socialist party, Miwa Jusō. In his capacity as an executive director from 1958 to 1962, Katayama played a particularly active role in preaching the gospel of New Life. Also serving as officers of the association were leaders of Japan's major women's organizations, notably the prewar suffragists Yamataka (Kaneko) Shigeri, Oku Mumeo, and Ichikawa Fusae.[74] The only significant political group that did not participate in the New Life Campaign Association was the small Communist party, which criticized this latest instance of government-run social education—just as it had fundamentally opposed the original Social Education Law in 1949.

As in earlier improvement campaigns, the New Life Campaign Association successfully incorporated widely held desires for modernization, social cohesiveness, and a strong state and national economy. The first National Conference on New Life agreed upon the following agenda in November 1955:

1. Simplification of Ceremonial Occasions
2. Elevation of Public Morality
3. Improvements in Food, Clothing, and Shelter
4. Rationalization of Savings and Household Accounts
5. Attention to Time (see Figure 13)
6. Elimination of Wastefulness
7. Improvements in the Functions and Customs of Daily Life
8. Improvements in Health and Sanitation

FIGURE 13. The New Life campaign, 1957: A youth association's clock exhorts passersby to pay "attention to time."

9. Defeat of Superstitious Customs
10. Campaigns to Eradicate Mosquitoes and Flies
11. Promotion of Healthy Entertainments
12. Campaigns for Mutual Assistance
13. Family Planning[75]

Several of the objectives above centered on community building and strengthening social solidarity.[76] Committed to "fostering public spiritedness" and mutual assistance, the New Life Campaign Association worked to propagate "social morality, traffic morality, and fire prevention thought." Activities to cultivate patriotism—or "elevate love of Homeland and humanity"—were also high on the list. In terms of crime prevention, the drives endeavored to "remove the sources of juvenile delinquency." The association's monthly newsletter regularly publicized communal efforts to improve public hygiene (see Figure 14).

Other activities aimed at extirpating customs that embarrassed urban middle classes and were thought to sully Japan's image in the eyes of

FIGURE 14. The New Life campaign, 1957: Fathers and children sweep the streets in a Tokyo neighborhood.

Western visitors. The influence of Christians, socialists, and women's groups was apparent in the New Life Campaign Association's programs to encourage "chastity education" and "thoughts of purity" in the schools and among youth groups. In a related effort to "elevate public morality" in 1956, the association promoted the New Life Campaign in Travel. Aided by women, high school students, and the Boy Scouts, campaign organizers attempted to alter the habits of the many Japanese who acted with little consideration for others once they had left their own neighborhoods. Littering and the male practice of stripping down to one's underwear on trains were obvious targets. Worried that foreign visitors to the 1964 Olympics in Tokyo would be appalled by unsightly and unsanitary urban neighborhoods, the association substantially expanded its activities after 1959, with emphasis on the well-funded Campaign to Beautify Japan.[77]

Despite firmer guarantees of the freedom of religion in the postwar constitution, middle-class and bureaucratic proponents of the New Life also hammered away at the "superstitious customs" of ordinary Japanese, much as they had before 1945. The campaigns even attacked the practice of purchasing and burning incense on the grounds of Buddhist temples; adherents commonly swirled the smoke around their bodies to cure disease or lessen pain. To New Life leaders, such customs revealed the "shocking wastefulness expended on excessive religious practices."[78]

The New Life Campaign Association put forward community building and modernization as important tasks in their own right, but many of the campaigns' activities remained focused, as they had under the Katayama cabinet and before 1945, on persuading the populace to save, be frugal, and work harder. Much of the campaigns' positive appeal lay in their promise to improve household finances by offering advice on how to reduce the enormous costs of Japanese ritual life—weddings, funerals, gift giving, and the large numbers of "empty formalities." New Life campaigns repeatedly singled out end-of-the-year and New Year's festivities. Activists urged "self-restraint" (*jishuku*) not only in throwing end-of-the-year parties, but also in purchasing New Year's pine decorations (*kadomatsu*) and Christmas trees. Campaigners further exhorted the populace to stop sending large numbers of New Year's cards merely "for the sake of formality."[79]

At the same time, the New Life drives unquestionably advanced the state's economic agenda. One of the highest priorities of the New Life campaign was to "encourage savings to their utmost," announced the education minister in 1955. Expanded productivity, rather than consumption, would be "the basis for the reproduction of the Japanese race," he continued.[80] The New Life Campaign Association worked closely with the Central Council for Savings Promotion, social education directors, and local women's groups to "rationalize household accounts" and augment national savings. Since 1959, the association and the Central Council have joined together with leading women's organizations to sponsor the annual National Women's Meeting on "New Life and Savings."[81] In addition to promoting national savings, the New Life campaigns emphasized production over consumption to persuade the people that hard work and frugality would stave off poverty and dependence on state assistance. Adopting the slogan "from a consuming prefecture to a producing prefecture" in 1954, the New Life campaign in Hiroshima appealed to those families receiving welfare benefits to return to an "independent life."[82]

New Life campaigns have involved hundreds of thousands of Japanese during the postwar era. Most participated as members of community youth and women's associations, neighborhood associations (*burakukai* or *chōnaikai*), and agricultural cooperatives (particularly the youth and women's sections). These local groups, in turn, commonly affiliated with New Life campaign councils at the prefectural and municipal levels. Councils had been established in every one of Japan's 47 prefectures by the end of 1956. Municipal councils were nearly as ubiquitous. According to a survey of 908 cities, towns, and villages in 1959, New Life campaign councils operated in 735 (81 percent) of these municipalities. By 1978, fully 65 percent of the nation's municipal governments were subsidizing local New Life activities. According to the New Life Campaign Association's nationwide survey of public opinion in 1957, as many as 38 percent of the respondents replied that they were currently taking part in New Life activities—led by efforts to eradicate mosquitoes and flies, eliminate formalities, and promote savings while reducing wastefulness.[83]

During the late 1960s and 1970s, the New Life Campaign Association deepened its local base by cementing ties with the grass-roots environmental and housewives' groups that sprang up as part of the widespread "citizens' movements."[84] Concerned about the breakdown of social solidarity amid rapid urbanization and industrialization, central authorities sponsored efforts at "community building," much as Home Ministry officials had done under the Local Improvement Campaign at the beginning of the century. In 1971, the New Life Campaign Association launched a drive to encourage "service to one's home town." The number of formally registered volunteers soared to more than one million in 1979; most took part as members of existing community groups. Their activities centered on tidying up roads, parks, shrines, and other public spaces—followed by serving as school-crossing guards, working with children and adolescents, and helping the recipients of social services.[85]

The New Life campaigns' most enduring legacy has been the "daily life schools" (seikatsu gakkō), which typically consist of short-term study groups of fifty to one hundred housewives in urban neighborhoods, villages, and towns. There were 2,063 such schools by 1981. Beginning in 1964, the New Life Campaign Association has actively coordinated and subsidized the operation of these study courses to elevate the "subjecthood (shutaisei) of those in charge of daily life"—that is, to permit housewives to educate themselves and speak their minds on such questions as consumer prices, product safety, welfare, and pollution. Participating women have been free to choose topics of immediate concern, yet the association and state officials have played a major role in selecting lecturers and influencing the course of study on a national basis. Not surprisingly, enrolled housewives have since the 1960s commonly studied techniques of financial "life planning" so as avoid destitution in old age, as well as methods of "rational" spending in an era of "mass consumption."[86]

"Turning Misfortunes into Blessings"

Although New Life campaigns and the government's related savings promotion efforts remained a normal part of civic life through the 1960s and 1970s, their persistence has attracted little scholarly attention. Most students of postwar Japanese history portray the early 1960s as the beginnings of a "consumer revolution."[87] After the cabinet of Ikeda Hayato unveiled what became the highly successful Plan to Double National Income in Ten Years in 1960, even the government appeared to favor increased consumer spending and marked improvements in living standards.[88] Concerted appeals to lead simple, frugal lives—particularly for the sake of the nation—presumably fell on deaf ears.

In fact, they did not. As Carol Gluck notes, notwithstanding the "emerging middle-class myth" of consumerism, life for large numbers of Japanese remained insecure.[89] Ordinary people continued to cope with high prices, inadequate public welfare, and an economy that depended on resources and markets beyond its borders. After a decade and a half of unprecedented economic growth, Japan in 1969 ranked second among non-Communist nations in terms of gross national product, but only twenty-second in per capita income.[90] New Life and savings campaigns thus retained their attractiveness as Japanese searched for new ways of rationalizing their lives within the limits set by a high-growth strategy, which, in actuality, restrained consumption in the interests of boosting savings and investment.

Throughout the twentieth century, the Japanese state and private groups have cooperated most effectively on behalf of social management in times of perceived crisis. This was true in the Russo-Japanese War, World War I, and the Fifteen Years' War, as well as in the "economic wars" and struggle for "national salvation" that followed the hostilities. In recent years, Japan's greatest crisis occurred in the form of the first "Oil Shock," when the OPEC nations embargoed oil in 1973–1974. The energy-dependent, export-oriented Japanese economy was beset by crippling inflation as oil prices soared. Japan's GNP, which had grown at an annual real rate of 9.44 percent from 1955 to 1973, abruptly declined 0.3 percent in 1974. At the level of everyday life, panic swept the nation in the face of skyrocketing prices and shortages of toilet paper and other daily necessities.

With the Oil Shock, the postwar strands of social management— savings promotion, social education, and New Life campaigns—came together with a force that led many Japanese to recall the austerity drives of the Pacific War and early postwar years.[91] Some officials greeted the

Oil Shock with barely suppressed glee, determined to reverse high-growth-era attitudes that held "consumption is beautiful." Prime Minister Tanaka Kakuei asked "each and everyone of our people to use this opportunity to refrain from wasting energy and to adopt the spirit of economizing."[92] The New Life Campaign Association had this to say: "We welcome this test, regarding it as an excellent opportunity to 'turn misfortune into a blessing,' and we will work to safeguard our own lives as we stabilize and better the lives of our posterity. We must deal resolutely with the problem of resources if we are to build a society in which we can live in true affluence. There can be no other way."[93]

The chief architect of the cabinet's policies to deflate prices by encouraging frugality was the deputy prime minister, Fukuda Takeo. As a young Bank of Japan official in 1946, he had supervised the first "National Salvation Savings Campaigns" and may have given them their name.[94] In the preface to the Economic Planning Agency's 1975 Whitepaper on National Life, Director-General Fukuda praised the Japanese people for stringent economizing during the previous year. Returning to the early postwar definition of "New Life" as getting by on less, Fukuda approvingly observed a long-term "change in consciousness of people's life from the past mass consumption and attitude to dispose [sic] things easily during the period of rapid growth to a more rational way of life through economizing."[95]

The government clearly had a hand in manufacturing this consciousness. The Prime Minister's Office structured public opinion polls so as to give respondents few choices but to agree with the statements: "We must try and economize even more" and "Economizing will not ruin the quality of life in terms of betterment of life, in terms of convenience, and in terms of spiritual well-being." Granted additional publicity by the media, the government then touted these surveys as proof that the people themselves believed "that greater affluence is not necessarily a good thing," and "that there is a need to put an appropriate limit to it."[96]

Only someone living the life of a hermit could have missed the austerity campaigns that swept the Japanese archipelago following the first Oil Shock. With the formation of the Central Coordinating Council of the People's Campaign to Value Resources and Energy in April 1974, government officials once again played a indispensable part in forging a broad coalition among private associations for the national good. The 113 participating groups represented consumers, women, educators, businesses, the media, and local governments. There was, in the words of Japan's largest women's organization, a remarkable "consensus among officials and private groups" on the council in support of conserving resources and energy.[97]

To disseminate their message, organizers of the People's Campaign to Value Resources and Energy deployed the many postwar mechanisms of social management. The Central Council for Savings Promotion got off to an early start in January 1974 with the Special Savings Campaign to Restrain Prices. The council mobilized its vast network of social education officials, 1,326 local savings promotion leaders, and 530 model savings districts. Hovering above the four largest cities were 133 advertising balloons. The nation's schools were again the site of vigorous efforts to teach children how to "value goods and money." And women's groups, which met together with savings promotion officials at the national and prefectural levels, eagerly conveyed to the neighborhoods the imperative to economize and keep household accounts.[98]

Other organizations, including the New Life Campaign Association, similarly exhorted the populace to practice frugality. They also urged citizens to conserve resources and energy—both to lessen Japan's dependence on foreign suppliers and to confront the nation's worsening environmental problems. The large national newspapers proved particularly helpful in spreading the word. The *Mainichi shimbun* in 1975 sponsored the first annual contest among elementary and junior high school students for the best essays on "Valuing Goods" in the interests of conservation.

Aided by a 2-million-yen special grant from the government, the New Life Campaign Association launched its own three-year Campaign to Value Resources in 1974. This updated version of the New Life campaign reached down to the community level—assisted by local women's associations, block associations (*chōnaikai*), and the recently created daily life schools. The campaign promoted recycling and water-conservation techniques while repeating the familiar imperative to avoid wastefulness, exercise restraint in consumption, and simplify ceremonial occasions. Campaign leaders were intent on creating "energy-conservation lifestyles," and they were prepared to go to great lengths to do so. During 1980 and 1981, local activists conducted nationwide "inspections" of 11,733 and 10,669 homes, respectively. According to the official history of the New Life Campaign Association, the campaign did much to change daily habits. Japanese were cutting back, even in the number of times they opened their refrigerators.[99]

The persistence of large-scale moral suasion campaigns into the early 1980s is evidence of significant continuity in relations between the Japanese state and society throughout the twentieth century. Yet it also raises important questions; whether and to what extent the postwar campaigns influenced actual behavior may be the thorniest. We know, for example, that postwar Japanese households have saved a substantial portion of their disposable income, ranking among the world's best savers. Household savings rates reached 21 to 23 percent in 1974–1978, at the height of the economizing campaigns. By most accounts, high rates of household savings fueled massive investment in industry, dampened inflation, and contributed mightily to Japan's postwar "economic miracle."[100]

Similarly, although household consumption of energy did not decline absolutely during the years of the most active conservation campaigns (1974–1980), the rate of increase slowed considerably from that of the preceding high-growth era. According to a poll by the Prime Minister's Office in 1980, a total of 83 percent replied that they were "concerned" or "very concerned" with economizing on energy.[101] Thanks to household conservation efforts and substantial energy saving in industry, Japan was able to import 11 percent less oil in 1980 than in the previous year, despite a healthy growth in GNP of 3.8 percent.[102]

Anecdotal evidence further suggests that a great many Japanese not only received the campaigns' messages, but often attempted to act upon them in daily life. In the wake of the first Oil Shock, one American scholar witnessed the impact of exhortation on a farm woman whose husband was a local Socialist leader. The male head of the local Agricultural Cooperative branch lectured members of the women's section, his suggestions smacking of "traditional Confucian moralism." Observed the incredulous American: "Haruko, however, who was usually so practical and independent-minded, listened respectfully as the speaker exhorted women to greater frugality, enjoining them to make their own clothes and to use water sparingly." When Haruko told her friend that she would try to spend less money, the scholar retorted:

> "But you don't seem extravagant as it is, . . . "Where would you economize?"
> "Toilet paper."
> "Toilet paper?"
> "People used to use newspaper. And I could save on food, too. . . ."[103]

It is possible that, in the absence of campaigns, the Japanese people might have saved just as much money and consumed just as little energy because of economic and institutional factors, such as high energy prices or preferential tax treatment of savings. However, such claims have been greeted with skepticism by the government agencies that generously funded the many suasion drives.[104] Central Council for Savings Promotion officials observed that Americans responded to inflation in the late 1970s by consuming more and taking on greater debt, whereas Japanese increased their rate of household savings in the face of the similarly inflationary environment following the 1973 and 1979 Oil Shocks. In the words of the Central Council in 1981, "we are convinced that maintaining a steady *savings attitude* in our household economy will definitely contribute to building up a firm foundation for achieving price stability and for improving productivity and our living standard."[105] Whether the campaigns induced Japanese to save more or not, their significance in terms of state-society relations is beyond dispute. Like their interwar and wartime predecessors, the postwar campaigns brought together government and private organizations in cooperative endeavors to influence everyday behavior.

Of course, as in the interwar period, the interests of the postwar state and participating groups were not necessarily identical. The Socialist party in the Lower House opposed the revision of the Social Education Law in 1959, when ruling conservatives and the Ministry of Education seemed determined to strip local groups involved in social education activities of their remaining autonomy. Citizens' movements and "daily life schools" likewise challenged the government's pro-business, high-growth policies by demanding antipollution measures and protection of consumers from unsafe products and foods.[106]

Nonetheless, in these and other cases, private groups and the government generally agreed on the fundamentals. The right wing of the Socialist party consistently supported and even initiated the New Life campaigns, social education programs, and officially sponsored efforts to strengthen social solidarity. And by the early 1970s, local environmental and New Life groups frequently cooperated with the government, which had come to embrace the cause of reducing pollution. Both sides recognized the compatibility of campaigns to induce conservation and campaigns to encourage economizing in daily life. Coinciding interests made alliances on behalf of social management all the more potent in the postwar era. The common quest to influence public behavior remained very much alive, even if some of the mechanisms and relationships changed in the years following Japan's defeat.

Sexual Politics and the
Feminization of Social Management

IN THE DECADES since 1945, popular interpretations of postwar Japan on both sides of the Pacific have clustered around two poles. At one end stand those who insist that a "New Japan" arose from the ashes of defeat—a Japan that would gradually adopt American-style values and institutions. Countering this vision of convergence, others highlight the existence of an immutable "national character," which over the centuries made the Japanese unique in the world and will continue to do so.

Both interpretations, however, are flawed. Contemporary Japan neither lacks a prewar history nor is it merely the carryover of an ancient society. The postwar era makes little sense unless placed within the context of important developments that emerged in the late nineteenth and early twentieth centuries. These developments distinguished state and society in imperial Japan (1868–1945) from their premodern antecedents. Likewise, prewar and wartime changes in social relations and political economy powerfully affected postwar Japan, as recent "transwar" scholarship demonstrates.[1] In the moral suasion campaigns, for example, evolving technologies of statecraft and expanding networks of intermediary groups enabled the government to continue intervening in everyday life beyond World War II and well into the late twentieth century. Similar continuities and changes have occurred since 1945 in the patterns of state-society relations in the areas of women's groups, prostitution, religion, and welfare.

POSTWAR WOMEN AND THE STATE

When American Occupation officials spoke of "emancipating" Japanese women after World War II, they meant not only emancipation from "feudal" customs but also liberation from a highly controlling state. Ironically, the state's ability to manage postwar Japanese society has relied to a greater extent than before 1945 on the active involvement of women and women's groups. The twentieth-century history of Japanese women is usually told as the story of interwar "progress," wartime setbacks, and postwar liberation and democratization. Yet for our purposes, it is more an evolutionary story of developing relationships between the state and women after 1920 that, if anything, grew stronger in the postwar era.

Indeed, the middle decades of the twentieth century—cutting across eras of war and peace—witnessed a remarkable shift in the gendered nature of state-society relations. During the early part of the century, males were overwhelmingly the ones who dealt directly with the state on a daily basis. Men were the conscripts, of course, but they also fulfilled public roles in their capacities as household heads, welfare-related district commissioners, and members of the myriad semiofficial organizations, ranging from agricultural cooperatives to reservists' associations.

The procession of interwar industrialization and wartime mobilization steadily removed adult males from the public life of their communities. These trends continued during the postwar years, as more and more men became blue-collar workers and salaried employees, working outside their neighborhoods and even in different locales.[2] Aside from the dwindling numbers of full-time farmers and shopkeepers who remain active in agricultural cooperatives and trade associations, today few Japanese men regularly come in contact with institutions of the state.

For a great many Japanese women, on the other hand, "the state" became a familiar presence in everyday life, both during and after World War II. As housewives and mothers, women gradually emerged as the state's primary intermediaries in managing society. They have been the ones who assist the schools in socializing children, serve in the PTAs, and take the popular "mothers' classes" and other social education courses at the citizens' public halls. Women have also formed the nuclei of the many local groups that participate in the ever-present national campaigns to promote savings, "New Life," traffic safety, and crime prevention. In the realm of volunteer social work, women have gradually replaced males as the influential district commissioners (renamed "welfare commissioners" in the postwar era). Women constituted 2 percent of commissioners in 1928 and 6 percent in 1942. Yet by 1992, they accounted for fully 46 percent of the 189,965 welfare commissioners.[3]

Regrettably, few students of gender relations have explored the political implications of these seemingly mundane relationships between women and the state. Much as historians equate the prewar "women's movement" with suffragist groups, accounts of postwar Japanese women focus narrowly on their role in electoral politics and oppositional movements. Looking back in 1977 on "the principal political activities" of early postwar women's groups, the veteran suffragist Ichikawa Fusae chose to profile only those organizations that demanded suffrage and gender equality, or that opposed the government's various attempts to revive aspects of the presurrender order.[4]

Scholars and journalists have devoted particular attention to the influence of women in party politics and elections.[5] Not surprisingly, the story has been one of occasional progress punctuated by frequent disappointments. Although women won thirty-nine seats in the first Lower House elections held under universal suffrage in 1946, their numbers declined to fifteen in 1947 and have not exceeded twelve to this day. In the pessimistic words of one historian, "the postwar years have produced few campaigns capable of capturing the imagination and interest of a significant number of [Japanese] women."[6]

We err, however, in defining women's activism in "politics" too narrowly. Millions of Japanese women have participated in what they regard as bona fide women's organizations, even if contemporary Americans would not consider such groups to be part of a "women's movement." The largest women's federations in the postwar era, as before 1945, have been composed of local women's associations and groups of housewives.

Be they local associations or explicitly "political" national organizations, Japanese women's groups have been less interested than American counterparts in the quest for strict gender equality. Having begun to extend the domestic sphere into public life before and during World War II, organized women preferred to advance a distinct "women's politics," in which they sought influence on the basis of their widely recognized identities as housewives, mothers, neighborhood activists, and guardians of public morality. Despite occasional tensions with state officials, their interests have generally coincided with those of postwar bureaucrats. The result has been the largely unseen but highly significant strengthening of earlier alliances between women and the state.

Many of these alignments solidified under the Allied Occupation and during the 1950s. The first months following Japan's defeat witnessed a flurry of national-level organizing by veterans of the interwar women's movements. Ichikawa Fusae and other prominent prewar suffragists set about reviving the campaign for women's suffrage, culminating in the formation of the New Japan Women's League (Shin Nihon Fujin Dōmei) in November 1945. Having survived the war intact, the Japanese Women's Christian Temperance Union similarly resumed its leadership of the movement to abolish licensed prostitution.

Several other women's groups appeared on the postwar scene for the first time, encouraged—directly or indirectly—by SCAP's policy to further the democratization of women's organizations. The best known was probably the Women's Democratic Club (Fujin Minshu Kurabu), led by

influential women in the Socialist and Communist parties.[7] Article 5 of
the Police Law of 1900, it will be recalled, had prevented women from
joining political parties, but the Japanese government, on orders from
SCAP, abrogated the entire law on November 21, 1945. The major parties thereupon sponsored women's sections, the most active emerging in
the Socialist party. After the Diet enacted a universal women's suffrage
law in December 1945, women assumed formal political roles as party
organizers and candidates. Women's sections also sprang up in labor
unions throughout Japan. In August 1946, only one year after Japan's
defeat, some 964,000 women belonged to unions, and accounted for
nearly one-fourth of all organized workers.[8]

Although these diverse groups insisted on their "autonomy" from the
state, they commonly defined the interests of women much as bureaucrats
and middle-class women had since the 1920s—as centered on home management, motherhood, and local civic life.[9] To be sure, left-wing women's
groups devoted a good deal of attention to improving the lot of women
workers, who constituted a significant portion of the labor force. In 1947,
these organizations lobbied successfully for the establishment of the
Women's and Minors' Bureau in the Ministry of Labor, and they strongly
supported the passage of the Labor Standards Law, which legislated both
equal pay and special protection for women workers.[10]

Nonetheless, most women's organizations sought to incorporate
women into the political process not simply because, as citizens, women
were entitled to the same rights as men but because—they argued—wives
and mothers were ultimately responsible for the stability of "daily life."
The picture they presented was not of the leisured, full-time housewife
but of the great mass of Japanese women, who struggled during and after
the war to maintain their families while toiling in the fields, factories, and
shops. Amid the deprivations of the early postwar years, many women
headed households before husbands and brothers returned from war, if
they returned at all. Endemic food shortages, in a sense, transformed
most adult women into "housewives." They were the ones, according
to women's leaders, who stood in line several hours a day to receive
rations.[11] Even the Women's Democratic Club, which initially focused its
appeals on working women, increasingly represented the Japanese
woman as "a consumer as well as a producer, a mother and a housewife
as well as a worker, and if either one of these two phases is neglected, the
woman's life as a whole can never be improved and her status is never
raised."[12]

It is equally noteworthy that Ichikawa Fusae's New Japan Women's
League, the leading postwar suffragist organization, demanded the vote
not as an end but a means to represent the voice of housewives and
mothers in politics. Although Ichikawa had once insisted on equal rights

for women and men, she had since the 1930s based her claims for women's political participation on their special abilities to "purify" and domesticate politics.[13] In its founding principles in November 1945, the New Japan Women's League mentioned neither gender equality nor working women. Rather, once suffrage was achieved, the first priority would be "to make direct connections between politics and the kitchen, work for the stabilization of daily life, and promote rationalization and use of cooperative means in household life." The influence of the prewar daily improvement movement on the suffragists was apparent. In one of its earliest acts during spring 1946, the league mounted a campaign to assist women in coping with food shortages by teaching them how to keep household accounts and even how to build their own scale to measure rationed rice.[14]

In choosing to emphasize women's special abilities to manage everyday life, postwar women's groups invariably allied with sympathetic state officials who seemed equally intent on improving daily life. Women's leaders had, for the most part, served the wartime regime in the Greater Japan Women's Association (1942–1945) and home-front mobilization efforts, and they entered the postwar era accustomed to cooperating with the state. On August 25, 1945, just ten days after the Japanese decision to surrender, Ichikawa Fusae and other prominent women organized the Women's Committee on Postwar Countermeasures (Sengo Taisaku Fujin Iinkai). Most accounts portray the committee as the genesis of the postwar suffrage movement, playing up the "liberal" and "independent" cast of the leaders—Ichikawa, Yamataka (Kaneko) Shigeri, Akamatsu Tsuneko, and Kawasaki Natsu.[15]

Yet a more careful reading clarifies that the Women's Committee on Postwar Countermeasures was not intended to challenge the state. Ichikawa deliberately invited some seventy women "who had occupied positions of leadership during the war." The invitees included several leaders of the defunct Greater Japan Women's Association and other wartime organizations, plus two women officials from the Ministry of Health and Welfare's National Health Section, which had overseen the Greater Japan Women's Association.[16]

The progressive founders of the Women's Committee were themselves no exception, each having openly collaborated with the wartime government. Ichikawa Fusae, who had held high-ranking posts in the Greater Japan Women's Association and sat on various mobilization councils, would be purged by SCAP in 1947 for her wartime activities. Akamatsu Tsuneko, a well-known socialist feminist, had worked in the Greater Japan Industrial Patriotic Association, the state-run labor front that had supplanted autonomous labor unions in 1940. Yamataka Shigeri, who went on to lead the postwar National Federation of Regional Women's Organizations (Zen Chifuren), had been the suffrage movement's most enthusiastic proponent of collaboration between 1935 and 1945. She had joined with bureaucrats on behalf of "election purification," assisted the wartime Ministry of Finance in encouraging women to save and be frugal, and worked for the wartime Ministry of Health and Welfare board that provided "guidance" to the families of war dead.[17]

When the Women's Committee held its general meeting on September 11, the quest for suffrage was but a minor issue of discussion. Participants instead concerned themselves with an array of urgent problems that faced women in the wake of Japan's defeat. Their five-point program was more in keeping with wartime social mobilization than with the "New Japan":

1. Let's continue wearing *mompe* [peasant pantaloons worn by most women during the war] on a daily basis as the functional clothes best suited to [re]building.

2. Along with working for increased production of food, let's offset insufficiencies by the way we prepare and eat food.

3. Let's continue saving, firmly warn [the people] against exchanging money for goods, and fight inflation.

4. Let's thank returning soldiers for their efforts from the bottom of our hearts and warmly welcome them back.

5. Let's put up a resolute front before the Allied Forces of Occupation, taking pride in Japanese womanhood [that is, safeguarding women from the sexual desires of foreign troops].[18]

Clearly the mission of women's groups to manage the lives of ordinary women had survived defeat and the demise of authoritarian rule.

Nor did women's leaders necessarily wish to abandon the wartime model of a state-supported, hierarchically organized national women's federation. The Ministry of Health and Welfare broached the subject of creating a national federation to replace the disbanded Greater Japan Women's Association soon after the Japanese surrender. At an October 2 meeting with former women officers of the wartime association—including the ubiquitous Ichikawa Fusae—the chief of the ministry's National Health Section recommended the formation of an umbrella organization so that the "opinions of women, who are presently the ones responsible for the stabilization and maintenance of national life" could be reflected in postwar administration. Rather than be offended by this bureaucratic attempt to organize women, the assembled women quickly agreed on the blueprint for a "Japan Women's Cooperation Association" (Nihon Fujin Kyōryokukai). After some debate, they resolved to create a central federation that would be based on the thousands of existing local women's associations, which the wartime regime had so recently mobilized.[19]

The Japan Women's Cooperation Association was formally inaugurated on November 6, 1945, and undoubtedly would have endured had it not been for SCAP's opposition. Referring to the defunct Greater Japan Women's Association, American officials criticized the Cooperation Association as "nothing but a replica of the old bureaucratic body." Funds for the new association came straight from the wartime body's remaining one million yen—monies that were controlled by the Ministry of Health and Welfare. Intense pressure from the Occupation persuaded the Japan Women's Cooperation Association to dissolve itself in January 1946.[20]

But this did not occur before several notable figures from the so-called autonomous women's groups had endorsed this latest partnership with the government. Yamataka Shigeri and Kawasaki Natsu, who subsequently became a Socialist member of parliament, played major roles in designing the body's hierarchical structure, and they both served on its central council. The original proposal for forming the Japan Women's Cooperation Association came from none other than Kubushiro Ochimi, the veteran head of the Women's Christian Temperance Union. Kubushiro urged women to organize the association to deal with the pressing problems of food and the sexual dangers posed by the occupying forces.[21]

The failure of the Japan Women's Cooperation Association severed many of the bonds between the bureaucracy and women's groups, yet the advent of New Life campaigns provided new opportunities for looser alliances. Except for Communist associations, women's groups embraced "New Life" as one of their most important missions—especially after the cabinet of the Christian socialist Katayama Tetsu launched its New Life campaign in 1947.

Some 180 representatives of women's organizations were invited to the prime minister's residence that July to form a women's council on behalf of the government-sponsored People's Campaign to Build a New Japan. The Women's Christian Temperance Union responded enthusiastically, calling on all women—in the parlance of wartime Japan—to "cooperate with national policy" (kokusaku ni kyōryoku). Assisted by the government, WCTU leaders rallied other women's organizations to mount a women's New Life campaign, which concentrated on elevating the "spirit of cooperation," teaching women how to improve nutrition, and simplifying ceremonial occasions. From the perspective of WCTU leaders, the women were not simply following the authorities. Rather, their role was to "spur on the government while cooperating with it," and in so doing, they would "develop one big women's movement nationwide that will establish New Life and truly build the New Japan." Also participating in this campaign was the venerable Hani Motoko, whose *Fujin no tomo* had been urging women to rationalize daily life since the early twentieth century. Composed of some 6,000 housewives in 140 branches, Hani's Friendship Society (Tomonokai) contributed to the drive by devising methods to "eliminate waste not only in food but in everything."[22]

In addition, many Socialist women looked favorably on the New Life campaigns, in part because "New Life" was associated from the start with the Socialist party and the Socialist-led Katayama cabinet. An influential supporter was Katō (Ishimoto) Shizue, prewar Japan's foremost proponent of birth control and one of the most progressive women elected to Lower House in 1946. Once in the Diet, she wrote to Madame Chiang Kai-shek, asking the leader of China's New Life movement to give Japanese women advice on starting their own.[23] To Katō and her followers, New Life campaigns also offered a means of teaching ordinary women about birth control and thus liberating them from the "slavish lot which is theirs." Knowledge of birth control, argued Katō, would enable them "to plan their lives" and "be freed from animal sexual desire."[24] She echoed the views of other Socialist champions of New Life, who maintained that Japanese women had developed more slowly than men because of "extremely unscientific home lives."[25]

Progressive national women's groups helped develop "connections between politics and the kitchen" in the public's mind. However, the real task of mobilizing ordinary housewives and mothers fell to new types of grass-roots organizations that sprang up in the late 1940s and 1950s. The popularity of these self-identified housewives' associations reflected both socioeconomic change and the positive value that rank-and-file women attached to the status of "housewife." The decades from the 1910s to the 1970s—except for the war years—mark Japan's "era of the housewife," observes the historian Kano Masanao. More and more women aspired to marry well-paid husbands and take on the essentially middle-class role of managing household affairs full-time. What was once a merely "dream" among daughters of workers, farmers, and shopkeepers became the socially recognized norm during the high-growth era of the 1950s and 1960s.[26] Although in 1955 close to 60 percent of the nation's women aged 15 and older participated in the labor force, by 1975 fewer than 46 percent of all Japanese women were employed.[27] Reinforcing the image of woman as wise mother and frugal homemaker were the mass-circulation housewives' magazines. *Shufu no tomo* had already established a substantial readership before World War II, but by 1952, according to one survey, it had become the third most popular magazine of any type in Japanese households, closely followed by three other housewives' magazines.[28]

More than any other early postwar group, the Japan Housewives Association (Shufu Rengōkai or Shufuren) defined the emerging relationship between women and power. The nationwide federation was founded in 1948 after housewives waged campaigns to eliminate the sale of faulty matches and lower the official prices of milk and other rationed necessities. The organization inherited some of the traits of those interwar groups that had sought to influence government policy by virtue of women's control over the household economy. Led by Oku Mumeo, a prewar activist of socialist leanings, however, the Housewives Association introduced a spirit of militancy not found in the prewar middle-class associations.[29] Housewives were encouraged to consider themselves "workers in the kitchen" who should "put the voice of the kitchen into politics."[30] The new symbol of "housewives' power" was the white-aproned demonstrator carrying a giant rice scoop (*shamoji*) as her placard. In recent decades, the Housewives Association has become famous for aggressive campaigns against price fixing and unsafe products.

Although scholars portray the Housewives Association as a fiercely independent consumer organization,[31] the group developed in close cooperation with the state, and its efforts to manage daily life went well beyond consumer protection. The federation grew rapidly during the late 1940s in part because of support from the government's Price Agency. Attempting to stabilize prices, the authorities relied on the Housewives Association to inform neighborhood women of the officially set prices and to dissuade them from turning to the black market.[32] Oku herself had energetically worked with the wartime regime on behalf of what she perceived as common projects to improve the lives of women. In addition to serving in the Imperial Rule Assistance Association and Greater Japan Women's Association, she had lectured women on the need to save, and was employed by the Ministry of Health and Welfare to help develop a female labor force in war-related industries.[33]

During the 1950s, savings and New Life campaigns repeatedly brought the Housewives Association and the state together. Future generations might claim Oku as the founder of Japan's consumers' movement, but the Oku of that time was more inclined to advise its members: "In place of consumption, strive for a life filled with imagination and resourcefulness. Unless the clever housewife maintains her household, this country will not rise."[34] The link between the housewife's frugality and economic nationalism filled the pages of the association's newsletter during this period. "Rationalization of daily life" was touted as the key to overcoming Japan's economic dependence on the United States. Calling on women in 1959 to "work hard to create national power," Oku revealed a managerial agenda worthy of turn-of-the-century Home Ministry bureaucrats: "We must thoroughly eliminate the waste in daily life and *cultivate many people* who will curb the dissipation of national power."[35]

The authorities would have been hard pressed to find a more willing ally in their campaigns to mold popular economic behavior. From the start, the Housewives Association did its part to "heighten the desire to save." Women were exhorted to budget wisely and, to help them along, the association distributed its own "housewives' notebooks" and account books. The government also received the association's support in the ongoing campaign to dampen the public's expectations of more expansive welfare programs. Although her federation lobbied for greater social security, Oku counseled that a "housewives' savings movement" remained the best means of improving life: "In this small nation, this nation without resources, this overpopulated nation, the state obviously cannot provide much [social] security."[36] The Housewives Association's propensities were particularly evident in New Life campaigns to discourage lavish expenditures on Christmas and New Year's festivities. Added to the normal end-of-the-year rituals in the late 1950s was that of association members cruising the streets in sound trucks, calling out to pedestrians to exercise "self-restraint."[37]

Nor did leaders of the Housewives Association balk at becoming a formal part of the state's apparatus for managing society. In 1954, Oku Mumeo eagerly accepted an invitation to become a member of the Central Council for Savings Promotion. Two years later she consented to sit on the first board of directors of the New Life Campaign Association. She and her successors have actively served on both councils ever since. And when officials opened a new savings drive, they could count on the Housewives Association to print parables of thrifty women in its newsletter and to cooperate on several other fronts.[38] Far from regarding their incorporation as co-optation, association leaders strove to participate in as many government commissions as possible, so as to maximize "the voice of women" in policies relating to daily life.[39]

The degree of cooperation between the government and putatively progressive groups like the Housewives Association is certainly noteworthy. Yet the vast majority of Japanese women participated in official programs of social management as members of residentially based women's associations (*chiiki fujinkai*). According to one government survey in 1949, some 6.1 million women belonged to women's organizations nationwide. Of the total of 8,853 groups, more than 90 percent (or 8,093) were residential or "regional" women's associations.[40] Most later affiliated with the National Federation of Regional Women's Organizations (Zen Chifuren), which claimed 7.8 million members and nearly 24,000 individual associations by the early 1960s. Many of these women also belonged to other local women's organizations linked to national federations. The National Council of War Widows' Organizations (Zenkoku Mibōjin Dantai Kyōgikai) recorded 870,000 members in the early 1960s, and the women's sections of the Agricultural Cooperatives (Nōkyō) boasted approximately 3 million members at the end of the 1970s.[41]

These postwar groups bore a striking resemblance to interwar and wartime women's associations. They usually enrolled most adult women living within a town, village, or urban neighborhood, and they increasingly formed the lowest level in national hierarchies—topped by prefectural federations and central organizations. The revival of the presurrender type of women's associations caught Occupation officials by surprise. Determined to democratize women's organizations, SCAP had sought to sever the historical ties between state-supported national federations and local women's groups. The Americans encouraged the growth of clubs made up of women with similar interests, rather than residentially based associations in which women had little choice but to join. Military Government Teams were instructed to stop Japanese officials from subsidizing women's associations. Local associations would be permitted to form only loose liaison councils, not the constraining prefectural federations of the past.[42]

Had SCAP succeeded in this program, the postwar Japanese women's movement might have evolved more autonomously from the state. However, as the Occupation neared its end in 1952, it was apparent that the Americans had failed to transform the organizational patterns of imperial Japan. Despite SCAP's opposition to prefectural federations of women's associations, such federations had been organized in fully 70 percent of Japan's forty-seven prefectures by the end of 1951. In some locales, women's associations succeeded in removing wives of officials and other elite women from leadership positions, or they protested attempts by prefectural governments to use the associations to carry out official tasks.[43] Nevertheless, most wartime women's associations continued essentially intact or quickly reconstituted themselves with minor changes. The Occupation eventually softened its initial hard line against the formation of national federations. War widows' organizations and women's sections of the agricultural cooperatives were allowed to establish national councils in 1950 and 1951, respectively. Facing greater resistance from SCAP, prefectural federations of residential women's associations chose to wait out the Occupation. In July 1952, their leaders inaugurated the National Federation of Regional Women's Organizations (Zenkoku Chiiki Fujin Dantai Renraku Kyōgikai or Zen Chifuren).[44]

The presurrender mode of women's organization resurfaced for several reasons. First, as we have seen, the Japanese government quietly thwarted

SCAP, instructing prefectural officials to revitalize residential women's associations in the months after defeat. Individual ministries had vested interests in retaining the services of local women as their "subcontractors" in various programs to manage society. These ranged from savings and New Life campaigns to social education and rural improvement.[45]

Second, the separation of males from local life during the war created in every village, town, and ward a core of civic-minded women who were eager to retain leadership. These women saw nothing problematic about collaborating with the authorities to revive the neighborhood associations or running their organizations' operations out of prefectural or municipal offices. They were more likely to resent interference from their foreign occupiers than from Japanese officials. Tensions abounded as Military Government Teams pressured prefectural women's federations to reconstruct themselves as American-style "democratic" organizations.[46] From the perspective of left-wing women, the persistence of local wartime leaders indicated a "lack of independent thinking" among Japanese women. The critics, however, granted that residential organizations had established strong foundations among the masses of women.[47]

Finally, Occupation officials themselves soon recognized the futility of destroying long-standing patterns of cooperation between Japanese authorities and local women. Like the Japanese government, SCAP found itself conversely encouraging the organization of local women's associations to accomplish other objectives of the Occupation. Well-organized women seemed the perfect vehicle for disseminating "social education" about the new constitution and electoral system, assisting American-style agricultural extension workers, and building a peaceful New Japan.[48]

The National Federation of Regional Women's Organizations' ties to the bureaucracy and conservative parties were obvious from its inception. The federation's inaugural meeting in July 1952 featured opening addresses by the welfare minister and the acting education minister of Yoshida Shigeru's conservative cabinet. Championing nationalist causes, the federation pledged to "mount vigorous campaigns to mitigate the sentences or win the release of convicted war criminals and to secure the return of all Japanese territory" taken by the Allied powers after World War II. In the late 1960s, the organization openly allied with right-wing groups to demand the reversion of the four northern islands seized by the Soviets in 1945.[49] Although the National Federation of Regional Women's Organizations was ostensibly nonpartisan, conservative candidates commonly mobilized local affiliates to drum up support.[50]

Government subsidies gave residential women's associations an added incentive to cooperate with the authorities. To take subsidies for carrying out "social education" activities and public policies struck most women's groups as perfectly normal. In one notable episode in 1957, the National

Federation of Regional Women's Organizations consolidated prefectural affiliates into seven regional "blocs." The initiative behind this major restructuring appears to have come from the state. By no coincidence, the costs of instituting the blocs were defrayed by a generous grant of 500,000 yen from the Central Council for Savings Promotion, which envisioned the new units as vital links in its national network. Officials would not be disappointed. Over the next decades, National Federation leaders came together regularly in bloc meetings—primarily to map out savings promotion strategies.[51]

The National Federation of Regional Women's Organizations by no means served as handmaid to the state on every issue. Together with the Housewives Association, the National Federation often took the lead, especially when advancing the political influence of women as wives and mothers. The founding of the New Life Campaign Association in 1955 owed much to initiatives by the two women's federations. During the preceding five years, both had sponsored several New Life women's conferences, as well as exhibitions of new kitchen products and labor-saving stratagems. Yamataka Shigeri, chairwomen of the National Federation, reminded male politicians that her organization had conducted its own New Life activities long before the government institutionalized the campaigns. Regarding New Life as essentially a movement by and for women, Yamataka became one of the New Life Campaign Association's first executive directors, and she proudly served on its board over the next two decades.[52]

In other instances, the National Federation of Regional Women's Organizations opposed conservative policies with unexpected fervor. In 1954, politicians in the ruling Liberal Party recommended altering the postwar constitution and revised Civil Code (1948) so as to resurrect aspects of prewar family law. They hoped to subordinate individual family members and real property to the authority of the "household" (*ie*)—in most cases, meaning the patriarch. The National Federation joined the Housewives Association and other women's groups to squelch this attempt to "revive the family system." What united the organizations was not so much a deep-seated belief in individual rights as the fear that the Japanese woman, who had evolved as the mainstay of the family, would be relegated to her former lowly position.[53]

"ECONOMIZING MAMAS ARE ON THE RISE"

Since the 1960s, many observers have predicted the rise of a women's movement eager to assert its autonomy from the conservative establishment and bureaucratic state. From their perspective, all signs point to the

gradual disappearance of the housewives' and residential women's associations that had so often functioned as the lowest level of administration.
As large numbers of housewives reentered the work force beginning in the
1970s, they had less time to devote to local civic associations. The proliferation of high-rise apartments and increased mobility further chipped
away at the communal solidarity underlying residential associations.[54]
Even the Housewives Association and the National Federation of Regional Women's Organizations, which had previously striven to "rationalize" consumption, increasingly mounted consumerist campaigns to resist price increases and improve product safety. The 1970s also witnessed
the appearance of more self-consciously feminist groups. The "second-
wave" feminists questioned the cozy relationships between the older
women's groups and the state, and they sought to advance the position of
women in the workplace and political life, as well as within the domestic
sphere.[55]

These trends notwithstanding, reports of the death of women as state
agents have, to paraphrase Mark Twain, been exaggerated. The gendered
basis of Japanese women's participation in public life has not fundamentally changed since the interwar era, even if new elements have appeared.
Whether they work outside the home or not, wives are still held responsible for education, household finances, and the health and welfare of their
families and communities. The imperative to ally with the authorities to
make improvements in these areas may have diminished, but it has hardly
disappeared.

Savings promotion remains one key arena of cooperation. In retrospect, the 1950s marked not the high point but the beginning of institutionalized ties between women's groups and the government. To com-
memorate the wedding of Crown Prince (and present emperor) Akihito in
1959, leading women's groups co-organized the first annual "National
Women's Meeting for 'New Life and Savings.'" The annual meetings
continue to this day, sponsored by the Central Council for Savings Promotion and the state-funded New Life Campaign Association—with the
full cooperation of the Housewives Association, the National Federation
of Regional Women's Organizations, the National Council of Agricultural Cooperative Women's Organizations, the National Council of War
Widows' Organizations, and other groups.

The government-sponsored "women's meetings" attracted hundreds
of organized women from the start. Attendees listened to speeches by
officials and experts while discussing strategies for fostering savings and
economizing at the grass roots. Remarkably enough, delegates continued
to struggle with the challenge of reducing expenditures on ritual life well
into the 1980s, a decade of growing affluence.[56] The zeal with which
women's groups took part in the annual meetings flowed not only from

their desire to improve daily life. As a former chief secretary of the House-wives Association observed, savings promotion officials accomplished for women's organizations what the women had failed to do by them-selves. The New Life and savings meetings provided the opportunity for the major groups, which had previously quarreled with one another, to unify around a cause.[57] It is more than a little ironic that the Japanese "women's movement" was in part forged within the crucible of the state.

Alliances between organized women and the state became strained in the late 1960s and early 1970s, when public resentments about wors-ening pollution burst into a full-fledged environmental movement. Women's groups, including affiliates of the Housewives Association and the National Federation of Regional Women's Organizations, furnished much of the dynamism behind these "citizens' movements." Many activ-ists had grown disillusioned with the entrenched Liberal Democratic party and found themselves forming alliances with left-wing local govern-ments and parties.[58] Antipollution protests meshed well with the orga-nized womens' long-standing identification with daily life. The Oil Shock of 1973–1974 occasioned unprecedented criticism of official policies from an environmentalist standpoint. Meeting in January 1974, the Housewives Association, the National Federation of Regional Women's Organizations, and other associations attacked the government and busi-ness community for having pursued high-growth economic strategies with little commitment to conserving and recycling resources. They in-sisted that the authorities also do something about soaring prices and crippling shortages in daily necessities.[59]

As it turned out, environmentally minded women and the bureaucrats soon discovered common ground. Contrary to the predictions of many, the Oil Shock had the effect of stimulating a new round of cooperative arrangements between women's organizations and the state. Many of the measures the women proposed as solutions to environmental problems revitalized the economizing messages of the earlier New Life campaigns. Their prescriptions accorded nicely with the bureaucracy's own desire to restrain consumption and decrease Japanese dependence on resources from abroad. Wholeheartedly supporting the idea of nationwide cam-paign to persuade the populace to "value resources and energy," the Housewives Association took issue with the government only for being a Johnny-come-lately to the fight against "mass production" and "mass consumption." The self-proclaimed consumer group even criticized the Liberal Democratic cabinet for attempting to stimulate consumer demand as part of the government's counter-recession policy.[60]

The Oil Shock afforded women's groups the opportunity to reassert their power to change the daily habits of the nation. Working through its local associations, the National Federation of Regional Women's Organizations embarked on a campaign to encourage recycling and economizing on water and energy, to foster the spread of markets for exchanging un-needed goods, and—of course—to support the "simplification of ceremonial occasions." The Japanese people are not known for consuming vast quantities of food, which is relatively expensive, yet one of the federation's activities in 1976 involved surveying 20,000 homes and 1,000 restaurants in a drive to induce economizing on food. Federation women were dismayed to discover that 51 percent of respondents regularly left some of their rice, while a whopping 65 percent admitted to not finishing everything else on their plate.[61] In view of these efforts at social micromanagement after the Oil Shock, it is little wonder that women's groups in the mid-1970s recalled feeling "as if we were returning to the era immediately following defeat. The realization that we'd soon be up to our necks in overproduction and overconsumption spurred on the movement to reexamine daily life."[62] But to some critics, the incessant calls to "economize" that were sounded in housewives' magazines and the campaigns recalled the war itself.[63]

And as in the war and immediate postwar eras, the leading women's groups avidly cooperated with the state. In 1975, women's and consumers' organizations enthusiastically responded to the government's invitations to join the Central Council of the People's Campaign to Value Resources and Energy. Yamataka Shigeri, the indefatigable proponent of cooperation for more than a half century and head of the National Federation of Regional Women's Organizations, presided over the Central Council of the People's Campaign until her death in 1977.[64] The Housewives Association continued to criticize the ministries for subsidizing and stage-managing the "people's campaign." Yet it, too, openly accepted official monies from the Economic Planning Agency to conduct surveys of "waste" in housewives' lives. The Housewives Association was obviously intent on creating, as well as measuring, economic norms. To the obvious delight of the bureaucrats, the association reported that the great majority of housewives surveyed had shifted from "wasteful modes to economizing modes," following the Oil Shock.[65] The findings of another of its surveys was summed up in the association newsletter's exuberant headline: "Economizing Mamas Are on the Rise."[66]

As we fathom Japan in the 1990s, Americans might contemplate the consequences of the historically close connections between the Japanese government's anticonsumption policies and the major postwar women's groups. The consumer movement, which significantly overlaps with the women's federations and their affiliates, does not necessarily share its American counterpart's interest in lowering prices as the highest priority. In Japanese urban neighborhoods, groups that call themselves "consumers' organizations" often spend much of their time working with the

authorities to promote savings, recycling, and other environmental projects.[67] Their priorities may be related to the fact that consumer information centers, operated by central and local governments, have trained and
certified leaders of local consumers' groups since the late 1960s. At its
annual seminar for consumers' leaders, the Japan Consumer Information
Center sets a national agenda for participating groups. Seminars in the
last several years have emphasized such environmental activities as recycling and improving the safety of agricultural produce.[68] When one
also considers that farm women make up a significant portion of the large
national women's federations, it is not surprising that prominent consumers' groups strenuously opposed efforts to liberalize the import of rice
over the last two decades. Japanese rice sold for as much as five times
the U.S. price prior to the government's partial liberalization in 1993.
The Housewives Association, nevertheless, supported protectionist policies, claiming that foreign rice posed health hazards to Japanese consumers, endangered the livelihood of farmers, and eroded Japan's "self-
sufficiency."[69]

In addition to helping shape economic behavior, women's groups
continue to play highly visible roles in managing local society on other
fronts. Parent-teacher associations, which Americans established under
the Occupation, enable activist women and the centrally administered
schools to instruct mothers in child rearing, hygiene, and household management.[70] In the area of social work, housewives today constitute the
core of more than 4 million local volunteers. Efforts on behalf of crime
prevention and traffic safety date back to World War II, when women
assumed responsibilities for self-policing at the neighborhood level. Although SCAP nominally disbanded the wartime neighborhood associations, it did not prevent postwar police officials from creating "mother's
societies" (*haha no kai*) to act as their eyes and ears in maintaining
order.[71] The nation's semiannual traffic-safety campaigns vividly harness
the regulatory propensities of local women, as illustrated by a mid-1970s
description of the city of Kurashiki's "traffic safety mother's association":

> The mothers don yellow sashes and hold yellow flags to help children cross
> streets near schools, urge pedestrians to use pedestrian bridges over railroad
> tracks, and actively participate in traffic-safety campaigns. During one cam-
> paign in Kurashiki, the mothers lined up along a busy street for the purpose
> of "glaring at and embarrassing" drivers who violated the law.[72]

Whether organized women should have aligned themselves so intimately with the state's objectives remains a crucial question as women's
leaders contemplate the future. Many bristle at charges that they have
dutifully followed the lead of postwar governments. They prefer to highlight their dynamic role in persuading bureaucrats and politicians to im-

prove daily life. Seeking to empower women as the mainstays of family, community, and society, the major groups generally believe they have done a better job of protecting women from economic insecurity and marginalization than American feminists who insist on equality of opportunity and the elevation of women as individuals. Nevertheless, the persistent patterns of interdependence between women's organizations and the state have, without question, constrained the development of a more autonomous women's movement in postwar Japan. Recognizing the problem, women's leaders have struggled to maintain their independence while collaborating with the government in pursuit of common goals. That is why mainstream groups so often protested bureaucratic interference, even as they participated in official campaigns. The inherent tensions led Housewives Association officers in 1958 to conclude in words that resonate today: "When one takes money [subsidies], one cannot say what one would like. That's the state of the supposedly autonomous women's associations."[73]

The ramifications for state-society relations are equally profound. As men withdrew from civic life over the past half century, women's groups provided the indispensable intermediaries in nearly every one of the state's programs of social management. What gave these interventionist efforts added force was, ironically, postwar democratization. In contrast to top-down mobilization by the wartime regime, larger numbers of women in a far greater variety of groups organized their own campaigns for their own reasons—even if most drives ultimately intersected with those of the state. There were, however, instances in which the state and women's organizations clashed in their respective attempts to manage society. It is to those that we next turn.

"ARE THERE NO MOTHERS IN TOKYO?": REGULATING POSTWAR SEXUALITY

Although women gained the vote in 1946, women's groups in postwar Japan remained wary of pursuing their interests primarily through "politics," by which they meant elections, parties, and the parliamentary process.[74] One can point to remarkably few pieces of important legislation that passed due to agitation by a concerted women's movement. Convinced that male politicians in the Diet invariably marginalized "women's issues," women's leaders—much as before World War II—found it more efficacious to influence policymaking in alliance with bureaucrats and by participating in the authoritative commissions attached to various ministries and agencies.

To many in the media, the House of Councilors' election in 1989 signaled the dawning of a new "era of women" in politics. Women won an
unprecedented twenty-two seats in the so-called Madonna Boom. The
ruling Liberal Democratic party lost control of the upper house for
the first time in its thirty-four-year history, reportedly having incurred the
wrath of the nation's homemakers.[75] In retrospect, however, the 1989
election did not mark the advent of an oppositional women's bloc or a
fundamental redefinition of gender roles. Rather, the large women's
groups, which had historically supported the ruling party and bureaucracy on most issues, temporarily chastised the Liberal Democratic party
for its many perceived affronts against Japanese women in their roles as
housewives and mothers. As savers and consumers, women protested
the cabinet's introduction of a 3 percent consumption tax; as farmers or
consumer activists, they opposed the government's moves toward im-
porting allegedly unhealthy foreign rice; and as champions of civic
"purity," they were appalled by the latest money scandal involving LDP
politicians.

Yet the issue that most united women, progressive and conservative,
was one of sexual morality. Shortly before the election, Prime Minister
Uno Sōsuke was revealed not only to have kept a geisha as a mistress, but
(worse in the eyes of many Japanese) to have treated her callously, to the
point of failing to give her a traditional parting gift when he ended the
affair. More than fifty women's groups, including the Housewives Association and the Japanese Women's Christian Temperance Union, collectively protested Uno's behavior, and scores of women heckled the prime
minister whenever he spoke. Uno resigned in disgrace after his party suffered unprecedented defeat in the upper house election.[76]

Never before had women's organizations played such a prominent role
in political change. But in many respects, their attack on the prime minister's infidelities was simply the latest development in the twentieth-
century evolution of a women's movement that most successfully influenced politics and policy when it acted as the guardian of public morality.

The postwar identification of women with moral reform would not
have been obvious in the early years of the century. Men in the Salvation
Army and Purity Society participated in the movement to abolish licensed
prostitution just as vigorously as women. The abolitionist camp was held
together, above all, by its Protestant core, rather than by a feminism that
rallied women of various ideological stripes. As late as the 1920s, Ichikawa Fusae and other suffragists distanced themselves from what they
regarded as the WCTU's moralistic preoccupation with prostitution.[77]
Local women's associations generally accepted prostitution as a normal
part of the household economy of the poor.

In the course of the 1930s and war years, however, non-Christian

women's organizations joined Protestant groups on behalf of moral reform. From Ichikawa's League for Women's Suffrage to the bureaucratically organized women's federations, they demanded not only the abolition of licensed prostitution but also tougher regulation of cafés, dance
halls, and the chastity of young women and men.[78] Activists increasingly
asserted women's natural role as mothers and moral regulators. Concerned about the rising number of male students who frequented cafés,
mah-jongg parlors, and pool halls in the mid-1930s, the WCTU's
Kubushiro recalled asking herself: "Are there no mothers in Tokyo?"[79]

Organized women emerged from World War II with a firmer resolve to
curb prostitution, yet they confronted a state that remained committed to
the essentials of the presurrender system of licensed prostitution. In August 1945, the Home Ministry established the Recreation and Amusement Association and mobilized as many as seventy thousand Japanese
"comfort women" to serve the occupying forces, still convinced that mar-
ginal women could be used to prevent rape and the spread of venereal
disease. Officially recognized prostitution was a bit much for the Americans. The United States command soon placed the "amusement centers"
off-limits to military personnel, and the RAA was disbanded. SCAP further ordered the Japanese government to abolish the institution of licensed prostitution and to nullify all contracts that, directly or indirectly,
bound women to prostitution. On February 2, 1946, with great reluctance, the Home Ministry abrogated the Rules Regulating Licensed Prostitutes of 1900, the legal basis of licensed prostitution for nearly half a
century.[80]

In the ensuing months, Japanese authorities scrambled to replace the
defunct institution of licensed prostitution with a looser regulatory regime. They were no more inclined to take a laissez-faire approach than
their predecessors had been, following the promulgation of Ordinance
Liberating Prostitutes in 1872. Officials voiced alarmed at the appearance
of tens of thousands of unregulated "streetwalkers" (*yami no onna*) or
"pan-pan girls," as American servicemen called them. Many were former
"comfort women" forced onto the streets after the RAA's "amusement
centers" were shut down, although most were amateurs. Like the café
waitresses and unlicensed prostitutes of the interwar era, streetwalkers
posed a greater threat to the state, and to middle-class society, than licensed prostitutes. Scattered throughout the cities, they were difficult to
police and more likely to carry venereal diseases. Unlike the idealized
licensed prostitute, the pan-pan girl was commonly regarded as anything
but the self-sacrificing victim of family poverty. In one survey of 5,225
streetwalkers arrested in May 1947, only 47 percent claimed to have been
motivated by hardships in their lives, while fully 24 percent replied that
they had taken up prostitution out of "curiosity."[81]

On November 14, 1946, the government adopted a new policy that was to regulate prostitution for the next twelve years. To a certain extent, officials aimed at protecting prostitutes. Contracts of prostitution and agreements to repay advance money would be recognized as void, and those who contractually obligated women to work as prostitutes would be punished. To prevent women from falling into prostitution, the authorities pledged to grant public assistance to poor women on a broader scale. And for the first time, the government established in the major cities and elsewhere "women's welfare centers," which were designed to retrain former prostitutes in "proper living" and "healthy work."[82]

These protective features aside, the new policy rested upon the assumptions and practices of the past, as officials explained at the time: "Prostitution, from the viewpoint of society, is a necessary evil. It protects ordinary girls, sequesters these zones of prostitution from the rest of society, and curbs the spread of venereal disease. We therefore grant de facto recognition (*mokunin*) to these activities."[83] Brothels were summarily redesignated "special bars and restaurants"; licensed quarters became "special zones regulated by the police"; and former licensed prostitutes were thenceforth termed "entertainers" (*settaifu*). Prostitutes working in the special zones remained subject to periodic, compulsory medical examinations. The special zones soon became known as "red-line zones" because of the color used to demarcate them on police maps. Much as the interwar police had also attempted to regulate unlicensed areas, other concentrations of prostitutes were marked off with a "blue line."[84] In 1952, nearly four hundred of the prewar licensed quarters continued to operate as red-line zones; the number of prostitutes working in all red-line zones totaled approximately forty-five thousand.[85]

The government's regulatory policy, moreover, retained the prewar penchant for vigorously suppressing streetwalkers, who practiced their trade outside the recognized establishments and zones. Police were empowered to arrest anyone who they had reason to believe was a "habitual prostitute." Those detained were compelled to undergo medical inspections and, if found to be infected, would be sent to the hospital for treatment. Police arrested 17,871 suspected prostitutes nationwide during the first five months of 1947 alone. False arrests of young working women occurred frequently.[86]

The principle of accepting and regulating prostitution easily survived the Occupation's reform efforts, in a word, because supporters were many and detractors few. Even United States military authorities tacitly acknowledged the advantages of having GIs spend their time in well-policed establishments with medically inspected prostitutes, rather than picking up free-lance streetwalkers.[87] Nor was most of the Japanese public ready to abandon a venerable Japanese institution. In a poll by the government's National Public Opinion Survey Office in 1949, 70 percent of respondents favored the policy of regulating prostitution by means of the special zones. As justifications, they cited the time-honored litany. Not only did supervised prostitution safeguard ordinary girls and limit the spread of venereal disease, but "in these days of marital problems, it is a necessary evil that satisfies the instincts of males." As antiprostitution proponents sadly admitted, many well-educated people and mothers were among those who believed that the existence of prostitution protected respectable girls.[88]

Besides, Japanese political culture continued to tolerate extramarital liaisons with prostitutes, geisha, and mistresses at the highest levels of power. While on the campaign trail shortly after the war, a rival candidate accused Miki Bukichi, a leading conservative politician, of behaving shamefully when he returned home from Tokyo accompanied by three mistresses. "The number of women was *five*, not three," corrected Miki to raucous applause.[89]

But if the Americans and most of Japanese society accepted the existence of officially recognized prostitution, more and more women's groups did not. The struggle against prostitution soon involved nearly every major women's organization in Japan. In 1951, the WCTU and four other women's groups formed the Council to Oppose the Revival of the System of Licensed Prostitution. They feared that the government and conservative parties would reinstate the prewar system once the Occupation ended. Imperial Ordinance Number 9 (1947) had theretofore constrained brothel prostitution, punishing those who caused women to prostitute themselves or who concluded contracts to that effect. Yet the measure—along with other Occupation-era ordinances—was scheduled to lapse six months after the restoration of Japanese sovereignty in April 1952. Swelling to include eighty groups, the antiprostitution forces persuaded the Diet to enact the ordinance into law in 1952 after gathering an unprecedented 960,000 signatures.

Emboldened, they turned their sights on the passage of a statute that would outlaw prostitution itself. A familiar face, Kubushiro Ochimi of the WCTU, headed the renamed Council to Promote the Enactment of an Antiprostitution Law, but the alliance drew in many new elements from the larger women's movement. In addition to Ichikawa Fusae's Japanese League of Women's Voters, the Housewives Association, and the national PTA, the most noteworthy recruit was the generally conservative National Federation of Regional Women's Organizations, which rallied its millions to bring about a "nation without prostitution."[90]

The consolidation of a Japanese women's movement around the cause of antiprostitution may be explained in several ways. At the most elemental level, prostitution became bound up with deep-seated Japanese

anxieties about racial contamination and racial subordination by the occupying forces. Matrons who had not been particularly disturbed when
prostitution seemed a matter between Japanese men and women expressed new-found disgust for postwar prostitution, which they often
equated with the young women who mixed with American servicemen
during the Occupation and 1950s. Safeguarding Japanese women from
rapacious GIs loomed as the most urgent issue among the influential
figures who organized the Women's Committee on Postwar Countermeasures in August 1945. In a widely read women's magazine in 1946, the
distinguished suffragist and physician Takeuchi Shigeyo further warned
of the "eugenic problem of mixed blood." Unions with the foreigners
resulted in a "difficult delivery" for the mother, judged Dr. Takeuchi,
so "chastity must be prized for the sake of our descendants."[91] During
the 1950s, antiprostitution groups focused much of their attention on
the problems of "mixed-blood children" and the rampant prostitution
surrounding the more than two thousand U.S. military installations,
which remained after the Occupation as the result of the Korean War and
lingering Cold War.[92]

The growing clout of the antiprostitution movement was also related
to postwar democratization. Divided into left-wing and right-wing parties between 1951 and 1955, Japanese socialists were nonetheless unified
in fervently supporting the enactment of antiprostitution legislation. Socialists had been a minor force in the interwar Diet, but they emerged as
a formidable political force standing between the two major conservative
parties from 1946 to 1955. In addition, although women candidates
failed to win many Diet seats despite postwar enfranchisement, female
members of parliament overcame party divisions in 1953 to form a vocal
bloc in favor of eliminating prostitution. As in other policy areas,
women's groups took advantage of their new inclusion in several government commissions, while informally allying with sympathetic officials.
The creation of the Women's and Children's Bureau (Ministry of Labor),
in particular, offered women a bureaucratic advocate that had not existed
in the prewar era. In December 1952, the bureau's advisory Women's and
Minors' Problems Commission played a pivotal role in advancing the
fortunes of antiprostitution legislation. Chaired by the socialist Diet-
woman, Kamichika Ichiko, the commission recommended an end to regulation and an outright ban on prostitution.[93]

Finally, prostitution emerged squarely as a "women's issue" as Japanese women took to regarding themselves primarily as mothers, and
women's groups attacked prostitution in terms of its ill effects on the
sexual mores of daughters and sons. In 1955, a number of women's
leaders came together to form the Mothers' Congress (Hahaoya Taikai).
The new organization prominently demanded the extirpation of prostitu-

tion, the abolition of military bases, and the protection of children from sexually explicit movies, comics, and toys.[94] Intent on inculcating a "new morality" among young people, the maternalist movement overlapped significantly with the New Life campaigns. The New Life Campaign Association similarly pledged to eradicate prostitution and stimulant drugs, "foster concepts of purity," "encourage healthy entertainments," and "eliminate harmful publications, movies, and other materials."[95] Leaders of the National Federation of Regional Women's Organizations grew so incensed at the prevalence of pornographic movies that in 1955 they founded the Sakura Film Company. Commissioned to produce films for children and mothers, the outfit was billed as the "mothers' production" company because nearly all of its stock was held by mothers. How to purge one's community of disease-carrying insects was the subject of its first widely distributed movie, "Sayonara, Mosquitoes and Flies."[96]

In their determination to wipe out—rather than deregulate—all forms of commercial sex, postwar women inherited earlier Christian propensities to rely on the state to impose their own vision of public morality. Just as prewar abolitionists have generally been depicted as liberals, most scholars uncritically portray the postwar antiprostitution movement as the champion of "human rights."[97] In actuality, few postwar women's leaders recognized the right of the prostitute to practice her trade if she so chose. The Japanese women's movement was often more eager than the state itself to manage the sexuality of prostitutes and their customers.

Influential women recommended a highly suppressive policy from the start. Responding to the Home Ministry's request for advice in autumn 1946, the WCTU's Kubushiro Ochimi advocated the prohibition of "acts of prostitution by anyone." She urged the police to register "habitual prostitutes" on "black lists," insisting that the authorities be given powers to inspect the homes of such women "at any time of the day."[98] Chaired by the WCTU's Gauntlett Tsune and including Ichikawa Fusae and other leading women, the government's advisory Central Council for Women's Welfare advanced a similar position the following year. The body recommended that the police be empowered to arrest suspected prostitutes and enter any premises frequented by them. The council also favored revising the Venereal Disease Prevention Law to allow the "compulsory examination of those suspected of prostitution." Most influential were the proposals for sweeping rehabilitative policies that would morally reform prostitutes and teach them a "proper trade." The council recommended enactment of legislation that would permit compulsory incarceration in a "women's home . . . because very few fallen women would presently enter a women's home . . . on their own."[99]

The contours of the women's movement's antiprostitution legislation emerged in recommendations made by the Women's and Minors'

Problems Commission in 1952. Its report served as the basis of the several "bills to punish prostitution," which Dietwomen and the socialist parties introduced from 1953 to 1955. Along with subsequent "bills to punish prostitution," the commission's proposed legislation would have criminalized the act of prostitution in all its aspects—punishing the customer, those who profited from the prostitution of others, and the prostitute herself. In addition, those women who prostituted themselves for economic reasons would be placed in rehabilitative facilities and trained in "proper trades," whereas "those deficient in spirit and the flesh [i.e., sexually deviant] . . . should be placed in long-term protective facilities and be [actively] supervised."[100]

The conservative parties fought to defend the early postwar system of regulation, but the specter of thousands of local women's associations campaigning against pro-prostitution candidates nationwide wore down their resistance. After the Democratic and Liberal parties blocked the socialists' bill to punish prostitution in July 1955, the Democratic party's Hatoyama cabinet promised to offer its own measure. The Liberal and Democratic parties merged to form the Liberal Democratic party that November. In May 1956, the Diet enacted the LDP government's bill. The Antiprostitution Law went into effect on April 1, 1957, except for the penal provisions, which were enforced on April 1, 1958. The statute effectively proscribed large-scale brothel prostitution, and it eliminated the openly regulated zones of the prewar and early postwar eras. The Antiprostitution Law severely punished those in "the business" of furnishing places for prostitution or making others prostitute themselves. The act of prostitution itself was not made a punishable offense, unless the prostitute solicited a client in public.[101]

Although the socialists and most women's groups eventually endorsed the government's antiprostitution bill in 1956, they vociferously criticized the lack of criminal sanctions against the prostitute and her customer. They also lobbied to strengthen the provisions establishing rehabilitative institutions for ex-prostitutes. It was not a "Law to Prohibit Prostitution," sighed WCTU leaders, but merely a "Law to Curb Prostitution."[102]

One might have expected the socialists to have adopted a liberal perspective toward acts of prostitution, representing the prostitute as a worker compelled to eke out a living in a harsh economic structure. At least that was the way that many prostitutes regarded themselves. In early 1956, some 4,500 "entertainers" in red-line zones formed the Federation of Tokyo Women Employees' Unions (Tōkyō-to Joshi Jūgyōin Kumiai Rengōkai) for the purposes of improving working conditions and resisting legislative efforts to abolish their livelihood. But if they expected sympathy from the Socialist party, they were sadly mistaken. The antiprostitution forces dismissed the entertainers' federation as a front for the prostitution industry, and the two male labor organizers who had helped form the union were summarily expelled from the Socialist party.[103]

The socialists instead approached the problem of prostitution with the same moral absolutism and statist propensities as middle-class women's groups. The socialist Dietwomen Kamichika Ichiko was chief sponsor of the 1955 "bill to punish prostitution." Kamichika had not always been a paragon of middle-class morality. As a young woman in 1916, she shot and wounded the anarchist Ōsugi Sakae, a married man with whom she was having an affair, after Ōsugi jilted her for another prominent feminist. By 1955, however, Kamichika was insisting that prostitutes be punished so as to "cause women to reflect on their deeds." This well-known feminist accorded no rights to prostitutes, for they undermined the dignity of middle-class women. Therefore, "we must punish the estimated five hundred thousand prostitutes to protect the life styles of forty million housewives."[104]

In his critique of the government's antiprostitution bill in 1956, the socialist Lower House member Inomata Kōzō similarly argued that if the state considered prostitution an evil and a crime, "it therefore should be punished." The measure should also single out "habitual prostitutes" for more severe penalties, he urged. In a bizarre twist, the socialist deputy urged the bill's drafters to unshackle the state: "If we do not give the authorities the legal power to investigate prostitutes and their customers as suspects, how will the authorities be able to conduct raids on these people?"[105]

For their part, bureaucrats and conservative politicians were no more opposed to managing sexuality than socialists and women's groups. Nonetheless, having lost the battle to preserve a de facto licensed system in the form of red-line zones, representatives of the government sounded uncharacteristically liberal in their opposition to rounding up thousands of prostitutes. It was neither practical nor compassionate for women's groups to treat the estimated 500,000 prostitutes as criminals, asserted the ruling Democratic party in 1955, because most young women turned to the trade out of poverty brought on by war, food shortages, and other catastrophes beyond their control.[106] Responding to socialist demands for the arrests of prostitutes and customers, the parliamentary vice minister of justice explained that "in today's times when human rights are respected," gathering evidence of sexual acts would invariably "infringe on human rights." The government would punish public solicitation, but "we have no intention of breaking in on couples and catching them in the act."[107]

Although women's groups celebrated the passage of the Antiprostitution Law as a watershed in the political history of Japanese women, we might more fully reflect on its impact on actual policies toward illicit sexuality. With the enforcement of the Antiprostitution Law in 1958, women's organizations won a victory of sorts. They had broken the back of the regulatory approach that had governed Japan's pleasure quarters for centuries. No longer would prostitution be a legitimate industry recognized by the state. Nor would the authorities maintain the powers to register and inspect prostitutes—to the frustration of present-day Japanese officials who wish to limit the spread of AIDS.[108] Determined to change the mores of the nation, middle-class women's leaders were particularly pleased that the Antiprostitution Law condemned prostitution as contrary to "the dignity of human beings, sexual morals, and good manners of society," even if it did not punish most acts of prostitution.

Women's organizations were less successful when it came to managing the morality of lower-class women. The antiprostitution movement had long lobbied for a law that would have sent thousands of displaced or arrested prostitutes to nationally funded rehabilitation facilities. Under the Antiprostitution Law, subsidized women's groups operated some of these facilities, and prefectures and municipalities employed part-time "women's consultants" to discern "women needing rehabilitation." The government, on the other hand, did not envision guidance and rehabilitative facilities as a central element in its antiprostitution policies. Those placed in women's protective facilities in the law's first year of enforcement totaled only 2,400 women, a tiny fraction of the 133,000 officially estimated prostitutes in 1957.[109]

During the 1960s, Dietwomen joined opposition parties in several failed attempts to strengthen the morally reformative aspects of the Antiprostitution Law. The first such revision in 1961 was sponsored, interestingly enough, by the progressive heroes of the prewar women's movement—Akamatsu Tsuneko, Ichikawa Fusae, and Oku Mumeo. Their amendments would have permitted imprisonment or fining of prostitutes and customers. They would have also extended the term of incarceration in guidance facilities for prostitutes deemed unable to return to society.[110]

The women's movement failed, above all, to transform the morality of a society that tolerated prostitution as a normal sexual outlet for husbands and single men alike. This fact of Japanese life, in turn, enfeebled efforts to destroy the resilient sex industry. According to one official survey, more than two-thirds of the proprietors forced out of the prostitution business in 1958 simply converted their operations to restaurants, inns, cabarets, bars, cafés, and other establishments in which prostitution probably continued.[111] The most visible of the new forms of prostitution were the Turkish baths, or "soaplands" as they came to be called in the 1980s, after Turkish diplomats protested. As the Prime Minister's Office explained in 1973 with bureaucratic precision, Turkish baths were places where "in the privacy of individual bathrooms, nearly naked 'Miss Turkos' offer customers such services as washes, massages," and commonly sexual intercourse.[112] In 1981, officials counted 18,342 women working in private-room bathhouses. By the early 1970s, resourceful entrepreneurs had discovered another way of organizing prostitution—sex tours to neighboring Asian countries. In 1991 alone, nearly 2 million Japanese men traveled to Thailand, South Korea, or Taiwan, the vast majority of whom visited prostitutes as part of package deals.[113]

Rather than admit defeat, women's groups have remained united in their struggle to stamp out prostitution in all of its manifestations. Led by Ichikawa Fusae and stalwarts in the WCTU, they attempted to outlaw Turkish bathhouses during the 1960s and 1970s. Turkish baths, they charged, were tantamount to the revival of licensed prostitution, for under the Public Morals Enterprises Law, police were able to concentrate and regulate the bathhouses within designated zones. Women's organizations have also joined together since the early 1970s in several unsuccessful campaigns to stop Japanese travel agencies from operating sex tours.[114]

The issue of prostitution divided middle-class women and the state as no other question has in postwar Japan, pitting the proponents of two very different styles of social management. This contentious relationship is not at all like the partnership prevailing during the 1930s and war years, when women and other moral reformers allied with the regime to shut down cafés and police young people. That alliance had led to a more sweeping regulation of morality than either the authorities or women's groups could have accomplished by themselves. The clash over prostitution after 1945 further contrasts with the cooperative relationships between women and the state in other areas of postwar life, in which common interests in inculcating "economic morality" and orderly behavior resulted in the extraordinarily effective management of society.

In the end, the contest over how to regulate sexual morality resulted not in the triumph of one type of social management over the other, but in the overall weakening of the postwar state's ability to interfere in the realm of illicit sexuality. Women's groups generally frustrated the authorities' historical preference for tightly monitoring and even encouraging prostitution within special zones. The government, for its part, blunted the suppressive potential of the women's movement's moral crusade because officials were sentimentally and pragmatically opposed to eradicating the "necessary evil." Neither side intended to liberalize Japanese society, yet the loosening of controls was the consequence of their ongoing skirmishes.

Managing Spiritual Life and
Material Well-Being

CHANGING RELATIONS BETWEEN
STATE AND RELIGION

IN CONTRAST with other areas, relations between the state and postwar religions exhibit the clearest signs of a rupture with the presurrender past. In none of the other areas we have considered did the Allied Occupation so effectively sever the ties between government and private groups, nor so powerfully guarantee the autonomy of these groups from official interference. Only in recent years have there been major movements to revive aspects of prewar managerial policies toward religions, and their success in rolling back the Occupation settlement remains to be seen.

The role of religion in social management before 1945 varied over time and according to the type of religious group. After being ignored and in some cases persecuted by the state after 1868, the established Buddhist, Christian, and Shinto sects and denominations gradually emerged as active intermediaries in the government's many moral suasion campaigns. They did so alongside the state-controlled Shinto shrines. The established religions tolerated and frequently sought substantial state regulation of their activities, particularly when official intervention and recognition seemed to further their interests. The so-called new religions, on the other hand, suffered increasing marginalization and outright suppression, even as the established religious bodies assumed roles within the governing apparatus. In the 1930s, the state's "campaigns to eradicate the evil cults" became all the more virulent because of strong support from the established religions, the press, and some of the nations' most modern-thinking men and women. The final and shortest-lived development in these dynamic relationships was the wartime elevation of State Shinto and the draconian consolidation of the established religions.

The triangular relationships among the state, established religions, and new religions that existed before World War II would probably have continued after 1945 had it not been for decisive intervention by SCAP. Nearly all religious groups welcomed the Occupation's disestablishment of State Shinto, as well as firmer guarantees of religious freedom from the types of control imposed by the wartime regime. The established religions were less enthusiastic, however, about terminating long-standing cooperative arrangements with the state. In the early months of the Occupation, the Ministry of Education routinely mobilized "religious associations of various sects" in nationwide social education campaigns aimed at inculcating a sense of "service to the state and society" among youth, women, and laborers. Heartened by the government's expressed intent to "cultivate religious sentiment" as part of the campaigns, religious organizations participated as actively in these and later New Life campaigns as they had in the past. Christian groups were often the most avid.[1]

Moreover, the established religions were no more eager to apply the freedom of religion to all religions and clergy than they had been before the war. After SCAP in October 1945 ordered the abrogation of the wartime Religious Organizations Law (1939), many sects and denominations demanded that the state continue to regulate and "recognize" religious bodies by means of a new statute. Buddhist and Shinto organizations again looked to the government to protect their hierarchies from secession by constituent units. Equally remarkable, a number of religious groups (including six Christian denominations) pressed for a new ordinance that would impose special controls, if not outright prohibition, on "unhealthy or injurious" sects—a reference to the new religions.[2]

Occupation officials could well have resigned themselves to the persistence of close ties between the government and religions, much as they tacitly recognized the continued existence of the wartime residential women's associations. Instead the Americans resolved to make fundamental changes in state-religion relations. And in this they succeeded. Their passion flowed from Allied outrage over the wartime role of State Shinto in fostering ultranationalism while compelling Japanese of all other religions to worship at the shrines. The Department of War film, "Know Your Enemy—Japan," tersely summed up U.S. thinking on Shinto at the time:

> Now on the surface, Shintoism seems to be a nice quaint religion for a nice quaint people, and in the olden days, it used to be just that. But today, there's a diabolical joker in Shintoism, for since about 1870, the state has forced into the teachings of Shinto a mad, fanatical doctrine—a doctrine that has brought suffering and death to untold millions of innocent Asiatics, and now, to thousands upon thousands of Americans.[3]

SCAP's immediate goal was not to disband shrine Shinto as a religion but rather to transform it into a bona fide creed, totally removed from government control. In the "Shrine Directive" of December 15, 1945, SCAP banned any form of official sponsorship of, control over, or financial support to Shinto or Shinto shrines. The wartime Shrine Board was abolished, and for the first time since 1877 the Home Ministry lacked the power to employ the nationwide system of shrines in its far-ranging programs of social management. Shrines were placed on an equal footing with other religious bodies. Prewar Shinto leaders and former Home Ministry officials thereupon founded the nongovernmental Association of Shinto Shrines (Jinja Honchō) to administer most of the shrines.[4]

Determined to prevent the Japanese government from ever again patronizing one cult to the detriment of other religions, the Occupation's legal specialists drafted one of most unconditional guarantees of the freedom of religion in the world. The Meiji Constitution of 1889 had ambiguously proclaimed the freedom of religious belief "within limits not prejudicial to peace and order, and not antagonistic to their [the Japanese people's] duties as subjects." In contrast, Article 20 of the constitution of 1946 guaranteed freedom of religion "to all," further banning the state and its organs from conducting "religious education or any other religious activity." In addition, Japan's postwar constitution separated not only shrine Shinto but all religions from the state more thoroughly than any of its Western counterparts. Article 89, as we have seen, prohibited the expenditure of public funds either to maintain religious institutions or religious associations or to finance private charitable and educational enterprises—including those run by religious organizations. Such provisions went beyond even United States constitutional law, which condoned the use of public funds, say, to pay chaplains in the armed forces and support religiously run social services.[5] The new constitution profoundly altered the mechanisms of presurrender social management, eliminating religious bodies and the shrines as major agents of the state.

Within the realm of statutory law, the Occupation further stripped the state of its prewar powers to police the internal affairs of religious organizations. No longer could the authorities determine which religions should be legally recognized and which constituted "pseudo religions." Enacted toward the end of the Occupation, the Religious Corporation Law (Shūkyō Hōjinhō) of 1951 effectively protected postwar religions from the type of official interference experienced before 1945. The law's main purpose was to permit religious organizations to register as incorporated entities and thereby own property and conduct business affairs that advanced the work of the religion. Other laws were concurrently amended to exempt or partially exempt religious corporations from taxation. Although SCAP's Religious and Cultural Resources Division did not initiate the legislation, its officers insisted on inserting several safeguards against interventionist acts by the state. The Religious Corporation Law barred the authorities from mediating or interfering "in religious matters such as faith, discipline, usages, etc." Religious organizations also gained certain rights not enjoyed by other groups in Japanese society. A religious corporation could bring suit against tax officials if they conducted raids that disrespected the "religious characteristics and customs" of the religion or interfered with the "freedom of faith."[6]

The Religious Corporation Law did give the state some powers. The government was permitted to dissolve a religious organization *as a corporation* if the group perpetuated "acts which clearly can be recognized as having violated laws and ordinances and have done considerable harm to public welfare." However, unlike the Religious Organizations Law of 1939, the Religious Corporation Law did not grant the competent minister of state the power to make that determination. Rather this became a matter for the courts, with the religious corporation given the opportunity to protest and have a judgment suspended.[7] The process is such that not one religious corporation was disbanded for having committed the stipulated acts in the forty-four years following the law's passage in 1951.

The Occupation thus granted postwar religious organizations a remarkably strong constitutional-legal position, which bore little resemblance to that of their prewar predecessors. The most apparent result has been the unfettered proliferation of new religions. Several of the Shintoist sects suppressed during the 1930s and war years resurfaced and expanded under the favorable conditions after 1945. These included Ōmotokyō, Sekai Kyūseikyō, Hommichi (formerly Tenri Hommichi), and Hitonomichi Kyōdan, which changed its name to PL Kyōdan (short for "Perfect Liberty"). Other burgeoning religions were newer and derived from the Buddhist Lotus tradition—notably Reiyūkai, Risshō Kōseikai, and Sōka Gakkai. Whereas the largest interwar new religions had counted fewer than half a million believers, Risshō Kōseikai attracted one million adherents by 1955, and conservative estimates of Sōka Gakkai's membership in the late 1960s started at three to five million individuals. These sects thrived amid early postwar dislocations, rapid urbanization, and the declining attractiveness of established Buddhism. They also succeeded in offering positive roles to large numbers of housewives and other women.[8] Furthermore, encouraged by the ease of registering as independent corporations, many groups and temples simply seceded from established Buddhist and Shinto organizations.[9]

In addition, the Occupation empowered new societal forces that act as watchdogs against conservative attempts to harness religion in the service of social management. Isolated and persecuted, the new religions had exercised little political influence in the prewar era. Their position in postwar politics stands in marked contrast. In 1951, leading new religions banded together to form the Union of New Religious Organizations in Japan, united by their obvious interests in protecting the principles of religious freedom and separation of religion and state. The rapidly expanding Sōka Gakkai went further, running candidates for public office since the mid-1950s. In 1964, Sōka Gakkai founded its own political party, the Kōmeitō (Clean Government party). Capable of mobilizing millions of loyal voters, the Kōmeitō established itself as the third largest party in the Lower House during the 1970s. Schisms within the Liberal Democratic party in 1993 ushered in the present era of fluid alignments among the parties. In the reconsolidation that followed, Kōmeitō became a key rival of the LDP, due to its central position within the New Frontier party (Shinshintō, established 1994). Few of the new religions could be considered politically radical, and since the early 1970s several have contributed heavily to the Liberal Democratic party and recently to the other conservative parties. At the same time, the growing influence of the sects within these parties repeatedly inhibited conservative efforts to revise the Religious Corporations Law and otherwise to weaken the separation of state and religion.[10]

The fate of the ruling party's attempts to revive aspects of State Shinto is a case in point. Many in the LDP and right-wing circles deeply resented the Occupation's separation of state and Shinto. Echoing the imperial officials of the past, they maintained that the shrines were not religious but rather should be the sites of public rituals designed to foster a sense of belonging to the nation state. Their attention centered on reinstating government support for the Yasukuni Shrine, which has enshrined the spirits of Japan's war dead since its establishment in 1869. On five separate occasions between 1969 and 1974, the LDP introduced legislation to make Yasukuni a state-supported institution. Since 1976, prime ministers and their cabinets have also routinely paid tribute to the nation's war dead at annual ceremonies commemorating Japan's surrender in 1945, although every prime minister but Nakasone Yasuhiro in 1985 claimed to be doing so as a private individual.

Western and Asian media have long reported these developments as evidence of a resurgence of the old Japan. But the bigger story may be that efforts to resuscitate the prewar style of spiritual management have continually run into a brick wall. The Yasukuni Shrine bills went down to defeat all five times because of impassioned resistance from the Kōmeitō, other opposition parties, and a coalition of religious groups. Christian and certain Buddhist denominations were joined by the ever-vigilant Union of New Religious Organizations, led by Risshō Kōseikai and PL Kyōdan. Conservatives and their religious opponents will probably continue to skirmish over the issue of the state and Shinto. But, as Helen Hardacre remarks, in contrast to the prewar situation, "no single party has hegemony in formulating the content of tradition and the meaning of its symbols."[11]

The Occupation settlement has generally held firm concerning the state and Shinto, yet major tensions persist in the state and public's relations with the new religions. The principle of nonintervention in the affairs of the burgeoning sects did not come naturally to the Japanese bureaucracy. Although SCAP disbanded the Special Higher Police and its "religions police" in 1945, American officials were dismayed to learn that the Attorney General's Office operated a special section for the investigation of religious bodies as late as spring 1951. Several new religions—including the prewar victims Tenri Hommichi and PL Kyōdan—once again experienced campaigns of intimidation and even threats of dissolution at the hands of investigators during the last years of the Occupation.[12] Nor did the rest of society necessarily discard prewar images of the new religions as superstitious "cults" that rejected science and fleeced the wealth of followers.[13] The opulence of some sects today further convinces much of the public that new religions, in general, operate as mere fronts for greedy confidence men who take advantage of the postwar freedom of religion and their groups' tax-exempt status.

The meteoric rise of Sōka Gakkai injected an additional element into society's long-standing hostility toward new religions. The sect became notorious during the 1950s for its aggressive proselytizing methods, which sometimes involved surrounding a person's home and even using violence. Pressures to vote for the group's candidates at election time were also brought to bear on members and nonmembers alike. As the Kōmeitō grew into a major political force, the press and intellectuals expressed alarm at the appearance of a religiously based party. The Kōmeitō, they feared, would impose a theocracy should it come to power. After the Sōka Gakkai and Kōmeitō employed bribery and intimidation to prevent the sale of two books critical of their organizations in 1969, the Socialist and Communist parties pressed for a parliamentary investigation of their rival.[14] The Sōka Gakkai thereafter periodically came in for public criticism, but no mass movement surfaced to demand tighter restrictions on religious organizations.

That is, until 1995. On March 20, a terrorist act in the Tokyo subways brought the Japanese public's deep-seated anxieties about new religions to the surface. The carefully orchestrated nerve-gas attack killed 12 people and sent more than 5,500 to hospitals. Police quickly uncovered evidence linking the crime to Aum Shinrikyō (Aum Supreme Truth), a 10,000-member sect under the charismatic leadership of Asahara Shōkō

FIGURE 15. Police apprehend Asahara Shōkō, leader of Aum Shinrikyō, May 1995.

(see Figure 15). Confessions by Aum leaders subsequently established that the sect had previously carried out a series of kidnappings and murders. Aum functioned as a veritable government within a government, stockpiling deadly Sarin gas, smuggling in a Russian helicopter, and even forming its own ministries in imitation of the hated Japanese state.[15]

The heinous and random nature of Aum's alleged crimes did a great deal to soften postwar Japanese society's inhibitions against using state power to regulate religious organizations. Reminiscent of the prewar raids on Ōmotokyō, tens of thousands of police raided some two hundred Aum facilities nationwide, acting on orders to use "every legal means possible" to establish a connection to the gassing. More than two hundred adherents were arrested in the next two months, most on unrelated minor charges, including traffic violations.[16] The police investigation drew overwhelming praise from the public—the only open criticism, observed one press account, coming from "politicians, lawyers, and TV commentators urging them [the police] to step up their inquiry."[17] By late June, a total of 223 prefectural and municipal assemblies had adopted resolutions or requests calling on the government to disband Aum.[18]

In the ensuing months, attention shifted from the fate of Aum to a fundamental reexamination of the postwar legal structure that had seemingly permitted a violent cult to operate for years as a legally registered religious corporation. To be sure, the state possessed an array of laws that could be applied to apprehend religious leaders and disband religious corporations should they be linked to criminal activity, particularly of a violent nature. And in 1995, officials showed little hesitation in enforcing them against Aum. Having secured court approval under the provisions of the Religious Corporation Law of 1951, the government revoked Aum's status as a religious corporation and began seizing the group's assets. The assets would be liquidated and transferred to the cult's victims and their families as compensation. The authorities also commenced proceedings to destroy the organization itself, using the Subversive Activities Prevention Law of 1952. Enacted to control left-wing groups but never before enforced, the law would empower the state to stop Aum from propagating its dogma, collecting donations, and conducting most other activities.[19]

The availability of these legal weapons did not, however, deter politicians, bureaucrats, and leading newspapers from demanding the revision of the Religious Corporation Law so as to grant the government greater powers of supervision over religious bodies.[20] Their campaign received strong support from the Japanese people, who as in the interwar era looked to the state to safeguard society from the perceived transgressions of heterodox religions. According to a much-cited poll by the *Yomiuri shimbun* in June 1995, fully 85 percent of those surveyed favored revisions in the Religious Corporation Law, while only 11 percent opposed changes.[21]

Buoyed by public opinion, the government introduced to the Diet a bill to amend the Religious Corporation Law in autumn 1995. Changes were proposed in two areas. Religious corporations that operated in more than one prefecture would be placed under the jurisdiction of the central government's Cultural Affairs Agency, a part of the Ministry of Education. Most nationwide religious organizations had theretofore registered with a single prefectural office, making it difficult for authorities to monitor their activities in other prefectures. The proposed centralization of authority, explained one LDP Diet member, would strengthen the government's ability to "supervise and guide" religious corporations under the law.[22] Second, the bill required religious corporations to submit records of their financial conditions to the Cultural Affairs Agency or prefectural officials. If the authorities suspected a group of expending monies on nonreligious activities, they would be empowered to question its representatives. To discourage the misuse of an organization's funds, the legislation also guaranteed access to these documents by members and other concerned parties.[23] Government spokesmen insisted that the amendments did not sanction interference in the religious affairs of groups.

Several of Japan's influential religious organizations thought otherwise. Their opposition to the cabinet's revision bill transformed this debate over state and religion into the most contentious issue facing Japanese politics in autumn 1995. When the Ministry of Education presented the draft revision bill to its fifteen-member advisory Juridical Persons Council, seven of the eleven representatives of religious bodies reportedly voiced either opposition or requests for more cautious deliberation. The government chose to ignore their pleas. Leading denominations from all three major religions—Sōka Gakkai, Konkōkyō, and United Church of Christ in Japan—denounced the revisions in absolute terms. Many others, led by Tenrikyō and the Buddhist sect Tendaishū, accepted some of the changes, yet opposed the hasty effort to transform the forty-four-year-old law. Religious organizations—particularly new religions—were not keen on exposing their sometimes questionable financial practices to official scrutiny. But they also warned that changes in the Religious Corporation Law would open the door to re-creating the prewar mechanisms used to police and oppress religions. Critics further charged the Liberal Democratic party, the largest party in Murayama Tomiichi's coalition cabinet, with promoting the revisions for political reasons—that is, to permit the government to eviscerate the fundraising ability of Sōka Gakkai, whose Kōmeitō had become the dominant force within the opposition New Frontier party.[24]

Indeed, alarm at the growing political power of the new religions united the LDP, the Socialist party, and the Japan Communist party behind the effort to revise the Religious Corporation Law.[25] Although the media were puzzled by this alliance of conservatives and leftists, it bore a remarkable resemblance to the coalition of bureaucrats and secular progressives who supported the state's campaigns to manage and suppress new sects during the interwar era. The cabinet's bill targeted not only violent cults like Aum, but also, as LDP leaders acknowledged, those religious groups—namely, the Sōka Gakkai—that supported parties seeking to come to power. In the words of the party's secretary-general Katō Kōichi, "It's OK for religious organizations to be interested in politics, especially issues like *human rights, peace and social welfare*, but when they try to get into the core of public power, it's another story. We have to protect our authority of government from the dominance of a specific religious organization."[26] Led by Prime Minister Murayama, the Socialist party unequivocally supported the LDP's revision initiative, despite the Left's postwar history of vocally defending the separation of state and religion. The Socialists may have simply been attempting to appease their coalition cabinet partners, the Liberal Democrats, although that would not explain support by the Communists, who were most definitely out of power. The Left's endorsement of stronger state controls over religious bodies derived in large part from its decades-old rivalry with the new religions to win over working-class and lower-middle-class Japanese.

The ruling coalition succeeded in enacting the revision of the Religious Corporation Law in December 1995. Only time will tell whether the passage of the amended law signaled a return to substantial controls over religious organizations. But one thing is certain: at century's end, yet another of the Occupation's efforts to check Japanese propensities to manage society is under attack.

Fashioning a "Japanese-Style Welfare Society"

The postwar evolution of Japanese welfare policy has had its own controversies. Debates center not on whether to retain or jettison early postwar reforms, but on the fate of more recent changes. Whereas Occupation authorities aggressively separated state and religion, they were less intent on revamping the Japanese government's prewar policies with respect to poverty and welfare. In the absence of transformative pressures from SCAP, social welfare programs expanded only modestly during the 1950s and 1960s, while retaining many of the managerial and tightfisted aspects of the prewar system. During those decades, as Table 2 indicates, the Japanese government spent a far smaller proportion of its gross domestic product than Western counterparts on social security (including public social insurance, health care, social services, and public assistance).

What happened next has been the subject of widely varying interpretations. In the early 1970s, the government sponsored major expansions in health care, pensions, and various programs for the elderly. No sooner had it done so than the Japanese economy experienced the Oil Shock of 1973–1974, and conservative elites proclaimed the new imperative of reining in previous welfare commitments. By 1979, Liberal Democratic governments openly embraced the goal of fashioning a distinctive "Japanese-style welfare society," in which the state need not provide European levels of support because the Japanese family system and traditional communal solidarity remain strong.

The actual impact of these dramatic policy changes is open to question. Is Japanese welfare indeed developing along a path different from that taken by European welfare states? In the 1980s, many observers took government leaders at their word when they pledged to institute a "Japanese-style welfare society." Scholars commonly expected Japanese social programs to maintain a "distinctive welfare mix," which would set them apart from European counterparts for the foreseeable future.[27] Others dissented, noting the steady expansion of Japanese social spending since the early 1970s. For them, the big story has been the conservatives' failure

TABLE 2

Social Security Expenditure as a Percentage of GDP

	1960	1970	1980	1990	1992
Japan	4.9%	5.6%	11.1%	12.4%	12.4%
United States	6.8	9.3	12.4	14.1	15.6
United Kingdom	10.8	13.7	18.3	19.8	22.8
West Germany*	15.4	17.1	25.0	23.8	27.3
France	13.2	15.1	23.5	26.0	27.3
Sweden	10.9	18.6	30.4	32.6	37.1

Sources: International Labour Office, *The Cost of Social Security, 1978–1980*, pp. 56–59, and *The Cost of Social Security, 1984–1986*, pp. 79–84; Organisation for Economic Co-operation and Development, *Social Expenditure Statistics of OECD Member Countries*, p. 19.

* 1992 figure is for the united Germany.

to stop Japan from taking on the trappings of a modern welfare state. John Campbell recently predicted that by 2010 Japan's expenditure on social security (as a percentage of GDP) would place it in the intermediate ranks of Western industrial nations—above the United States, Canada, and the United Kingdom, though well below France, Germany, and Sweden. To Campbell, talk of a distinctive Japanese trajectory is just that—talk. The "Japanese-style welfare society," he insists, "is essentially ideology, evocations of a past ideal, whether real or mythical, by a conservative elite hoping to obscure a reality that has already changed."[28]

My historical study of twentieth-century Japanese welfare suggests that ideology does matter. This is particularly true when those ideologies have been manufactured or appropriated by elites to dampen popular expectations of state assistance and, conversely, to encourage familial and communal support. Contemporary Japanese society and the government are, without question, a good deal more committed to state-sponsored welfare than either was at the century's start. Nonetheless, the precise shape and limitations of the Japanese welfare system remain influenced by the persistence of prewar attitudes and institutions.

If the Occupation did not embark on a wholesale reformation of Japanese welfare policies in 1945, this was no doubt because American political culture shared some of Japan's misgivings about the type of comprehensive welfare states that were gaining favor in European nations at the time. SCAP provided emergency relief to the myriad victims of food shortages, unemployment, and other war-related dislocations, but it was reluctant to institute or expand universal programs for old-age pensions and national health insurance. In some respects, presurrender Japan had

advanced further toward the ideal of universal coverage than had its occupiers. The Japanese people had been more or less covered by a National
Health Insurance Law since 1938, whereas contemporary Americans
were not—and still are not. Although many in SCAP's Public Health and
Welfare Section (PH&W) were "New Dealers" who had participated in
social reforms in the United States, they were constrained by conservative
watchdogs back home. Fearing that the Occupation would promote progressive social security programs, the American Medical Association in
1948 dispatched a delegation to Japan to criticize PH&W's alleged ex-
perimentation with health insurance schemes that the American public
opposed.[29] In the area of public assistance, PH&W's social work experts
brought with them ideas of individual responsibility that would hardly
have displeased prewar Japanese bureaucrats. As explained by the chief
of the section's Public Assistance and Child Welfare Branch, recipients
had a "responsibility" to get off welfare as fast as possible to relieve the
taxpayers, who were "one's friends and neighbors." Able-bodied members of recipient families should be required to find work, he insisted.[30]

Nevertheless, the Occupation did introduce some changes that departed from prewar welfare policy. At the prodding of SCAP, the Ministry of Health and Welfare drafted and the Diet enacted the Daily Life
Security Law of 1946. Revised in 1950, the measure remains the center-
piece of public assistance legislation to this day. In formulating the law,
American officials sought, above all, to eliminate the discriminatory and
preferential aspects of presurrender relief programs. The Relief and Protection Law of 1929 had permitted the authorities to deny assistance if
they deemed applicants to be able-bodied or of bad character. Moreover,
some of the indigent—particularly the families of dead or wounded servicemen—had been singled out for preferential treatment and more generous assistance. In contrast, the Daily Life Security Law covered most
categories of the needy, superseding the Relief and Protection Law, Military Assistance Law, and other presurrender relief measures. It further
established, in principle, the entitlement of the needy to public assistance,
regardless of the cause of one's predicament.

The Occupation also introduced the concept of a legal "right" to request support from the state. The postwar constitution of 1946 included
Article 25, which stated that

> All people have the right to maintain the minimum standards of whole-
> some and cultured living.
> In all spheres of life, the State shall use its endeavors for the promotion
> and extension of social welfare and security, and of public health.

Although the origins of Article 25 are obscure, it appears that the Americans inserted the guarantee of an individual's right to a minimum living

standard.[31] Article 25 did not immediately result in the Japanese government's recognition of a right to claim state assistance. Nor did it prevent the authorities from systematically providing levels of support inadequate to maintain "the minimum standards of wholesome and cultured living."[32] On the other hand, Japanese claimants could, for the first time, legally contest relief policies on constitutional grounds. The government was eventually compelled to raise the levels of public assistance significantly in the wake of a series of cases, beginning with the highly publicized suit brought by Asahi Shigeru in 1957.[33]

Although eager to democratize the principles behind social welfare, Occupation authorities proved less willing or able to reform the moralistic and managerial nature of prewar Japanese policies toward poverty. In the making of the Daily Life Security Law of 1946, Ministry of Health and Welfare bureaucrats effectively undercut SCAP directives to assist all of the needy, regardless of the cause of their misfortune. Article 2 of the enacted law prominently excluded the following from receiving assistance:

1. Persons who, in spite of their being capable of doing so, have no will to work or persons who neglect work or persons who make no effort maintaining their living.

2. Persons of indifferent behavior.[34]

These clauses gave administrators broad discretion in determining eligibility, and they recalled the prewar Relief and Protection Law, under which the Home Ministry had denied benefits to those whose "conduct is conspicuously bad or lazy." Ministry of Health and Welfare officials obtained PH&W's understanding that "indifferent behavior" would be defined as "drinking, gambling, and whoring."[35] Wary of recognizing a right to relief, ministry officials likewise excluded from the Daily Life Security Law any provision for applicants to appeal decisions denying them assistance.

In 1950, the government substantially revised the Daily Life Security Law, in large part to conform with Article 25 of the postwar constitution. The right to a minimum standard of "wholesome and cultured living," which had theretofore existed only on paper, was given meaning by the establishment of an appeals process. Yet the Daily Life Security Law of 1950 preserved the spirit of the original law on several counts. The amended measure offered livelihood assistance only when applicants could not be adequately maintained by their families. Under the revised Civil Code (1948), "direct blood relatives and siblings" and "relatives living together" remained obligated, as before 1945, to support their own. In addition, the new public assistance law echoed prewar policy in its emphasis on fostering "independence" or "self-reliance" (*jiritsu*) among recipients.[36]

The most remarkable continuities with presurrender practice occurred as a product of the Occupation's decision to retain the system of district commissioners. These volunteer visitors to the poor had functioned since the 1920s as the state's primary "caseworkers" and grass-roots administrators of poor relief. Their existence profoundly disturbed the Americans, who were suspicious of them for their vital role in mobilizing neighborhoods during the war. At a more fundamental level, the Occupation sought an end to the practice of entrusting public welfare programs to unsalaried individuals within the community.

However, just as SCAP eventually permitted the residential women's associations of wartime Japan to regroup and carry out the Occupation's objectives, PH&W acceded to the Ministry of Health and Welfare's pressures to deputize the commissioners as the unpaid administrators of public assistance programs. By the stroke of a pen in 1946, the nation's "district commissioners" (*hōmen iin*) became "welfare commissioners" (*minsei iin*). Their national federation, the All-Japan League of District Commissioners, just as effortlessly changed its name to the All-Japan League of Welfare Commissioners. Some 127,000 strong at the end of 1946, the welfare commissioners repeatedly thwarted SCAP's attempts to destroy their influence. Hoping to supplant the generally untrained volunteers, PH&W instituted programs to educate a new corps of professional social work officials. Yet the urgency of Japan's postwar welfare needs and the obvious economy of relying on unpaid activists made the welfare commissioners an attractive alternative to professional caseworkers. Tokyo in 1950, for example, employed a mere 52 social workers, as opposed to the 4,492 volunteer welfare commissioners.[37]

The persistence of the welfare commissioner system has had far-reaching consequences for postwar Japanese welfare. For all of SCAP's efforts to establish consistent principles by law, public assistance programs were often carried out by a presurrender generation of local notables, which had little inclination to abandon the moralistic and restrictive approaches of the past.[38] The Daily Life Security Law of 1946, in particular, gave welfare commissioners major powers to "assist" local officials in determining eligibility and the amount of relief to be granted. To the dismay of Occupation authorities, many commissioners took it upon themselves to reform the poor as they saw fit. According to the regional welfare officer Martin Sherry in 1949, welfare commissioners routinely granted recipients assistance at levels well below that to which they were entitled, believing that anything more generous would discourage self-reliance. Commissioners often withheld appropriate assistance from families on the grounds that the male head was either lazy, of bad character, or did not work hard enough. When Sherry investigated, he found that many of these "lazy" men were actually ill and incapable of working. American officials were equally bothered by the tendency of welfare commissioners to regard public assistance as their personal gift to those below them.[39]

Under pressure from SCAP, the revised Daily Life Security Law of 1950 delegated the tasks of determining eligibility and assistance levels to municipal officials called social welfare secretaries. Welfare commissioners, nonetheless, continued to play important roles in assisting and rehabilitating the poor in their new legal capacity as a "cooperative entity." Other welfare laws in the 1940s and 1950s granted them similar powers to deal directly with juvenile delinquents, the elderly, the physically disabled, the mentally retarded, former prostitutes, and others. A survey recorded 5,136,711 interventions by the commissioners in 1961, the majority of which (52 percent) involved consultations with their charges, followed by various certification activities (20 percent) and help in securing assistance monies (11 percent).[40]

Public assistance in the postwar era thus retained significant features of the prewar system, while gradually expanding to meet the needs of lower-income Japanese. On the one hand, social workers and public officials increasingly took over the provision of assistance and social services, and during the 1950s and 1960s the Ministry of Health and Welfare emerged as an advocate of extending public assistance to all eligible persons. The levels of general assistance have risen substantially since 1961, both in absolute terms and as a percentage of the average consumption expenditure of the lowest-income quintile. At the same time, the proportion of the population receiving public assistance steadily declined, in no small part because postwar recovery and sustained economic growth dramatically reduced the numbers of Japanese living in poverty.[41]

On the other hand, the declining percentage of recipients may also be attributed to efforts at managing the thought and behavior of the Japanese people. As in the prewar years, the postwar state and intermediary groups have frequently intervened to discourage the development of dependency on official aid. Pressed by a Ministry of Finance eager to retrench public assistance expenditures in the mid-1950s, the Ministry of Health and Welfare conducted a successful nationwide campaign to cut recipients from the rolls. The government's objectives were not only to save money but also to "reinforce the work ethic and to limit the notion of a right to a minimum standard of living," in the words of one scholar.[42] During the 1970s and 1980s, when the government again strove to slash overall spending, national and local welfare officials pointedly refrained from encouraging eligible low-income individuals to apply for public assistance. Toward this end, officials occasionally fanned the flames of long-standing public hostility to material poor relief. Although fraudulent claims were remarkably small at the time, the Ministry of Health and Welfare exploited sensational reports of abuse in 1980, suggesting that organized crime was bilking the public assistance system to a significant degree.[43]

Moreover, the government deployed a particularly harsh system of means-testing to inhibit the poor from requesting assistance—one that persisted well into the 1990s. Recent Ministry of Health and Welfare guidelines require applicants to sell off belongings that cannot be considered "necessities" or that are not owned by at least 70 percent of households in the applicant's district. In 1994, officials in the city of Okegawa compelled a seventy-nine-year-old woman to dispose of her air-conditioner—termed a "luxury"—as a condition for receiving public assistance. After suffering through summer temperatures that soared above 100 degrees Fahrenheit inside her tiny apartment, the woman was rushed to the hospital in a state of acute dehydration.[44]

Supported by such policies, official and media campaigns built upon prewar diatribes against "excessive assistance" to shape popular attitudes. The resulting social stigma associated with public assistance clearly has had its effect on the needy. Postwar surveys suggest that lower-income Japanese are much more reluctant than those in Western nations to request assistance from the state. According to one study, only 24 to 28 percent of the lower-income households that were technically eligible for public assistance actually received such benefits between 1975 and 1982. In contrast, some 65 to 75 percent of their British counterparts received comparable assistance during those years.[45] The fact that one's own neighbors, notably the welfare commissioners, had a hand in administering the system further discouraged many from applying for public assistance, just as it had before 1945. In a survey of former recipients in 1956, more than half reported a "shrinking of personal pride," several because "their neighbors talked."[46] Having observed life in a Tokyo ward in 1951, Ronald Dore similarly noted that the needy could not simply file for assistance at a public office but typically made requests to the powerful local welfare commissioner, much as one would ask a personal favor; such favors invariably incurred personal debts.[47]

If policies and attitudes toward general assistance for the poor reveal a striking inheritance from prewar days, the postwar development of universal social programs has been much more the story of change. The emergence of a substantial left-wing parliamentary opposition created a new political force for expanded social security. Although a group of scholars and bureaucrats had been calling since the late 1940s for a national pension system that would cover the entire population, it took the Socialist party's demands for such a system in 1955 to prod the ruling

Liberal Democratic party into sponsoring legislation. The National Pension Law was enacted in 1959. A National Health Insurance Law, which effectively applied to all citizens, had passed the previous year. Both measures fell short of providing adequate benefits, however.

As general poverty declined during the 1960s, public attention shifted to the plight of older people, who constituted the core of the nation's poorest and unhealthiest. Leftist parties again took the lead. In 1969, the Socialist- and Communist-supported governor of Tokyo, Minobe Ryōkichi, introduced free medical care for the elderly, and pressures grew for a similar system at the national level. Seeking to arrest a steady drop in their popularity, the governing Liberal Democrats signed on to a major expansion in universal programs. Even the conservatives had come to embrace the task of transforming Japan into a "welfare state." The Diet enacted free medical care for the elderly in 1972, and in 1973 the government committed itself to marked increases in pension benefits.[48]

JAPAN'S "AGING-SOCIETY CRISIS"

The celebration of 1973 as the "first year of welfare" was short-lived, to say the least. In the wake of the Oil Shock later that year, bureaucrats, businessmen, and conservative politicians questioned how the government would finance the costly commitments of the early 1970s in an era of slower economic growth. By 1975, a "reexamination of welfare" (fukushi minaoshi) was in full swing. With the full cooperation of the media, the government launched a campaign to convince the public of the existence of a new crisis—namely, the "aging-society problem" (kōreika shakai mondai). Old people, who had recently been the object of expanded welfare policies, suddenly became the problem.[49] Few Japanese today would be unable to recite the following jeremiad: Japan, which has had a relatively small percentage of elderly, currently possesses the most rapidly aging society among the advanced nations; its shrinking base of younger working people will be hard-pressed to pay for pensions and old-age care as Japan becomes the oldest population sometime around 2025. Most industrialized societies face similar problems, yet the Japanese public has been persuaded that their "aging-society crisis" is unique and calls for special sacrifices.[50]

Having defined the problem, Japanese elites required several years to formulate a solution. In 1979, the government of Ōhira Masayoshi boldly charted a new course. No longer would Japan unthinkingly trod upon the road taken by Western welfare states. The time had come for the nation to "choose and create its own path. . . . Japan aims for the realization of a new welfare society that may be described as Japanese-style."[51]

What spokesmen meant by a "Japanese-style welfare society" was not always clear. At first glance, they seemed to be advocating the type of free-market individualism that was associated at the time with Prime Minister Margaret Thatcher in Britain and President Ronald Reagan in the United States. During the 1980s, business leaders and the Liberal Democratic party pursued "administrative reform" efforts to shrink the size of government. The welfare state came in for particular criticism, for it was regarded as "obstructing the spirit of independence, self-help, and responsibility for oneself."[52] The extravagant welfare state was to be replaced by a smaller, "efficient government" and a "vital welfare society" (*katsuryoku fukushi shakai*). This new welfare society would be driven by the "creative vitality of a free economy and society."[53]

Despite the apparent similarities, the vision of a Japanese-style welfare society was something more than a warmed-over version of Thatcherism and Reaganism.[54] Japan's new welfare policy owed much to indigenous attitudes dating back to the early twentieth century, if not before. When the LDP's Fukuda Takeo warned in 1975 that the "completion of the social security system might lead to a citizenship losing its sense of independence, and to the production of lazy people," he invoked language once used by Meiji-era bureaucrats to criticize poor relief.[55] Likewise, Japanese leaders have long sought to draw upon the nation's "distinctive" social structure in designing an alternative system to the European welfare state. The alleged incompatibility of Western models with Japanese culture lay at the heart of the Home Ministry's denunciations of English- and German-style poor laws nearly one hundred years ago.

The late 1970s ushered in the most recent wave of Japanese exceptionalism, with conservative politicians and publicists again warning of the perils of becoming like the Europeans. This time, the models were a good deal more malignant. The public was soon bombarded with accounts of the "English disease" and "Swedish disease," both of which the Japanese were sure to contract if they kept expanding the welfare state. As explained by a provocative LDP pamphlet in 1979, the "English disease" was essentially a case of "economic diabetes" brought on by "slicing up the economic pie (GNP) . . . , rather than making it bigger." In their single-minded pursuit of social leveling and enhanced social security, the British had lost the very creativity and work ethic that gave Japan its "special vitality."

Reports of the "Swedish disease" were, in a sense, more chilling. Thanks to high-level welfare and ample pensions, Swedish old people lived independently of their families—often in state-supported nursing homes and other institutions. Yet the lives they lived, charged the LDP pamphlet, were marked by "loneliness and isolation" and "cold-hearted human relationships." Large numbers of pensioners lived alone (many having never married), rarely if ever visited by family. Aged Swedes were depicted as "passing the day staring at the walls" or sitting on park benches "utterly ignored"—the victims of an "extremely individualistic" society. In view of trends toward nuclear families, the same fate apparently threatened Japan's elderly, except that the Japanese could fall back on a culture of warm human relationships. While acknowledging the somewhat idealized nature of its portrait, the LDP pointed to the good life of Japanese old people:

> there may not be many parks, but the elderly have small gardens; [the man] has a wife; they have grandchildren, they have a son and his wife; they have fishing companions and *go* partners. If healthy, they even travel to other countries. And they live out their lives having celebrated sixtieth and seventieth birthdays and golden anniversaries, enjoying the blessings of those around them.[56]

Japan's mission, declared the governing party, was to "mobilize the special wisdom of the Japanese people to avoid a [Swedish-style] aging society lacking that warm glow."[57]

The LDP's talk of mobilizing society and its attack on individualism alerts us to other differences between the "Japanese-style welfare society" and conservative ideals in contemporary Britain and the United States. Although Japanese proponents emphasized the importance of individual effort, most parted company with American conservatives concerning the roles of the state and intermediary groups. Few Japanese conservatives seriously considered placing the ultimate responsibility for the citizenry's well-being in the hands of the individual and the marketplace. As in the prewar era, leaders of the Japanese state have sought to limit expenditure on social programs while actively managing and coordinating "private" welfare mechanisms. The government, by widespread agreement, also serves as the provider of last resort to those who lack sufficient familial support. In a 1977 report, the Economic Planning Agency held out hope for the development of individual "independence and spontaneity in the future." But "we do not expect our country to become a Western-style individualistic society. It therefore is necessary to make the best use of our intermediary groups (*chūkan shūdan*), such as families and local communities, and continue to strive for the optimal mix of individualism and groupism."[58]

The vision is striking, but to what extent has the government since 1979 acted upon its pronouncements to implement a distinctively Japanese welfare policy? One of the most concrete programs to stimulate individual "vitality" aims at encouraging the elderly to work beyond the age of sixty-five. The Japanese approach often surprises Westerners. European polities generally discourage old-age employment in order to maximize jobs for younger people. Americans are fond of insisting on "workfare, not welfare" for able-bodied recipients of public assistance, though few would suggest such a solution for their aged parents. In contrast, since the days of the Relief Regulations of 1874, Japanese elites have frequently warned that state assistance robs even the elderly of the "spirit of independence" and the will to work.[59] Nor did suspicions of retired old people die following World War II. In a much-publicized incident in 1972, Labor Minister Hara Kenzaburō termed residents of old-age homes a "stagnant pool of self-seekers" who are "so ready to become a burden to others." The labor minister pledged to work toward "a situation where *everyone* can be self-sufficient and not have to depend on anyone else."[60] Since the 1980s, a series of government white papers have adopted somewhat gentler language in urging the elderly to live economically "independent" lives. In a "welfare vision" jointly drafted by the Ministry of Labor and Ministry of Health and Welfare in 1988, the elderly were put on notice that they would "not only be the objects of protection and assistance." By creating opportunities and programs, the ministries would enable them to "participate in society" and "contribute to society." Simply put, old people should work.[61]

Beginning in the 1970s, the government played a key role in persuading companies to raise their mandatory retirement ages, and officials have since exhorted and subsidized employers to hire, retain, and retrain older workers. Other programs established organizations that locate and administer part-time jobs for retired people. Some 36 percent of Japanese males aged sixty-five and older were working in 1987, compared to only 16 percent and 4 percent in the United States and France, respectively, in 1984.[62] Do Japanese old people continue working because of a cultural predisposition to diligence, because they lack adequate pensions, or as a result of the government's old-age employment policies? The question does not particularly trouble Japan's social managers, for the three factors reinforce each other and significantly relieve popular demands on the state for increased welfare.

"Japanese-style" welfare policies and the nation's most important intermediate group—the family—are similarly interrelated. The Ministry of Health and Welfare's 1978 white paper heralded the "three-generation family" as Japan's "hidden asset in welfare."[63] Although the proportion of elderly who reside with their children has declined since 1960, an impressive 56 percent of those aged sixty-five and older were living with their children in 1993, rather than on their own or in institutions. Comparable figures in most Western nations by the late 1980s were well below 20 percent.[64] If anything, the current Japanese figures underestimate the degree of familial care. Many old couples live near their children, and, as they age or become incapacitated, they often return to one of their children's homes to be nursed.[65] According to the Ministry of Health and Welfare's 1992 survey of bedridden elderly, an astounding 86 percent were being nursed at home by a child's spouse (invariably a daughter-in-law), their own child, their own spouse, or another relative. In only 8 percent of the cases did someone outside of the family primarily provide the care.[66] The Japanese state has thus evaded some, if not much, of the costs incurred by Western polities in supporting nursing homes and long-term hospitalization.

As in the area of old-age employment, the government's welfare policies may simply be honoring the Japanese people's cultural preference to take care of their own. Yet the state has had much to do with bolstering and even manipulating this culture. Recent changes have sorely taxed the ability of Japanese families to care for the aged, and the media is filled with plaintive accounts of middle-aged children and daughters-in-law. Not only are the elderly living longer (often incapacitated), but the growing phenomenon of working wives and the small size of urban Japanese homes places additional strains on households.

The family would have declined as the primary welfare institution at a much faster clip had it not been for managerial efforts by the state. First, central and local governments have since the 1970s assisted families with dependent elderly through such measures as preferential tax treatment and low-interest loans to build appropriate housing for three-generation families.[67] Second, because officials are determined to prevent the Swedish-style institutionalization of old people on a massive scale, they have worked hard to persuade the populace of the "naturalness" of caring for one's parents or parents-in-law. One strategy, employed over the past twenty years, has been to commission opinion polls that purportedly demonstrate an overwhelming popular preference for living with one's children in old age. The media then reads these polls back to the public, who become all the more convinced that family-based welfare is essentially a "Japanese" trait. In a recent poll done in 1992, a rather high 72 percent of respondents of all ages replied that, should they become incapacitated, they would like to remain at home. Only 12 percent preferred to enter an institution. Never ones to sit back while the people make their own choices, Ministry of Health and Welfare officials editorialized: "if effective measures are devised to expand in-home services and lessen the burden on care-givers, *we should be able to raise the percentage of those choosing to live at home even further.*"[68]

To maintain the family support unit, officials have devoted considerable effort to mollifying the middle-aged wives who bear the greatest burden in caring for the aged. Beginning in the early 1990s, the Ministry of Health and Welfare and other agencies reported, with increasing alarm, on the rapid rise of unmarried women between the ages of 25 and 34.

"Women Stay Single; Will Impact Social System, Too," headlined one story in the normally sedate *Asahi shimbun*. The anticipated shortage of mothers and daughters-in-law, suggested the article, would exacerbate Japan's problems of declining birth rates and caring for the "aging society."[69] Acknowledging the physical and mental toll exacted on married women who nurse parents and parents-in-law, the government in 1990 announced a major initiative to hire more home helpers and expand other in-home services. The "Gold Plan" promised, among other things, a total of 100,000 home helpers (since expanded to the goal of 170,000) and 10,000 local day service centers for the elderly by 1999. To some observers, the Gold Plan signifies the end of attempts at forging the "Japanese-style welfare society" and the resumption of the government's commitment to a growing welfare state.[70]

For all the fanfare surrounding the Gold Plan, however, the fact remains that the Japanese state relies on married women to perform the bulk of Japan's welfare services.[71] The Ministry of Health and Welfare had hired only 69,000 home helpers by the end of the 1993 fiscal year and had built a mere 1,800 day service centers. Even if the plan were to meet its goal of 170,000 home helpers by 1999, the helpers would amount to only 13 per 10,000 people, as compared to 87 per 10,000 in Sweden (1992).[72]

Far from relieving wives of their burdens, various agencies and local governments have found new ways of mobilizing women on behalf of the nation's welfare needs. Recruiting local volunteers to help the elderly, as we shall see, is one such activity. Playing upon popular fears of inadequate pensions, savings-promotion officials have concurrently run well-attended seminars on "life planning" since the 1970s. Targeted at housewives and local women's groups, the seminars teach methods of coping with the "aging society" by increasing household savings.[73] Although the Japanese government has expanded in-home services for the elderly, it demonstrates little eagerness to replace the family with the types of widespread institutional care that have characterized Western welfare states.

In addition to the family, proponents of Japanese-style welfare extolled two other intermediary organizations—the local community and the business enterprise. As skeptics rightly note, the enterprise's contributions to overall welfare are limited. Company pension and benefit levels generally lag behind those in large American corporations, and only a minority of Japan's work force qualify for such benefits. Skeptics are less persuasive when they dismiss the roles played by communal intermediaries.[74] The state's mobilization of local communities remains significant in the area of social services. The nearly eighty-year-old system of welfare commissioners is alive and well. They numbered 189,965 nationwide in 1992. Since the 1960s, welfare commissioners have increasingly focused on assisting the elderly. They frequently visit the homes of the elderly and handicapped, arrange for home helpers, and, when necessary, help place their charges in institutions.[75]

Recognizing the limits of depending on a fairly small number of welfare commissioners in each neighborhood, officials stepped up efforts to recruit welfare volunteers on a massive scale during the 1980s and 1990s. In 1993, the National Social Welfare Council, which assists the Ministry of Welfare in coordinating social services locally, counted 4,690,000 volunteers and 56,000 participating groups nationwide. The term "volunteer" (*borantea*) is somewhat of a misnomer if it suggests service independent of bureaucratic supervision. The government has recruited many of these volunteers from the ranks of the women's associations, old-age clubs, and other local groups that have cooperated in national campaigns throughout the postwar era. Individuals and groups officially register as volunteers at "volunteer centers" administered by local social welfare councils. Since the latter half of the 1980s, the Ministry of Health and Welfare and the National Social Welfare Council have aggressively sponsored various training courses for volunteers and their leaders. As evidenced by survey data in the early 1990s, volunteers are overwhelmingly women (75 percent), some 61 percent of whom described themselves as housewives. The majority of men were retirees or self-employed.[76]

The impact of millions of volunteers on the provision of social services cannot be underestimated. Like the welfare commissioners, volunteers today spend most of their time helping the elderly and, to a lesser extent, the handicapped and children. Volunteers typically provide in-home services, such as bringing food, bathing their charges, and cleaning house. In short, Japanese volunteers and welfare commissioners continue to perform many of the tasks done by paid social workers elsewhere. Accordingly, observes one scholar, Japanese municipalities have gotten by with far fewer social workers and lower welfare expenditures than Western European cities.[77] Japanese officials are more explicit, envisioning volunteer activities—along with public services—as "the bases upon which the vital welfare society will be built."[78]

The viability of the "Japanese-style welfare society" is often judged by whether the government has successfully reversed trends toward expanded public services and greater social spending. That may be too unreasonable a test, for few higher civil servants over the last twenty years expected the state to do less as the numbers of elderly soared. Indeed, expenditures on social security (measured by Japanese authorities as a proportion of national income) have grown from 13.7 percent in 1990 to 16.3 percent in 1993.[79] Officials have instead focused on slowing the rate of growth of welfare spending, in spite of rising needs. And in this they have been quite successful. Welfare policies, of course, continue to depend on families and communal intermediaries, and the government has recently expanded in-home services as a relatively inexpensive alternative to long-term institutionalization.

The state also remains adept at using moral suasion to defuse popular demands for more generous welfare. Years of pounding away at the "English disease" and "Swedish disease" have produced a populace that apparently desires relief from the costs of privately supporting the elderly, yet is not eager to pay European levels of taxation to finance such a welfare state.[80] The authorities sometimes appear to have done their job too well. It took LDP cabinets more than a year to overcome popular opposition and enact a 3 percent consumption tax in 1988, even though much of the anticipated revenue was ostensibly earmarked for welfare expenses. When Prime Minister Hosokawa Morihiro in 1994 attempted to raise the consumption tax to 7 percent, calling it a "national welfare tax," he similarly ran into formidable opposition from the general public and his coalition partners, the Socialists. The Ministry of Finance eventually settled for a 5 percent tax, which will not go into effect until 1997.[81]

Whatever the short-term consequences, campaigns to raise public consciousness of the tradeoffs between taxation and welfare benefits have made it easier for the bureaucracy to chip away at earlier commitments to welfare expansion. In 1985, with scarcely a whimper from the public and opposition parties, the Ministry of Health and Welfare substantially cut future pension benefits while hiking current contributions. The bureaucracy's attempts to raise the age of eligibility at which one begins receiving pensions encountered more resistance during the 1980s. Nonetheless, the Ministry of Health and Welfare's proposal to raise the age from sixty to sixty-five sailed through the Diet in 1994 (the change to be phased in between 2001 and 2013). Cutting back universal entitlements has been a highly contentious issue in France, the United States, and other polities in the mid-1990s. Japan's successful reductions are projected to result in significantly lower rates of social spending and taxation than would have otherwise been the case.[82]

This book ends, as it began, with an examination of Japanese welfare. The well-being of a people was, is, and always will be a major issue for state and society—whether one is discussing Tokugawa-era villages or an aging Japan in the year 2025. The issue is, moreover, inextricably linked to the phenomenon of social management, for redistributing wealth invariably gives rise to efforts to influence the thought and behavior of recipients. As Japan approaches the twentieth-first century, the nation's welfare policies exhibit both the limits and resiliency of the long-standing drive to manage society.

The limits are apparent. Japanese officials would like families and communities to bear much of the welfare burden directly. They also hope to persuade all women to marry (assuming that all men desire marriage), produce enough children to maintain the population, and nurse parents-in-law or parents. But as one official in 1990 conceded somewhat sadly, after being asked if the government would revive the wartime policy of encouraging women to "give birth and multiply" for the sake of the nation: "It isn't such an easy matter to get Japanese women to bear children."[83] Obviously the state has not managed to reverse fundamental social trends. Young women are becoming more independent, and many are postponing, if not ruling out, marriage; birth rates have fallen below replacement levels; and communities no longer dig into their pockets to aid their less fortunate. Growing numbers of urban men, and even women, scarcely know their neighbors.

Nonetheless, social management has had a profound impact in reshaping welfare programs, deflating popular expectations, and constraining the costs of welfare from rising even further. Contemporary Japan is hardly unique among industrialized societies in experiencing rapid urbanization, declining birth rates, a rising percentage of working wives, and decreasing rates of marriage. Demographic changes that in other societies compelled massive state expenditures on institutions and health care for the elderly could conceivably have produced the same results in Japan, had the state and cooperative groups not undertaken policies to forestall their consequences on several fronts. If the state had devoted major resources to enabling the elderly to obtain institutional care and live independently, would a majority of old people still be living in their children's cramped homes? Just as the prewar regime did a great deal to re-create and modernize communal welfare institutions of the early modern era, postwar governments continue to experiment with new forms of community self-help, such as welfare commissioners and the rapidly expanding network of grass-roots volunteers.

What may be most distinctive about the present-day management of welfare is the cooperation of the media. Japanese need only glance at the headlines or turn on the television to be reminded of the Western-style social disintegration and economic stagnation that awaits the nation, should they fail to rein in their appetite for state-funded welfare. Although families bear their welfare burdens with rising bitterness, the populace shows few signs of demanding alternatives to family-based care. Japanese policymakers may not have prevented a welfare state from emerging in fact, but they have retained the ability to manage the growth of social programs to a degree that their Western counterparts would surely envy.

Epilogue

Japan is changing all right—but not by becoming like us.
Japan is simply looking for new ways to remain itself.

—Thomas L. Friedman, *New York Times*, 3 March 1996

T HE JAPAN described in the pre-
ceding chapters is not the Japan that many American visitors see. It is not
the Japan of anonymous commuters in a Tokyo rush hour but rather the
Japan of the neighborhood, the housewife, and the women's magazine.
Nor would Americans be likely to hear much about the persistence of
social management from Japanese informants. Officials are eager to appear accommodating toward Washington's demands for economic deregulation and greater consumption, and they have little incentive to talk
about their state's ongoing interventions or promotion of savings—least
of all in English. Japanese women's leaders, who have long recognized the
benefits of cooperating with the state in certain areas, hesitate to explain
these relationships to disapproving American visitors, and instead highlight their groups' opposition to authority.

Most of all, to those who habit the frenetic world of Japanese urban
life (particularly males), the nation described in this book is the Japan of
the past. Indeed, we may never again see the great moral suasion campaigns that characterized Japanese statecraft between 1900 and the
1970s. Growing affluence in the 1980s made the populace less receptive
to messages of austerity. There were some even within the government
who hinted at a new direction. Headed by former Bank of Japan governor
Maekawa Haruo, a cabinet-level commission in 1986 recommended
policies designed to expand popular consumption and improve the quality of Japanese life.[1] Household savings rates, which had peaked at 23
percent in 1976, fell throughout the booming 1980s. Where once newspapers and radio programs gave tips on how to "rationalize" life, the
media gushed with celebratory stories of conspicuous consumption. The
American commentator James Fallows remembers being taken to lunch
in 1988 at one of Tokyo's French restaurants. Dessert consisted of choco-

late mousse. The waiter reappeared with "some kind of grinder, and instead of cinnamon or flaked chocolate he began decorating my mousse with shavings of pure gold."[2]

The 1980s also witnessed a sustained decline in many of the institutions that had directed or mediated twentieth-century campaigns of social management. The goal of "New Life," which had so appealed to a less prosperous generation in the early postwar decades, gradually lost meaning, and in 1982, the New Life Campaign Association renamed itself the Association to Build the Japan of Tomorrow (Ashita no Nihon o Tsukuru Kyōkai). The new association no longer received the generous level of state funding once enjoyed by its predecessor.[3] The Central Council for Savings Promotion was likewise compelled to reduce its operations. In 1987, it, too, adopted a new name, the Central Council for Savings *Information*. The wartime phrase "savings promotion" (*chochiku zōkyō*) had become something of an embarrassment, at a time when the United States government was criticizing the Japanese for "excess saving."[4] Meanwhile, at the societal level, the National Federation of Regional Women's Organizations and its residential women's associations had lost much of their former vitality as agents of the state. Younger women participated less in the residential associations, as they took on jobs or joined other groups based on similar interests, such as hobbies or the cooperative purchase of organic food.

The era of rapidly rising affluence was not to last forever. The so-called bubble economy of the 1980s soon burst, replaced by the prolonged recession that began in 1991 and continued through 1995. The widespread sense of crisis and pessimism in Japan today occasioned a return to more visible efforts to manage society. Just as state officials following the Oil Shock of 1973–1974 demonized the previous high-growth era as one of unrestrained mass consumption and shallow materialism, bureaucrats and the media currently tout the "collapse of the bubble economy" as a moral lesson for the Japanese people. Only by returning to the habits of diligence, thrift, and conservation of resources—officials argue—will the nation maintain its position in world markets and preserve social stability.[5] The public, for its part, appears once again receptive to messages of frugality. Women's magazines are filled with tips on economizing, and one of 1994's best sellers was entitled "How to Live the Frugal Life." Contrary to most predictions, household savings rates have leveled off and even trended upward since 1989.[6]

Moreover, nationwide campaigns to influence the populace are far from dead in the 1990s. As officials of the renamed Central Council for Savings Information readily admit, the state's project of savings promotion has not fundamentally changed.[7] The growing demands of the "aging society," asserts the agency's literature, makes the task of saving all the more urgent. The Central Council continues to direct the savings promotion activities of prefectural and municipal governments, prefectural savings promotion committees, social education officers, 1,253 professional "life planning and savings advisors," and thousands of volunteers. Fearing that the younger generation will abandon habits of thrift, the Central Council and the Ministry of Education also maintain efforts to teach schoolchildren to "value goods and money."[8] New Life campaigns persist, as well. Working to rebuild communal solidarity and further recycling efforts, the Association to Build the Japan of Tomorrow maintains prefectural councils in all forty-seven prefectures. The organization presently aims to create a society of "true affluence based on a balance between the material and spiritual"—meaning a society that eschews excessive consumption and the singular pursuit of self-interest.[9] At the grass-roots level, the "daily life schools" of housewives are thriving, and they often constitute the leadership in the government's 526 "life planning and savings districts."[10]

This is not to say that the programs of social management operate essentially as they had during the early postwar years. The history of modern Japanese governance is one of ongoing efforts to adapt managerial mechanisms to changing circumstances. We have only to recall the early twentieth century, when concerns over the breakdown of early modern communal structures prompted the appearance of new state-assisted intermediaries—district commissioners, women's associations, and even Christian social workers and moral reformers. Prominent among recent changes in social management has been the growing role of the media. A gradual shift occurred during the century from direct forms of managing society (through intermediaries) to indirect management, by which the state and organizations employed nationwide media to convey their messages. Television, newspapers, and magazines serve as the primary vehicles in the present age. The government relies heavily on the media in the current campaign to persuade the populace to bear the brunt of the "aging-society problem." Indirect management is also playing a greater part in normalizing savings and consumption patterns. Today's busy housewife, who often works part time, need not be instructed in the ways of thrift by a neighborhood leader, when she can turn to standardized household account books, which are distributed annually by major women's magazines, the Central Council for Savings Information, and other government agencies.[11]

In addition, although some intermediaries have declined, other groups have arisen to take their place in managerial projects. Unpaid social work is no longer performed exclusively by the fewer than 200,000 local welfare commissioners, but also by the more than 4 million volunteers. Although the national women's federations have become less active in promoting savings, the Central Council for Savings Information has recently deputized smaller, more locally based women's groups to lead campaigns in its "life planning and savings districts." These ad hoc groups often take the form of hobby and sports clubs, consumer cooperatives, recyling associations, and study associations (*benkyōkai*)—the very groups to which younger women have transferred their allegiance in recent years.[12] At the same time, we err in thinking that the old national networks of residental women's organizations have simply disappeared. Some 5 to 6 million women still belonged to affiliates of the National Federation of Regional Women's Organizations as late as 1992.[13]

In today's world, one invariably judges and compares, and it may be impossible to remain value-neutral about the Japanese practices of social management that seem so foreign to Americans. I was once asked by a Japanese colleague (a Marxist, no less) why I spent so much time studying postwar savings campaigns. After all, he reasoned, "if it's good for people to save money, what's wrong with encouraging savings?" Others might well ask: What's wrong with neighborhood groups assisting the elderly, watching out for criminal activity, helping in the schools, or getting people to conserve resources and avoid running up consumer debt? The fact is that many Americans would welcome such local activism if it contributed, as it seems to have done in the Japanese case, to low crime rates, overall social stability, and a strong industrial base financed by abundant sources of investment capital.

Signs of disintegration in our own society have prompted leading thinkers to ponder whether federal and state governments might similarly harness the energies of community groups to ameliorate social problems. None has been as influential as Robert Putnam. The Harvard social scientist points to the ominous decline in American "civic engagement"—be it participation in PTAs or bowling leagues. In previous work on Italy, Putnam demonstrated that governments function most effectively in locales rich in civic organizations. He offers few concrete suggestions on how government might rebuild local "social capital" in the United States, although he does refer to past examples of community building, notably agricultural extension programs and Head Start.[14]

In the 1980s, Americans were fond of looking to Japan for solutions to their own problems. However, before we discover another attractive model in the form of social management, let us reflect on the nature of Japanese civic participation in light of both history and questions of democracy. American communitarians like Putnam envision the reinvigoration of American "civic tradition" occurring from the bottom up. Japanese civic engagement, though vital, may not be what they have in mind. Although civic activism has evolved during the postwar era, local organizational efforts and the organizations themselves remain embedded in the state-society relations of imperial Japan.

Neither the Occupation nor Japanese progressives succeeded in severing the links between the central government and the groups that enroll the bulk of public-spirited citizens. Is it possible to speak of the proliferation of community groups as a manifestation of grass-roots democracy when so many got their start, or at least maintained themselves, due to official encouragement, outright subsidies, and governmental coordination? When the National Federation of Regional Women's Organizations takes a large subsidy from the state to set up regional blocs that administer savings drives, or when seemingly independent consumers' and housewives' groups all happen to encourage savings and recycling in the same week throughout the country, we are obviously talking about a different notion of local autonomy than that put forward by Americans.

The benefits of managing intermediaries, who in turn manage everyday life, are undeniable. Twentieth-century Japan is a striking case of a resource-poor nation that could never have become the modern world's first non-Western military power and achieved the postwar "economic miracle," had it not so effectively mobilized its society in war and peace. From the perspective of democracy, however, the drawbacks of this style of governance are equally apparent. Few popular groups, before, or after World War II, enjoyed the autonomy that would have enabled them to challenge the state's agenda in fundamental ways. If the leaders of a community group are trained in government-sponsored seminars, or if the group receives official recognition and subsidies to "rationalize" daily life or conserve resources, it not so easy, say, for its members to protest the state's role in maintaining consumer prices at higher levels than in most other industrialized nations.

Postwar Japan would seem to present an enigma. It is a polity whose democratic institutions and firm guarantees of civil liberties coexist with a broad-based commitment to managing society. There are in the world today many non-Western nations that organize the populace into hierarchal associations and attempt to regulate everyday life. Yet few have successfully reshaped the mores of their people or created active popular support for their programs.[15] How do we explain the extraordinary willingness of the Japanese people to manage their own lives and make real sacrifices for the sake of the nation state during the twentieth century?

We could, of course, fall back on cultural stereotypes of the Japanese as submissive to authority. Such explanations do not begin to account, however, for the tensions pervading the state-society relations profiled in this book. Youth associations and women's organizations commonly resented official interference, even as they cooperated with the government in New Life and social education activities; the postwar women's movement continued the century-long battle against a state that would not do more to suppress prostitution and the extramarital sexuality of males; consumers' groups occasionally took on the government in potent movements against price fixing and unsafe products; and families increasingly complain about the task of caring for the elderly in a society with inadequate welfare services.

Yet far from obstructing official efforts, these tensions may be one of the keys to understanding the efficiency of Japanese social management. The intermediary activists in this study have not always blindly obeyed the dictates of the state. Often they have acted from their own managerial impulses or in pursuit of what they deemed to be their own interests. Whatever the motivation, their active collaboration more often than not strengthened the state's capacity to regulate society to a greater degree than if a small cadre of bureaucrats had simply imposed its will from above. The new middle classes allied with the state to advance their status as the bearers of Western knowledge and as those best able to modernize the mores of ordinary Japanese. The old middle classes assumed such roles as welfare commissioners in a quest to govern their communities. Seeking to empower themselves as mothers and housewives, organized women similarly took center stage in official campaigns to better daily life, improve child rearing, and sometimes to control illicit sexuality.

Perhaps the true genius of the Japanese state lies in its ability to marry the currents of democratization and social management. The bureaucrats might have ruled solely by force or in alliance with local notables and business interests. Instead, their campaigns increasingly incorporated a variety of rising social forces—including lower-middle-class community leaders, middle-class professionals, organized women, and even prominent feminists and social democrats. The steady expansion of popular participation in these managerial efforts was not confined to periods of overt democracy in the 1920s and postwar years but, if anything, accelerated during the war years of 1937–1945, when the government by necessity recruited masses of civic leaders from among women and relatively humble folk.

The resiliency of social management in the present day is also closely bound up with the continued hold of Japanese nationalism. Since the Meiji Restoration, most Japanese have regarded the nation state not only as the engine of progress, but also as the best means of protecting the Japanese people from what was, and still is, perceived to be a hostile outside world. Few Japanese in the twentieth century have embraced the sort of American-style free-market liberalism that conceives of the world as borderless and the individual as the basic unit of economic well-being.[16] The belief persists that the Japanese people must regulate themselves, make sacrifices, or at least "rationalize" their behavior for the greater good. Japan at the end of the twentieth century remains, in some ways, as it was at the start: a nation at war in peace.[17] The press commonly reports on U.S.-Japanese economic relations in terms of "trade wars," and criticism of Japanese policy is often described as "Japan-bashing" by the mighty United States. Japanese are also constantly made aware of the debilitating ideological forces that threaten to invade, lest they fail to manage their own society. The "Swedish disease" and "English disease" were bad enough, but they are nothing to compare with the "American disease"—which is marked by crime, drugs, divorce, growing income inequality, self-indulgence, and the overall unwillingness to do anything to avert social breakdown.[18]

Faced with a choice between American-style laissez-faire and the substantial regulation of economy and society, most Japanese would still respond much as a high-ranking, American-trained official of the Ministry of Finance did recently: "I'm not a nationalist in the narrow sense of the word, but too much deregulation would create great confusion. . . . It's naked market forces against cultures. It would be the end of Japanese-style capitalism if we pushed this kind of change too far. Japan would be split, as America is split."[19] As long as this profound sense of national solidarity and vulnerability persists, Japan's broadly based acceptance of social management will continue.

Notes

PREFACE

1. "Babies, Rice Farms and Diplomas," *New York Times*, 20 June 1990, sect. A, p. 24.

INTRODUCTION

1. Quoted in Jacques Donzelot, *Policing of Families*, 7.

2. James Leiby, "Social Control and Historical Explanation," in Walter I. Trattner, ed., *Social Welfare or Social Control?*, 97–99.

3. Francis F. Piven and Richard A. Cloward, *Regulating the Poor*; for a guide to the literature, see Stanley Cohen and Andrew Scull, "Introduction: Social Control in History and Sociology," in *Social Control and the State*, 1–16.

4. Michel Foucault, *Discipline and Punish*, 178; also 135–37, 179, 224.

5. See F. M. L. Thompson, "Social Control in Victorian Britain"; and Gareth Steadman Jones, "Class Expression versus Social Control? A Critique of Recent Trends in the Social History of 'Leisure,'" in Cohen and Scull, *Social Control and the State*, 39–49.

6. See Laura Engelstein, "Combined Underdevelopment."

7. Michel Foucault, "Governmentality" and *The History of Sexuality*, 1:89; Peter Miller and Nikolas Rose, "Governing Economic Life."

8. For a classic discussion of the emperor system, see Inoue Kiyoshi, *Tennōsei*.

9. See Carol Gluck, *Japan's Modern Myths*, chap. 1. Nor did loyalty to the emperor figure prominently in the recollections of Japanese who ostensibly fought in his name between 1931 and 1945. See Haruko Taya Cook and Theodore F. Cook, *Japan at War*, 16.

10. Except Gluck, *Japan's Modern Myths*, 3, 313 n. 1: her translation is "influence" or "civic education."

11. See *Kōjien*, 2d ed. (1969), 565, 567.

12. See Kenneth B. Pyle, "Technology."

13. Chochiku zōkyō chūō iinkai, *Chochiku undōshi*, 2; see also James Edward Ketelaar, *Of Heretics and Martyrs*, 120.

14. Gluck, *Japan's Modern Myths*, 111–12, 120–21.

15. Inoue Tomoichi, *Rekkoku no keisei to minsei* (1901), quoted in Miyachi Masato, "Nichirō zengo," 6:132–33.

16. Nakamura Masanori and Suzuki Masayuki, "Kindai tennōsei kokka no seiritsu," 12, 16–17.

17. Inoue Tomoichi, "Kanka kyūsai jigyō," 1–2, 8–9.

18. *The Japan Year Book*, 1911, p. 496.

19. Wilbur M. Fridell, *Japanese Shrine Mergers*, 46–48.

20. See Pyle, "Technology," 58–62; Gluck, *Japan's Modern Myths*, 197–99, 200–1.

21. Naimushō shakaikyoku, "Shōhi setsuyaku ni tsuite," 1–2; also Akazawa Shirō, *Kindai Nihon no shisō dōin*, 17–18; Nakajima Kuni, "Taishō-ki ni okeru 'seikatsu kaizen undō,'" 58.

22. "Kyōka undō," 56; also 57, 64–65, 75, 85.

23. Shibamura Atsuki, "Daitoshi ni okeru kenryoku," 66, 68; Akazawa, *Kindai Nihon no shisō dōin*, 23–24.

24. See Nakajima, "Taishō-ki ni okeru 'seikatsu kaizen undō.'"

25. "Ie no hikari gurafu: Seikatsu kaizen dayori," *Ie no hikari* 10 (October 1934); see also Itagaki Kuniko, *Shōwa senzen, senchūki no nōson seikatsu*, 16–32, 167–79.

26. On the growth of bureaucracy, see Masumi Junnosuke, *Nihon seitōshi ron*, 4:165.

27. "Shōhi setsuyaku shōrei shisetsu ni kansuru ken, Shakaikyokuchō yori shōkai kaitō."

28. Mombushō, *Kyōka dōin jisshi gaikyō*, 202–31; selected posters may be found in the preface and in Naimushō shakaikyoku shakaibu, *Kinken shōrei undō gaikyō*.

29. W. Elliot Brownlee, "Social Investigation and Political Learning in the Financing of World War I," in Michael J. Lacey and Mary O. Furner, eds., *The State and Social Investigation in Britain and the United States*, 343–54; on "morale," see Nikolas Rose, *Governing the Soul*, chap. 2.

30. Naimushō shakaikyoku, "Shōhi setsuyaku ni tsuite," 2; Pyle, "Technology," 57, 59.

31. Senzenki kanryōsei kenkyūkai (Hata Ikuhiko), ed., *Senzenki Nihon kanryōsei no seido, soshiki, jinji*, 686–88, 692.

32. Sheldon Garon, *State and Labor*, 80–82.

33. For example, Takayoshi Matsuo, "The Development of Democracy in Japan," and Sharon L. Sievers, *Flowers in Salt*, chap. 8.

34. See Thomas R. H. Havens, *Valley of Darkness*.

35. Karel van Wolferen, "An Economic Pearl Harbor?" *New York Times*, 2 December 1991, sect. A, p. 17; also his *The Enigma of Japanese Power*.

36. Gluck, *Japan's Modern Myths*.

37. William Miles Fletcher, III, *The Search for a New Order*.

38. Yoshimi Yoshiaki, *Kusa no ne no fuashizumu*, Nagahama Isao, *Kokumin*

seishin sōdōin no shisō to kōzō, 7–9; Takahashi Hikohiro, ed., *Minshū no gawa no sensō sekinin*; Hirota Teruyuki, "Senjiki shomin no shinjō to ronri."

39. Desley Deacon, *Managing Gender*, 3–10; Donzelot, *Policing of Families*, 96–99, 121–22, 128–29.

40. Hata Ikuhiko, *Kanryō*, 9–15; Chalmers Johnson, *MITI*, 36–40.

41. For the parties' role in policymaking during this era, see Garon, *State and Labor*.

42. Hata, *Kanryō*, 9.

43. Peter Duus, "Liberal Intellectuals," 437.

44. Kenneth Pyle, "Advantages of Followership"; Garon, *State and Labor*, 27.

45. Cf. Byron K. Marshall, *Academic Freedom*, 92–93.

46. Sharon H. Nolte, *Liberalism in Modern Japan*, 222–23; Garon, *State and Labor*, 49, 113–14, 161–62.

47. Duus, "Liberal Intellectuals," 437.

48. Ryusaku Tsunoda, William Theodore de Bary, and Donald Keene, eds., *Sources of Japanese Tradition*, 2:137.

49. See Sheldon Garon, "Rethinking Modernization and Modernity in Japanese History."

50. Joan Wallach Scott, *Gender and the Politics of History*, 3, 29; also 6, 10, 23–24.

51. Theda Skocpol, *Protecting Soldiers and Mothers*; also Linda Gordon, "Social Insurance and Public Assistance."

CHAPTER ONE
THE EVOLUTION OF "JAPANESE-STYLE" WELFARE

1. For example, M[aurice] B. Bruce, *The Coming of the Welfare State*; cf. D. Fraser, "The English Poor Law and the Origins of the British Welfare State," in W. J. Mommsen ed., *The Emergence of the Welfare State in Britain and Germany, 1850–1950*, 9–10.

2. Inoue, "Kanka kyūsai jigyō," 2.

3. Inoue Tomoichi, *Kyūsai seido*, 172.

4. Hugh Heclo, *Modern Social Politics*, 17, 46–64.

5. Ikeda Yoshimasa, *Nihon shakai fukushishi*, 92–93; Yoshida Kyūichi, *Nihon shakai jigyō*, 76.

6. Inoue, *Kyūsai seido*, 119, 167, 169, 184–86.

7. Ursula R. Q. Henriques, *Before the Welfare State*, 1.

8. Ikeda, *Nihon shakai fukushishi*, 93. One *kan* = approximately 1,000 coins.

9. Herman Ooms, *Charismatic Bureaucrat*, 51–53.

10. Miyata Noboru, "Nōson no fukkō undō," 221.

11. Irwin Scheiner, "Benevolent Lords and Honorable Peasants"; Anne Walthall, *Social Protest*, 55–57.

12. Stephen Vlastos, *Peasant Protests*, 41; also 15–16, 39–40.

13. Quoted in Ikeda, *Nihon shakai fukushishi*, 94; for other thinkers, see 94–95.

14. Yoshida, *Nihon shakai jigyō*, 102.

15. Herman Ooms, *Tokugawa Ideology*, 119–20, also 156; for Tokugawa-era criticism of idleness, see Yoshida Kyūichi, "Kinsei jukyō no fukushi shisō," in his *Shakai fukushi no Nihonteki tokushitsu*, 66, 79, 92.

16. Quoted in Ikeda, *Nihon shakai fukushishi*, 95.

17. Yoshida, *Nihon shakai jigyō*, 97–99; Vlastos, *Peasant Protests*, 11–12.

18. Arne Kalland, *Fishing Villages in Tokugawa Japan*, 252–53, 263–64.

19. Ikeda, *Nihon shakai fukushishi*, 115–16.

20. Walthall, *Social Protest*, 57.

21. Yoshida, *Nihon shakai jigyō*, 85.

22. Ikeda, *Nihon shakai fukushishi*, 101–2.

23. James L. McClain, *Kanazawa*, 127–29.

24. Daniel Botsman, "Punishment and Power," 23–31; also Tetsuo Najita, *Visions of Virtue*, 180, 194, 199–200.

25. Ikeda, *Nihon shakai fukushishi*, 124–27, for Osaka's mutual assistance network, see 120–22; Yoshida, *Nihon shakai jigyō*, 85–86.

26. See Helen Hardacre, "Creating State Shintō, 38–40.

27. Cited by Thomas C. Smith, "Ōkura Nagatsune and the Technologists," 140.

28. Kanzō Uchimura, "Ninomiya Sontoku—A Peasant Saint," in the *The Complete Works of Kanzō Uchimura*, 2:69.

29. Sontoku Ninomiya, *Sage Ninomiya's Evening Talks*, 41–42, 59; Thomas R. H. Havens, "Religion and Agriculture in Nineteenth-century Japan," 101.

30. Robert N. Bellah, *Tokugawa Religion*, 126–31.

31. Yoshida, *Nihon shakai jigyō*, 116–17.

32. Ikeda, *Nihon shakai fukushishi*, 160.

33. Miyata, "Nōson no fukko undō," 221.

34. Cited by Peter Duus, *The Rise of Modern Japan*, 77.

35. W. Dean Kinzley, "Japan's Discovery of Poverty," 12–13.

36. Ishida Takeshi, "Kindai Nihon in okeru 'shakai fukushi' kanren kannen no hensen," 183.

37. Proclamation of 9 December 1867, quoted in Ogawa Masaaki, "Jukkyū kisoku," 262.

38. Yoshida, *Nihon shakai jigyō*, 133.

39. Ogawa, "Jukkyū kisoku," 263, 272–74; Andrew Fraser, "Local Administration: The Example of Awa-Tokushima," in Marius B. Jansen and Gilbert Rozman, eds., *Japan in Transition*, 124.

40. P[aul] Mayet, *Agricultural Insurance*, 257, 270, 276–77, 288, 293, 386–88; also supplement: "Opinions of the Press," 2, 4–5, 6–7, 14–16.

41. See Harry D. Harootunian, "The Economic Rehabilitation of the Samurai."

42. Shakai hoshō kenkyūjo, *Nihon shakai hoshō zenshi shiryō* (hereafter cited as NSHZS), 4:6.

43. Ogawa, "Jukkyū kisoku," 264, 266–67, 270–71.

44. Ikeda, *Nihon shakai fukushishi*, 182–83; also 164, 181–84.

45. NSHZS, 4:6–7.

46. Ogawa, "Jukkyū kisoku," 305, 307–8.

47. Yoshida Kyūichi, "Meiji ishin ni okeru kyūhin seido," in Nihon shakai jigyō daigaku and Kyūhin seido kenkyūkai, eds., *Nihon no kyūhin seido*, 87–89; Ikeda, *Nihon shakai fukushishi*, 304.

48. Italics added. Ogawa, "Jukkyū kisoku," 299–300.

49. Gertrude Himmelfarb, *Idea of Poverty*, 111–12.

50. Toshio Tatara, "1400 Years of Japanese Social Work," 199–205; see also Earl H. Kinmouth, *The Self-Made Man in Meiji Japanese Thought*.

51. Cited by Yoshida, *Nihon shakai jigyō*, 141; also Yoshida, "Meiji ishin," in Nihon shakai jigyō daigaku, *Nihon no kyūhin seido*, 61.

52. Quoted in Ogawa, "Jukkyū kisoku," 309.

53. *Tōkyō nichinichi shimbun*, 12 December 1884, quoted in Ogawa, "Jukkyū kisoku," 312–33.

54. See Heclo, *Modern Social Politics*, 60, 62–63.

55. Yoshida, "Meiji ishin," in Nihon shakai jigyō daigaku, *Nihon no kyūhin seido*, 90.

56. Quoted in Kawai Eijirō, *Meiji shisōshi no ichidammen*, 162.

57. Horikoshi Kansuke, in R. H. P. Mason, "Debate on Poor Relief," 17.

58. Ogawa, "Jukkyū kisoku," 313–14.

59. Tatara, "1400 Years of Japanese Social Work," 87.

60. Yoshida, "Meiji ishin," in Nihon shakai jigyō daigaku, *Nihon no kyūhin seido*, 62.

61. *Asahi shimbun*, 3 September 1885. I am indebted to Andrew Fraser for sharing this source and many others on Tokushima prefecture.

62. Yoshida Kyūichi, *Nihon hinkonshi*, 176, 177–78; for other surveys, see 174–83.

63. Ikeda, *Nihon shakai fukushishi*, 176–77.

64. Ichibangase Yasuko and Takashima Susumu, *Shakai fukushi no rekishi*, 29–30.

65. Ikeda, *Nihon shakai fukushishi*, 285–89; Garon, *State and Labor*, 25–27; Pyle, "Advantages of Followership."

66. Kubota Shizutarō, "Himmin kyūsai seido iken," *Shakai*, no. 11 (December 1899), in Nihon shakai jigyō daigaku, ed., *Kubota Shizutarō ronshū*, 155–58.

67. Cf. Kinzley, "Japan's Discovery of Poverty," 12–13.

68. *Dai Nihon teikoku gikai shi*, vol. 1, 1st Diet, Lower House, 6 December 1890, p. 472.

69. Tatara, "1400 Years of Japanese Social Work," 99; Mason, "Debate on Poor Relief," 8–10, 13.

70. Mason, "Debate on Poor Relief," 14–16, 18–19.

71. Tatara, "1400 Years of Japanese Social Work," 100–2.

72. Committee hearing of 7 March 1902, quoted in Ogawa Masaaki, "Sangyō shihon kakuritsu-ki no kyūhin seido," in Nihon shakai jigyō daigaku, *Nihon no kyūhin seido*, 119.

73. Inoue, *Kyūsai seido*, 185–86.

74. Ibid., 168, 191.

75. Ibid., 171.

76. Tokonami Takejirō, "Jizen jigyō no san-yōgi to shinkōshin," 2–3.

77. Himmelfarb, *Idea of Poverty*, chap. 6.

78. Inoue, *Kyūsai seido*, 190; also 186–89.

79. Ikeda, *Nihon shakai fukushishi*, 304, 311, 312.

80. Inoue, *Kyūsai seido*, 172–73.

81. Ibid., 317–18, 535–36; Ichiki Kitokurō (vice minister), "Wagakuni ni okeru jikei kyūsai jigyō to jizen kyōkai to no kankei," 16.

82. Sidney and Beatrice Webb, *The Prevention of Destitution*, 317.

83. Quoted in Heclo, *Modern Social Politics*, 83.

84. Inoue, "Kanka kyūsai jigyō," 11.

85. Ikeda, *Nihon shakai fukushishi*, 382.

86. Tokonami Takejirō, "Kanka kyūsai jigyō tōkyokusha no kokoroe," 20–21.

87. Inoue, "Kanka kyūsai jigyō," 2; also Miyachi Masato, "Nichirō zengo," 6:131–33.

88. Shakai fukushi chōsa kenkyūkai, *Senzenki shakai jigyō shiryō shūsei*, 18:1–3.

89. Nakagawa Kiyoshi, "Senzen no Nihon no hinkon no seikaku," in Yoshida, *Shakai fukushi no Nihonteki tokushitsu*, 293, 298.

90. Diary entry of 14 September 1911, in George Feaver, ed., *The Webbs*, 72–73.

91. Andrew Gordon, *Labor and Imperial Democracy*, part 1, chap 2.

92. NSHZS, 4:11; Ikeda, *Nihon shakai fukushishi*, 311–12.

93. Pyle, "Technology," 58, 61–62.

94. Ichibangase and Takashima, *Shakai fukushi no rekishi*, 40–41; Miyachi, "Nichirō zengo," 6:157.

95. Kiyoura Keigo, "Jizen jigyō ni taisuru shokan," 3, 5–6.

96. Ikeda, *Nihon shakai fukushishi*, 343, 348–49, 352–53.

97. Endō Kōichi, "'Shokutaku' to shite no Tomeoka."

98. Takabayashi Takashi, "Meiji-ki ni okeru hōtoku undō ni tsuite," 51–54;

Ikeda, *Nihon shakai fukushishi*, 160. For a favorable assessment of Ninomiya by Protestant missionaries, see Albert H. Abbott, "Introduction," in Robert Cornell Armstrong, ed., *Just before the Dawn*, xv.

99. Tomeoka Kōsuke, "Jizen jigyō no kako 45 nen," 19.

100. Quoted in Ikeda, *Nihon shakai fukushishi*, 379.

101. Diary entry of 23 August 1911, in Feaver, *The Webbs*, 35; Ogawa, "Sangyō shihon kakuritsu-ki," in Nihon shakai jigyō daigaku, *Nihon no kyūhin seido*, 146–47 n. 1.

102. Ikeda, *Nihon shakai fukushishi*, 304, 380–82, 383–85.

103. Quoted in Michael Lewis, *Rioters and Citizens*, 29–30, 73.

104. Yoshida Kyūichi, *Gendai shakai jigyōshi*, 129.

105. Sally Ann Hastings, *Neighborhood and Nation*, 41–49; Garon, *State and Labor*, 77–78, 94–95.

106. Garon, *State and Labor*, 73–89.

107. Yamazaki Iwao, "Kyūgo jigyō sokushin no kyūmu," 128.

108. Naimushō shakaikyoku hogoka, "Tōkyō-shi narabi Yokohama-shi ni okeru kyūmin kyūjo shisetsu shisatsu no kansō," 102.

109. "Shakai jigyōka kondankai," 73–74.

110. Yoshida, *Gendai shakai jigyōshi*, 142–43, 144.

111. Tago Ichimin, "Shakai shinsatsu no hitsuyō to shakai jigyōka yōsei kikan setchi no kyūmu," 3.

112. Tomeoka Kōsuke, "Shakai hōshi no seishin," *Shakai jigyō* (August 1925), quoted in Yoshida, *Gendai shakai jigyō*, 143–44.

113. Quoted in Ishida Takeshi, "Kindai Nihon in okeru 'shakai fukushi,'" 196–97.

114. Yoshida, *Gendai shakai jigyō*, 95.

115. Ibid., 131–33; "Kaisetsu," NSHZS, 6:1,124–25.

116. Ikeda Hiroshi (chief, Bureau of Social Affairs), "Ōsaka hōmen iin sōkai ni saishite issho o saisu," 48.

117. Suzuki Kisaburō, cited by Shibata Keijirō, "Hōmen jigyō hattatsushi bekken," part 2, *Shakai jigyō* 20 (February 1937), in NSHZS, 6:1,292.

118. Fujino Megumi, "Honkoku hōmen iin seido yōron," part 1, *Shakai jigyō* 9.11 (February 1926), in NSHZS, 6:1,223.

119. Fujino, "Honkoku hōmen iin," part 3, *Shakai jigyō* 10. 2 (May 1926), in NSHZS, 6:1,231.

120. Ozawa Hajime, "Hōmen iin seido," 59.

121. Ibid., 57.

122. Shibamura, "Daitoshi ni okeru kenryoku," 67; Ōmori Makoto, "Toshi shakai jigyō," 65–68.

123. I am grateful to Narita Ryūichi for sharing his survey of district commissioners in Yokohama, ca. 1927.

124. Niimura Kiichi, "Hōmen jigyō no shin-bun'ya," 6.

125. Ōmori, "Toshi shakai jigyō," 71–72.

126. Naimushō shakaikyoku, *Honkoku shakai jigyō gaiyō*, 1933, in NSHZS, 6:1,179.

127. House of Peers, 56th Diet, 22 March 1929, in NSHZS, 4:27.

128. Yamazaki Iwao (Social Bureau), *Kyūhin seido yōgi*, 287; for details on the Relief and Protection Law and the campaigns to enact and effect it, see Ikeda, *Nihon shakai fukushishi*, 688–702.

129. Shigeta Shin'ichi, "Senjika ni okeru kōteki fujo no dōkō," in Nihon shakai jigyō daigaku, *Nihon no kyūhin seido*, 272–73.

130. Rōdōshō, *Rōdō gyōseishi*, 1:583; also, 580, 585. See Andrew Gordon, "The Right to Work in Japan."

131. Ikeda, *Nihon shakai fukushishi*, 735–42.

132. See Endō Kōichi, "Senjika hōmen iin katsudō no seikaku to tokuchō."

133. Yoshida, *Gendai shakai jigyōshi*, 287; Ishida, "Kindai Nihon in okeru 'shakai fukushi,'" 208–9, 211.

134. John Creighton Campbell, *How Policies Change*, xi; Kent E. Calder, *Crisis and Compensation*, 349.

CHAPTER TWO
DEFINING ORTHODOXY AND HETERODOXY

1. Murakami Shigeyoshi, *Kindai Nihon no shūkyō*, 126.

2. Italics added. Miyachi Masato, "Ōmotokyō fukei jiken: Shinkō shūkyō to tennōsei ideorogii," in Wagatsuma Sakae, ed., *Nihon seiji saiban shiroku: Taishō*, 297.

3. For example, Miyachi Masato, *Tennōsei no seiji shiteki kenkyū*; Haga Noboru, *Meiji kokka to minshū*; Takeda Kiyoko, *Tennōsei shisō to kyōiku*. For a suggestive reinterpretation, see Gluck, *Japan's Modern Myths*.

4. See Inoue, *Tennōsei*.

5. Martin Collcutt, "Buddhism: The Threat of Eradication," in Jansen and Rozman, *Japan in Transition*, 143–67; Ketelaar, *Heretics and Martyrs*, chap. 2.

6. Joseph M. Kitagawa, *Religion in Japanese History*, 242–43.

7. Bunkachō bunkabu shūmuka, *Meiji ikō shūkyō seido*, 125–28.

8. Wakahara Shigeru, "Wagakuni ni okeru shūkyō seisaku," 97–100.

9. Nakajima Michio, "'Meiji kempō taisei' no kakuritsu to kokka no ideorogii seisaku," 172.

10. *Chūgai nippō*, 27 May 1913, p. 3.

11. Akazawa Shirō, "1920 nendai no shūkyō hōan," 77–78; cf. Hideo Kishimoto, ed., *Japanese Religion in the Meiji Era*, 278.

12. Kōmoto Mitsugi, "'Shisō kokunan,'" 319, 321; also Fridell, *Japanese Shrine Mergers*; Helen Hardacre, *Shintō and the State*, 109–10, 128–32.

13. Kōmoto, "'Shisō kokunan,'" 321–25.

14. "Naimushō jinja tōkyoku dan."

15. Akazawa, "1920 nendai no shūkyō hōan," 77.

16. Endō, " 'Shokutaku' to shite no Tomeoka," 300–1.

17. Ikeda, *Nihon shakai fukushishi*, 343; Yoshida, *Nihon shakai jigyō*, 166.

18. Hara Takashi, 26 December 1911, *Hara Takashi nikki*, 3:208.

19. For corporatism in Japan, see T. J. Pempel and Keiichi Tsunekawa, "Corporatism Without Labor? The Japanese Anomaly," in Philippe C. Schmitter and Gerhard Lehmbruch, eds., *Trends Toward Corporatist Intermediation*, 231–70.

20. Miyachi, "Nichirō zengo," 6:156–58.

21. Quoted in Doi Akio, "Sankyō kaidō," part 2, 88.

22. Akazawa, *Kindai Nihon no shisō dōin*, 16, 109–10.

23. *Chūgai nippō*, 23 May 1919, p. 3.

24. Keishitsu Teisei, ed., *Nihon bukkyōshi*, 3:433–34.

25. Mombushō, *Kyōka dōin*, 4, and passim.

26. Cited by Akazawa, "1920 nendai no shūkyō hōan," 78.

27. Doi, "Sankyō kaidō," part 1, 99, 105.

28. Wakahara, "Wagakuni ni okeru shūkyō seisaku," 97, 127.

29. Doi, "Sankyō kaidō," part 1, 95.

30. *Chūgai nippō*, 12 June 1928, p. 2.

31. Robert Cornell Armstrong, "The Three Religions Conference," 272.

32. Akazawa, "1920 nendai no shūkyō hōan," 79–80; Bunkachō, *Meiji ikō shūkyō seido*, 191.

33. House of Peers, special committee on the religions bill, in *Tōkyō asahi shimbun*, 23 February 1926, p. 3.

34. Keishitsu, *Nihon bukkyōshi*, 3:431–32. In the government's preliminary Commission on a Religions System in 1926, Buddhist representatives introduced an amendment to remove all religious elements from state shrines, only to withdraw it after the Ministry of Finance offered to increase the acreage of temple lands to be returned. Akazawa, "1920 nendai no shūkyō hōan," 83–84.

35. Akazawa, "1920 nendai no shūkyō hōan," 80–81, 85.

36. *Chūgai nippō*, 2 May 1926, p. 2; 2 June 1926, p. 2; 11 August 1926, p. 2. Saneharu Ojima, "The Religious Organizations Bill," 111–12.

37. *Japan Christian Quarterly* 2.2 (April 1927):110.

38. *Tōkyō asahi shimbun*, 3 February 1927, p. 2; 8 March 1927, p. 2; 14 March 1929, p. 3: 15 March 1929, p. 3; 16 March 1929, p. 3.

39. See remarks by former home minister and career bureaucrat, Mizuno Rentarō, in *Teikoku gikai kizokuin iinkai giji sokkiroku*, 52nd Diet, "Shūkyō hōan," 1st sess., 2 February 1927, pp. 2–4. Upon becoming minister of education later that year, Mizuno similarly resisted calls to reintroduce the religions bill. *Chūgai nippō*, 1 June 1928, p. 3.

40. Watanabe Osamu, "Tennōsei kokka chitsujo," 238.

41. Akazawa, "1920 nendai no shūkyō hōan," 90; Ojima, "Religious Organizations Bill," 109, 116.

42. Murakami, *Kindai Nihon no shūkyō*, 108, 111.

43. Based on middling estimates from several official surveys. See Shihōshō keijikyoku, *Saikin ni okeru ruiji shūkyō*, 104–5; Watanabe Osamu, "Fuashi-zumu-ki no shūkyō tōsei," 141 n. 45, 151 n. 70; Thomas Peter Nadolski, "Socio-Political Background," 189–90.

44. Kano Masanao, *Taishō demokurashii no teiryū*, 26–28.

45. Murakami, *Kindai Nihon no shūkyō*, 108–11; Nadolski, "Socio-Political Background," 20.

46. Winston Davis, *Dojo*, 99–114.

47. When officials questioned thirty arrested members of Tenri Kenkyūkai in 1928 as to why they initially joined the parent sect Tenrikyō, a majority replied that they had sought healing for themselves (13) or for a close relative (10). Miyachi Masato, "Tenri Kenkyūkai fukei jiken," in Wagatsuma, *Nihon seiji saiban shiroku: Shōwa-zen*, 265.

48. Miyachi Masato, "Hitonomichi kyōdan fukei jiken," in Wagatsuma, *Nihon seiji saiban shiroku: Shōwa-kō*, 252–54; Murakami, *Kindai Nihon no shūkyō*, 113–14.

49. Nadolski, "Socio-Political Background," chap. 2.

50. Yamano Haruo and Narita Ryūichi, "Minshū bunka to nashonarizumu," 276.

51. Miyachi, "Hitonomichi," in Wagatsuma, *Nihon seiji saiban shiroku: Shōwa-kō*, 257–58.

52. Nadolski, "Socio-Political Background," 195–96.

53. Watanabe, "Tennōsei kokka chitsujo," 210.

54. Directive of 3 March 1919, quoted ibid., 214.

55. Ibid., 234–35, 238–39; Miyachi, "Tenri Kenkyūkai," in Wagatsuma, *Nihon seiji saiban shiroku: Shōwa-zen*, 258–90.

56. Karasawa Toshitatsu to Special Higher Police section chiefs, 25 February 1936, quoted in Watanabe, "Fuashizumu-ki no shūkyō tōsei," 121 n. 1.

57. Nagano Wakamatsu, "Shūkyō keisatsu," 20.

58. Murakami, *Kindai Nihon no shūkyō*, 125–26; Nadolski, "Socio-Political Background," 264.

59. Watanabe, "Fuashizumu-ki no shūkyō tōsei," 127–31; Miyachi Masato, "Dai niji Ōmotokyō jiken," in Wagatsuma, *Nihon seiji saiban shiroku: Shōwa-kō*, 95–140.

60. Watanabe, "Fuashizumu-ki no shūkyō tōsei," 137–38, 146–47, 155–57; Murakami, *Kindai Nihon no shūkyō*, 129–30.

61. Especially Kurihara Akira, "1930 nendai no shakai ishiki to Ōmoto."

62. Norman Cohn, *The Pursuit of the Millennium*, 14.

63. Kano, *Taishō demokurashii no teiryū*, 57–58.

64. Report by Special Higher Police, n.d., cited by Watanabe, "Fuashizumu-ki no shūkyō tōsei," 125 n. 10.

65. Miyachi, "Tenri Kenkyūkai," in Wagatsuma, *Nihon seiji saiban shiroku: Shōwa-zen*, 265.

66. Murakami, *Kindai Nihon no shūkyō*, 115.

67. Davis, *Dojo*, 13.

68. Ōmoto 70-nenshi hensankai, ed., *Ōmoto 70-nenshi*, 2:185; Nadolski, "Socio-Political Background," 254.

69. Watanabe, "Fuashizumu-ki no shūkyō tōsei," 117, 122–24 n. 5.

70. Shihōshō keijikyoku, *Hitonomichi kyōdan jiken no kenkyū*, 266; Ikeda Akira, ed., *Hitonomichi kyōdan fukei jiken kankei shiryō shūsei*, 934.

71. Ōmoto 70-nenshi hensankai, *Ōmoto 70-nenshi*, 1:602–7, 2:399–403; Murakami, *Kindai Nihon no shūkyō*, 102.

72. Ōyama Ikuo, "Shakai mondai to shite mitaru saikin ni okeru meishin ryūkō no keikō"; Sakai Toshihiko, "Meishinteki genshō no shakaiteki kansatsu," and Kawakami Hajime, "Paranoia to jibun," both in Nakamura Kokyō, *Ōmotokyō no kaibō*, foreword, 33–38, 41–44.

73. Nakamura, *Ōmotokyō no kaibō*; Ōmoto 70-nenshi hensankai, *Ōmoto 70-nenshi*, 1:483, 527, 541, 551; for other prominent critics of Ōmotokyō, see 1:483–85.

74. Nakamura Kokyō, "Giji shūkyō wa subete sagi nari," 77.

75. *Chūgai nippō*, 7 July, 31 August 1920, p. 3; for New Buddhists, see Keishitsu, *Nihon bukkyōshi*, 3:358–62.

76. Takashima Beihō, "Jashūkyō," 419.

77. Ibid., 412, 419.

78. Nadolski, "Socio-Political Background," 6.

79. Nagano, "Shūkyō keisatsu," 15, 22–25.

80. Nadolski, "Socio-Political Background," 172, 181–82, 264–65.

81. Miyachi, "Hitonomichi," in Wagatsuma, *Nihon seiji saiban shiroku: Shōwa-kō*, 261; Murakami, *Kindai Nihon no shūkyō*, 114, 127.

82. Nagano, "Shūkyō keisatsu," 15, 24.

83. Wakahara, "Wagakuni ni okeru shūkyō seisaku," 128.

84. See Garon, *State and Labor*, chap. 3; Nagano Wakamatsu, *Nagano Wakamatsu shi danwa dai 1-kai sokkiroku*, 10–11.

85. Nagano, "Shūkyō keisatsu," 23–25.

86. See Helen Hardacre, *Lay Buddhism in Contemporary Japan*.

87. See Brenda M. Bolton, "Mulieres Sanctae," 141, 143, 154; Natalie Zemon Davis, "City Women and Religious Change," in her *Society and Culture in Early Modern France*, 65–66.

88. Nagano, "Shūkyō keisatsu," 25.

89. Miyachi, "Hitonomichi," in Wagatsuma, *Nihon seiji saiban shiroku: Shōwa-kō*, 256.

90. Shihōshō keijikyoku, *Hitonomichi kyōdan jiken no kenkyū*, 264–65, 293.

91. Nagano, "Shūkyō keisatsu," 16–17.

92. Ibid., 15.

93. Shihōshō keijikyoku, *Saikin ni okeru ruiji shūkyō*, 14.

94. Matsuzaka Hiromasa (chief, Criminal Affairs Bureau), in *Shisō kenkyū shiryō tokushū* 62 (1939), cited by Watanabe, "Fuashizumu-ki no shūkyō tōsei," 157–58 n. 85.

95. On the distinction between state and societal corporatism, see Philippe C. Schmitter, "Still the Century of Corporatism?" in Schmitter and Lehmbruch, *Trends Toward Corporatist Intermediation*, 20.

96. Forced revisions in the creeds of Tenrikyō and Nichiren Buddhism are discussed by Watanabe, "Fuashizumu-ki no shūkyō tōsei," 153.

97. House of Peers, special committee on the religious organizations bill, 8 February 1939, cited ibid., 160.

98. Ibid., 161.

CHAPTER THREE
THE WORLD'S OLDEST DEBATE?

1. Itō Hidekichi, *Nihon haishō undōshi*, 169–78.

2. Vern Bullough and Bonnie Bullough, *Women and Prostitution*, 45–46, 55–56, 59–61, 91–93; Itō Hidekichi, *Kōtōka no kanojo*, 34–35.

3. Abraham Flexner, *Prostitution in Europe*, 4; see also John F. Decker, *Prostitution*, 74–76.

4. Hugh Borton, "Memorandum Prepared by the Inter-Divisional Area Committee on the Far East," 9 May 1944, in U.S. Department of State, *Foreign Relations of the United States: Diplomatic Papers, 1944*, 5:1,258–59.

5. Yamamoto Shun'ichi, *Nihon kōshōshi*, 3–5.

6. Ibid., 5.

7. Ibid., 238–39, also 202.

8. *Nihon fujin mondai shiryō shūsei* (hereafter cited as NFMSS), 1:38–39; Yamamoto, *Nihon kōshōshi*, 74–87.

9. Yoshimi Kaneko, *Baishō no shakaishi*, 18–20.

10. Yamamoto, *Nihon kōshōshi*, 109, 112, 121, 156.

11. Yamamoto, *Nihon kōshōshi*, 129–30.

12. D. Eleanor Westney, *Imitation and Innovation*, 50; Alain Corbin, *Women for Hire*, 88–93.

13. Yamamoto, *Nihon kōshōshi*, 163, 292, 296, 365.

14. Kusama Yasoo, "Wagakuni ni okeru kōshō," 62.

15. Corbin, *Women for Hire*, 115, also 11, 37–38, 85–86, 115–17; see also Mary Gibson, *Prostitution and the State in Italy*, 33, 223–24.

16. Nishimura Miharu, "Baishun mondai," 112; Kusama, "Wagakuni ni okeru kōshō," 65.

17. Yamamoto, *Nihon kōshōshi*, 370.

18. Ruling of 21 May 1900, in U. G. Murphy, *Social Evil*, 142.

19. For the more limited role of indebtedness in French brothels, see Corbin, *Women for Hire*, 68, 78–79.

20. J. Mark Ramseyer, "Indentured Prostitution in Imperial Japan," 90.

21. Murphy, *Social Evil*, 118–19, 132.

22. Ibid., 63–117.

23. Yonekura Akira, "Hōritsu kōi," part 17, 60:34–35; part 16, 59:35–40.

24. Yamamuro Gumpei, "Kyūseigun Kieko-ryō kaisetsu ni saishite," 6.

25. Nishimura, "Baishun mondai," 112.

26. Kusama Yasoo, *Tomoshibi no onna*, 2:807.

27. NFMSS, 1:516–17.

28. Yamamoto, *Nihon kōshōshi*, 389.

29. League of Nations, *Commission of Enquiry*, 104–7.

30. Yoshimi, *Baishō no shakaishi*, 142; NFMSS, 1:509–10.

31. Mark R. Shaw, "Temperance and Purity Notes," 93.

32. Kusama, *Tomoshibi no onna*, 2:833–34; for other surveys, see 2:831–38; Yamamoto, *Nihon kōshōshi*, 520.

33. Kusama, *Tomoshibi no onna*, 2:838, 841–43, 846.

34. Ibid., 2:834–35.

35. Alexandre-Jean-Baptiste Parent-Duchâtelet, *De la prostitution dans la ville de Paris*, 3d ed. (1857), 1:584, quoted in Flexner, *Prostitution in Europe*, 21.

36. Yamamoto, *Nihon kōshōshi*, 389–90.

37. Kusama, *Tomoshibi no onna*, 2:1,069–71.

38. Kusama Yasoo, "Zegen to yūkakugyōsha no jitsujō," *Taisei* 8 (March 1927), reprinted in Kusama, *Kindai toshi kasō shakai*, 1:199–200; Kusama, "Kaihō sareta shōgi no yukue," *Kaizō* 16 (July 1934), ibid., 1:526; cf. Ramseyer, "Indentured Prostitution," 102.

39. League of Nations, *Commission of Enquiry*, 105.

40. Kusama, *Tomoshibi no onna*, 2:1,172–75.

41. Robert J. Smith and Ella Lury Wiswell, *The Women of Suye Mura*, 140–42.

42. Corbin, *Women for Hire*, 81; Kusama, *Tomoshibi no onna*, 2:1,004–5.

43. Calculated from figures for annual customer visits in Yamamoto, *Nihon kōshōshi*, 518; NFMSS, 1:516–17; Wakita Haruko, Hayashi Reiko, and Nagahara Kazuko, eds., *Nihon joseishi*, 261.

44. Ujihara Sukezō, *Baishōfu*, 134–35.

45. Gibson, *Prostitution and the State*, 33.

46. Joseph Ernest de Becker, *The Nightless City*, 202–3.

47. Tanabe Hisa, "Harimise no kōshi no naka kara," 43; see also Takemura Tamio, *Haishō undō*, 60–61.

48. Takemura, *Haishō undō*, 60–64.

49. Judith R. Walkowitz, *Prostitution and Victorian Society*; Corbin, *Women for Hire*, 214–20; David J. Pivar, *Purity Crusade*, 67, 85, 96–98, 118–19.

50. Nihon kirisutokyō fujin kyōfūkai, *Nihon kirisutokyō fujin kyōfūkai*, 35–37, 93, 98–110; Sievers, *Flowers in Salt*, 92–98.

51. Itō, *Kōtōka no kanojo*, 257–59, 275–76.

52. See Walkowitz, *Prostitution and Victorian Society*, 99–101.

53. Nihon kirisutokyō fujin kyōfūkai, *Nihon kirisutokyō fujin kyōfūkai*, 70.

54. Itō, *Kōtōka no kanojo*, 332–34.

55. Joseph Ernest de Becker, *Annotated Civil Code of Japan*, 3:73–75, 4:11–13, 41–42; Wakita, Hayashi, and Nagahara, *Nihon joseishi*, 193–94.

56. Japan, *The Criminal Code of Japan*, 132.

57. Nihon kirisutokyō fujin kyōfūkai, *Nihon kirisutokyō fujin kyōfūkai*, 51, 62–65, 331–32.

58. Ibid., 52–53.

59. Uemura Masahisa, *Gyokusekishū* (1887), quoted in Harada Kiyoko, "Kirisutokyō to sono shūhen no josei-kan," 64; also, Itō, *Kōtōka no kanojo*, 332–33.

60. Nihon kirisutokyō fujin kyōfūkai, *Nihon kirisutokyō fujin kyōfūkai*, 62–64.

61. Yoshimi, *Baishō no shakaishi*, 48; Itō, *Kōtōka no kanojo*, 334; Kataoka Shōichi, ed., *Haishō ka*, 58–59; Augustine, quoted in Fernando Henriques, *Prostitution and Society*, 2:25.

62. Yamamoto, *Nihon kōshōshi*, 3–4, 58–59, 200–1.

63. Kusama, *Tomoshibi no onna*, 2:1,072, 1,079.

64. Itō, *Kōtōka no kanojo*, 377–81; Gunpei Yamamuro, "The Social Evil in Japan."

65. Ujihara, *Baishōfu*, 144–45, 352–53.

66. Fukumi Takao, *Teitō ni okeru baiin no kenkyū*, 6–8.

67. Hasegawa Yasushi, "Haishō ronsha," 94–95,

68. Fukuzawa Yukichi, "Hinkō ron" (1885), translated in *Fukuzawa Yukichi on Japanese Women*, 87–88.

69. Funada Naka, speech to the National Federation of the Brothel Trade, 19 February 1935, in NFMSS, 1:500.

70. Hasegawa, "Haishō ronsha," 93–94, 97–98.

71. Corbin, *Women for Hire*, 19; Gibson, *Prostitution and the State*, 19–23.

72. *The Daily News* (London), 2 July 1896, p. 7.

73. Kusama, *Tomoshibi no onna*, 2:846.

74. Kusama Yasoo, *Furōsha to baishōfu no kenkyū* (1927), reprinted in Kusama, *Kindai kasō minshū seikatsushi*, 1:126.

75. Ujihara, *Baishōfu*, 355.

76. Kataoka, *Haishō ka*, 50.

77. Takemura, *Haishō undō*, 45–46.

78. Yamamoto, *Nihon kōshōshi*, 423–24.

79. See Garon, *State and Labor*, chap. 3.

80. *Tōkyō asahi shimbun*, 26 April 1926, p. 2; 26 April 1926 (evening ed.), p. 2; 30 April 1926 (evening ed.), p. 2; 4 May 1926, p. 2.

81. Nihon kirisutokyō fujin kyōfūkai, *Nihon kirisutokyō fujin kyōfūkai*, 512–32.

82. Itō Hidekichi, "Miuri bōshi undō to sono shisetsu gaiyō," 27.

83. Itō, *Kōtōka no kanojo*, 609–10, 616–25.

84. Matsumiya Yahei, *Saikin no haishō undō*, 3–5, 15–16; League of Nations, *Commission of Enquiry*, 96.

85. Itō Hidekichi, "Sekai no baishō seisaku," 10–11.

86. Itō, *Nihon haishō undōshi*, 329.

87. NFMSS, 1:43.

88. Corbin, *Women for Hire*, 315–16.

89. *Teikoku gikai shūgiin giji sokkiroku*, 59th Diet, 14 February 1931, pp. 295–96.

90. *Tōkyō asahi shimbun*, 23 March 1935, p. 13.

91. Kubushiro Ochimi, "Tsutsushimite kishū ryōin ni uttau," 7.

92. Nishimura Miharu, "Kaisetsu," 9.

93. Takemura, *Haishō undō*, 178–79.

94. Kusama, *Tomoshibi no onna*, 2:850.

95. See Miriam Silverberg, "The Modern Girl as Militant," in Gail Lee Bernstein, ed. *Recreating Japanese Women*, 239–66.

96. Kanō Mikiyo, *Onnatachi no "jūgo,"* 37–38.

97. Ōbinata Sumio, *Tennōsei keisatsu to minshū*, 203–5.

98. *Tōkyō asahi shimbun*, 25 December 1934, evening ed., 2.

99. *Kakusei* 24 (October 1934):39, (November 1934):31.

100. *Kakusei* 25 (March 1935):38.

101. Kagawa Toyohiko, "Haishō undō no kompon seishin," 7–8.

102. Ieda Sakichi, "Junketsu Nihon no fukkō to kensetsu," 27.

103. Takashima Beihō, "Gendai josei o hihansu," 13.

104. Abe Isoo, "Jinkō mondai to danjo mondai," 3.

105. Murakami Yūsaku, "Jiji hyōron," 26–27.

106. *Kakusei* 27 (August 1937):24, (November 1937):31; 28 (March 1938): 27.

107. Takashima Beihō, "Kokumin seishin sōdōin to fūkyō mondai," 4.

108. Ozaki Yukio, "Kokumin dōtoku no kōjō o hakare," 5.

109. Takemura, *Haishō undō*, 183–88.

110. Nihon kirisutokyō fujin kyōfūkai, *Nihon kirisutokyō fujin kyōfūkai*, 652–55.

111. Kubushiro Ochimi, *Haishō hitosuji*, 258.

112. Takemura, *Haishō undō*, 189–90.

113. *Kakusei* 32 (September 1942):28; Murakami Yūsaku, "Kōkyū kyōraku kyūshi shokan," 7.

114. George Hicks, *The Comfort Women*, 19–20, 34–35, 44–45, chap. 4, and passim.

115. Yamamoto, *Nihon kōshōshi*, 632–33.

116. Katsuo Ryūzō, cited by Nishi Kiyoko, *Senryōka no Nihon fujin seisaku,* 107.

117. Sally Ann Hastings, *Neighborhood and Nation,* 33, 54, 58; *Kirisutokyō jimmei jiten,* 1986 ed., s.v. "Yamamuro Gumpei."

118. Masutomi Masasuke, "Ōkuma naikaku to Kyōfūkai," 13–14.

119. For example, "Kokusan aiyō shijō zadankai."

120. Corbin, *Women for Hire,* 218–20, 226.

121. Gibson, *Prostitution and the State,* 48–51, 91–92.

122. Walkowitz, *Prostitution and Victorian Society,* 245–52; Brian Harrison, "State Intervention and Moral Reform," 313–14.

123. Pivar, *Purity Crusade,* 7, 97–98, 210–12.

124. Barbara Meil Hobson, *Uneasy Virtue,* 139–53, 165–83; Mark Thomas Connelly, *The Response to Prostitution,* 141–43.

CHAPTER FOUR
INTEGRATING WOMEN INTO PUBLIC LIFE

1. Most recently, Bernstein, *Recreating Japanese Women*; and Joseishi sōgō kenkyūkai, ed., *Nihon josei seikatsushi.*

2. Kano Masanao, *Fujin, josei, onna,* 74–75; also 52–53.

3. Sievers, *Flowers in Salt,* xi–xii; see also Mikiso Hane, trans. and ed., *Reflections on the Way to the Gallows,* 1–2.

4. For example, Ichikawa Fusae, ed., *Nihon fujin mondai shiryō shūsei* (hereafter cited as NFMSS), vol. 2; Ichikawa Fusae, *Ichikawa Fusae jiden*; Kodama Katsuko (supervised by Ichikawa), *Fujin sanseiken undō shōshi.*

5. Kathleen Susan Molony, "One Woman Who Dared"; Dee Ann Vavich, "Japanese Woman's Movement"; Patricia Murray, "Ichikawa Fusae and the Lonely Red Carpet."

6. Dorothy Robins-Mowry, *Hidden Sun,* 88–89; Vavich, "Japanese Woman's Movement," 426–27.

7. Suzuki Yūko, *Feminizumu to sensō*; Kano, *Fujin, josei, onna,* 79–80.

8. Ichikawa, *Ichikawa Fisae jiden,* 268.

9. Nihon kirisutokyō fujin kyōfūkai, *Nihon kirisutokyō fujin kyōfūkai,* 498.

10. Fujime Yuki, "Zen Kansai fujin rengōkai," 71–74; Abe Tsunehisa, "1920 nendai no fujinkai," in Joseishi sōgō kenkyūkai, ed., *Nihon joseishi,* 5:75–113; Gregory M. Pflugfelder, "Politics and the Kitchen."

11. Paula Baker, "The Domestication of Politics," 622.

12. Sievers, *Flowers in Salt,* chap. 3.

13. Shiraishi Reiko, "1920–30 nendai Nihon ni okeru fujin kankei rippō ni tsuite no ikkōsatsu," 38–39.

14. NFMSS, 2:132–34, 139–40.

15. Ōi Shizuo and Takahashi Tokutarō, *Chian keisatsuhō shakugi*, 22; also 25.

16. *Dai Nihon teikoku gikai shi* (hereafter cited as DNTGS), vol. 1, 1st Diet, Lower House, 1 March 1890, pp. 1,049, 1,058.

17. Translation of *Onna daigaku* appears in Atsuhara Sakai, "Kaibara-Ekiken and 'Onna Daigaku' "; see also Jennifer Robertson, "The Shingaku Woman," in Bernstein, *Recreating Japanese Women*, 91–92, 95.

18. Mariko Asano Tamanoi, "Songs as Weapons," 794.

19. Ibid., 803; Robertson, "Shingaku Woman," in Bernstein, *Recreating Japanese Women*, 94; Pivar, *Purity Crusade*, 170.

20. Fukuzawa Yukichi, "Onna daigaku hyōron," *Jiji shimpō*, 1 April–23 July 1899, in *Fukuzawa Yukichi on Japanese Women*, 201–2, 208.

21. Quoted in Margit Maria Nagy, "How Shall We Live?", 25.

22. Cf. Sharon H. Nolte and Sally Ann Hastings, "The Meiji State's Policy toward Women, 1890–1910," in Bernstein, *Recreating Japanese Women*, 157. They assert that because Article 5 prohibited military men, teachers, and priests— as well as women—from joining political associations, "the grouping implied that women were like civil servants whose political activity would be inappropriate or whose responsibilities so weighty as to preclude their participation."

23. Muramatsu Tsuneichirō, in DNTGS, vol. 9, 31st Diet, Lower House, 30 January 1914, p. 270.

24. Sotozaki Mitsuhiro, *Nihon fujinronshi*, 1:200–4.

25. For example, Kudō Yukitomo, in DNTGS, vol. 4, 10th Diet, Lower House, 2 March 1897, p. 456.

26. Kano Masanao, "Fusen kakutoku dōmei no seiritsu to tenkai, 68.

27. Chino Yōichi, *Kindai Nihon fujin kyōikushi*, 109, 133.

28. Ichikawa Fusae, "Chian keisatsuhō dai 5-jō shūsei no undō," 23–24.

29. Shimoda Utako, "Niwa no oshie," *Fujo zasshi* 3.5 (1 March 1893), quoted in Chino, *Kindai Nihon fujin kyōikushi*, 105–6.

30. Mitsui Kōsaburō, *Aikoku fujinkaishi*, 1, 4.

31. Saji Emiko, "Gunji engo to katei fujin—shoki aikoku fujinkai ron," in Kindai joseishi kenkyūkai, ed., *Onnatachi no kindai*, 116–43; also Sally A. Hastings, "Women Educators and the Patriotic Women's Society"; Chino, *Kindai Nihon fujin kyōikushi*, 128.

32. Chino, *Kindai Nihon fujin kyōikushi*, 141–60.

33. Ibid., 167–68; Hane, *Reflections on the Way to the Gallows*, 15; Margit Nagy, "Middle-Class Working Women During the Interwar Years," in Bernstein, *Recreating Japanese Women*, 201–4, 208.

34. Sievers, *Flowers in Salt*, chap. 8.

35. DNTGS, vol. 12, 44th Diet, House of Peers, 26 March 1921, pp. 1,158–59.

36. For example, Molony, "One Woman Who Dared," 148–49.

37. *Josei dōmei* 6 (March 1921):71.

38. Ichikawa Fusae, *Watakushi no fujin undō*, 68, 70–71, 79–80, 90–91.

39. Tabuchi Toyokichi, in DNTGS, vol. 12, 43rd Diet, Lower House, 19 July 1920, pp. 482, 483; also Takahashi Motokichi, in *Teikoku gikai shūgiin iinkai giroku*, 43rd Diet, Petitions committee, lst section, 1st sess., 12 July 1920, p. 7.

40. For a similar assessment of the arguments for suffrage and the revision of Article 5, see Sharon H. Nolte, "Women's Rights and Society's Needs," 696, 708. To Nolte, most proponents in the Diet justified suffrage in terms of service to society, rather than service to the state, whereas I view their conceptions of state and society as intertwined.

41. Tabuchi, in DNTGS, vol. 12, 43rd Diet, Lower House, 19 July 1920, pp. 483, 484.

42. DNTGS, vol. 12, 44th Diet, Lower House, 5 February 1921, p. 1,342.

43. *Teikoku gikai shūgiin iinkai giroku*, 43rd Diet, "Chian keisatsuhō-chū kaisei hōritsuan," 2nd sess., 21 July 1920, p. 4.

44. Kawamura Takeji, in *Teikoku gikai kizokuin iinkai giji sokkiroku*, 44th Diet, "Chian keisatsuhō-chū kaisei hōritsuan," 1st sess., 13 March 1921, pp. 1, 3.

45. Ibid., 1.

46. Rinji gunji chōsa iinkai, *Ōshusen to kōsen kakkoku fujin* (1917), 1, 80, quoted in Chino, *Kindai Nihon fujin kyōikushi*, 175; for similar reports by the Ministry of Education, see 174–75.

47. Naimushō chihōkyoku, *Senji rekkoku chihō shiryō*, 40, 43–44.

48. Nakajima, "Taishō-ki ni okeru 'seikatsu kaizen undō,'" 58.

49. Kathleen S. Uno, "Women and Changes in the Household Division of Labor," in Bernstein, *Recreating Japanese Women*, 17–18, 27, 32–34.

50. Smith and Wiswell, *Women of Suye Mura*, 180–82.

51. Abe, "1920 nendai no fujinkai," 78.

52. Saitō Michiko, "Hani Motoko no shisō—kaji kakei ron chūshin ni," in Kindai joseishi kenkyūkai, ed., *Onnatachi no kindai*, 150.

53. Kano Masanao, *Fujin, josei, onna*, 25–26; Chizuko Ueno, "The Japanese Women's Movement," 172–73.

54. Itagaki, *Shōwa senzen, senchūki no nōson seikatsu*, ii–iii, 32–36.

55. *Tōkyō asahi shimbun*, 2 October 1920, p. 5.

56. Naimushō shakaikyoku, *Zenkoku shojokai, fujinkai no gaikyō*, 2, 4.

57. Nakajima, "Taishō-ki ni okeru 'seikatsu kaizen undō,'" 57, 59–60, 63–65, 68–69; Chino, *Kindai Nihon fujin kyōikushi*, 186–87.

58. Nakajima, "Taishō-ki ni okeru 'seikatsu kaizen undō,'" 55, 60, 71.

59. Tago Ichimin, *Shinjidai no fujin*, 144.

60. Sally A. Hastings, "From Heroine to Patriotic Volunteer," Nagy, "How Shall We Live?" 131–32, 240–41.

61. Kyōchōkai, ed., *Saikin no shakai undō*, 712; Chino, *Kindai Nihon fujin kyōikushi*, 240–41.

62. *Tōkyō asahi shimbun*, 2 October 1929, p. 7.

63. Fukushima Shirō, "Yūshi irai no fujin no chikara."

64. For Hiratsuka's role in the feminist "debate over the protection of motherhood" (1916–1918), see Laurel Rasplica Rodd, "Yosano Akiko and the Taishō Debate over the 'New Woman,'" in Bernstein, *Recreating Japanese Women*, 189–98.

65. Italics added. [Hiratsuka] Raichō, "Shakai kaizō ni taisuru fujin no shimei," 4, 10.

66. Ichikawa, *Watakushi no fujin undō*, 17–20.

67. Reprinted in NFMSS, 2:179–81.

68. Suzuki Yūko, *Joseishi o hiraku*, 2:30–33.

69. See William L. O'Neill, *The Woman Movement*, 14, 33–36, 43; Pivar, *Purity Crusade*, 6, 170; Baker, "Domestication of Politics," 625, 632; in the Japanese context, see Nolte, *Liberalism in Modern Japan*, 118–28.

70. Chino, *Kindai Nihon fujin kyōikushi*, 180–81; Nakajima, "Taishō-ki ni okeru 'seikatsu kaizen undō,'" 60–61, 69.

71. Saitō, "Hani Motoko no shisō," in Kindai joseishi kenkyūkai, *Onnatachi no kindai*, 147–53, 157, 159, 166–67.

72. Chino, *Kindai Nihon fujin kyōikushi*, 181.

73. Quoted in Fujime, "Zen Kansai fujin rengōkai," 83.

74. *Josei dōmei*, 2 (November 1920):43.

75. Fujime, "Zen Kansai fujin rengōkai," 84.

76. Ibid., 71, 75–76, 80–82.

77. Molony, "One Woman Who Dared," 214.

78. Matsuyama Jirō, "Fujin kōminken-an no suii," 89.

79. "Bijaku na fujin undō," *Tōkyō asahi shimbun*, 17 February 1929, p. 3.

80. Kodama, *Fujin sanseiken undō*, 211–12.

81. "Zen Kansai fujin rengōkai hombu daihyōsha zadankai," *Fujin* 7. 2 (February 1930):53; also Onda Kazuko, "Zen Kansai fujin rengōkai," 7.

82. Shindō Tokuko, "Jūnin o kanjitsuzu," 12.

83. *Jiji shimpō*, 18 June 1928, in NFMSS, 2:294–95.

84. Speeches by Yamamasu Norishige and Nishioka Takejirō, in *Teikoku gikai shūgiin iinkai giroku*, 58th Diet, "Shisei-chū kaisei hōritsuan," 1st sess., 9 May 1930, p. 2.

85. Saji Emiko, "Hamaguchi naikaku," 17–18.

86. *Teikoku gikai shūgiin giji sokkiroku*, 58th Diet, no. 11, 8 May 1930, p. 192.

87. *Tōkyō asahi shimbun*, 9 March 1930, p. 3.

88. Finance Minister Inoue Junnosuke, quoted in Saji, "Hamaguchi naikaku," 3; see also 1–4.

89. Ibid., 4.

90. [Ichikawa Fusae], "Kotoshi no aki."

91. Sakamoto Makoto, "Hamaguchi kinshuku naikaku o mukaete," 4.

92. Saji, "Hamaguchi naikaku," 4–5.

93. "Shōhi keizai kōenkai," 10.

94. "Naishō no enzetsu."

95. Hasama Shigeru, *Chihō jichi*, 66–67.

96. Ichikawa Fusae, "Fuken to shichōson to wa, dō chigau ka," 19.

97. Hasama Shigeru, *Chihō jichisei kōwa*, 68; also Tsugita Daisaburō, in *Teikoku gikai kizokuin iinkai giji sokkiroku*, 59th Diet, "Shisei-chū kaisei hōritsuan," 2nd sess., 9 March 1931, p. 8.

98. Tazawa Yoshiharu, "Fujin kōminken no igi," 26; Saji, "Hamaguchi naikaku," 9–10.

99. Tago Ichimin, in *Teikoku gikai shūgiin iinkai giroku*, 58th Diet, "Shisei-chū kaisei hōritsuan," 1st sess., 9 May 1930, p. 6.

100. Suematsu Kaichirō, in *Teikoku gikai shūgiin iinkai giroku*, 58th Diet, "Shisei-chū kaisei hōritsuan," 1st sess., 9 May 1930, pp. 10, 12.

101. *Teikoku gikai kizokuin iinkai giji sokkiroku*, 59th Diet, "Shisei-chū kaisei hōritsuan," 1st sess., 5 March 1931, p. 3.

102. Ichikawa Fusae, "Seifu narabi ni Seiyūkai teian no fujin kōminken-an ni taisuru watakushidomo no taido," 7.

103. Kodama, *Fujin sanseiken undō*, 205–6.

104. Ichikawa Fusae, Sakamoto Makoto, and Kaneko Shigeri, "Seigen kōminken-an o megurite," 9–10; *Fusen* 5.4 (April 1931): 35.

105. "Fujin kōminken to fujin sanseiken to izure ga taisetsu ka," 14.

106. Onda, "Zen Kansai fujin rengōkai," 9.

107. Ichikawa Fusae, "Zenkoku chōsonchōkai no fujin kōminken hantairon ni bakusu," *Fusen* 4.11 (December 1930), in NFMSS, 2:397–98.

108. Molony, "One Woman Who Dared," 284–85.

109. Statement of 4 November 1930, in NFMSS, 2:395–96.

110. Italics added. Fukami Kiyoshi, in *Teikoku gikai shūgiin giji sokkiroku*, 58th Diet, no. 12, 10 May 1930, p. 229.

111. Umezono Atsuhiko, in *Teikoku gikai kizokuin iinkai giji sokkiroku*, 59th Diet, "Shisei-chū kaisei hōritsuan," 2nd sess., 9 March 1931, pp. 4–5.

112. *Teikoku gikai kizokuin giji sokkiroku*, 59th Diet, no. 38, 24 March 1931, p. 628.

113. Interviews with Kimura Masayoshi (Seiyūkai) and Yamamoto Tatsuo (home minister), in *Fusen* 6.8 (August 1932):17–18, 21.

114. Kanō, *Onnatachi no "jūgo"*, 45; Fujii Tadatoshi, *Kokubō fujinkai*, 127–28; also 91–106.

115. Chino, *Kindai Nihon fujin kyōikushi*, 268–69.

116. Nihon kirisutokyō fujin kyōfūkai, *Nihon kirisutokyō fujin kyōfūkai*, 623–29; Fujii, *Kokubō fujinkai*, 121–22; Nagahara Kazuko and Yoneda Sayoko, *Onna no Shōwashi*, 30–31.

117. Kano Masanao, "Fuashizumuka no fujin undō," Molony, "One Woman Who Dared," 322–43.

118. Ichikawa Fusae, "Jichisei e no fujin kyōryoku," 4–5.

119. "Sōsenkyo to fusen kakutoku dōmei."

120. Ichikawa Fusae, "Shōwa jūnen ni okeru fusen undō no shinten," 4.

121. Molony, "One Woman Who Dared," 296–98; Ichibangase Yasuko, "Boshi hogohō seitei sokushin undō no shakaiteki seikaku ni tsuite," 38–39.

122. Yoshiko Miyake, "Doubling Expectations: Motherhood and Women's Factory Work under State Management in Japan in the 1930s and 1940s," in Bernstein, *Recreating Japanese Women*, 270–73.

123. Mitsui Reiko, *Gendai fujin undōshi nempyō*, 63; Suzuki Yūko, *Feminizumu to sensō*, 17–19.

124. Ichikawa Fusae, "Kokumin sōdōin to fujin."

125. Ichikawa Fusae, "Watakushi no koro," 23.

126. Suzuki, *Feminizumu to sensō*, 47–53, 76–86, 143–45.

127. Kanō, *Onnatachi no "jūgo"*, 45–46.

CHAPTER FIVE
RE-CREATING THE CHANNELS OF MORAL SUASION

1. Quoted in David John Lu, ed., *Sources of Japanese History*, 2:176–77.

2. Ronald H. Spector, *Eagle against the Sun*, 505.

3. John W. Dower, *War without Mercy*, 297–99.

4. To borrow a phrase from James B. Crowley, *Japan's Quest for Autonomy*.

5. Masataka Kosaka, *100 Million Japanese*, 45; Supreme Commander for the Allied Powers (hereafter cited as SCAP), *History of the Nonmilitary Activities*, no. 7: "The Purge," 29–30.

6. "Tensei jingo," *Asahi shimbun*, 22 February 1946, p. 1.

7. J. Victor Koschmann, "The Debate on Subjectivity in Postwar Japan."

8. SCAP, *History of the Nonmilitary Activities*, no. 6: "Local Government Reform," 44, 52–55; for the role of New Deal thought in the Occupation's welfare policies, see Tatara, "1400 Years of Japanese Social Work," 344, 411–12, 459–60, 494.

9. Usui Masahisa, ed., *Shakai kyōiku*, 13; also John W. Dower, "Peace and Democracy in Two Systems: External Policy and Internal Conflict," in Andrew Gordon, ed., *Postwar Japan as History*, 3–4.

10. Garon, *State and Labor*, 234.

11. Yoshida Shigeru, *Sekai to Nihon* (1962), quoted in John W. Dower, *Empire and Aftermath*, 364.

12. For accounts of Left-Right conflict during the 1950s, see John W. Dower, "Peace and Democracy," in Gordon, ed., *Postwar Japan as History*, 5, 18–20; George R. Packard, *Protest in Tokyo*; Kosaka, *100 Million Japanese*, 127–29, 134–36, 157–99.

13. For example, Gerald L. Curtis, *The Japanese Way of Politics*, 16–18, 35–37.

14. United States, State Department, Interim Research and Intelligence Section, [and] Research and Analysis Branch, "Control of Inflation," Report— R & A no. 2,451, 1 October 1945, reprinted in Ōkurashō zaiseishishitsu, *Shōwa zaiseishi: Shūsen kara kōwa made*, 20: 491–92.

15. Ōkurashō zaiseishi hensanshitsu, *Shōwa zaiseishi*, 11:234–36; savings rates appear in Charles Yuji Horioka, "Consuming and Saving," in Gordon, *Postwar Japan as History*, 283.

16. Chochiku zōkyō chūō iinkai, *Chochiku undōshi*, 13, 126.

17. Chochiku zōkyō chūō iinkai, *Chochiku hakusho*, 215–16.

18. Chochiku zōkyō chūō iinkai, *Chochiku undōshi*, 22–25.

19. Chochiku zōkyō chūō iinkai, *Chochiku hakusho*, 241.

20. Central Council for Savings Promotion, *Savings and Savings Promotion Movement*, 37–39; Central Council for Savings Information, *Savings Trend and Savings Promotion Movement*, 15, 19–20.

21. Chochiku zōkyō chūō iinkai, *Chochiku hakusho*, 242, 246.

22. Chochiku zōkyō chūō iinkai, *Chochiku undōshi*, 44–45.

23. Italics added. Chochiku zōkyō chūō iinkai, *Chochiku hakusho*, 217.

24. Ibid., 230; Chochiku zōkyō chūō iinkai, *Chochiku undōshi*, 33–34.

25. Chochiku zōkyō chūō iinkai, *Chochiku undōshi*, 51–52; Chochiku kōhō chūō iinkai, *Chochiku seikatsu sekkei fukyū oyobi chiku no shiori.*

26. Central Council for Savings Promotion, *Savings and Savings Promotion Movement*, 33–34.

27. Chochiku zōkyō chūō iinkai, *Chochiku undōshi*, 17, 18, 162.

28. Ibid., 55–56; Chochiku zōkyō chūō iinkai, *Chochiku hakusho*, 248–49.

29. Central Council for Savings Information, *Savings Trend and Savings Promotion Movement*, 17.

30. J. E. Thomas, *Learning Democracy*, 3–4, 84–87.

31. SCAP, Civil Information and Education Section, Education Division, *Education in the New Japan*, 2:9.

32. Usui, *Shakai kyōiku*, 127–28.

33. Thomas, *Learning Democracy*, 90.

34. Usui, *Shakai kyōiku*, 6–7, 11; in English, see SCAP, *Education in the New Japan*, 1:125–26.

35. Usui, *Shakai kyōiku*, 15.

36. Directive of 13 November 1945, quoted in John M. Nelson, "Adult Education," 127.

37. Cited and analyzed by Nelson, ibid., 121–23, 129–30.

38. Ibid., 163–64, 192–94.

39. Thomas, *Learning Democracy*, 129.

40. Usui, *Shakai kyōiku*, 114–15, 117–18; Nelson, "Adult Education," 61.

41. "Government Subsidy of Social Education Projects," 28 February 1948,

Civil Information and Education Records, SCAP, Box no. 5374, Sheet no. CIE(B)-02958, in Ogawa Toshio and Niimi Hideyuki, eds., *Nihon senryō to shakai kyōiku*, 242.

42. "Yakusho no himotsuki ga shimpai."

43. Usui, *Shakai kyōiku*, 193–94.

44. Ibid., 127–29.

45. Ibid., 154–55; Thomas, *Learning Democracy*, 76–77.

46. Usui, *Shakai kyōiku*, 206–7.

47. Ibid., 190, 192–93, 202.

48. Nelson, "Adult Education," 198.

49. Yokoyama Hiroshi and Kobayashi Bunjin, *Shakai kyōikuhō seiritsu katei shiryō shūsei*, 39–40.

50. Usui, *Shakai kyōiku*, 107, 115.

51. Yokoyama and Kobayashi, *Shakai kyōikuhō seiritsu katei*, 40–41.

52. Thomas, *Learning Democracy*, 95–99, makes a similar point.

53. Garon, "Rethinking Modernization," 354–58.

54. Text appears in Shin seikatsu undō kyōkai, *Shin seikatsu undō kyōkai 25 nen no ayumi* (hereafter cited as SSUK), 220–21.

55. Ibid., 221.

56. SCAP, *Summation of Non-Military Activities in Japan*, no. 26 (November 1947):281.

57. SSUK, 220–21.

58. SCAP, *Summation of Non-Military Activities in Japan*, no. 23 (August 1947):21, 23.

59. SSUK, 220.

60. Usui, *Shakai kyōiku*, 67.

61. Ibid., 41.

62. SSUK, 220–21.

63. SCAP, *Summation of Non-Military Activities in Japan*, no. 21 (June 1947):258.

64. Garon, "Rethinking Modernization," 355; Kagawa regularly contributed to the cooperative movement's magazine, *Ie no hikari*, in and around 1934.

65. Statement of 1 June 1947, in SCAP, *Summation of Non-Military Activities in Japan*, no. 20 (May 1947):28.

66. New Year's message, in SCAP, *Summation of Non-Military Activities in Japan*, no. 28 (January 1948):27.

67. "Senjika no fujin mondai o kataru zadankai," 278, 280.

68. SSUK, 3.

69. Usui, *Shakai kyōiku*, 67–68; SSUK, 3.

70. SSUK, 4–6.

71. See report ibid., 222–24.

72. Statement of 22 August 1955, ibid., 226.

73. Ibid., 7, 149–50.

74. Ibid., 6–7, 171–73; Katayama Tetsu, "Kyōikuteki sochi kōzeyo," *Shin seikatsu tsūshin*, April 1958, p. 2.

75. SSUK, 8.

76. These objectives were elaborated upon in the New Life Campaign Association's agenda of 31 March 1956, ibid., 230–32.

77. Ibid., 11, 13, 103–4, 230–31.

78. "Komatta meishin," *Shin seikatsu tsūshin*, March 1956, p. 5.

79. SSUK, 230–31.

80. Cited ibid., 225.

81. Chochiku zōkyō chūō iinkai, *Chochiku undōshi*, 53–54, 59–60.

82. *Shin seikatsu tsūshin*, January 1956, p. 5.

83. SSUK, 8–10, 142–43, 147.

84. See Margaret A. McKean, *Environmental Protest*.

85. SSUK, 121–23.

86. Ibid., 67–69, 73, 75, 93.

87. For example, Marilyn Ivy, "Formation of Mass Culture," in Gordon, *Postwar Japan as History*, 249.

88. Laura E. Hein, "Growth Versus Success: Japan's Economic Policy in Historical Perspective," in Gordon, *Postwar Japan as History*, 114.

89. Carol Gluck, "The Past in the Present," in Gordon, *Postwar Japan as History*, 75–76.

90. Koji Taira, "Dialectics of Economic Growth, National Power, and Distributive Struggles," in Gordon, *Postwar Japan as History*, 173–74.

91. Zenkoku chiiki fujin dantai renraku kyōgikai (hereafter cited as Zen chifuren), *Zen chifuren*, 132.

92. Chochiku zōkyō chūō iinkai, *Chochiku undōshi*, 96.

93. SSUK, 129.

94. Chochiku zōkyō chūō iinkai, *Chochiku undōshi*, 15.

95. Japan, Economic Planning Agency, *Whitepaper on National Life, 1975: Change of Consumer's Behavior and Generation*, preface.

96. Ibid., 6, 9, 132, 133.

97. Zen chifuren, *Zen chifuren*, 132.

98. Chochiku zōkyō chūō iinkai, *Chochiku undōshi*, 97–99, 103–4.

99. SSUK, 130–32, 136–38, 205.

100. Kazuo Sato, "Saving and Investment."

101. Keizai kikakuchō, *Kokumin seikatsu hakusho*, 137–38, 155–57.

102. SSUK, 139.

103. Gail Lee Bernstein, *Haruko's World*, 138–39.

104. Toyama Shigeru, *Kin'yūkai kaiko 50 nen*, 75–76; interview with Central Council for Savings Information officials—Abiko Yuichi, Ishikawa Osamu, and Watanabe Hiroshi—21 July 1992, Bank of Japan, Tokyo.

105. Italics added. Central Council for Savings Promotion, *Savings and Savings Promotion Movement*, 24.

106. See consumerist and environmental resolutions passed by annual conventions of the daily life schools movement, 1970–1981, in SSUK, 94–102.

CHAPTER SIX
SEXUAL POLITICS AND THE FEMINIZATION OF
SOCIAL MANAGEMENT

1. See Richard J. Samuels, *The Business of the Japanese State*, and *"Rich Nation, Strong Army"*; John W. Dower, *Japan in War and Peace*; Garon, *State and Labor*; Andrew Gordon, *The Evolution of Labor Relations in Japan*; and Johnson, *MITI and the Japanese Miracle*.

2. Anne E. Imamura, *Urban Japanese Housewives*, 2–3, 10; Theodore C. Bestor, *Neighborhood Tokyo*, 92.

3. Naimushō shakaikyoku shakaibu, *Fujin hōmen iin ni kansuru chōsa*; Shakai hoshō kenkyūjo, *Nihon shakai hoshō zenshi shiryō*, 6:1,125; Kōseishō, *Kōsei hakusho*, 1995, p. 317.

4. Ichikawa Fusae, "Kaisetsu," in NFMSS, 2:72–78.

5. For example, Susan J. Pharr, *Political Women in Japan*.

6. Janet E. Hunter, *The Emergence of Modern Japan*, 154.

7. Helen M. Hopper, *New Woman*, 176–81.

8. Itō Yasuko, *Sengo Nihon joseishi*, 51–52, 58.

9. For a similar argument, see Kathleen S. Uno, "The Death of 'Good Wife, Wise Mother'?" in Gordon, *Postwar Japan as History*, 308–9.

10. Hopper, *New Woman*, 205–9; see also Gail Nomura, "The Allied Occupation of Japan."

11. Yoshioka Yayoi, in "On Female Suffrage," *Sunday Mainichi Weekly*, 27 January 1946, Press Translations, no. 1,527 (26 February 1946):2, Allied Translator and Interpreter Section, SCAP, National Archives and Records Administration (hereafter cited as NARA), Suitland, Md. I am grateful to Harald Fuess and Jamie Hood for sharing these documents.

12. "Purport of the Democratic Women's Society," ca. spring 1947, Women's Affairs Activities File, Civil Information and Education Section (hereafter cited as WAAF, CI&E), SCAP, Box 5,250, Record Group 331, NARA.

13. Molony, "One Woman Who Dared," 352.

14. Kodama Katsuko, *Oboegaki*, 20, 22–23.

15. Robins-Mowry, *Hidden Sun*, 87; Itō, *Sengo Nihon joseishi*, 46.

16. Kodama, *Oboegaki*, 9, 11.

17. Suzuki, *Feminizumu to sensō*, 146–61.

18. NFMSS, 2:769.

19. *Yomiuri hochi shimbun* and *Mainichi shimbun*, both of 3 October 1945, in NFMSS, 2:774–75.

20. "Women's Organizations," ca. February 1946, p. 1, WAAF, CI&E, SCAP, Box 5,250, RG 331, NARA; Kodama, *Oboegaki*, 12; *Mainichi shimbun*, 16 January 1946, in NFMSS, 2:775.

21. *Yomiuri hochi shimbun*, 3 October 1945, in NFMSS, 2:774.

22. Munakata Masako, "Shin seikatsu undō fujin kyōgikai ni tsuite"; *Aiiku*, 25 January 1948, translated in "Women's Movement," pp. 5–6, WAAF, CI&E, SCAP, Box 5,250, RG 331, NARA.

23. Misao Kuwaye, "Women Diet Members in the 90th and 91st Diet Sessions," Memorandum to the Chief, Government Section, 25 February 1947, p. 6, Political Affairs Division, Government Section, SCAP, in Makoto Iokibe, ed., *Occupation of Japan*, 3–A–476.

24. *Jiyū kōron*, n.d., in "Birth Control," Publications Analysis, no. 33 (27 April 1946):3–4, Media Analysis Division, Civil Information and Education Section, SCAP.

25. Morito Tatsuo (education minister, Katayama cabinet), *Fujin kurabu*, n.d., in "Women in Japan," Publications Analysis, no. 151 (8 March 1948): 7, Analysis and Research Division, Civil Information and Education Section, SCAP.

26. Kano, *Fujin, josei, onna*, 25–27.

27. Mary C. Brinton, *Women and the Economic Miracle*, 27–28.

28. *Shūkan asahi*, 8 June 1952, cited by Ochiai Emiko, "Bijuaru imeeji to shite no onna—sengo josei zasshi ga miseru sei-yakuwari," in Joseishi sōgō kenkyūkai, ed., *Nihon josei seikatsushi*, 5:206.

29. For Oku's prewar activities, see Akiko Tokuza, "Oku Mumeo."

30. Zen chifuren, *Zen chifuren*, 14; *Asahi jimbutsu jiten: Gendai Nihon*, 1990 ed., s.v. "Oku Mumeo."

31. Robins-Mowry, *Hidden Sun*, 190–210.

32. "Shufuren no rekishi," in Shufu rengōkai, *Shufuren 15 shūnen kinen*; *Shufuren dayori* 1 (5 December 1949):1.

33. Suzuki, *Feminizumu to sensō*, 162–86.

34. Oku Mumeo, "Shin seikatsu e."

35. Italics added. Oku Mumeo, "Kokusaiteki na chūritsu."

36. Oku Mumeo, "Shufu chochiku no undō"; Funada Fumiko, "Kotoshi no mokuhyō."

37. *Shufuren dayori* 115 (15 December 1958):2.

38. Ibid. 88 (15 September 1956):4.

39. "Shufu rengōkai ni gosanken kudasai."

40. Women's Section, Women's and Minor's Bureau, Labor Ministry, "On Survey of Women's Organizations," 1949, pp. 1–2, WAAF, CI&E, SCAP, Box 5,250, RG 331, NARA.

41. Fujioka, *Women's Movements*, 67; Robins-Mowry, *Hidden Sun*, 152.

42. Zen chifuren, *Zen chifuren*, 19.

43. For example, SCAP, *Summation of Non-military Activities in Japan*, no. 27 (December 1947):339.

44. Zen chifuren, *Zen chifuren*, 15–16, 20.

45. Tabe Shin'ichi, "Chiiki fujin dantai," 261.

46. Zen chifuren, *Zen chifuren*, 16–17, 19.

47. Kamichika Ichiko, in *Fujin minshū shimbun*, 10 June 1948, translated in "Residential Women's Organizations," p. 3, WAAF, CI&E, SCAP, Box 5,250, RG 331, NARA.

48. Itō, *Sengo Nihon joseishi*, 73–74.

49. Zen chifuren, *Zen chifuren*, 22, 76–77.

50. Tabe, "Chiiki fujin dantai," 263, 265; for ties between the LDP and one women's section of the Agricultural Cooperatives, see Bernstein, *Haruko's World*, 136–38.

51. Zen chifuren, *Zen chifuren*, 56–57.

52. Zen chifuren, *Zen chifuren*, 20, 51–52; "Nempyō," in Shufu rengōkai, *Shufuren 15 shūnen kinen*.

53. Zen chifuren, *Zen chifuren*, 36–37.

54. Imamura, *Urban Japanese Housewives*, 9–10, 51–53, 111–12, 123–24; Tabe, "Chiiki fujin dantai," 262–63, 268, 272.

55. Uno, "Death of 'Good Wife, Wise Mother'?" in Gordon, *Postwar Japan as History*, 312–15.

56. *"Shin seikatsu to chochiku,"* 20, 48–49.

57. Interview with Katsube Mieko, Tokyo, 30 July 1992.

58. McKean, *Environmental Protest*, 109, 185, 191, 197.

59. Zen chifuren, *Zen chifuren*, 131.

60. "'Shigen to enerugii' kansei undō wa okotowari."

61. Zen chifuren, *Zen chifuren*, 133.

62. Zen chifuren, *Zen chifuren*, 132–33.

63. Kanō Mikiyo, *Onnatachi no "jūgo"*, 254–55.

64. Zen chifuren, *Zen chifuren*, 132.

65. "Rōhi ni tsuite."

66. "Setsuyaku mama ga zōka shita."

67. Imamura, *Urban Japanese Housewives*, 124–26.

68. Nobuyuki Oishi, "Consumer Groups."

69. Interview with Katō Masayo (Japan Housewives Association), Tokyo, 24 June 1992; Wolferen, *Enigma of Japanese Power*, 52–53.

70. Thomas, *Learning Democracy*, 104–5.

71. R. P. Dore, *City Life in Japan*, 273–76.

72. Walter L. Ames, *Police and Community in Japan*, 44; also 42–43. See also Bestor, *Neighborhood Tokyo*, 142, 171.

73. "Yakusho no himotsuki ga shimpai."

74. Hopper, *New Woman*, 182, 186, 196, 201.

75. Tomoaki Iwai, "'The Madonna Boom,'" 105.

76. *Washington Post*, 19 July 1989, sect. D, p. 1.

77. See "Chihō yūzei zadankai," *Fusen* 4.3 (March 1930):23–24.

78. See Chapter Three. On Ichikawa's participation in the abolitionist Association to Prevent the Evil of Prostitution in 1933–1934, see NFMSS, 1:485, 486–87.

79. Kubushiro, *Haishō hitosuji*, 258.

80. Yamamoto, *Nihon kōshōshi*, 634–38; Yoshimi, *Baishō no shakaishi*, 196–97.

81. Yoshimi, *Baishō no shakaishi*, 210; also 207.

82. Text of vice ministers' decision appears in Yamamoto, *Nihon kōshōshi*, 639–41.

83. Ibid., 639.

84. Yoshimi, *Baishō no shakaishi*, 207.

85. Rōdōshō fujin shōnenkyoku, "Baishun mondai no taisaku ni kansuru tōshinsho," 27 December 1952, in NFMSS, 1:577.

86. Yoshimi, *Baishō no shakaishi*, 210–11; for cases of false arrest, see *Nippon Times*, 2 July 1948, pp. 1–2.

87. Fujiwara Michiko, "Kichi no shūhen," *Asahi shimbun*, 24 July 1952, evening, in NFMSS, 1:675–76.

88. Report by the Women's and Minor's Problems Commission, Ministry of Labor, 27 December 1952, in NFMSS, 1:579–80.

89. Sataka Makoto, *Ryō-Nihonshugi no seijika*, 173–74. I am grateful to Funabashi Yōichi for sharing this passage.

90. Zen chifuren, *Zen chifuren*, 31–32; Nihon kirisutokyō fujin kyōfūkai, *Nihon kirisutokyō fujin kyōfūkai*, 715–17, 719.

91. *Fujin kurabu*, n.d., translated in "Birth Control," Publications Analysis, no. 33 (27 April 1946), p. 3, Media Analysis Division, Civil Information and Education Section, SCAP, RG 331, NARA.

92. Nihon kirisutokyō fujin kyōfūkai, *Nihon kirisutokyō fujin kyōfūkai*, 717–18.

93. NFMSS, 1:66; also 588.

94. Fujioka, *Women's Movements*, 82–83; also Uno, "Death of 'Good Wife, Wise Mother'?" in Gordon, *Postwar Japan as History*, 303–4, 308–9.

95. Objectives of 31 March 1956, in Shin seikatsu undō kyōkai, *Shin seikatsu undō kyōkai 25 nen*, 230–31.

96. Zen chifuren, *Zen chifuren*, 47–49.

97. Abolitionist and antiprostitution movements are subsumed under the title of "human rights" in NFMSS, vol. 1.

98. Kubushiro Ochimi, "Fūki seisaku ni kansuru ikensho," 4.

99. "Tenraku josei no kōsei fukushi ni kansuru fujin fukushi chūō renraku iinkai hōkokusho," 11 December 1947, in NFMSS, 1:558–60.

100. Rōdōshō fujin shōnenkyoku, "Baishun mondai," in NFMSS, 1:577.

101. NFMSS, 1:68, 665; translation of law appears in Japan, Ministry of Justice, *Materials Concerning Prostitution*, 32–39.

102. Nihon kirisutokyō fujin kyōfūkai, *Nihon kirisutokyō fujin kyōfūkai*, 728; NFMSS, 1:68, 707–8.

103. Yuki Shiga-Fujime, "The Prostitutes' Union," 19–20.

104. Kamichika Ichiko, *Sayonara ningen baibai* (Tokyo: Gendaisha, 1956), quoted ibid., 10–11; the incident with Ōsugi is described by Sievers, *Flowers in Salt*, 185.

105. *Kokkai shūgiin hōmu iinkai giroku*, 24th Diet, 32nd and 33rd sess., 1956, in Yamamoto, *Nihon kōshōshi*, 665, 666–67.

106. Statement of 15 August 1955, in NFMSS, 1:661–62.

107. Matsuhara Kazuhiko, in *Kokkai shūgiin hōmu iinkai giroku*, 24th Diet, 32nd and 33rd sess., 1956, in Yamamoto, *Nihon kōshōshi*, 666, 674.

108. Stephan M. Salzberg, "Japanese Response to AIDS," 257 n. 56, 265.

109. Baishun taisaku shingikai, *Baishun taisaku*, 82; Ichikawa Fusae, "Kaisetsu," NFMSS, 1:69; also Salzberg, "Japanese Response to AIDS," 261.

110. NFMSS, 1:72, 750–51.

111. Baishun taisaku shingikai, *Baishun taisaku*, 90–91, 93–96.

112. NFMSS, 1:801.

113. Aya Takada, "Despite AIDS, Japanese Continue Asian Sex Tours"; figure on bathhouse women from Salzberg, "Japanese Response to AIDS," 258 n. 60.

114. NFMSS, 1:74–75, 771–73, 811, 813–14; Nihon kirisutokyō fujin kyōfūkai, *Nihon kirisutokyō fujin kyōfūkai*, 782–83, 808–17.

CHAPTER SEVEN
MANAGING SPIRITUAL LIFE AND MATERIAL WELL-BEING

1. Directives of 25 September, 6 November, and 13 November 1945, in Nelson, "Adult Education," 122, 125, 127–28; Munakata, "Shin seikatsu undō," 3.

2. William P. Woodward, "Religion-State Relations," 656, 658; SCAP, *History of the Nonmilitary Activities*, monograph no. 32: "Religion," 39.

3. U.S. Department of War, Information and Education Division, "Know Your Enemy—Japan," War Department Orientation Film, Official O.F.–10 (1945; distributed by National Audiovisual Center, Washington, D.C.).

4. Hardacre, *Shintō and the State*, 136–37.

5. Woodward, "Religion-State Relations," 651–52.

6. William P. Woodward, "Religious Juridical Persons Law," part 1, pp. 430–32; part 4, pp. 307, 309–10.

7. Woodward, "Religious Juridical Persons Law," part 1, p. 464, also p. 433; for text of Religious Organizations Law, see SCAP, *History of the Nonmilitary Activities*, monograph 32, p. 6.

8. Shigeyoshi Murakami, *Japanese Religion*, 138–46; James W. White, *Sokagakkai and Mass Society*, 28, 58–60; Hardacre, *Shintō and the State*, 143.

9. SCAP, *History of the Nonmilitary Activities*, monograph no. 32, pp. 38–39.

10. Shimamura Yoshinobu, "Shūkyō hōjinhō minaoshi," 181; Murakami, *Japanese Religion*, 147, 151–53, 162, 165.

11. Hardacre, *Shintō and the State*, 159, also 143–47; Murakami Shigeyoshi, *Gendai shūkyō to seiji*, 131.

12. William P. Woodward, *The Allied Occupation of Japan*, 181–82, 181 n. 1.

13. Murakami, *Japanese Religion*, 141, 144–45.

14. Lawrence Ward Beer, *Freedom of Expression in Japan*, 328, 382–87; Daniel A. Métraux, *The Soka Gakkai Revolution*, 55–59.

15. *Daily Yomiuri*, 17 May 1995, p. 6.

16. "Keisatsu kokka ka, kyōaku tero shakai ka," 10.

17. *Nikkei Weekly*, 24 April 1995, p. 1.

18. Kyodo News Service, Japan Economic Newswire, 30 June 1995.

19. *Nikkei Weekly*, 18 December 1995, p. 1.

20. See editorial, *Yomiuri shimbun*, 18 October 1995, p. 3.

21. *Yomiuri shimbun*, 27 June 1995, pp. 1, 13.

22. Shimamura, "Shūkyō hōjinhō minaoshi," 178–79.

23. *Mainichi Daily News*, 14 October 1995, p. 12.

24. Ibid., *Japan Times*, 9 September 1995, p. 3.

25. *Daily Yomiuri*, 21 October 1995, p. 2.

26. Italics added. Quoted in *Los Angeles Times*, 16 October 1995, part A, p. 1.

27. Naomi Maruo, "The Development of the Welfare Mix in Japan," 68, 75–77; also Hirokuni Tabata, "Japanese Welfare State: Its Structure and Transformation," in *Japanese "Welfare State" Today*, 24–26; Ezra F. Vogel, *Japan as Number One*, 184–203.

28. Campbell, *How Policies Change*, 21; also 4, 10–11.

29. Tatara, "1400 Years of Japanese Social Work," 344, 346, 348–49.

30. Irvin Markuson, lecture to In-Service Training Institute at Japan School of Social Work, October 1949, cited ibid., 481–82.

31. Tatara, "1400 Years of Japanese Social Work," 402.

32. Deborah Joy Milly, "Poverty and the Japanese State," 165; Ishida Takeshi, *Nihon no seiji to kotoba*, 1:241.

33. *Sengoshi daijiten*, 1991 ed., s.v. "Asahi soshō," by Hiraoka Kōichi.

34. Text of law appears in Tatara, "1400 Years of Japanese Social Work," 614–24.

35. Milly, "Poverty and the Japanese State," 123–24, 123 n. 19.

36. For these and other continuities, see Yoshida, *Gendai shakai jigyōshi*, 450–51; Milly, "Poverty and the Japanese State," 179; Tatara, "1400 Years of Japanese Social Work," 399–401; for discussion of the Civil Code, see Paul Martin Lewis, "Family, Economy and Polity," 235–36.

37. Tatara, "1400 Years of Japanese Social Work," 415–24; Zenkoku minsei iin jidō iin kyōgikai, *Minsei iin seido 70-nenshi*, 177.

38. Ishida Takeshi, "Nihon ni okeru fukushi kannen," 4:50.

39. Martin Sherry, "Some Critical Observations on Japanese Welfare Practices," in *Basic Papers on Social Work*, ed. Ministry of Welfare and the Japan Social Work School (1949), cited by Ishida, "Nihon ni okeru fukushi kannen," 50–51.

40. Zenkoku minsei iin jidō iin kyōgikai, *Minsei iin seido 70-nenshi*, 169–70, 184–86, 210–12.

41. Arthur Gould, *Capitalist Welfare Systems*, 45; Yoshiya Soeda, "The Development of the Public Assistance System in Japan, 1966–73," in *Japanese "Welfare State" Today*, 32, 56.

42. Milly, "Poverty and the Japanese State," 193–94.

43. Soeda, "Development of the Public Assistance System," in *Japanese "Welfare State" Today*, 55–56, 60, 62.

44. *Mainichi Daily News*, 7 September 1994.

45. Soeda, "Development of the Public Assistance System," in *Japanese "Welfare State" Today*, 55–57.

46. Koji Taira, "Public Assistance in Japan," 107.

47. Dore, *City Life in Japan*, 70.

48. Campbell, *How Policies Change*, 62–72, 126–28, 133–34, 152–56; Ishida, "Nihon ni okeru fukushi kannen," 52.

49. Campbell, *How Policies Change*, 210–14.

50. Takashima, *Chō-kōrei shakai no fukushi*, 16.

51. Keizai kikakuchō, *Shin-keizai shakai nanakanen keikaku*, 11; translated version appears in T. J. Pempel, *Policy and Politics*, 165–66.

52. Rinji gyōsei chōsakai jimukyoku, *Rinchō kinkyū teigen: Rinji gyōsei chōsakai daiichiji tōshin* (1981), 35, quoted in Ishida, "Nihon ni okeru fukushi kannen," 55.

53. Keizai kikakuchō, *Shin-keizai shakai nanakanen keikaku*, 11.

54. Cf. Joji Watanuki, "Is There a 'Japanese-type Welfare Society'?" 264–65.

55. Fukuda Takeo, *Zoku: Kore kara no Nihon sokoku shinseiron* (1976), quoted in Campbell, *How Policies Change*, 215. See Chapter One above.

56. Jiyū minshutō, *Nihongata fukushi shakai*, 23.

57. Ibid., 12, 21–23, 25–26; for media discussions of the "English disease" and related maladies, see Kenneth B. Pyle, "The Future of Japanese Nationality," 240.

58. Keizai kikakuchō kokumin seikatsu seisakuka, *Sōgō shakai seisaku o motomete, fukushi shakai e no ronri* (1977), 59, quoted in Ishida, "Nihon ni okeru fukushi kannen," 54.

59. In 1912, Tokonami Takejirō, vice minister of home affairs, opposed an old-age pensions bill on similar grounds. Quoted in Yoshida, *Nihon shakai jigyō*, 199.

60. Italics added. Quoted in Pempel, *Policy and Politics*, 160–62.

61. "Chōju-fukushi shakai o genjitsu suru tame no shisaku no kihonteki kan-gaekata to mokuhyō ni tsuite," 25 October 1988, in Zenkoku shakai fukushi kyōgikai, *Shakai fukushi no dōkō, 1991*, pp. 5–6; see also Economic Planning Agency's 1994 white paper on national life, summarized in *Daily Yomiuri*, 22 November 1994, p. 6.

62. Campbell, *How Policies Change*, 7, 18, chapter 8.

63. Kōseishō, *Kōsei hakusho, 1978*, p. 91.

64. *Daily Yomiuri*, 2 May 1994, p. 2; Kōseishō 50-nenshi henshū iinkai, *Kōseishō 50-nenshi*, 2:708; Toshitani Nobuyoshi, "Fukushi to kazoku," 4:188; Campbell, *How Policies Change*, 6–7.

65. Takashima, *Chō-kōrei shakai*, 112–13.

66. Kōseishō, *Kōsei hakusho, 1995*, pp. 196–97.

67. Campbell, *How Policies Change*, 19.

68. Italics added. Kōseishō, *Kōsei hakusho, 1995*, p. 196; see also ibid., *1978*, p. 59.

69. *Asahi shimbun*, 17 June 1992, p. 5. Between 1975 and 1993, the propor-tion of women aged 25–29 who were not married rose from 21 percent to 45 percent, and, in the 30–34 cohort, from 8 percent to 16 percent. Kōseishō, *Kōsei hakusho, 1995*, p. 249.

70. Campbell, *How Policies Change*, 21, 246–47, 251.

71. For an excellent analysis of Japanese women, welfare, and the state, see Margaret Lock, *Encounters with Aging*, 119–34.

72. *Nikkei Weekly*, 16 October 1995, p. 2; *Daily Yomiuri*, 19 March 1994, p. 6.

73. Central Council for Savings Information, *Savings Trend and Savings Pro-motion Movement*, 16–18; interviews with Namba Shuntarō (deputy secretary, Central Council for Savings Information), Tokyo, 2 July 1992, and Shimizu Hatoko (chief secretary, Japan Housewives Association), Tokyo, 24 June 1992; William W. Kelly, "Finding a Place in Metropolitan Japan," in Gordon, ed., *Post-war Japan as History*, 198–99.

74. Watanuki, "Is There a 'Japanese-type Welfare Society'?" 266; Campbell, *How Policies Change*, 21.

75. Gould, *Capitalist Welfare Systems*, 51–52; Zenkoku minsei iin jidō iin kyōgikai, *Minsei iin seido 70-nenshi*, 715–30.

76. Kōseishō, *Kōsei hakusho, 1992*, p. 96–98, and *Kōsei hakusho, 1995*, p. 327; also Zenkoku shakai fukushi kyōgikai, *Shakai fukushi no dōkō, 1991*, pp. 831–83.

77. Maruo, "Development of the Welfare Mix," 69–71.

78. Zenkoku shakai fukushi kyōgikai, *Shakai fukushi no dōkō, 1991*, p. 367.

79. Kōseishō, *Kōsei hakusho, 1995*, pp. 254–55.

80. Stephen J. Anderson, *Welfare Policy and Politics*, 115.

81. *Nikkei Weekly*, 21 March 1994, p. 3, and 16 October 1995, p. 2; Campbell, *How Policies Change*, 243–44.

82. See Campbell, *How Policies Change*, 330–41; Peter S. Heller, Richard Hemming, and Peter W. Kohnert, *Aging and Social Expenditure*, 8; *Nikkei Weekly*, 21 March 1994, p. 3; *Mainichi Daily News*, 3 November 1994, p. 16.

83. *Mainichi shimbun*, 19 October 1990, quoted in Lock, *Encounters with Aging*, 131–32.

Epilogue

1. Kenneth B. Pyle, *Japanese Question*, 93.

2. James Fallows, *Looking at the Sun*, 11.

3. Interview with Katsube Mieko.

4. Interview with Toyama Shigeru (former chairman of the Central Council for Savings Promotion), Tokyo, 2 July 1992.

5. Interviews with Toyama Shigeru and with Abiko Yuichi, Ishikawa Osamu, and Watanabe Hiroshi.

6. Bill Powell, "The Age of Hubris Ends"; *New York Times*, 15 September 1995, sect. A, p. 4.

7. Interviews with Toyama Shigeru and Namba Shuntarō.

8. Central Council for Savings Information, *Savings Trend and Savings Promotion Movement*, 16–20; Leslie Helm, "Frugality? Phooey! Some Economists Suggest Japan Should Save Less and Spend More," *Los Angeles Times*, 5 September 1993, sect. D, p. 3.

9. Ashita no Nihon o tsukuru kyōkai, *Furusato tsukuri undō o suishin suru*.

10. Interview with Yoshida Hiroshi (secretariat, Central Council for Savings Information, Tokyo, 27 July 1992.

11. Interview with Tabe Hiroko (Home-Living Improvement Training Institute, Ministry of Agriculture, Forestry, and Fisheries), Tokyo, 2 July 1992.

12. Interview with Namba Shuntarō.

13. Interview with Tanaka Sato (chief secretary, Tokyo Federation of Women's Organizations), Tokyo, 29 July 1992.

14. Robert D. Putnam, "Bowling Alone"; "The Strange Disappearance of Civic America"; and *Making Democracy Work*.

15. Putnam, *Making Democracy Work*, 90–91; see also Gregory J. Kasza, *The Conscription Society*.

16. Johnson, *MITI*, chap. 1; Fallows, *Looking at the Sun*, chap. 4.

17. David Williams, *Japan*, 119.

18. Pyle, *Japanese Question*, 51.

19. Sakakibara Eisuke, in *New York Times*, 3 January 1995, sect. A, p. 6.

Bibliography

Place of publication is Tokyo unless otherwise noted.

Abe Isoo. "Jinkō mondai to danjo mondai" [Population question and male-female question]. *Kakusei* [Purity] 32 (March 1942):1–4.

Abe Tsunehisa. "1920 nendai no fujinkai" [Local women's associations in 1920s]. In *Nihon joseishi*, edited by Joseishi sōgō kenkyūkai, 5:75–113. Tōkyō daigaku shuppankai, 1982.

Akazawa Shirō. *Kindai Nihon no shisō dōin to shūkyō tōsei* [Ideological mobilization and control of religion in modern Japan]. Azekura shobō, 1985.

————. "1920 nendai no shūkyō hōan—shūkyō tōsei o meguru shotaikō" [Religions bills in 1920s—conflicts over control of religion]. *Rekishigaku kenkyū* 500 (January 1982):79–93, 102.

Ames, Walter L. *Police and Community in Japan*. Berkeley and Los Angeles: University of California Press, 1981.

Anderson, Stephen J. *Welfare Policy and Politics in Japan: Beyond the Developmental State*. New York: Paragon House, 1993.

Armstrong, Robert Cornell. *Just before the Dawn: The Life and Work of Ninomiya Sontoku*. New York: Macmillan, 1912.

————. "The Three Religions Conference." *Japan Christian Quarterly* 3.3 (July 1928):271–80.

Asahi jimbutsu jiten: Gendai Nihon [Asahi biographical encyclopedia: Contemporary Japan]. 1990 ed.

Asahi shimbun.

Ashita no Nihon o tsukuru kyōkai [Association to Build the Japan of Tomorrow]. *Furusato tsukuri undō o suishin suru* [Promoting campaign to build home towns]. Pamphlet. Ashita no Nihon o tsukuru kyōkai, 1991.

Baishun taisaku shingikai [Commission on Policies toward Prostitution]. *Baishun taisaku no genkyō* [Policies toward prostitution at present]. Baishun taisaku shingikai, 1959.

Baker, Paula. "The Domestication of Politics: Women and American Political Society, 1780–1920." *American Historical Review* 89.3 (June 1984):620–47.

Beer, Lawrence Ward. *Freedom of Expression in Japan: A Study in Comparative Law, Politics, and Society*. Kodansha International, 1984.

Bellah, Robert N. *Tokugawa Religion: The Values of Pre-Industrial Japan.* Boston: Beacon Press, 1957.

Bernstein, Gail Lee. *Haruko's World: A Japanese Farm Woman and Her Community.* Stanford: Stanford University Press, 1983.

———, ed. *Recreating Japanese Women, 1600–1945.* Berkeley and Los Angeles: University of California Press, 1991.

Bestor, Theodore C. *Neighborhood Tokyo.* Stanford: Stanford University Press, 1989.

Bolton, Brenda M. "Mulieres Sanctae." In *Women in Medieval Society*, edited by Susan Mosher Stuard, 141–58. Philadelphia: University of Pennsylvania Press, 1976.

Botsman, Daniel. "Punishment and Power in the Tokugawa Period." *East Asian History* (Australian National University), 3 (June 1992):1–32.

Brinton, Mary C. *Women and the Economic Miracle: Gender and Work in Postwar Japan.* Berkeley and Los Angeles: University of California Press, 1993.

Bruce, M[aurice] B. *The Coming of the Welfare State.* London: B. T. Batsford, 1961.

Bullough, Vern, and Bonnie Bullough. *Women and Prostitution: A Social History.* Rev. ed. Buffalo, N.Y.: Prometheus Books, 1987.

Bunkachō bunkabu shūmuka [Cultural Affairs Agency, Cultural Affairs Bureau, Religious Affairs Section]. *Meiji ikō shūkyō seido hyakunenshi* [100-year history of religions systems from Meiji era]. Hara shobō, 1983.

Calder, Kent E. *Crisis and Compensation: Public Policy and Political Stability in Japan, 1949–1986.* Princeton: Princeton University Press, 1988.

Campbell, John Creighton. *How Policies Change: The Japanese Government and the Aging Society.* Princeton: Princeton University Press, 1992.

Central Council for Savings Information. *Savings Trend and Savings Promotion Movement in Japan.* Central Council for Savings Information, 1992.

Central Council for Savings Promotion. *Savings and Savings Promotion Movement in Japan.* Central Council for Savings Promotion, 1981.

Chino Yōichi. *Kindai Nihon fujin kyōikushi* [History of women's education in modern Japan]. Domesu shuppan, 1979.

Chochiku kōhō chūō iinkai [Central Council for Savings Information]. *Chochiku seikatsu sekkei fukyū oyobi chiku no shiori* [Guide to savings and life-planning extension work and districts]. Pamphlet. Chochiku kōhō chūō iinkai, ca. 1992.

Chochiku zōkyō chūō iinkai [Central Council for Savings Promotion]. *Chochiku hakusho: Antei seichō no tame ni, chochiku no riron to jitai* [Savings white paper: Toward stable growth—theory and practice of savings]. Chochiku zōkyō chūō iinkai, 1963.

———. *Chochiku undōshi: Chozōi 30 nen no ayumi* [History of savings campaigns: 30 years of Central Council for Savings Promotion]. Chochiku zōkyō chūō iinkai, 1983.

Chūgai nippō [Daily news at home and abroad].

Cohen, Stanley, and Andrew Scull, eds. *Social Control and the State*. New York: St. Martin's Press, 1983.

Cohn, Norman. *The Pursuit of the Millennium: Revolutionary Millenarians and Mystical Anarchists of the Middle Ages*. London: Granada Publishing, 1970.

Connelly, Mark Thomas. *The Response to Prostitution in the Progressive Era*. Chapel Hill: University of North Carolina Press, 1980.

Cook, Haruko Taya, and Theodore F. Cook. *Japan at War: An Oral History*. New York: New Press, 1992.

Corbin, Alain. *Women for Hire: Prostitution and Sexuality in France after 1850*. Cambridge: Harvard University Press, 1990.

Crowley, James B. *Japan's Quest for Autonomy: National Security and Foreign Policy, 1930–1938*. Princeton: Princeton University Press, 1966.

Curtis, Gerald L. *The Japanese Way of Politics*. New York: Columbia University Press, 1988.

Dai Nihon teikoku gikai shi [Records of Imperial Diet of Greater Japan]. 18 vols. Dai Nihon teikoku gikai shi kankōkai, 1926–1930.

The Daily News (London).

Daily Yomiuri.

Davis, Natalie Zemon. *Society and Culture in Early Modern France*. Stanford: Stanford University Press, 1975.

Davis, Winston. *Dojo: Magic and Exorcism in Modern Japan*. Stanford: Stanford University Press, 1980.

Deacon, Desley. *Managing Gender: The State, the New Middle Class and Women Workers 1830–1930*. Melbourne: Oxford University Press, 1989.

De Becker, Joseph Ernest. *Annotated Civil Code of Japan*. 4 vols. London: Butterworth, 1909–1910.

―――. *The Nightless City, or the "History of the Yoshiwara Yūkwaku"*. 3d ed. rev. Yokohama: M. Nossler, [1905].

Decker, John F. *Prostitution: Regulation and Control*. Littleton, Colo.: Fred B. Rothman, 1979.

Doi Akio. "Sankyō kaidō—seiji, kyōiku, shūkyō to no kanren ni oite" [Assembly of Three Religions and its relation to politics, education, and religion]. 2 parts. *Kirisutokyō shakai mondai kenkyū*: part 1, 11 (March 1967):90–115; part 2, 14–15 (March 1969):72–93.

Donzelot, Jacques. *The Policing of Families*. Translated by Robert Hurley. New York: Pantheon, 1979.

Dore, R. P. *City Life in Japan: A Study of a Tokyo Ward*. Berkeley and Los Angeles: University of California Press, 1958.

Dower, John W. *Empire and Aftermath: Yoshida Shigeru and the Japanese Experience, 1878–1954*. Cambridge: Council on East Asian Studies, Harvard University, 1979.

―――. *Japan in War and Peace: Selected Essays*. New York: New Press, 1993.

Dower, John W. *War without Mercy: Race and Power in the Pacific War*. New York: Pantheon, 1986.

Duus, Peter. "Liberal Intellectuals and Social Conflict in Taishō Japan." In *Conflict in Modern Japan*, edited by Tetsuo Najita and J. Victor Koschmann, 412–40. Princeton: Princeton University Press, 1982.

———. *The Rise of Modern Japan*. Boston: Houghton Mifflin, 1976.

Endō Kōichi. "Senjika hōmen iin katsudō no seikaku to tokuchō" [Character and distinctive aspects of wartime activity by district commissioners]. *Shakai jigyōshi kenkyū* 4 (October 1976):15–41.

———. "'Shokutaku' to shite no Tomeoka Kōsuke—Naimu gyōsei to jizen jigyō" [Tomeoka Kōsuke as a "commissioned officer"—Home Ministry administration and charity work]. *Meiji Gakuin ronsō*, nos. 352–53: *Shakaigaku, shakai fukushigaku kenkyū* 65–66 (March 1984):243–310.

Engelstein, Laura. "Combined Underdevelopment: Discipline and the Law in Imperial and Soviet Russia." *American Historical Review* 98.2 (April 1993):338–53.

Fallows, James. *Looking at the Sun*. New York: Pantheon Books, 1994.

Feaver, George, ed. *The Webbs: The 1911–12 Travel Diary*. Houndmills, Basingstake, Hampshire: Macmillan, 1992.

Fletcher, William Miles, III. *The Search for a New Order: Intellectuals and Fascism in Prewar Japan*. Chapel Hill: University of North Carolina Press, 1982.

Flexner, Abraham. *Prostitution in Europe*. Montclair, N.J.: Patterson Smith, 1914.

Foucault, Michel. *Discipline and Punish: The Birth of the Prison*. Translated by Alan Sheridan. New York: Vintage Books, 1977.

———. "Governmentality." In *The Foucault Effect: Studies on Governmentality*, edited by Graham Burchell, Colin Gordon, and Peter Miller, 87–104. London: Harvester Wheatsheaf, 1991.

———. *The History of Sexuality: An Introduction*. Translated by Robert Hurley. Vol. 1. New York: Pantheon, 1978.

Fridell, Wilbur M. *Japanese Shrine Mergers 1906–12: State Shinto Moves to the Grass Roots*. Sophia University, 1973.

Friedman, Thomas L. "Land of the Rising Sun (Inc.)." *New York Times*, 3 March 1996, sect. E, p. 15.

Fujii Tadatoshi. *Kokubō fujinkai* [National Defense Women's Association]. Iwanami shoten, 1985.

Fujime Yuki. "Zen Kansai fujin rengōkai no kōzō to tokushitsu" [Structure and distinctiveness of Federation of Women's Associations of Western Japan]. *Shirin* 71.5 (September 1988):71–100.

"Fujin kōminken to fujin sanseiken to izure ga taisetsu ka" [Which is more important: women's civic rights or national women's suffrage?]. *Fusen* [Women's suffrage] 4.10 (November 1930):14–18.

Fukumi Takao. *Teitō ni okeru baiin no kenkyū* [Study of prostitution in the imperial capital]. Hakubunkan, 1928.

Fukushima Shirō. "Yūshi irai no fujin no chikara" [Women's power since dawn of history]. *Fujo shimbun* [Women and girls' newspaper], 11 May 1917, p. 1.

Fukuzawa, Yukichi. *Fukuzawa Yukichi on Japanese Women: Selected Works.* Edited and translated by Eiichi Kiyooka. University of Tokyo Press, 1988.

Funada Fumiko. "Kotoshi no mokuhyō: Katei no kagakuka e—mainichi no seikatsu o hansei" [This year's goal: Bringing science to the home—thinking about everyday life]. *Shufuren dayori* [Housewives Association news] 10 (1 January 1950):2.

Garon, Sheldon. "Rethinking Modernization and Modernity in Japanese History: A Focus on State-Society Relations." *Journal of Asian Studies* 53.2 (May 1994):346–66.

————. *The State and Labor in Modern Japan.* Berkeley and Los Angeles: University of California Press, 1987.

Gibson, Mary. *Prostitution and the State in Italy, 1860–1915.* New Brunswick, N.J.: Rutgers University Press, 1986.

Gluck, Carol. *Japan's Modern Myths: Ideology in the Late Meiji Period.* Princeton: Princeton University Press, 1985.

Gordon, Andrew. *The Evolution of Labor Relations in Japan: Heavy Industry, 1853–1955.* Cambridge: Council on East Asian Studies, Harvard University, 1985.

————. *Labor and Imperial Democracy in Prewar Japan.* Berkeley and Los Angeles: University of California Press, 1991.

————, ed. *Postwar Japan as History.* Berkeley and Los Angeles: University of California Press, 1993.

————. "The Right to Work in Japan: Labor and the State in the Depression." *Social Research* 54.2 (Summer 1987):247–72.

Gordon, Linda. "Social Insurance and Public Assistance: The Influence of Gender in Welfare Thought in the United States, 1890–1935." *American Historical Review* 97.1 (February 1992):19–54.

Gould, Arthur. *Capitalist Welfare Systems: A Comparison of Japan, Britain and Sweden.* London: Longman, 1993.

Haga Noboru. *Meiji kokka to minshū* [Meiji state and the people]. Yūhikaku, 1974.

Hane, Mikiso, trans. and ed. *Reflections on the Way to the Gallows: Rebel Women in Prewar Japan.* Berkeley and Los Angeles: University of California Press, 1988.

Hara Takashi. *Hara Takashi nikki* [Hara Takashi's diary]. Edited by Hara Keiichiro. Vol. 3. Fukumura shuppan kabushiki kaisha, 1965.

Harada Kiyoko. "Kirisutokyō to sono shūhen no josei-kan" [View of women by Christianity and its following]. In *Josei kaihō no shisō to kōdō: Senzenhen,* edited by Tanaka Sumiko, 62–80. Jiji tsūshinsha, 1976.

Hardacre, Helen. "Creating State Shintō: The Great Promulgation Campaign and the New Religions." *Journal of Japanese Studies* 12.1 (Winter 1986):29–63.

———. *Lay Buddhism in Contemporary Japan: Reiyūkai Kyōdan*. Princeton: Princeton University Press, 1984.

———. *Shintō and the State, 1868–1988*. Princeton: Princeton University Press, 1989.

Harootunian, Harry D. "The Economic Rehabilitation of the Samurai in the Early Meiji Period." *Journal of Asian Studies* 19.4 (August 1960):433–44.

Harrison, Brian. "State Intervention and Moral Reform in Nineteenth-century England." In *Pressures from Without in Early Victorian England*, edited by Patricia Hollis, 289–322. London: Edward Arnold, 1974.

Hasama Shigeru. *Chihō jichi* [Local self-government]. Shakai kyōiku kōshūkai kōgiroku, vol. 13. Gizaikai, 1928.

———. *Chihō jichisei kōwa* [Lectures on local self-government system]. Teikoku chihō gyōsei gakkai, 1929.

Hasegawa Yasushi. "Haishō ronsha ni tadasu" [Setting the abolitionists straight]. In *Shōgi sompai no dan'an* [Pros and cons on licensed prostitution], edited by Saka Tsunesaburō, 92–102. Shakai kenkyūkai, 1900.

Hastings, Sally Ann. "From Heroine to Patriotic Volunteer: Women and Social Work in Japan, 1900–1945." *Working Papers on Women in International Development*, no. 106. East Lansing: Office of WID, Michigan State University, 1985.

———. *Neighborhood and Nation in Tokyo, 1905–1937*. Pittsburgh: University of Pittsburgh Press, 1995.

———. "Women Educators and the Patriotic Women's Society." Paper presented to Annual Meeting of the Association for Asian Studies, Chicago, 7 April 1990.

Hata Ikuhiko. *Kanryō no kenkyū* [Study of bureaucrats]. Kōdansha, 1983.

Havens, Thomas R. H. "Religion and Agriculture in Nineteenth-century Japan: Ninomiya Sontoku and the Hōtoku Movement." *Japan Christian Quarterly* 38.2 (Spring 1972):98–105.

———. *Valley of Darkness: The Japanese People and World War Two*. New York: W. W. Norton, 1978.

Heclo, Hugh. *Modern Social Politics in Britain and Sweden*. New Haven: Yale University Press, 1974.

Heller, Peter S., Richard Hemming, and Peter W. Kohnert. *Aging and Social Expenditure in the Major Industrial Countries, 1980–2025*. Washington, D.C.: International Monetary Fund, 1986.

Henriques, Fernando. *Prostitution and Society*. Vol. 2: *Prostitution in Europe and the New World*. London: MacGibbon & Kee, 1963.

Henriques, Ursula R. Q. *Before the Welfare State: Social Administration in Early Industrial Britain*. London: Longman, 1979.

Hicks, George. *The Comfort Women: Japan's Brutal Regime of Enforced Prostitution in the Second World War*. New York: W. W. Norton, 1994.

Himmelfarb, Gertrude. *The Idea of Poverty: England in the Early Industrial Age.* New York: Vintage Books, 1983.

[Hiratsuka] Raichō. "Karyūbyō danshi kekkon seigenhō seitei ni kansuru seigan undō" [Petition movement for enactment of law restricting men with venereal diseases from marrying]. *Josei dōmei* [Women's league] 1 (October 1920):30–36.

———. "Shakai kaizō ni taisuru fujin no shimei" [Women's mission on behalf of social reconstruction]. *Josei dōmei* 1 (October 1920):2–11.

Hirota Teruyuki. "Senjiki shomin no shinjō to ronri—Shōwa senji taisei no nenaite no bunseki" [Sentiments and logic of common people in wartime—analysis of the agents of 1931–1945 wartime system]. In *"Kindai Nihon" no rekishi shakaigaku: Shinsei to kōzō,* edited by Tsutsui Kiyotada, 169–99. Bokutakusha, 1990.

Hobson, Barbara Meil. *Uneasy Virtue: The Politics of Prostitution and the American Reform Tradition.* New York: Basic Books, 1987.

Hopper, Helen M. *A New Woman of Japan: A Political Biography of Katō Shidzue.* Boulder, Colo.: Westview Press, 1996.

Hunter, Janet E. *The Emergence of Modern Japan: An Introductory History since 1853.* London: Longman, 1989.

Ichibangase Yasuko. "Boshi hogohō seitei sokushin undō no shakaiteki seikaku ni tsuite" [Social policy of movement promoting enactment of Mother-Child Protection Law]. *Shakai fukushi* (Nihon joshi daigaku) 14 (1967):29–51.

Ichibangase Yasuko and Takashima Susumu. *Shakai fukushi no rekishi* [History of social welfare]. Vol. 2 of *Kōza shakai fukushi.* [Social welfare]. Yūhikaku, 1981.

Ichikawa Fusae. "Chian keisatsuhō dai 5-jō shūsei no undō" [Movement to revise Art. 5 of Police Law]. Part 1. *Josei dōmei* [Women's league] 1 (October 1920): 23–30.

———. "Fuken to shichōson to wa, dō chigau ka" [What's really the difference between prefectural and municipal levels?]. *Fusen* [Women's suffrage] 4.9 (October 1930):19–24.

———. *Ichikawa Fusae jiden: Senzenhen* [Autobiography of Ichikawa Fusae: Prewar Years]. Shinjuku shobō, 1974.

———. "Jichisei e no fujin kyōryoku" [Women's cooperation with local governments]. *Fusen* 7.7 (July 1933):4–7.

———. "Kokumin sōdōin to fujin" [National mobilization and women]. *Josei tembō* [Women's view] 11.10 (October 1937):2.

———. "Kotoshi no aki" [This autumn]. *Fusen* 3.9 (September 1929):1.

———. "Seifu narabi ni Seiyūkai teian no fujin kōminken-an ni taisuru watakushidomo no taido" [Our position toward the government's and Seiyūkai's proposed civic rights bills]. *Fusen* 5.2 (February 1931):6–9.

———. "Shōwa jūnen ni okeru fusen undō no shinten" [Progress of women's movement in 1935]. *Fusen* 9.12 (December 1935):4–5.

Ichikawa Fusae. *Watakushi no fujin undō* [My women's movement]. Akimoto shobō, 1972.

———. "Watakushi no koro" [My turn]. *Josei tembō* 11.9 (September 1937):22–23.

Ichikawa Fusae, Sakamoto Makoto, and Kaneko Shigeri. "Seigen kōminken-an o megurite" [On the limited civic rights bill]. *Fusen* 5.3 (March 1931):8–17.

Ichiki Kitokurō. "Wagakuni ni okeru jikei kyūsai jigyō to jizen kyōkai to no kankei" [Relation between charity and relief works and the Charity Association in our country]. *Jizen* [Charity] 1.1 (July 1909):13–17.

Ieda Sakichi. "Junketsu Nihon no fukkō to kensetsu" [Reconstructing and constructing a Pure Japan]. *Kakusei* [Purity] 26 (January 1936):26–27.

Ikeda Akira, ed. *Hitonomichi kyōdan fukei jiken kankei shiryō shūsei* [Collection of materials relating to Hitonomichi Kyōdan lèse-majesté case]. San'ichi shobō, 1977.

———, ed. *Ōmoto shiryō shūsei* [Collection of materials on Ōmoto]. 3 vols. San'ichi shobō, 1982–1985.

Ikeda Hiroshi. "Ōsaka hōmen iin sōkai ni saishite issho o saisu" [Letter to general meeting of Osaka district commissioners]. *Shakai to kyūsai* [Society and relief] 4.9 (December 1920):48–51.

Ikeda Yoshimasa. *Nihon shakai fukushishi* [History of Japanese social welfare]. Kyoto: Hōritsu bunkasha, 1986.

Imamura, Anne E. *Urban Japanese Housewives: At Home and in the Community.* Honolulu: University of Hawaii Press, 1987.

Inoue Kiyoshi. *Tennōsei* [Emperor system]. Tōkyō daigaku shuppankai, 1958.

Inoue Tomoichi. "Kanka kyūsai jigyō no yōkō" [Essentials of reformatory and relief work]. *Jizen* [Charity] 3.3 (January 1912):1–17.

———. *Kyūsai seido yōgi* [Outline of poor relief systems]. Hakubunkan, 1909.

International Labour Office. *The Cost of Social Security.* Geneva: International Labour Organisation, 1985–1992.

Iokibe, Makoto, ed. *Occupation of Japan.* Microform. Bethesda, Md.: Congressional Information Service, 1987.

Ishida Takeshi. "Kindai Nihon in okeru 'shakai fukushi' kanren kannen no hensen" [Changing conceptions of social welfare in modern Japan]. In Ishida, ed., *Kindai Nihon no seiji bunka to gengo shōchō*, 175–232. Tōkyō daigaku shuppankai, 1983.

———. "Nihon ni okeru fukushi kannen no tokushitsu" [Distinctive aspects of the Japanese conception of welfare]. In *Fukushi Kokka* [Welfare state], edited by Tōkyō daigaku shakai kagaku kenkyūjo, 43–58. Tōkyō daigaku shuppankai, 1984.

———. *Nihon no seiji to kotoba* [Politics and language in Japan]. Vol. 1: *"Jiyū" to "fukushi"* ["Liberty" and "welfare"]. Tōkyō daigaku shuppankai, 1989.

Itagaki Kuniko. *Shōwa senzen, senchūki no nōson seikatsu: Zasshi 'Ie no hikari' ni miru* [Farm life in Shōwa era, before and during World War II, as seen in magazine *Ie no hikari*]. Mitsumine shobō, 1992.

Itō Hidekichi. *Kōtōka no kanojo no seikatsu* [Life of women beneath the red lights]. Jitsugyō no Nihonsha, 1931.

——. "Miuri bōshi undō to sono shisetsu gaiyō" [Survey of movement to stop daughter-selling and its progress]. Part 1. *Kakusei* [Purity] 25 (January 1935): 16–29.

——. *Nihon haishō undōshi* [History of Japanese movement to abolish licensed prostitution]. 1931; reprint Fuji shuppan kabushiki kaisha, 1982.

——. "Sekai no baishō seisaku" [Prostitution policies throughout world]. *Kakusei* 26 (December 1936):9–13.

Itō Yasuko. *Sengo Nihon joseishi* [History of women in postwar Japan]. Ōtsuki shoten, 1974.

Iwai, Tomoaki. "'The Madonna Boom': Women in the Japanese Diet." *Journal of Japanese Studies* 19.1 (Winter 1993):103–20.

Jansen, Marius B., and Gilbert Rozman, eds. *Japan in Transition: From Tokugawa to Meiji*. Princeton: Princeton University Press, 1986.

Japan. *The Criminal Code of Japan*. Translated by William J. Sebald. Kobe: Japan Chronicle Press, 1936.

——. Economic Planning Agency. *Whitepaper on National Life, 1975: Change of Consumer's Behavior and Generation*. Economic Planning Agency, 1975.

——. Ministry of Justice. *Materials Concerning Prostitution and Its Control in Japan*. Ministry of Justice, 1957.

Japan (Nippon) Times.

The Japan Year Book, 1911. Japan Year Book Office, 1911.

Japanese "Welfare State" Today. Annals of the Institute of Social Science 32 (1990). Institute of Social Science, University of Tokyo, 1991.

Jiyū minshutō. *Nihongata fukushi shakai* [Japanese-style welfare society]. Kenshū sōsho 8. Jiyū minshutō kōhō iinkai shuppankyoku, 1979.

Johnson, Chalmers. *MITI and the Japanese Miracle: The Growth of Industrial Policy, 1925–1975*. Stanford: Stanford University Press, 1982.

Joseishi sōgō kenkyūkai, ed. *Nihon josei seikatsushi*. 5 vols. Tōkyō daigaku shuppankai, 1990.

Kagawa Toyohiko. "Haishō undō no kompon seishin" [Fundamental spirit of abolitionist movement]. *Kakusei* [Purity] 26 (January 1936):7–8.

Kalland, Arne. *Fishing Villages in Tokugawa Japan*. Richmond, Surrey: Curzon Press, 1995.

Kano Masanao. "Fuashizumuka no fujin undō—Fusen kakutoku dōmei no baai" [Women's movement under fascism—case of League for Women's Suffrage]. In *Kindai Nihon no kokka to shisō*, edited by Ienaga Saburō kyōju Tōkyō kyōiku daigaku taikan kinen ronshū kankō iinkai, 306–27. Sanshōdō, 1979.

——. *Fujin, josei, onna: Joseishi no toi* [Questions in women's history]. Iwanami shoten, 1989.

Kano Masanao. "Fusen kakutoku dōmei no seiritsu to tenkai—'Manshū jihen' boppatsu made" [Formation and development of League for Women's Suffrage—until "Manchurian incident"]. *Nihon rekishi* 319 (December 1974):68–85.

————. *Taishō demokurashii no teiryū* [Undercurrents in Taishō democracy]. Nihon hōsō shuppan kyōkai, 1973.

Kanō Mikiyo. *Onnatachi no "jūgo"* [Women's experience on the "home front"]. Chikuma shobō, 1987.

Kasza, Gregory James. *The Conscription Society: Administered Mass Organizations.* New Haven: Yale University Press, 1995.

Kataoka Shōichi, ed. *Haishō ka, sonshō ka* [Abolish licensed prostitution or keep it?]. Baishōfu mondai kenkyūkai, 1925.

Kawai Eijirō. *Meiji shisōshi no ichidammen—Kanai Noburu o chūshin to shite* [One aspect of Meiji intellectual history—profiling Kanai Noburu]. 1941; reprint Shakai shisōsha, 1969.

"Keisatsu kokka ka, kyōaku tero shakai ka" [Police state, or a brutal, terrorist society?]. *AERA* 375 (22 May 1995):10–11.

Keishitsu Teisei, ed. *Nihon bukkyōshi* [History of Japanese Buddhism]. Vol. 3. Kyoto: Hōsōkan, 1967.

Keizai kikakuchō [Economic Planning Agency]. *Kokumin seikatsu hakusho* [White paper on national life], 1980. Ōkurashō insatsukyoku, 1980.

————. *Shin-keizai shakai nanakanen keikaku* [New economic and social seven-year plan]. Ōkurashō insatsukyoku, 1979.

Ketelaar, James Edward. *Of Heretics and Martyrs in Meiji Japan: Buddhism and Its Persecution.* Princeton: Princeton University Press, 1990.

Kindai joseishi kenkyūkai, ed. *Onnatachi no kindai.* Kashiwagi shobō, 1978.

Kinmouth, Earl H. *The Self-Made Man in Meiji Japanese Thought.* Berkeley and Los Angeles: University of California Press, 1981.

Kinzley, W. Dean. "Japan's Discovery of Poverty: Changing Views of Poverty and Social Welfare in the Nineteenth Century." *Journal of Asian History* 22.1 (1988):1–24.

Kirisutokyō jimmei jiten [Encyclopedia of prominent Christians]. 1986 ed.

Kishimoto, Hideo, ed. *Japanese Religion in the Meiji Era.* Translated by John F. Howes. Obunsha, 1956.

Kitagawa, Joseph M. *Religion in Japanese History.* New York: Columbia University Press, 1966.

Kiyoura Keigo. "Jizen jigyō ni taisuru shokan" [Thoughts on charity work]. *Jizen* [Charity] 2.3 (January 1911):1–16.

Kodama Katsuko. *Oboegaki: Sengo no Ichikawa Fusae* [Memoir: Ichikawa Fusae in postwar era]. Shinjuku shobō, 1985.

————, (supervised by Ichikawa Fusae). *Fujin sanseiken undō shōshi* [Short history of women's suffrage movement]. Domesu shuppan, 1981.

"Kokusan aiyō shijō zadankai" [Magazine's round-table discussion on buying Japanese products]. *Fujin shimpō* [Women's news] 389 (August 1930): 26–33.

Kōmoto Mitsugi. "'Shisō kokunan' to jinja—Taishō-ki o chūshin ni shite" ["National crisis in thought" and the shrines in Taishō era]. In *Nihon ni okeru kokka to shūkyō*, edited by Shimode Sekiyo hakushi kanreki kinenkai, 315–35. Ōkura shuppan, 1978.

Kosaka, Masataka. *100 Million Japanese: The Postwar Experience.* Kodansha International, 1972.

Koschmann, J. Victor. "The Debate on Subjectivity in Postwar Japan: Foundations of Modernism as a Political Critique." *Pacific Affairs* 54.4 (Winter 1981–1982):609–31.

Kōseishō [Ministry of Health and Welfare]. *Kōsei hakusho* [White paper on welfare]. Ōkurashō insatsukyoku and Kōsei mondai kenkyūkai, 1978–1995.

Kōseishō 50-nenshi henshū iinkai. *Kōseishō 50-nenshi* [50-year history of Ministry of Health and Welfare]. Vol. 2. Kōsei mondai kenkyūkai, 1988.

Kubushiro Ochimi, "Fūki seisaku ni kansuru ikensho" [Position paper on public morals policy]. *Fujin shimpō* [Women's news] 563 (November 1946):4–6.

———. *Haishō hitosuji* [Story of abolitionist movement]. Chūō kōronsha, 1982.

———. "Tsutsushimite kishū ryōin ni uttau" [Appeal to gentlemen in both houses of Diet]. *Fujin shimpō* 337 (March 1926):6–9.

Kurihara Akira. "1930 nendai no shakai ishiki to Ōmoto—shakai fuan to ryōgisei no shūkyō" [Social consciousness and Ōmoto during 1930s—social unrest and a religion of dual meanings]. *Shisō* 624 (June 1976):31–47.

Kusama Yasoo. *Kindai kasō minshū seikatsushi* [Documents of lives of the lower-class populace in modern times]. 3 vols. Akashi shoten, 1987.

———. *Kindai toshi kasō shakai* [Lower-class society in modern cities]. 2 vols. Akashi shoten, 1990.

———. *Tomoshibi no onna, yami no onna* [Women in the bright lights; women of the dark]. 1937; reprinted in Kusama, *Kindai kasō minshū seikatsushi*, 2: 769–1,183. Akashi shoten, 1987.

———. "Wagakuni ni okeru kōshō oyobi shishō no genjō" [Present condition of licensed and unlicensed prostitutes in our country]. *Shakai jigyō* [Social work] 15.3 (June 1931):61–70.

Kyōchōkai, ed. *Saikin no shakai undō* [Recent social movements]. Kyōchōkai, 1929.

"Kyōka undō" [Moral suasion campaigns]. *Shakai kyōiku* [Social education] 2 (July 1925):55–94.

Lacey, Michael J., and Mary O. Furner, eds. *The State and Social Investigation in Britain and the United States.* Washington, D.C.: Woodrow Wilson Center Press and Cambridge University Press, 1993.

League of Nations. *Commission of Enquiry into Traffic in Women and Children in the East: Report to the Council.* Series of League of Nations Publications, IV.Social.1932.IV.8. Geneva: League of Nations, 1932.

Lewis, Michael. *Rioters and Citizens: Mass Protest in Imperial Japan*. Berkeley and Los Angeles: University of California Press, 1990.

Lewis, Paul Martin. "Family, Economy and Polity: A Case Study of Japan's Public Pension Policy." Ph.D. dissertation, University of California, Berkeley, 1981.

Lock, Margaret. *Encounters with Aging: Mythologies of Menopause in Japan and North America*. Berkeley and Los Angeles: University of California Press, 1993.

Los Angeles Times.

Lu, David John, ed. *Sources of Japanese History*. Vol. 2. New York: McGraw-Hill, 1974.

McClain, James L. *Kanazawa: A Seventeenth-Century Japanese Castle Town*. New Haven: Yale University Press, 1982.

McKean, Margaret A. *Environmental Protest and Citizen Politics in Japan*. Berkeley and Los Angeles: University of California Press, 1981.

Mainichi Daily News.

Marshall, Byron K. *Academic Freedom and the Japanese Imperial University, 1868–1939*. Berkeley and Los Angeles: University of California Press, 1992.

Maruo, Naomi. "The Development of the Welfare Mix in Japan." In *The Welfare State East and West*, edited by Richard Rose and Rei Shiratori, 64–79. New York: Oxford University Press, 1986.

Mason, R. H. P. "The Debate on Poor Relief in the First Meiji Diet." *Journal of the Oriental Society of Australia* 3.1 (January 1965):2–26.

Masumi Junnosuke. *Nihon seitōshi ron* [Historical study of Japanese political parties]. Vol. 4. Tōkyō daigaku shuppankai, 1968.

Masutomi Masasuke. "Ōkuma naikaku to Kyōfūkai." [Ōkuma cabinet and WCTU]. *Fujin shimpō* [Women's news] 202 (May 1914):12–14.

Matsumiya Yahei. *Saikin no haishō undō* [Abolitionist movement recently]. Kakuseikai, Fujin kyōfūkai haishō remmei, 1934.

Matsuo, Takayoshi. "The Development of Democracy in Japan: Taishō Democracy, Its Flowering and Breakdown." *Developing Economies* 4.4 (December 1966):612–37.

Matsuyama Jirō. "Fujin kōminken-an no suii—toku ni dai 59–gikai no shingi o chūshin to shite" [Ebb and flow of the women's civic rights bill—profiling debate in 59th Diet]. *Komazawa daigaku hōgaku ronshū* 7 (1970):81–118.

Mayet, P[aul]. *Agricultural Insurance in Organic Connection with Savings-banks, Land-credit, and the Commutation of Debts*. Translated by Arthur Lloyd. London: Swan Sonnenschein, 1893.

Métraux, Daniel A. *The Soka Gakkai Revolution*. Lanham, Md.: University Press of America, 1994.

Miller, Peter, and Nikolas Rose. "Governing Economic Life." *Economy and Society* 19.1 (February 1990):1–31.

Milly, Deborah Joy. "Poverty and the Japanese State: Politics, Technical Analysis, and Morality in Policymaking, 1945–1975." Ph.D. dissertation, Yale University, 1990.

Mitsui Kōsaburō. *Aikoku fujinkaishi* [History of Patriotic Women's Association]. Aikoku fujinkaishi hakkōsho, 1912.

Mitsui Reiko. *Gendai fujin undōshi nempyō* [Chronology of history of modern women's movements]. San'yōsha, 1963.

Miyachi Masato. "Nichirō zengo no shakai to minshū" [Society and the people during Russo-Japanese War]. In *Kōza Nihonshi*, edited by Rekishigaku kenkyūkai and Nihonshi kenkyūkai, 6:131–70. Tōkyō daigaku shuppankai, 1970.

————. *Tennōsei no seiji shiteki kenkyū* [Studies in political history of emperor system]. Azekura shobō, 1981.

Miyata Noboru. "Nōson no fukkō undō to minshū shūkyō no tenkai" [Campaigns to revive villages and development of popular religions]. In *Iwanami kōza: Nihon rekishi*, 13:209–45. Iwanami shoten, 1975.

Molony, Kathleen Susan. "One Woman Who Dared: Ichikawa Fusae and the Japanese Women's Suffrage Movement." Ph.D. dissertation, University of Michigan, 1980.

Mombushō [Ministry of Education]. *Kyōka dōin jisshi gaikyō* [Report on results of moral suasion mobilization]. Mombushō, 1930.

Mommsen, W. J., ed. *The Emergence of the Welfare State in Britain and Germany, 1850–1950*. London: Croom Helm, 1981.

Munakata Masako. "Shin seikatsu undō fujin kyōgikai ni tsuite" [Women's Council of New Life Campaign]. *Fujin shimpō* [Women's news] 571 (September 1947):2–3.

Murakami Shigeyoshi. *Gendai shūkyō to seiji* [Contemporary religion and politics]. Tōkyō daigaku shuppankai, 1978.

————. *Japanese Religion in the Modern Century*. Translated by H. Byron Earhart. University of Tokyo Press, 1980.

————. *Kindai Nihon no shūkyō* [Religion in modern Japan]. Kōdansha, 1980.

Murakami Yūsaku. "Jiji hyōron" [Thoughts on the times]. *Kakusei* 27 (December 1937):26–27.

————. "Kōkyū kyōraku kyūshi shokan" [Thoughts on suspending operations of high-class pleasure establishments]. *Kakusei* 34 (March 1944):7–9.

Murphy, U. G. *The Social Evil in Japan and Allied Subjects*. 3d ed. rev. [Tokyo]: Methodist Publishing House, 1908.

Murray, Patricia. "Ichikawa Fusae and the Lonely Red Carpet." *Japan Interpreter* 10.2 (Autumn 1975):171–89.

Nadolski, Thomas Peter. "The Socio-Political Background of the 1921 and 1935 Ōmoto Suppressions in Japan." Ph.D. dissertation, University of Pennsylvania, 1975.

Nagahama Isao. *Kokumin seishin sōdōin no shisō to kōzō: Senjika minshū kyōka no kenkyū* [Thought and structure of national spiritual mobilization: Study of wartime moral suasion among populace]. Akashi shoten, 1987.

Nagahara Kazuko and Yoneda Sayoko. *Onna no Shōwashi* [Women's Shōwa history]. Yūhikaku, 1986.

Nagano Wakamatsu. *Nagano Wakamatsu shi danwa dai 1-kai sokkiroku* [First interview with Nagano Wakamatsu]. Naiseishi kenkyū shiryō, no. 86. Naiseishi kenkyūkai, 1970.

———. "Shūkyō keisatsu ni tsuite" [On the religions police]. *Keisatsu kyōkai zasshi* [Bulletin of Police Association] 434 (July 1936):14–26.

Nagy, Margit Maria. "How Shall We Live?: Social Change, the Family Institution and Feminism in Prewar Japan." Ph.D. dissertation, University of Washington, 1981.

Naimushō chihōkyoku [Home Ministry, Bureau of Local Affairs]. *Senji rekkoku chihō shiryō* [Materials related to local affairs in the nations at war] 7. Naimushō, 1918.

"Naimushō jinja tōkyoku dan" [Interview with Home Ministry's shrines officials]. *Zenkoku shinshokukai kaihō* [Bulletin of National Shinto Priests Association] 209 (March 1916):29–31.

Naimushō shakaikyoku [Home Ministry, Bureau of Social Affairs]. "Shōhi setsuyaku ni tsuite" [On consumer thrift]. *Shakai jigyō* 6.7 (October 1922):1–11.

———. *Zenkoku shojokai, fujinkai no gaikyō* [Report on local maidens' associations and women's associations nationwide]. Naimushō, 1921.

Naimushō shakaikyoku hogoka [Home Ministry, Social Bureau, Protection Section]. "Tōkyō-shi narabi Yokohama-shi ni okeru kyūmin kyūjo shisetsu shisatsu no kansō" [Impressions upon inspecting assistance and services for the needy in Tokyo and Yokohama]. *Shakai jigyō* 10.5 (August 1926):102–5.

Naimushō shakaikyoku shakaibu [Home Ministry, Social Bureau, Social Division]. *Fujin hōmen iin ni kansuru chōsa* [Survey of women district commissioners]. Naimushō shakaikyoku shakaibu, 1930.

———. *Kinken shōrei undō gaikyō* [Report on Campaign to Encourage Diligence and Thrift]. Shakaikyoku, 1927.

"Naishō no enzetsu" [Home minister's speech]. *Fujin* [Woman] 6.10 (October 1929):1.

Najita, Tetsuo. *Visions of Virtue in Tokugawa Japan: The Kaitokudō Merchant Academy of Osaka.* Chicago: University of Chicago Press, 1987.

Nakajima Kuni. "Taishō-ki ni okeru 'seikatsu kaizen undō'" [Taishō-era "daily life improvement campaigns"]. *Shisō* (Nihon joshi daigaku shigaku kenkyūkai) 15 (October 1974):54–83.

Nakajima Michio. "'Meiji kempō taisei' no kakuritsu to kokka no ideorogii seisaku—kokka shintō taisei no kakuritsu katei" [Establishment of "Meiji constitutional order" and the state's ideological policy—establishing State Shinto system]. *Nihonshi kenkyū* 176 (April 1977):166–217.

Nakamura Kokyō. "Giji shūkyō wa subete sagi nari" [The quasi-religions are all frauds]. *Keisatsu kyōkai zasshi* [Bulletin of the Police Association] 444 (May 1937):77–81.

———. *Ōmotokyō no kaibō* [Ōmotokyō dissected]. Nihon shinri igakukai, 1920.

Nakamura Masanori and Suzuki Masayuki. "Kindai tennōsei kokka no seiritsu" [Formation of modern emperor-system state]. In *Taikei Nihon kokkashi*, edited by Hara Hidesaburō et al., 5:1–87. Tōkyō daigaku shuppankai, 1976.

Nelson, John M. "The Adult Education Program in Occupied Japan, 1946–1950." Ph.D. dissertation, Kansas University, 1954.

New York Times.

Nihon fujin mondai shiryō shūsei [Collected documents on Japanese women's issues]. 10 vols. Domesu shuppan, 1976–1981.

Nihon kirisutokyō fujin kyōfūkai, ed. *Nihon kirisutokyō fujin kyōfūkai hyaku-nenshi* [One-hundred-year history of Japanese Women's Christian Temperance Union]. Domesu shuppan, 1986.

Nihon shakai jigyō daigaku, ed. *Kubota Shizutarō ronshū* [Collected works of Kubota Shizutarō]. Nihon shakai jigyō daigaku, 1980.

Nihon shakai jigyō daigaku and Kyūhin seido kenkyūkai, eds. *Nihon no kyūhin seido* [Japan's poor relief system]. Keisō shobō, 1960.

Niimura Kiichi. "Hōmen jigyō no shin-bun'ya" [New fields of district commissioner work]. *Shakai fukuri* 15.2 (February 1931):2–7.

Nikkei Weekly.

Ninomiya, Sontoku. *Sage Ninomiya's Evening Talks*. Translated by Isoh Yamagata. Tokuno Kyokai, 1937.

Nishi Kiyoko. *Senryōka no Nihon fujin seisaku* [Policies toward women in occupied Japan]. Domesu shuppan, 1985.

Nishimura Miharu. "Baishun mondai ni kansuru chōsa—senzen" [Surveys of prostitution problem in prewar years]. *Shakai jigyōshi kenkyū* 8 (November 1980):109–29.

Nolte, Sharon H. *Liberalism in Modern Japan: Ishibashi Tanzan and His Teachers, 1905–1960*. Berkeley and Los Angeles: University of California Press, 1987.

———. "Women's Rights and Society's Needs: Japan's 1931 Suffrage Bill." *Comparative Studies in Society and History* 28.1 (October 1986):690–714.

Nomura, Gail. "The Allied Occupation of Japan: Reform of the Japanese Government's Labor Policy on Women." Ph.D. dissertation, University of Hawaii, Honolulu, 1978.

Ōbayashi Munetsugu. *Jokyū seikatsu no shin-kenkyū* [New research on lives of waitresses]. 1932; reprint *Kindai Fujin mondai meichō senshū: Shakai mondai hen*, vol. 3. Nihon tosho sentaa, 1983.

Ōbinata Sumio. *Tennōsei keisatsu to minshū* [Emperor-system police and the people]. Nihon hyōronsha, 1987.

Ogawa Masaaki. "Jukkyū kisoku no seiritsu—Meiji zettaishugi kyūhinhō no keisei katei" [Establishment of Relief Regulations—how the Meiji-era absolutist poor law came about]. In *Toseki seido to "ie" seido*, edited by Fukushima Masao, 259–319. Tōkyō daigaku shuppankai, 1959.

Ogawa Toshio and Niimi Hideyuki, eds. *Nihon senryō to shakai kyōiku: Shiryō to kaisetsu* [Occupation of Japan and social education: Documents and commentary]. Ōzorasha, 1991.

Ōi Shizuo and Takahashi Tokutarō. *Chian keisatsuhō shakugi* [Commentary on Police Law]. Keisatsu sōsho, no. 3. Hōchisha, 1920.

Oishi, Nobuyuki. "Consumer Groups: Advocates of What?" *Nikkei Weekly*, 23 August 1993, Economy section, p. 2.

Ojima, Saneharu. "The Religious Organizations Bill." *Japan Christian Quarterly* 4.2 (April 1929):108–18.

Oku Mumeo. "Kokusaiteki na chūritsu, kokunai de mo chūritsu" [Neutrality in domestic, as well as international, affairs]. *Shufuren dayori* [Housewives Association News] 119 (31 October 1959):1.

―――. "Shin seikatsu e" [Striving for New Life]. *Shufuren dayori* 52 (15 August 1953):1.

―――. "Shufu chochiku no undō" [Housewives' savings campaign]. *Shufuren dayori* 67 (15 November 1954):1.

Ōkurashō zaiseishi hensanshitsu. *Shōwa zaiseishi* [Financial history of Shōwa era]. Vol. 11. Tōyō keizai shimpōsha, 1957.

Ōkurashō zaiseishishitsu. *Shōwa zaiseishi: Shūsen kara kōwa made* [Financial history of Shōwa era: From defeat to peace treaty]. Vol. 20. Tōyō keizai shimpōsha, 1982.

Ōmori Makoto. "Toshi shakai jigyō seiritsuki ni okeru chūkansō to mimponshugi—Ōsaka hōmen iin seido no seiritsu o megutte" [Middle class and democracy in formative era of urban social work—case of creation of Osaka district commissioner system]. *Hisutoria* 97 (December 1982):58–74.

Ōmoto 70-nenshi hensankai, ed. *Ōmoto 70-nenshi* [70-year history of Ōmoto]. 2 vols. Kameoka: Ōmoto, 1964–1967.

Onda Kazuko. "Zen Kansai fujin rengōkai to kon-gikai ni okeru fusen kakutoku undō" [Federation of Women's Associations of Western Japan and women's suffrage movement during this Diet session]. *Fusen* [Women's suffrage] 3.3 (March 1929):6–7, 9.

O'Neill, William L. *The Woman Movement: Feminism in the United States and England*. London: George Allen and Unwin, 1969.

Ooms, Herman. *Charismatic Bureaucrat: A Political Biography of Matsudaira Sadanobu, 1758–1829*. Chicago: University of Chicago Press, 1975.

―――. *Tokugawa Ideology: Early Constructs, 1570–1680*. Princeton: Princeton University Press, 1985.

Organisation for Economic Co-operation and Development. *Social Expenditure Statistics of OECD Member Countries*, provisional version. Labour Market and Social Policy Occasional Paper no. 17. Paris: OECD, 1996.

Ōyama Ikuo. "Shakai mondai to shite mitaru saikin ni okeru meishin ryūkō no keikō" [Superstitious tendencies as a social problem: recent trends]. *Chūō kōron* [Central review] 35.10 (September 1920):64–86.

Ozaki Yukio. "Kokumin dōtoku no kōjō o hakare" [Let's elevate national morality] *Kakusei* 28 (September 1938):4–5.

Ozawa Hajime. "Hōmen iin seido no shakaiteki kinō ni tsuite" [Social functions of district commissioner system]. Part 1. *Shakai jigyō* [Social work] 9.7 (October 1925):56–59.

Packard, George R. *Protest in Tokyo: The Security Treaty Crisis of 1960.* Princeton: Princeton University Press, 1966.

Pempel, T. J. *Policy and Politics in Japan: Creative Conservatism.* Philadelphia: Temple University Press, 1982.

Pflugfelder, Gregory M. "Politics and the Kitchen: The Women's Suffrage Movement in Provincial Japan." Paper presented to Annual Meeting of the Association for Asian Studies, Chicago, 7 April 1990.

Pharr, Susan J. *Political Women in Japan: The Search for a Place in Political Life.* Berkeley and Los Angeles: University of California Press, 1981.

Pivar, David J. *Purity Crusade: Sexual Morality and Social Control.* Westport, Conn.: Greenwood Press, 1973.

Piven, Francis F., and Richard A. Cloward. *Regulating the Poor: The Functions of Public Welfare.* New York: Pantheon, 1971.

Powell, Bill. "The Age of Hubris Ends." *Newsweek* (30 January 1995):30.

Putnam, Robert D. "Bowling Alone: America's Declining Social Capital." *Journal of Democracy* 6.1 (January 1995):65–78.

———. *Making Democracy Work: Civic Traditions in Modern Italy.* Princeton: Princeton University Press, 1993).

———. "The Strange Disappearance of Civic America." *American Prospect* 24 (Winter 1996):34–48.

Pyle, Kenneth B. "Advantages of Followership: German Economics and Japanese Bureaucrats, 1890–1925." *Journal of Japanese Studies* 1.1 (Autumn 1974): 127–64.

———. "The Future of Japanese Nationality: An Essay in Contemporary History." *Journal of Japanese Studies* 8.2 (Summer 1982):223–63.

———. *The Japanese Question: Power and Purpose in a New Era.* Washington, D.C.: AEI Press, 1992.

———. "The Technology of Japanese Nationalism: The Local Improvement Movement, 1900–1918." *Journal of Asian Studies* 33.1 (November 1973):51–65.

Ramseyer, J. Mark. "Indentured Prostitution in Imperial Japan: Credible Commitments in the Commercial Sex Industry." *The Journal of Law, Economics, and Organization* 7.1 (Spring 1991):89–116.

Robins-Mowry, Dorothy. *The Hidden Sun: Women of Modern Japan.* Boulder, Colo.: Westview Press, 1983.

Rōdōshō [Ministry of Labor]. *Rōdō gyōseishi* [History of labor administration]. Vol. 1. Rōdō hōrei kyōkai, 1961.

"Rōhi ni tsuite—shufu no kujō chōsa kara" [Attitudes toward waste—survey of housewives' plight]. *Shufuren dayori* [Housewives Association news] 297 (15 May 1974):2.

Rose, Nikolas. *Governing the Soul: The Shaping of the Private Self*. London: Routledge, 1990.

Ryusaku Tsunoda, William Theodore de Bary, and Donald Keene, eds. *Sources of Japanese Tradition*. Vol. 2. New York: Columbia University Press, 1958.

Saji Emiko. "Hamaguchi naikaku no fujin kōminken mondai" [Women's civic rights under Hamaguchi cabinet]. *Nihonshi kenkyū* 292 (December 1986):1–25.

Sakai, Atsuhara. "Kaibara-Ekiken and 'Onna Daigaku.'" *Cultural Nippon* 7.4 (December 1939):50–56.

Sakamoto Makoto. "Hamaguchi kinshuku naikaku o mukaete" [Welcoming Hamaguchi's retrenchment cabinet]. *Fusen* [Women's suffrage] 3.8 (August 1929):4–5.

Salzberg, Stephan M. "The Japanese Response to AIDS." *Boston University International Law Journal* 9.2 (Fall 1991):243–85.

Samuels, Richard J. *The Business of the Japanese State: Energy Markets in Comparative and Historical Perspective*. Ithaca: Cornell University Press, 1987.

———. *"Rich Nation, Strong Army": National Security and the Technological Transformation of Japan*. Ithaca: Cornell University Press, 1994.

Sataka Makoto. *Ryō-Nihonshugi no seijika: Ima, naze Ishibashi Tanzan ka* [A politician with the right kind of Japanese nationalism: How do we explain Ishibashi Tanzan today?]. Tōyō keizai shimpōsha, 1994.

Sato, Kazuo. "Saving and Investment." In *The Political Economy of Japan*. Vol. 1: *The Domestic Transformation*, edited by Kozo Yamamura and Yasukichi Yasuba, 137–85. Stanford: Stanford University Press, 1987.

Scheiner, Irwin. "Benevolent Lords and Honorable Peasants." In *Japanese Thought in the Tokugawa Period 1600–1868: Methods and Metaphors*, edited by Tetsuo Najita and Irwin Scheiner, 39–62. Chicago: University of Chicago Press, 1978.

Schmitter, Philippe C., and Gerhard Lehmbruch, eds. *Trends Toward Corporatist Intermediation*. Beverly Hills: SAGE Publications, 1979

Scott, Joan Wallach. *Gender and the Politics of History*. New York: Columbia University Press, 1988.

Sengoshi daijiten [Encyclopedia of postwar history]. 1991 ed.

"Senjika no fujin mondai o kataru zadankai" [Round-table discussion of wartime women's issues]. *Bungei shunjū* 16.19 (November 1938):272–98.

Senzenki kanryōsei kenkyūkai (Hata Ikuhiko), ed. *Senzenki Nihon kanryōsei no seido, soshiki, jinji* [Structure, organization, and personnel of prewar Japanese bureaucracy]. Tōkyō daigaku shuppankai, 1981.

"Setsuyaku mama ga zōka shita—shufu no ishiki chōsa yori" [Economizing mamas are on the rise—survey of housewives' consciousness]. *Shufuren dayori* [Housewives Association news] 310 (15 June 1975):2–3.

Shakai fukushi chōsa kenkyūkai. *Senzenki shakai jigyō shiryō shūsei* [Collected documents on prewar social work]. Vol. 18. Nihon tosho sentaa, 1985.

Shakai hoshō kenkyūjo. *Nihon shakai hoshō zenshi shiryō* [Documents on early history of Japanese social security]. 7 vols. Shiseidō, 1981–1984.

"Shakai jigyōka kondankai" [Round-table discussion among social work specialists]. *Shakai jigyō* [Social work] 8.7 (October 1924):70–74.

Shaw, Mark R. "Temperance and Purity Notes." *Japan Christian Quarterly* 2.1 (January 1927):91–93.

Shibamura Atsuki. "Daitoshi ni okeru kenryoku to minshū no dōkō" [Big-city trends in power and the people]. In *Taishō-ki no kenryoku to minshū*, edited by Koyama Hitoshi, 46–72. Kyoto: Hōritsu bunkasha, 1980.

Shiga-Fujime, Yuki. "The Prostitutes' Union and the Impact of the 1956 Anti-Prostitution Law in Japan." *U.S.-Japan Women's Journal*, English Supplement, no. 5 (1993):3–27.

"'Shigen to enerugii' kansei undō wa okotowari" [We decline to participate in the officially created campaign for "resources and energy"]. *Shufuren dayori* [Housewives Association news] 308 (15 April 1975):2.

Shihōshō keijikyoku [Ministry of Justice, Criminal Affairs Bureau]. *Hitonomichi kyōdan jiken no kenkyū* [Study of Hitonomichi Kyōdan case]. Shisō kenkyū shiryō tokushū, no. 54. February 1939; reprint, Shakai mondai shiryō kenkyūkai. Shakai mondai shiryō sōsho. 1st series, vol. 9. Tōyō bunkasha, 1974.

———. *Saikin ni okeru ruiji shūkyō undō ni tsuite* [Pseudo religions movement recently]. Shisō kenkyū shiryō tokushū no. 96. 1941; reprint, Shakai mondai shiryō kenkyūkai. Shakai mondai shiryō sōsho. 1st series, vol. 27. Tōyō bunkasha, 1974.

Shimamura Yoshinobu. "Shūkyō hōjinhō minaoshi o habamu mono" [Those who thwart reexamination of Religious Corporation Law]. *Bungei shunjū* (July 1995):178–82.

"Shin seikatsu to chochiku" zenkoku fujin no tsudoi [National Women's Meeting for "New Life and Savings"] Chochiku zōkyō chūō iinkai, annual report 27 (March 1985).

Shin seikatsu tsūshin [New life report].

Shin seikatsu undō kyōkai. *Shin seikatsu undō kyōkai 25 nen no ayumi* [25 years of New Life Campaign Association]. Shin seikatsu undō kyōkai, 1982.

Shindō Tokuko. "Jūnin o kanjitsuzu" [Appreciating our vital mission]. *Fujin* [Woman] 7.5 (May 1930):11–12.

Shiraishi Reiko. "1920–30 nendai Nihon ni okeru fujin kankei rippō ni tsuite no ikkōsatsu" [One perspective on women-related legislation in Japan during 1920s and early 1930s]. *Handai hōgaku* 110 (March 1979):36–72.

"Shōhi keizai kōenkai" [Consumer economy lectures]. *Fujin* [Woman] 6.9 (September 1929):10–18.

"Shōhi setsuyaku shōrei shisetsu ni kansuru ken, Shakaikyokuchō yori shōkai kaitō" [List of programs for encouraging consumer thrift; response to inquiry from chief of Social Bureau]. [October] 1922. Unpublished document: Taishō, no. 1,292–50. Shakai. Saitama-ken gyōsei monjo. Saitama kenritsu bunshokan [Saitama prefectural archives]. Urawa.

Shufu rengōkai [Housewives Association]. *Shufuren 15 shūnen kinen* [Commemorating Housewives Association's 15 years]. Shufu rengōkai, 1963.

"Shufu rengōkai ni gosanken kudasai" [Please let Housewives Association participate in government]. *Shufuren dayori* [Housewives Association news] 120 (15 April 1959):1.

Sievers, Sharon L. *Flowers in Salt: The Beginnings of Feminist Consciousness in Modern Japan.* Stanford: Stanford University Press, 1983.

Skocpol, Theda. *Protecting Soldiers and Mothers: The Political Origins of Social Policy in the United States.* Cambridge: Belknap Press of Harvard University Press, 1992.

Smith, Robert J., and Ella Lury Wiswell. *The Women of Suye Mura.* Chicago: University of Chicago Press, 1982.

Smith, Thomas C. "Ōkura Nagatsune and the Technologists." In *Personality in Japanese History,* edited by Albert M. Craig and Donald H. Shively, 127–54. Berkeley and Los Angeles: University of California, 1970.

"Sōsenkyo to fusen kakutoku dōmei" [General election and League for Women's Suffrage]. *Fusen* [Women's suffrage] 4.2 (February 1930):24.

Sotozaki Mitsuhiro. *Nihon fujinronshi* [History of Japanese debates regarding women]. Vol. 1. Domesu shuppan, 1986.

Spector, Ronald H. *Eagle against the Sun: The American War with Japan.* New York: Vintage Books, 1985.

Supreme Commander for the Allied Powers. *History of the Nonmilitary Activities of the Occupation of Japan.* Historical Monographs. 55 monographs. Tokyo: SCAP, 1951.

———. *Summation of Non-Military Activities in Japan.* September/October 1945–August 1948.

———. Unpublished materials. Record Group 331. National Archives and Records Administration. Suitland, Md.

———. Civil Information and Education Section. Education Division. *Education in the New Japan.* 2 vols. Tokyo: SCAP, Civil Information and Education Section, 1948.

Suzuki Yūko. *Feminizumu to sensō: Fujin undōka to sensō kyōryoku* [Feminism and war: How women's leaders rallied behind war effort]. Marujusha, 1986.

———. *Joseishi o hiraku* [Unpacking women's history]. Vol. 2: *Yokusan to teikō* [Assisting and resisting imperial rule]. Miraisha, 1989.

Tabe Shin'ichi. "Chiiki fujin dantai no saisei to tenkai" [Revival and development of residential women's groups]. In *Kyōdō tōgi: Sengo fujin mondaishi,* edited by Ichibangase Yasuko, 257–74. Domesu shuppan, 1971.

Tago Ichimin. "Shakai shinsatsu no hitsuyō to shakai jigyōka yōsei kikan setchi no kyūmu" [Need for social diagnosis and urgent need to create institutes to train social workers]. *Shakai to kyūsai* [Society and relief] 3.1 (April 1919):1–7.

———. *Shinjidai no fujin* [Women in the new era]. Hakusuisha, 1920.

Taira, Koji. "Public Assistance in Japan: Development and Trends." *Journal of Asian Studies* 27.1 (November 1967):95–109.

Takabayashi Takashi. "Meiji-ki ni okeru hōtoku undō ni tsuite—sono myaku-raku o chūshin to shite" [Meiji-era hōtoku movement—profiling its leaders]. *Shakai jigyōshi kenkyū* 13 (September 1985):41–57.

Takada, Aya. "Despite AIDS, Japanese Continue Asian Sex Tours." *Reuter Asia-Pacific Business Report*, 26 October 1992.

Takahashi Hikohiro, ed. *Minshū no gawa no sensō sekinin* [The people's war responsibility]. Aoki shoten, 1989.

Takashima Beihō. "Gendai josei o hihansu" [Criticizing modern women]. *Kakusei* [Purity] 26 (June 1936):13.

———. "Jashūkyō wa naze hanjō suru ka" [Why have evil religions flourished?]. *Chūō kōron* [Central review] 51.1 (January 1936):411–19.

———. "Kokumin seishin sōdōin to fūkyō mondai" [National spiritual mobilization and the public morals question]. *Kakusei* 28 (February 1938):4–6.

Takashima Susumu. *Chō-kōrei shakai no fukushi* [Welfare in the super-aging society]. Kagaku zensho 36. Ōtuski shoten, 1990.

Takeda Kiyoko. *Tennōsei shisō to kyōiku* [Emperor-system thought and education]. Meiji tosho shuppan kabushiki kaisha, 1964.

Takemura Tamio. *Haishō undō* [Abolitionist movement]. Tokyo, 1982.

Tatara, Toshio. "1400 Years of Japanese Social Work from Its Origins through the Allied Occupation, 552–1952." Ph.D. dissertation, Bryn Mawr College, Graduate School of Social Work and Social Research, 1975.

Tamanoi, Mariko Asano. "Songs as Weapons: The Culture and History of *Komori* (Nursemaids) in Modern Japan." *Journal of Asian Studies* 50.4 (November 1991):793–817.

Tanabe Hisa. "Harimise no kōshi no naka kara" [Sitting behind brothel grating]. *Fujin kōron* [Women's review] 6.8 (July 1921):43.

Tazawa Yoshiharu. "Fujin kōminken no igi" [Significance of women's civic rights]. *Chihō gyōsei* [Local administration] 39 (January 1931):20–26.

Teikoku gikai kizokuin giji sokkiroku [Records of proceedings of House of Peers of Imperial Diet].

Teikoku gikai kizokuin iinkai giji sokkiroku [Records of committee proceedings of House of Peers].

Teikoku gikai shūgiin giji sokkiroku [Records of proceedings of Lower House of Imperial Diet].

Teikoku gikai shūgiin iinkai giroku [Records of committee proceedings of Lower House].

Thomas, J. E. *Learning Democracy in Japan: The Social Education of Japanese Adults*. London: SAGE Publications, 1985.

Thompson, F. M. L. "Social Control in Victorian Britain." *Economic History Review* 2d series, 34.2 (May 1981):189–208.

Tokonami Takejirō. "Jizen jigyō no san-yōgi to shinkōshin" [Three principles of charity work and religious belief]. *Jizen* [Charity] 1.3 (January 1910):1–13.

———. "Kanka kyūsai jigyō tōkyokusha no kokoroe" [Authorities' directives on reformatory and relief work]. *Jizen* 2.3 (January 1911):20–36.

Tokuza, Akiko. "Oku Mumeo and the Movements to Alter the Status of Women in Japan from the Taisho Period to the Present." Ph.D. dissertation, University of Michigan, 1988.

Tōkyō asahi shimbun.

Tomeoka Kōsuke. "Jizen jigyō no kako 45 nen" [Past 45 years of charity work]. *Jizen* [Charity] 4.2 (October 1912):14–28.

Toshitani Nobuyoshi. "Fukushi to kazoku" [Welfare and family]." In *Fukushi kokka* [Welfare state], edited by Tōkyō daigaku shakai kagaku kenkyūjo, 4:183–247. Tōkyō daigaku shuppankai, 1984.

Toyama Shigeru. *Kin'yūkai kaiko 50 nen* [Memoir of 50 years in world of finance]. Tōyō keizai shimpōsha, 1981.

Trattner, Walter I, ed. *Social Welfare or Social Control?* Knoxville: University of Tennessee Press, 1983.

Uchimura, Kanzō. *The Complete Works of Kanzō Uchimura.* Vol. 2. Kyobunkwan, 1972.

Ueno, Chizuko. "The Japanese Women's Movement: The Counter-values to Industrialism." In *The Japanese Trajectory: Modernization and Beyond*, edited by Gavan McCormack and Yoshio Sugimoto, 167–85. Cambridge: Cambridge University Press, 1988.

Ujihara Sukezō. *Baishōfu oyobi karyōbyō* [Prostitutes and venereal disease]. Keisatsu kyōkai zasshi, 1926.

United States. Department of State. *Foreign Relations of the United States: Diplomatic Papers, 1944.* 7 vols. Washington, D.C.: U.S. Government Printing Office, 1965–1967.

United States. Department of War. Information and Education Division. "Know Your Enemy—Japan." War Department Orientation Film. Official O.F.-10. 1945. Distributed by National Audiovisual Center, Washington, D.C.

Usui Masahisa, ed. *Shakai kyōiku* [Social education]. Vol. 10 of *Sengo Nihon no kyōiku kaikaku.* Tōkyō daigaku shuppankai, 1971.

Vavich, Dee Ann. "The Japanese Woman's Movement: Ichikawa Fusae, A Pioneer in Woman's Suffrage." *Monumenta Nipponica* 22.3–4 (1967):401–36.

Vlastos, Stephen. *Peasant Protests and Uprisings in Tokugawa Japan.* Berkeley and Los Angeles: University of California Press, 1986.

Vogel, Ezra F. *Japan as Number One: Lessons for America.* New York: Harper & Row, 1979.

Wagatsuma Sakae, ed. *Nihon seiji saiban shiroku* [Historical record of political trials in Japan]. 5 vols. Dai ichi hōki shuppan kabushiki kaisha, 1968–1970.

Wakahara Shigeru. "Wagakuni ni okeru shūkyō seisaku ni tsuite no yobiteki kenkyū" [Preliminary research on religions policy in our country]. *Aichi gakuin daigaku shūkyō hōsei kenkyūjo kiyō* 13 (1974):67–143.

Wakita Haruko, Hayashi Reiko, and Nagahara Kazuko, eds. *Nihon joseishi.* Yoshikawa kōbunkan, 1987.

Walkowitz, Judith R. *Prostitution and Victorian Society: Women, Class, and the State.* Cambridge: Cambridge University Press, 1980.

Walthall, Anne. *Social Protest and Popular Culture in Eighteenth-Century Japan.* Tuscon: University of Arizona Press, 1986.

Washington Post.

Watanabe Osamu. "Fuashizumu-ki no shūkyō tōsei—chian ijihō no shūkyō dantai e no hatsudō o megutte" [Control of religions during fascist era—inclusion of religious organizations under Peace Preservation Law]. In *Fuashizumu-ki no kokka to shakai.* Vol. 4: *Senji Nihon no hōtaisei,* edited by Tōkyō daigaku shakai kagaku kenkyūjo, 113–63. Tōkyō daigaku shuppankai, 1979.

———. "Tennōsei kokka chitsujo no rekishiteki kenkyū josetsu" [Introduction to historical research on emperor-system-state order]. *Shakai kagaku kenkyū* 30.5 (March 1975):88–286.

Watanuki, Joji. "Is There a 'Japanese-type Welfare Society'?" *International Sociology* 1.3 (September 1986):259–69.

Webb, Sidney, and Beatrice Webb. *The Prevention of Destitution.* London: Longmans, Green, 1911.

Westney, D. Eleanor. *Imitation and Innovation: The Transfer of Western Organizational Patterns to Meiji Japan.* Cambridge: Harvard University Press, 1987.

White, James W. *The Sokagakkai and Mass Society.* Stanford: Stanford University Press, 1970.

Williams, David. *Japan: Beyond the End of History.* London: Routledge, 1994.

Wolferen, Karel van. *The Enigma of Japanese Power: People and Politics in a Stateless Nation.* New York: Knopf, 1989.

Woodward, William P. *The Allied Occupation of Japan 1945–1952 and Japanese Religions.* Leiden: E. J. Brill, 1972.

———. "Religion-State Relations in Japan." Part 2. *Contemporary Japan* 24.10–12 (April 1957):640–76.

———. "Study on Religious Juridical Persons Law." 4 Parts. *Contemporary Japan* 25.3 (September 1958):418–70; 25.4 (March 1959):635–57; 26.1 (August 1959):96–115; 26.2 (December 1959):293–312.

"Yakusho no himotsuki ga shimpai" [Worrying about strings attached by government offices]. *Shufuren dayori* [Housewives Association news] 114 (15 November 1958):2.

Yamamoto Shun'ichi. *Nihon kōshōshi* [History of Japanese licensed prostitution]. Chūō hōki shuppan kabushiki kaisha, 1983.

Yamamuro Gumpei. "Kyūseigun Kieko-ryō kaisetsu ni saishite" [When we set up Salvation Army's Kieko Home]. *Kakusei* [Purity] 25 (January 1935):5–7.

Yamamuro Gumpei. "The Social Evil in Japan." *Missionary Review of the World* 46 (October 1923):801–4.

Yamano Haruo and Narita Ryūichi. "Minshū bunka to nashonarizumu" [Mass culture and nationalism]. In *Kōza Nihonshi*, edited by Rekishigaku kenkyūkai and Nihonshi kenkyūkai. 9:253–92. Tōkyō daigaku shuppankai, 1985.

Yamazaki Iwao. "Kyūgo jigyō sokushin no kyūmu" [Urgent need to promote relief and protection work]. *Shakai jigyō* [Social work] 11.10 (January 1928): 127–33.

———. *Kyūhin seido yōgi* [Outline of poor relief system]. Ryōsho fukyū, 1931.

Yokoyama Hiroshi and Kobayashi Bunjin. *Shakai kyōikuhō seiritsu katei shiryō shūsei* [Collected documents on formulation and enactment of Social Education Law]. Shōwa shuppan, 1981.

Yomiuri shimbun.

Yonekura Akira. "Hōritsu kōi—Kōjo ryōzoku ihan no hōritsu kōi." [Legal acts that violate public order and morals]. Parts 16–18. *Hōgaku kyōshitsu* 59 (August 1985):30–44; 60 (September 1985):28–42; 61 (October 1985):118–33.

Yoshida Kyūichi. *Gendai shakai jigyōshi kenkyū* [Historical study of contemporary social work]. Keisō shobō, 1979.

———. *Nihon hinkonshi* [History of poverty in Japan]. Kawashima shoten, 1984.

———. *Nihon shakai jigyō no rekishi* [History of Japanese social work]. Keisō shobō, 1966.

———, ed. *Shakai fukushi no Nihonteki tokushitsu* [Japanese features of social welfare]. Kawashima shoten, 1986.

Yoshimi Kaneko. *Baishō no shakaishi* [Social history of prostitution]. Yūsankaku shuppan, 1984.

Yoshimi Yoshiaki. *Kusa no ne no fuashizumu: Nihon minshū no sensō taiken* [Grass-roots fascism: Wartime experiences of the Japanese people]. Tōkyō daigaku shuppankai, 1987.

"Zen Kansai fujin rengōkai hombu daihyōsha zadankai" [Round-table discussion among representatives from Federation of Women's Associations of Western Japan headquarters]. *Fujin* [Woman] 7.2 (February 1930):52–55.

Zenkoku chiiki fujin dantai renraku kyōgikai. *Zen chifuren 30 nen no ayumi* [30 years of National Federation of Regional Women's Organizations]. Zenkoku chiiki fujin dantai renraku kyōgikai, 1986.

Zenkoku minsei iin jidō iin kyōgikai [National Council of Welfare and Children's Commissioners]. *Minsei iin seido 70-nenshi* [70-year history of welfare commissioner system]. Zenkoku shakai fukushi kyōgikai, 1988.

Zenkoku shakai fukushi kyōgikai [National Social Welfare Council]. *Shakai fukushi no dōkō* [Trends in social welfare], 1991. Zenkoku shakai fukushi kyōgikai, 1991.

Interviews

Abiko Yuichi, Ishikawa Osamu, and Watanabe Hiroshi. Bank of Japan. Tokyo. 21 July 1992.

Katō Masayo. Japan Housewives Association. Tokyo. 24 June 1992.

Katsube Mieko. Association to Build the Japan of Tomorrow. Tokyo. 30 July 1992.

Namba Shuntarō. Central Council for Savings Information. Tokyo. 2 July 1992.

Shimizu Hatoko. Japan Housewives Association. Tokyo. 24 June 1992.

Tabe Hiroko. Ministry of Agriculture and Forestry. Tokyo, 2 July 1992.

Tanaka Sato. Tokyo Federation of Women's Organizations. Tokyo, 29 July 1992.

Toyama Shigeru. Formerly Central Council for Savings Promotion. Tokyo. 2 July 1992.

Yoshida Hiroshi. Central Council for Savings Information. Tokyo. 27 July 1992.

Index

About the author

Sheldon Garon is Professor of History and East Asian Studies
at Princeton University. He is the author of *The State and
Labor in Modern Japan*, which was awarded the
1988 John K. Fairbank Prize.